AF836427

100 Years of the Infanticide Act

Legacy, Impact and Future Directions

Edited by
Karen Brennan
and
Emma Milne

•HART•
OXFORD • LONDON • NEW YORK • NEW DELHI • SYDNEY

HART PUBLISHING

Bloomsbury Publishing Plc

Kemp House, Chawley Park, Cumnor Hill, Oxford, OX2 9PH, UK

1385 Broadway, New York, NY 10018, USA

29 Earlsfort Terrace, Dublin 2, Ireland

HART PUBLISHING, the Hart/Stag logo, BLOOMSBURY and the Diana logo are trademarks of Bloomsbury Publishing Plc

First published in Great Britain 2023

Copyright © The editors and contributors severally 2023

The editors and contributors have asserted their right under the Copyright, Designs and Patents Act 1988 to be identified as Authors of this work.

All rights reserved. No part of this publication may be reproduced or transmitted in any form or by any means, electronic or mechanical, including photocopying, recording, or any information storage or retrieval system, without prior permission in writing from the publishers.

While every care has been taken to ensure the accuracy of this work, no responsibility for loss or damage occasioned to any person acting or refraining from action as a result of any statement in it can be accepted by the authors, editors or publishers.

All UK Government legislation and other public sector information used in the work is Crown Copyright ©. All House of Lords and House of Commons information used in the work is Parliamentary Copyright ©. This information is reused under the terms of the Open Government Licence v3.0 (http://www.nationalarchives.gov.uk/doc/open-government-licence/version/3) except where otherwise stated.

All Eur-lex material used in the work is © European Union, http://eur-lex.europa.eu/, 1998–2023.

A catalogue record for this book is available from the British Library.

A catalogue record for this book is available from the Library of Congress.

Library of Congress Control Number: 2023939761

ISBN: HB: 978-1-50996-164-1
ePDF: 978-1-50996-166-5
ePub: 978-1-50996-165-8

Typeset by Compuscript Ltd, Shannon

To find out more about our authors and books visit www.hartpublishing.co.uk. Here you will find extracts, author information, details of forthcoming events and the option to sign up for our newsletters.

100 YEARS OF THE INFANTICIDE ACT

This book provides the first comprehensive and detailed analysis of the Infanticide Act and its impact in England and Wales and around the world.

It is 100 years since an Infanticide Act was first passed in England and Wales. The statute, re-enacted in 1938, allows for leniency to be given to women who kill their infants within the first year of life. This legislation is unique and controversial: it creates a specific offence and defence that is available only to women who kill their biological infants. Men and other carers are not able to avail of the special mitigation provided by the Act, nor are women who kill older children.

The collection brings together leading experts in the field to offer important insights into the history of the law, how it works today, the impact and legacy of the statute and potential futures of infanticide laws around the world.

Contributors consider the Act in practice in England and Wales, the ways it has been portrayed in the British media, and justifications for and criticisms of the provision of special treatment for women who kill their infants within a year of birth.

It also looks at the criminal justice responses to infanticide in other jurisdictions, such as Australia, Ireland, Sweden and the USA.

For all women who battle the daily hardships of mothering their children. May you thrive!

FOREWORD

It seems safe to say that few scholars intend to become experts in the study of maternal filicide. There is something so profoundly disturbing about the act of a mother killing her child that most people, quite understandably, just look away. As a result, even though infanticide has always been a part of the human story, until relatively recently, there has been little concerted effort to grapple with the hard questions underlying its persistence in a meaningful way. The scholars whose contributions are gathered in this volume come from a variety of backgrounds and perspectives. Together, they have committed themselves to forging a deeper understanding of these troubling cases and the legal response to them – an understanding that enables readers to think more clearly about maternal filicide, and as importantly, lays a foundation for the creation of wiser laws and policies.

To this point, when news of a mother killing her child arises, the typical response in both the media and the legal system is to classify the perpetrators as 'mad' or 'bad'.[1] This tendency at once serves to label the mothers as aberrant, and to eliminate the need to interrogate the structural forces contributing to these crimes. Yet the reality is that, when one looks beyond the headlines, the patterns surrounding the cases are so striking that they call out for reckoning.

My own reckoning with maternal filicide began in the 1990s, when I became curious about the similarities in the facts underlying reports of mothers who kill their children in the USA.[2] As I started to notice the recurring storylines in these cases, I found myself searching through news items, medical articles and the academic literature on the subject, hoping to find a coherent analysis of the subject. What little I found lacked the sort of rigorous examination needed to provide a firm foundation upon which to begin to answer the questions I had, as a lawyer, about blameworthiness and prevention. In its absence, I found that the US criminal legal system responded to each case as if it were unique and unprecedented. The result was an incoherent body of law, in which strikingly similar cases, such as those involving neonaticide (the death of a newborn following an unattended birth), might just as easily receive a life sentence as a sentence of probation and counselling. The outcomes were so variable as to seem almost random.

[1] A Wilczynski, 'Images of Women Who Kill Their Infants: The Mad and the Bad' (1991) 2 *Women & Criminal Justice* 71, 73.

[2] See M Oberman, 'Mothers Who Kill: Coming to Terms with Modern American Infanticide' (1996) 34 *American Criminal Law Review* 1; M Oberman and CL Meyer, *When Mothers Kill: Interviews from Prison* (New York University Press 2008); CL Meyer and M Oberman, *Mothers Who Kill Their Children: Understanding the Acts of Moms from Susan Smith to the 'Prom Mom'* (New York University Press 2001).

From this perspective, when I first encountered the Infanticide Acts of 1922/1938, I was impressed by the consistent approach afforded to cases of maternal filicide. The offence/defence was originally enacted in response to jurors' intuition that these cases were different – that the perpetrators were somehow deserving of mercy. As a result, there was a pattern of jury nullification, wherein juries refused to convict when they knew the defendant would either face the death penalty, or that the sentence would be commuted. Indeed, in every case where a conviction was returned, the Home Secretary ultimately commuted the death sentence, despite it having been declared in open court by the trial judge. As described in Chapter 1, lawmakers viewed this response as a 'solemn mockery' of the death penalty, and, concerned that it undermined the Rule of Law in general, they enacted a law specific to cases involving mothers who killed their newly born babies.[3] This law created a separate crime of infanticide, which governed cases in which the defendant can show that the 'balance of her mind was disturbed' by reason of childbirth or lactation.[4] It had the effect of allowing the defendant to avoid the harsh sentences associated with murder, without requiring the defendant to establish the affirmative defence of insanity.

This outcome seemed to me a compassionate and pragmatic solution. Compassionate because its language was rooted in the reality that caring for an infant in the first year of life can take an enormous toll on one's mental health. Pragmatic because its impact was to replace the drawn out, sensational and costly response seen in the US with a consistent, efficient, and to my mind, just resolution.

Upon reflection, however, I ignored the obvious complications inherent in the approach to maternal filicide in England and Wales. Because it is rooted in politics, not science, there is no real clarity about what is meant by a disturbance in the balance of the mind, and little evidence to support the notion that childbirth or lactation would trigger such disturbance. Instead, in one key way, the Infanticide Acts' classification of these cases as a distinct form of homicide functions similarly to the piecemeal American counterpart: it enables those adjudicating these cases to look away from their underlying facts, thereby avoiding the need to grapple with the social and structural components driving maternal filicide.

This collection of essays, authored by the leading members of a growing cohort of maternal filicide experts from around the world, provides the tools for that long-overdue grappling. Indeed, this collection represents precisely the sort of rigorous and thoughtful analysis that is a precondition for any meaningful legal or policy responses to the ongoing phenomenon of maternal filicide. To be sure, like all good scholarship, many of these pieces raise more questions than they answer. Rather than a simplistic embrace or critique, they offer a nuanced, complicated assessment of the Infanticide Act upon its centenary. There is more work to be done,

[3] Infanticide Act 1922, which was replaced by the Infanticide Act 1938. For further detail, see ch 1 of this volume. The law was later extended to cover infant-victims up to the age of 12 months.

[4] Infanticide Act 1938.

but I can think of no better starting point for designing a better legal response to contemporary cases of maternal filicide than the rich and varied contributions included in this volume.

Michelle Oberman
Katharine & George Alexander Professor of Law
Santa Clara University

ACKNOWLEDGEMENTS

The editors would like to thank the authors for their dedication to this volume and for their wonderful contributions. We would also like to thank Hart Publishing for their commitment to this edited collection.

Emma Milne would like to thank Karen Brennan for the excellent idea and for asking her to be a co-editor. It's always a joy, Karen.

Karen Brennan would like to thank Emma Milne for her dedication to this project and for the many stimulating discussions we have had about infanticide law over the last few years. She would also like to thank Patrick for teaching her a thing or two about motherhood!

CONTENTS

PART III
CRIMINAL JUSTICE RESPONSES TO INFANTICIDE BEYOND ENGLAND AND WALES

LIST OF CONTRIBUTORS

Susan Ayres is Professor of Law at Texas A&M University, where she teaches family law, criminal law, race and the law, and other courses.

Dr Lynsey Black is Assistant Professor in Criminology at Maynooth University.

Dr Karen Brennan is a Senior Lecturer in Criminal Law and Evidence at the University of Essex.

Dr Rachel Dixon is a Lecturer in Law at the University of Hull, where she teaches criminal law and criminal justice.

David M Doyle is an Associate Professor of Law at Maynooth University.

Dr Daniel JR Grey is Principal Lecturer in History, University of Hertfordshire.

Dr Helen Howard is a Senior Lecturer in Law at Teesside University where she teaches criminal law and medical law.

Dr Maria Kaspersson is a Senior Lecturer in Criminology at the University of Greenwich where she teaches on criminological theory and violence.

Dr Arlie Loughnan is Professor of Criminal Law and Criminal Law Theory at the University of Sydney Law School.

Ronnie Mackay is Professor of Criminal Policy and Mental Health at Leicester De Montfort Law School.

Dr Emma Milne is Associate Professor in Criminal Law and Criminal Justice at Durham University.

Tony Ward is Professor of Law and Convenor of the Centre for Evidence and Criminal Justice Studies at Northumbria University, Newcastle upon Tyne.

TABLE OF CASES

Australia

Canada

England and Wales

United States of America

TABLE OF STATUTES

Australia

England and Wales

Ireland

New Zealand

Sweden

United States of America

1

100 Years of Infanticide: The Law in Context

KAREN BRENNAN AND EMMA MILNE

Michelle Oberman has observed:

> [A]cross a startling expanse of time and place, one remarkably consistent observation may be made: infanticide is not treated like other homicides. Despite moral condemnation of infanticide, there is considerable evidence that societies have refused to punish it as they do other homicides.[1]

This observation certainly applies to England and Wales, where, for just over a century, there has been special provision in the law that allows for lenient treatment of women who kill their babies. Even before the Infanticide Act was first enacted in 1922, women who killed their infants were already receiving leniency in ways that other killers were not.[2]

The Infanticide Act is unique, and arguably somewhat of an oddity in the criminal law, being both an offence and a partial defence that applies only to a particular category of killer and victim – mothers who kill their biological children aged under 12 months. As the statute states:

> Where a woman by any wilful act or omission causes the death of her child being a child under the age of twelve months, but at the time of the act or omission the balance of her mind was disturbed by reason of her not having fully recovered from the effect of giving birth to the child or by reason of the effect of lactation consequent upon the birth of the child, then, if the circumstances were such that but for this Act the offence would have amounted to murder or manslaughter, she shall be guilty of felony, to wit of infanticide, and may for such offence be dealt with and punished as if she had been guilty of the offence of manslaughter of the child.[3]

[1] M Oberman, 'Mothers Who Kill: Coming to Terms with Modern American Infanticide' (1996) 34 *American Criminal Law Review* 1, 7.

[2] As discussed in section II.

[3] Infanticide Act 1938, s 1(1). Section 1(2) allows for infanticide to be returned as a verdict on a murder or manslaughter charge.

In practice, the offence/defence allows for a woman who kills her own infant, while her mind is disturbed due to childbirth or lactation, to escape the mandatory life sentence imposed for murder and, in the vast majority of cases, not to be imprisoned. Infanticide is also now an alternative to a manslaughter charge or conviction.[4]

The meaning of the terms in the legislation is somewhat nebulous, and indeed the core aspect of the infanticide doctrine, broadly called the 'medical rationale', has never been subject to interpretation by the appeal courts in England and Wales.[5] The Infanticide Act has rarely been used in recent times.[6] And yet this unique legislation, which has clear roots in Victorian understandings of women and childbirth, remains on the statute books, relatively unchanged since re-enactment in 1938. Not only that, it has influenced the enactment of infanticide legislation around the world.

It is 100 years since the first Infanticide Act was passed in England and Wales. Over the last few decades, the legislation has weathered criticism and calls for abolition, and is considered by many to be a controversial and unnecessary law,[7] particularly in light of the introduction of the defence of diminished responsibility to the criminal law of England and Wales in 1957.[8] This book explores the impact, legacy and future of the infanticide statute in England and Wales as well as around the globe. It brings together experts who have previously made important contributions to our understanding of the Infanticide Acts 1922/1938 and other infanticide statutes around the world that are based on the 1922/1938 model. The authors offer important insights into our understanding of infanticide laws, in terms of the history of the law, its operation today, its impact and legacy, and the potential future of infanticide laws. There is limited published scholarly work on infanticide laws; therefore, this collection, through bringing together experts on this topic to discuss different aspects of it, seeks to start a conversation about the purpose and future of infanticide laws in England and Wales and across the world.

In this introductory chapter we put the Infanticide Act in context by providing: (i) an account of the social and historical background to the crime of infanticide and the enactment of this law; (ii) an overview of how the infanticide law has operated in practice; and (iii) a summary of the key debates and critiques of the infanticide law. In particular, we argue that in order to understand the meaning of infanticide legislation and its current and future role in the criminal law, it is essential to appreciate the socio-historical background to the enactment of the Infanticide Acts, as well as the circumstances in which this crime occurs and the

[4] Infanticide Act 1938, s 1(1) and (2) as amended by s 57 of the Coroners and Justice Act 2009.
[5] Discussed in section II.
[6] See discussion in section III.
[7] Criticisms of the law are discussed in section IV.
[8] Homicide Act 1957, s 2.

factors that contribute to it. Linked with this is the importance of appreciating the role of wider public sentiment in relation to this crime and the law.

We begin this chapter with a discussion of the nature of the crime of infanticide (the killing of a child aged under 12 months by its biological mother), focusing on the historical and contemporary 'infanticidal woman' and the social circumstances that contribute to this offence. We then explore the historical background to the enactment of the 1922 and 1938 Infanticide Acts in England and Wales, with a particular focus on the origins of the medical rationale. Following this, we consider how the Infanticide Act 1938 has been used in practice. We then provide an overview of the key debates that have arisen in relation to the Infanticide Act 1938, and laws around the world based on this model, in recent decades. We finish with an overview of the chapters in this collection.

I. Infanticidal Women

To understand the role of the Infanticide Act, and consider its place in the criminal law today, both in England and Wales and in other legal jurisdictions, it is important to understand a 'typical' case of infanticide. As we have already noted, the history of infanticide is central to an understanding of the offence/defence. Consequently, it is essential to analyse infanticidal women as they are today, as well as those from the past.

A. Historical Infanticide

The history of this law reveals the significant connection between the social causes of the crime, the public response to it and the reasons for the enactment of the infanticide legislation.[9] At the time of the enactment of the 1922 Infanticide Act, maternal infant murder was closely associated with 'illegitimate' pregnancy and unmarried motherhood. Infanticide had, since at least the early seventeenth century, been understood to be a crime of the unwed pregnant woman. It was believed she concealed her pregnancy, gave birth alone and then killed the child, in order to conceal the 'shame' of being pregnant outside of marriage.[10]

By the end of the nineteenth century, such women were most often perceived in a sympathetic light. It was recognised that social and economic pressures acted

[9] See discussion in section II.

[10] M Jackson, *New-Born Child Murder: Women, Illegitimacy and the Courts in Eighteenth-Century England* (Manchester University Press 1996); PC Hoffer and NEH Hull, *Murdering Mothers: Infanticide in England and New England, 1558–1803* (New York University Press 1981); A-M Kilday, *A History of Infanticide in Britain, c 1600 to the Present* (Palgrave Macmillan 2013); JM Beattie, *Crime and the Courts in England, 1660–1800* (Princeton University Press 1986).

on them, which led to their fatal actions.[11] At that time, unmarried motherhood brought with it the risk of social alienation, intense shame and severe financial difficulties. Sexual double standards and the operation of the Poor Laws meant that men rarely had to take moral or financial responsibility for the children they fathered outside of marriage.[12] Women, however, were expected to remain chaste until marriage and were held fully responsible when they strayed from society's sexual code. Motherhood was only permissible within wedlock. 'Fallen women' were thus left with few attractive options and little or no financial or social support.[13] Supporting both themselves and their babies without family or state assistance was incredibly difficult. Domestic servants were particularly at risk from unwed pregnancies, and indeed faced losing their positions, not only because of the difficulty of looking after a child while in a job that demanded working long hours and (possibly) the requirement to live at their employer's residence, but also because no 'respectable' family would be willing to employ/continue to employ a 'fallen woman'.[14] Nevertheless, Higginbotham maintains that killing the baby was not the most common reaction to pregnancy out of wedlock.[15] The majority of women would not have been able to conceal their pregnancy or the birth, and so killing the child would not have been an option. Instead, women relied on workhouses, charities and family to raise their illegitimate children.

During the Victorian period, a changing perception developed of women's 'madness' and its connection to childbirth. Since the middle of the sixteenth century, medical scholars believed that women's reproductive capacity could make them insane. During the Victorian era, this belief was further examined and theorised by psychiatrists, who added to observations already made of women's depression, disorientation, occasional 'craziness' and violent tendencies post-partum, as witnessed by men-midwives, midwives and medical professionals.[16]

[11] K Brennan, '"A Fine Mixture of Pity and Justice": The Criminal Justice Response to Infanticide in Ireland, 1922–1949' (2013) 31 *Law and History Review* 793; K Brennan, 'Murderous Mothers and Gentle Judges: Paternalism, Patriarchy, and Infanticide' (2018) 30 *Yale Journal of Law and Feminism* 139; EF Farrell, *'A Most Diabolical Deed': Infanticide and Irish Society, 1850–1900* (Manchester University Press 2013); A Loughnan, 'The "Strange" Case of the Infanticide Doctrine' (2012) 32 *OJLS* 685; E Rapaport, 'Mad Women and Desperate Girls: Infanticide and Child Murder in Law and Myth' (2006) 33 *Fordham Urban Law Journal* 527.

[12] MJ Wiener, *Men of Blood: Violence, Manliness and Criminal Justice in Victorian England* (Cambridge University Press 2004) 123–25.

[13] See, eg, LCB Seaman, *Victorian England: Aspects of English and Imperial History, 1837–1901* (Routledge 1990) 13–14; Kilday (n 10).

[14] WD Rubinstein, *Britain's Century: A Political and Social History 1815–1905* (Bloomsbury Academic 1998) 319–24; C Smout, 'Aspects of Sexual Behaviour on Nineteenth Century Scotland' in P Laslett, K Oosterveen and RM Smith (eds), *Bastardy and its Comparative History: Studies in the History of Illegitimacy and Marital Nonconformity in Britain, France, Germany, Sweden, North America, Jamaica and Japan* (Harvard University Press 1980) 192, 196.

[15] AR Higginbotham, '"Sin of the Age": Infanticide and Illegitimacy in Victorian London' (1989) 3 *Victorian Studies* 319.

[16] Kilday (n 10); D Rabin, 'Bodies of Evidence, States of Mind: Infanticide, Emotion and Sensibility in Eighteenth-Century England' in M Jackson (ed), *Infanticide: Historic Perspectives on Child Murder*

Such observations were the bases for the development of the condition of puerperal insanity or psychosis. It was argued that there were two forms of the illness: mania and melancholy. Mania was an overt aggression with unpredictable tendencies towards violence; melancholy resulted in general despondency and lethargy. It was believed that puerperal insanity could come on directly after birth, or in later months whilst the body was still lactating.[17]

By the 1830s, the relationship between puerperal insanity and infanticide was widely accepted and infanticide was seen as a symptom of the illness.[18] Kilday argues that this explanation for why women kill their children was widely appreciated by the authorities as it could be applied to all women – single/married, young/old, killing a new-born or an older infant.[19] Furthermore, by making the act of infanticide a symptom of a medical condition, rather than a crime, understanding of the infanticidal woman shifted from that of a rational act based on economic and social motives conducted by a 'fallen' single woman, to the medicalised temporary insanity that was a natural reaction of her body.[20] However, by the twentieth century, the focus on puerperal psychosis reduced in significance within the medical community. Medics begin to doubt the blanket response regarding the condition and medical discourse began to focus on the well-being of infants. The shame of being pregnant out of wedlock and the economic implications of illegitimacy become the focus of infanticide cases once again.[21] Nevertheless, the theory that pregnancy causes 'madness' in women continued to play its role in the understanding of infanticide, and consequently had an impact on the creation of the Infanticide Act in 1922, as discussed in section II.A.[22]

Far less research exists focusing on infanticidal women between 1938 (when the Infanticide Act was re-enacted) and the start of the twentieth century. A major reason for this is the challenge of accessing primary resources. Unlike older cases, more contemporary cases are embargoed due to the chance that the accused woman or her relatives may still be alive. Furthermore, there have been very few appeals relating to the offence/defence of infanticide, so very few criminal cases have been published by the courts. Nevertheless, as Grey argues, a key focus of infanticide, throughout the twentieth century, has been on infanticidal women as being unlike other offenders, and thus deserving of lenient treatment.[23]

and Concealment, 1500–2000 (Ashgate 2002) 73; C Quinn, 'Images and Impulses: Representations of Puerperal Insanity and Infanticide in Late Victorian England' in Jackson (ed) (this footnote) 193.

[17] Quinn (n 16); H Marland, *Dangerous Motherhood: Insanity and Childbirth in Victorian Britain* (Palgrave Macmillan 2004).

[18] H Marland, 'Getting Away with Murder?: Puerperal Insanity, Infanticide and the Defence Plea' in Jackson (ed) (n 16) 168; Kilday (n 10).

[19] Kilday (n 10).

[20] Marland (n 18).

[21] Kilday (n 10).

[22] See also discussion in ch 6 of this volume.

[23] See ch 4 of this volume.

B. The Twenty-First Century Infanticidal Woman

Today, 'Infanticide' as a phenomenon is perhaps more accurately referred to as 'maternal filicide of infants'. This form of killing needs to be divided into two categories due their distinct nature: the killing of a child in the first day of its life, and the killing of an older infant. We will outline the nature of these killings separately.

i. Newborn Child Killing

Newborn child killing, often known as 'neonaticide',[24] occurs following what Milne has termed a 'crisis pregnancy',[25] whereby the pregnancy causes the woman a crisis due to the context of her life. Women who experience crisis pregnancies are living in complex situations, notably experiencing intimate partner or family violence and abuse. The crisis caused by the pregnancy means she feels she cannot reveal the pregnancy due to fear of the response from those closest to her, and her feelings of shame and guilt about the pregnancy.[26] Other situations that result in a crisis pregnancy include living in complex personal situations that may include alcohol or substance abuse, and poverty and general economic depravations.[27] The consequence is that a woman feels unable to determine how to approach her pregnancy and what decisions to make about the future of the pregnancy/foetus/child, causing her a crisis.[28] Furthermore, the pregnancy is understood and conceptualised by the woman as an 'unauthorised' pregnancy. As in historical cases of infanticide, discussed in section I.A, society dictates who should or should not be having a child, at what point in their lives, or even at all. For example, younger women,[29] older women,[30] poor women, 'career' women[31] and disabled

[24] Coined by PJ Resnick, 'Murder of the Newborn: A Psychiatric Review of Neonaticide' (1970) 126 *American Journal of Psychiatry* 1414. Milne argues that 'neonaticide' is an imprecise term, and advocates that 'suspicious perinatal death' and 'suspected perinatal killing' cover the broad range of actions or inactions that occur in these cases, as well as the breadth of legal and criminal justice responses: E Milne, *Criminal Justice Responses to Maternal Filicide: Judging the Failed Mother* (Emerald Publishing Limited 2021).

[25] Milne (n 24).

[26] K Beyer, S McAuliffe Mack and JL Shelton, 'Investigative Analysis of Neonaticide: An Exploratory Study' (2008) 35 *Criminal Justice and Behavior* 522.

[27] CL. Meyer and M Oberman, *Mothers Who Kill Their Children: Understanding the Acts of Moms from Susan Smith to the 'Prom Mom'* (New York University Press 2001); N Vellut, JM Cook and A Tursz, 'Analysis of the Relationship between Neonaticide and Denial of Pregnancy Using Data from Judicial Files' (2012) 36 *Child Abuse and Neglect* 553.

[28] E Milne, 'Concealment of Birth: Time to Repeal a 200-Year-Old "Convenient Stop-Gap"?' (2019) 27 *Feminist Legal Studies* 139, 146–48.

[29] K Ellis-Sloan, 'Teenage Mothers, Stigma and Their 'Presentations of Self"' (2014) 19 *Sociological Research Online* 16; AT Geronimus, 'Damned If You Do: Culture, Identity, Privilege, and Teenage Childbearing in the United States' (2003) 57 *Social Science & Medicine* 881.

[30] M Weigel, 'The Foul Reign of the Biological Clock' *The Guardian* (London, 10 May 2016) at www.theguardian.com/society/2016/may/10/foul-reign-of-the-biological-clock (accessed 8 November 2020).

[31] K Christopher, 'Extensive Mothering: Employed Mothers' Constructions of the Good Mother' (2012) 26 *Gender & Society* 73.

women[32] are some examples of those often represented as being 'unfit' for motherhood. Furthermore, in some cultures, pregnancy outside of marriage continues to be unacceptable. Becoming pregnant in such 'unauthorised' contexts can also lead to crisis.[33]

As a consequence of the crisis, women can have limited knowledge of their pregnancies, concealing and/or denying the pregnancy not only from others, but also from themselves.[34] The result is that a woman will make no plans for the birth of the child[35] and is often surprised by the delivery, potentially misinterpreting the bodily sensation of birth as a bowel movement.[36] The nature of the birth means that the foetus/baby either dies prior to live birth, or dies from neglect post-birth or is violently killed by the woman post-birth. A review by Milne of cases from England and Wales between 2002 and 2019 indicates that homicide convictions, including infanticide, are generally only sought in cases where the mother has actively taken steps to end the life of the child; if live birth can be proved, cases of death due to neglect are most often prosecuted as child-cruelty cases.[37]

In instances whereby women act to kill the child, there is evidence that some women are not in control of their actions at the time of the killing. While scholars argue widely that women suspected of causing the death of a newborn child are not psychotic and that psychopathology is rare in these cases,[38] there is substantial evidence that women are motivated by fear and shame, and that the killing occurs due to panic following the unexpected birth.[39] One of the most comprehensive studies of the psychological conditions of women who actively took steps to kill a newborn child, conducted by Spinelli, concluded that the accused women experienced dissociative psychosis and/or dissociative hallucinations, occurring in the context of the shock of the birth, with all women in the study living in a context of social isolation, emotional neglect, leading chaotic lives, with bizarre and strained relationships with their parents.[40]

[32] A Frederick, 'Between Stigma and Mother-Blame: Blind Mothers' Experiences in USA Hospital Postnatal Care' (2015) 37 *Sociology of Health & Illness* 1127.

[33] Milne (n 24).

[34] Meyer and Oberman (n 27); Beyer, McAuliffe Mack and Shelton (n 26); S Hatters Friedman, S McCue Horwitz and PJ Resnick, 'Child Murder by Mothers: A Critical Analysis of the Current State of Knowledge and a Research Agenda' (2005) 162 *American Journal of Psychiatry* 1578.

[35] Vellut, Cook and Tursz (n 27).

[36] R Kaplan and T Grotowski, 'Denied Pregnancy' (1996) 30 *Australian and New Zealand Journal of Psychiatry* 861; M Brozovsky and H Falit, 'Neonaticide: Clinical and Psychodynamic Considerations' (1971) 10 *Journal of the American Academy of Child Psychiatry* 673.

[37] Milne (n 24) 9.

[38] PT d'Orbán, 'Women Who Kill Their Children' (1979) 134 *British Journal of Psychiatry* 560; S Amon et al, 'Potential Predictors in Neonaticide: The Impact of the Circumstances of Pregnancy' (2012) 15 *Archives of Women's Mental Health* 167; Meyer and Oberman (n 27).

[39] Beyer, McAuliffe Mack and Shelton (n 26); Milne (n 24).

[40] MG Spinelli, 'Neonaticide: A Systematic Investigation of 17 Cases' in MG Spinelli (ed), *Infanticide: Psychosocial and Legal Perspectives on Mothers Who Kill* (American Psychiatric Pub 2003) 105. See also CM Alder and J Baker, 'Maternal Filicide: More Than One Story to Be Told' (1997) 9 *Women and Criminal Justice* 15; Amon et al (n 38).

ii. The Killing of Older Infants

The context that surrounds the killing of older infants is different from that of newborn child deaths. A significant proportion of women who kill older infants experience mental health conditions that are directly connected to parenting an infant, such as postnatal depression.[41] Other research reports women killing their infants due to psychotic episodes that are not the result of changing hormones from the pregnancy and birth.[42] Further studies have identified killings occurring in the context of child abuse – where the death is not the intention but the consequence of the abuse.[43] However, as with murder-suicides and killings to take 'revenge' on a third party, killing in the context of child abuse is far less frequently committed by women compared to men.[44] It should also be remembered that women's acts of killing make up only a very small minority of all homicides.[45]

However, as with newborn child killing, the social and cultural factors that surround women's fatal acts towards their infants are significant. A review by Alder and Baker of Coroner's court files in Victoria Australia from 1978 to 1991 revealed that women who committed a fatal assault on their infants (excluding homicide-suicide) faced their own unique but invariably difficult situations, such as financial problems, exhaustion, frustration, depression, isolation and lack of practical support. The incident that led to the final assault was often child misbehaviour or crying, and the accused women expressed feelings of frustration at the lack of support from their partner to help parent a difficult baby.[46] They conclude that most of these cases were of mothers who had difficult babies and were struggling to cope in the circumstances in which they were expected to parent the child, resulting in a build-up of frustration. Numerous other studies have highlighted similar 'social stressors' and drawn similar conclusions from the analysis

[41] d'Orbán (n 38); Friedman, Horwitz and Resnick (n 34); V Dobson and BD Sales, 'The Science of Infanticide and Mental Illness' (2000) 6 *Psychology, Public Policy, and Law* 1098; S Hatters Friedman, J Cavney and PJ Resnick, 'Mothers Who Kill: Evolutionary Underpinnings and Infanticide Law' (2012) 30 *Behavioral Sciences & the Law* 585.

[42] T Porter and H Gavin, 'Infanticide and Neonaticide: A Review of 40 Years of Research Literature on Incidence and Causes' (2010) 11 *Trauma, Violence & Abuse* 99.

[43] D Bourget and P Gagné, 'Maternal Filicide in Quebec' (2002) 30 *Journal of the American Academy of Psychiatry and the Law Online* 345; S Hatters Friedman and JB Friedman, 'Parents Who Kill Their Children' (2010) 31 *Pediatrics in Review* 10; PJ Resnick, 'Child Murder by Parents: A Psychiatric Review of Filicide' (1969) 126 *American Journal of Psychiatry* 325; M Oberman, 'A Brief History of Infanticide and the Law' in MG Spinelli (ed), *Infanticide: Psychosocial and Legal Perspectives on Mothers Who Kill* (American Psychiatric Pub 2003) 3.

[44] D Bourget, J Grace and L Whitehurst, 'A Review of Maternal and Paternal Filicide' (2007) 35 *Journal of the American Academy of Psychiatry and the Law Online* 74; K Cavanagh, RE Dobash and RP Dobash, 'The Murder of Children by Fathers in the Context of Child Abuse' (2007) 31 *Child Abuse and Neglect* 731.

[45] See Milne and Turton for analysis of homicide data: E Milne and J Turton, 'Understanding Violent Women' in E Milne et al (eds), *Women and the Criminal Justice System: Failing Victims and Offenders?* (Palgrave Macmillan 2018) 119.

[46] Alder and Baker (n 40).

of maternal filicide of older infants.[47] As discussed in section IV.B, the specific experience of parenting a child is overwhelmingly experienced by women rather than men. Consequently, this is one of the key arguments for not extending infanticide to fathers.

II. The History of the Infanticide Act

In this section we will provide an account of the history behind the 1922/1938 Infanticide Acts. This will serve to provide a context for discussions of the law in different chapters in the book. To understand the offence/defence of infanticide, and thus assess its role in the criminal law over the last 100 years and how it has been applied to cases, it is necessary to understand the socio-historical and legal context in which the 1922/1938 Infanticide Acts were enacted. Thus, although the history cannot tell us what the law means today, since that is something for the courts and other users of this law to determine,[48] an appreciation of the origins of this law, which pays attention to the social and legal context of its enactment/re-enactment, is essential as it serves to reveal what legislators had in mind at the time they passed this law. Consequently, the history of infanticide provides an essential context for an analysis of this law in the twenty-first century.

In terms of the legal origins of the Infanticide Act 1922, numerous scholars have argued that its roots lie in the 1624 *Act to Prevent the Destroying and Murthering of Bastard Children* ('the 1624 Act'). This legislation applied only to unmarried women who were suspected of having killed their newborn children. For these women, the statute reversed the burden of proof of live birth.[49] Under English and Welsh law then – and now – legal personhood only commences after live birth.[50] Thus, the prosecution were required to prove a child had been born alive before they could prove a woman had murdered the child. The 1624 Act removed this requirement, instead requiring the woman to prove that the baby was stillborn with the testimony of a witness. Without producing proof of stillbirth, the woman could be convicted of murder, a capital offence. The Act made it much easier to convict unmarried women of murder. The law essentially meant that concealing

[47] Meyer and Oberman (n 27); M Oberman and CL Meyer, *When Mothers Kill: Interviews from Prison* (New York University Press 2008); M Smithey, *The Cultural and Economic Context of Maternal Infanticide: A Crying Baby and the Inability to Escape* (Emerald Publishing Ltd 2019); CF Lewis and SC Bunce, 'Filicidal Mothers and the Impact of Psychosis on Maternal Filicide' (2003) 31 *Journal of the American Academy of Psychiatry and the Law Online* 459.

[48] Such as, for example, the Crown Prosecution Service in how it decides on charging and plea negotiations.

[49] Parliament Papers, 1624 21 Jac 1 c27; cited in Kilday (n 10) 17–18.

[50] E Coke, *The Fourth Part of the Institutes of the Laws of England: Concerning the Jurisdiction of Courts*, 6th edn (Printed by W Rawlins, for Thomas Basset at the George near St Dunstans Church in Fleet-street 1644[1681]).

the birth of an illegitimate child who subsequently died provided 'almost conclusive evidence of the child's being murdered by its mother'.[51]

While the legal and social response to women suspected of newborn child murder during the seventeenth and eighteenth centuries had an impact on legal approaches in the nineteenth century, to say that the Infanticide Act 1922 developed from this law, or that the 1624 Act was a form of an infanticide law, is to misunderstand the history of the Infanticide Act and the role the legislation was seen to fulfil when enacted in the early twentieth century. Nevertheless, the significance of the 1624 Act for our history of the Infanticide Acts 1922/1938 is that the harshness of the 1624 Act slowly impacted wider perceptions of women suspected of killing their newborn children.[52] The perceived harshness of the 1624 Act meant that by the early nineteenth century it was effectively not being used, and unmarried women accused of killing their infants were tried as any other person accused of murder – with the prosecution obliged to prove live birth before they could convict a woman of the crime.[53] Consequently, there was a growing concern that unmarried women were getting away with murdering their newborn children due to public perception of the harshness and unfair treatment caused by the 1624 Act. Repeal of the law therefore became a priority for Lord Ellenborough, the Lord Chief Justice, as part of his efforts to consolidate and codify the criminal law: as he stated in his speech to Parliament, '[too] harsh was this law, as to oblige the Judges, in their construction of it, to admit proof of the child having been still-born'.[54]

Ellenborough's Act of 1803 reinstated the presumption of dead birth, thus ensuring that unwed women who were suspected of murdering their babies would be subject to the same evidential rules that applied in all cases of murder. The statute also created a separate misdemeanour of concealment of birth, which criminalised the concealment of the dead body of a baby, irrespective of how it had died and whether or not it had been born alive.[55] The importance of the concealment offence for the history of the infanticide law is the role it played in newborn child murder cases throughout the nineteenth century and up until the enactment of the 1922 Infanticide Act. Concealment of birth essentially provided a lenient alternative for jurors who did not want to convict women of the capital offence of murder but nonetheless sought to punish the woman rather than fully acquit her.[56] However, as a misdemeanour, punishable with a maximum of two years' imprisonment, concealment of birth was considered an inappropriate response to infanticide. Concealment of birth also provided a 'convenient stop-gap'

[51] W Blackstone, *Commentaries on the Laws of England*, vol 4 (11th edn, T Cadell 1791) 198.
[52] Jackson (n 10).
[53] ibid; Beattie (n 10).
[54] Reported in *The Times* (29 March 1803) 2.
[55] 43 Geo III, c 58, ss 3 and 4. This offence was twice amended in the 19th century and its current iteration is found in the Offences Against the Person Act 1861 (24 & 25 Vict, c 100), s 60. For a discussion of the history concealment of birth, see Milne (n 28); Milne (n 24).
[56] Higginbotham (n 15).

in cases where live birth could not be proved and so a murder conviction was impossible.[57]

The 1866 Royal Commission on Capital Punishment is arguably the appropriate starting point for considering the history of the Infanticide Acts 1922/1938, because it is in the evidence presented to the Commission that we can identify the chief problems with the law relating to maternal infanticide and thus the roots for eventual legislative reform in 1922.[58] The picture that emerged from the evidence before the 1866 Commission was that the harshness of the law, which treated newborn infanticide as murder and thus a capital crime, defeated its purpose. Essentially, the law was so out of touch with wider public sentiment that it was effectively being disregarded.[59] For example, Lord Wensleydale noted that in the 'great number' of cases he had presided over, he had never had 'one woman convicted, they always escaped; it was found that the child was not born alive'.[60] Sir George Bramwell called the prevailing legal practice a 'contrivance' whereby 'the mother is never found guilty in what is undoubtedly a case of infanticide'.[61] Related to this was what became known as the 'solemn mockery' (also known as the 'black-cap farce') of the death sentence, whereby in every case where a murder conviction was returned against a woman who killed her baby and she was duly sentenced to death by the judge, the Home Secretary commuted the death sentence. As the Rev Lord SG Osborne remarked, '[i]n nine cases out of ten, trying women for their lives for infanticide is a cruel farce' because 'no one for one moment believes that the woman will be executed'.[62] The last execution of a woman for infant murder was in 1849, and the last execution of a woman for newborn child murder was in 1832.[63]

Ultimately, three issues can be identified from the evidence given before the Commission.[64] First, live birth was often genuinely difficult to prove, and there was a gap in the law in terms of protecting foetuses/infants in that it was no crime to kill a foetus/child in the act of birth. Second, the law on murder was too harsh in the face of significant public sympathy for accused women: it was extremely

[57] D Seaborne Davies, 'Child-Killing in English Law – Part I' (1937) 1 *MLR* 203, 213.

[58] D Seaborne Davies, 'Child-Killing in English Law' in L Radzinowicz and JWC Turner (eds), *The Modern Approach to Criminal Law* (Macmillan 1945) 319. For further detail on the history behind the 1922/1938 Infanticide Acts starting with the 1866 Commission, see K Brennan, 'Infanticide Past and Present: Law, History and Culture' (PhD Thesis, University College Dublin 2006) chs 6 and 7.

[59] Seabourne Davies (n 57) 217–18.

[60] *British Parliamentary Papers*, 1866, vol 21, 101. Please note that page numbers refer to the entire volume, not individual reports, papers, etc.

[61] ibid 74.

[62] ibid 475.

[63] Wiener (n 12) 124–15.

[64] The Commission in its report identified live birth as the chief obstacle to the administration of justice, with the solemn mockery of the death sentence being a second issue. It recommended two reforms: (i) the creation of a new offence to address the issue of live birth and close the gap in the law whereby it was no offence to kill a foetus/child in the act of birth; (ii) to allow judges to record the death sentence in cases of infanticide. See *British Parliamentary Papers* (n 60) 50.

difficult to secure a capital conviction in cases of infanticide, which meant women were acquitted entirely or convicted of the much less serious offence of concealment of birth. Related to this, the 'born alive' rule was regularly exploited by medical witnesses, juries and indeed judges, to justify an acquittal on a murder charge for reasons of sympathy. Finally, there was the issue of the 'solemn mockery' of the death sentence, in cases where juries did convict of murder and the death sentence was passed but it was invariably commuted. It was the second and third issues, both of which related to the effective administration of justice in the face of significant public sympathy for women who killed their babies at birth, that ultimately led to the enactment of the 1922 Infanticide Act. In particular, the issue of the 'solemn mockery' was, according to Seabourne Davies, the key driving force behind the introduction of this law.[65]

Starting with the 1866 Law of Capital Punishment Amendment Bill and ending with the 1880 Draft Criminal Code Bill (no 2), there were several attempts in the nineteenth century to reform the law by addressing the problems identified by the 1866 Commission.[66] Attempts at reform were revived in 1908 as part of parliamentary discussions on the proposed Children's Act, and there were a number of further attempts between 1908 and 1911.[67] These proposals were almost always concerned with the killing of babies at or soon after birth by their mothers and adopted different approaches to addressing the problems in the law, ranging from measures that allowed the death penalty to be recorded in cases of maternal infanticide to creating new offences/defences to remove maternal infanticide from the general provisions on murder/capital punishment.[68] The Infanticide Act 1922 began as the Child Murder (Trial) Bill, with a proposal to allow the jury to convict women who killed their children of manslaughter rather than murder where the jury were of the opinion that 'she had not fully recovered from the effects of giving birth'.[69] During the Committee Stage, Viscount Birkenhead, the Lord Chancellor, proposed various amendments with the objective of bringing more 'precision' to the language of the Bill, including an age limit ('newlyborn') and the requirement that the balance of the woman's mind must be disturbed, the purpose of this being to provide a connection between her act in killing the child and the fact that she had not fully recovered from the effect of giving birth. He also proposed creating a new substantive offence on this basis, called 'infanticide'. His amendments were all accepted.[70] The 1922 Act created the offence/partial defence of infanticide, which

[65] Seabourne Davies (n 58) 339. The gap in the law in cases where live birth could not be proved was addressed separately through the new offence of child destruction, which was created by the Infant Life Preservation Act 1929.

[66] For detail on these legislative attempts, see D Seaborne Davies, 'Child-Killing in English Law – Part II' (1938) 1 *MLR* 269. See also Brennan (n 58), chs 6 and 7.

[67] See generally Seabourne Davies (n 66); Brennan (n 58) chs 6 and 7.

[68] See generally Seabourne Davies (n 66); Brennan (n 58) chs 6 and 7.

[69] Seabourne Davies (n 66); Brennan (n 58) 215–19.

[70] HL Deb 16 May 1922, vol 50, cols 440–41; HL Deb 25 May 1922, vol 50, cols 758–62, 767–68. For summary of discussion in Parliament on the Bill and the amendments proposed, see Brennan (n 58) 215–19.

applied where a woman by a wilful act or omission killed her 'newlyborn' child at a time when 'she had not fully recovered from the effect of giving birth to such child and by reason thereof the balance of her mind was then disturbed'.[71]

The first case in which the 1922 Act was used was at Lincoln Assizes in October 1922, where 19-year-old domestic servant Emma Temple pleaded guilty to murdering her newborn infant. She was sentenced by Lush J to four months' imprisonment. The judge stated that although he felt sorry for the accused girl and believed that one would say that she had already suffered sufficient punishment, he felt that she should be given this sentence in order to deter others from the crime.[72] It was not long, however, before problems emerged with the 1922 Act, the central issue being the scope of infanticide in terms of the age of the victim. As Seaborne Davies has argued, '[t]he words "newly-born" … [became] decisive of the whole scope of the reform'.[73] The result of this was 'an invitation to a recurrence of the mischiefs which reformers for sixty years before the Act had attempted to correct'.[74]

The immediate trigger for the 1938 statute was the 1936 case of *Hale*. Mrs Hale had been tried for the murder of her 3-week-old infant.[75] After the birth of her first child, she had developed 'symptoms bordering on puerperal insanity', and this recurred after the birth of her second child, the victim. At her trial, Viscount Dawson of Penn gave evidence stating that she was suffering from puerperal insanity and did not know what she was doing at the time she killed her infant. The trial judge, Humphries J, stated that he was bound by the decision of the Court of Criminal Appeal in *O'Donoghue*,[76] where it was held that a judge was correct to tell a jury that an infant just over 4 weeks old 'was not, and could not be, a newly-born child within the meaning of the [Infanticide Act 1922]'.[77] The infanticide law could not, therefore, apply. Following the direction of the trial judge, the jury found Mrs Hale not guilty of murder but guilty of the act charged, for which she was not responsible in law, and the judge directed that she be detained at His Majesty's pleasure.[78]

There was a failed attempt at extending the law on infanticide in 1936, which ended with the abdication crisis, to explicitly take account of social circumstances and extend the age limit of the victim to 8 years.[79] Two years later, Viscount Dawson of Penn, who had given evidence at the *Hale* trial, introduced to Parliament a

[71] Infanticide Act 1922, s 1(1) and (2).
[72] Reported in 'New Infanticide Act: Judge on First Case' *The Times* (London, 31 October 1922) 9.
[73] Seabourne Davies (n 58) 338.
[74] ibid 339.
[75] *R v Hale*, The Times, 22 July 1936, 13.
[76] *R v O'Donoghue* (1927) 20 Cr App R 132.
[77] *Hale* (n 75) 13.
[78] ibid. See also Seabourne Davies (n 58) 337–38. Ward notes the verdict was 'designed to soften the stigma of being declared "guilty but insane"': see T Ward, 'The Sad Subject of Infanticide: Law, Medicine and Child Murder, 1860–1938' (1999) 8 *Social and Legal Studies* 163, 172.
[79] Seabourne Davies (n 66) 286.

new infanticide proposal. When presenting the 1938 Bill to Parliament, Dawson recalled that in *Hale*, 'it was so obviously discordant with the Judge's feelings to try this woman for murder that when he summed up he expressed the hope that some amendment of the infanticide law would be made'.[80] Dawson subsequently referred the issue of infanticide to a committee of experts in the Royal College of Physicians. The 1938 Bill was the product of their 'united wisdom'.[81] The Bill proposed to extend infanticide to cover babies up to 12 months, with an extension of the mitigation framework to include a disturbance in the balance of the mind caused by the effect of lactation consequent upon birth; it was passed without amendment. Like the 1922 Act, this proposal was concerned with the 'solemn mockery' and the administration of justice, and, related to this, not putting women through either the declaration of a capital sentence or the stigma and consequences of an insanity verdict.[82] Unlike the 1922 statute, which was focused on the killing of newborn 'illegitimate' babies, usually at a secret, unassisted birth in situations where the mother was unlikely to have been mentally ill,[83] the 1938 law was focused on the killing of older infants in situations where the mother could be said to be suffering from a mental illness.

The Infanticide Act 1938 has since been amended once to make it clear that the accused must be guilty of either murder or manslaughter before the infanticide offence/defence can apply.[84] This followed the *obiter* view of the Court of Appeal in *Gore*, where it was held that it was not necessary to prove the mens rea for murder in order to rely on infanticide, the mental element for infanticide being expressed in the requirement that the woman's act or omission that caused death was 'wilful'.[85] There has been very little case law on the statute. Judge LJ, in *obiter* comments in *Kai-Whitewind*, implied that social circumstances are not part of the doctrine when, after stating that the only relevant factors for consideration are birth and lactation, he highlighted as an area of concern in an upcoming Law Commission review the question of whether infanticide should 'extend to circumstances subsequent to birth, but connected with it, such as the stresses imposed on a mother by the absence of natural bonding with her baby: in short whether the current definition of infanticide reflects modern thinking'.[86] The only time the Infanticide Act 1938 has come before the appeal courts for interpretation is in the case of *Tunstill*,[87] where the Court of Appeal interpreted the phrase 'by reason of'

[80] HL Deb 22 March 1938, vol 108, cols 294–95.

[81] ibid 308. For detail on the parliamentary debates on the 1938 Bill/Act, see Brennan (n 58) 223–27.

[82] For summary of debates highlighting these issues as key in the 1938 reform, see Brennan (n 58) 223–27.

[83] Ward (n 78).

[84] Coroners and Justice Act 2009, s 57(2).

[85] *R v Gore (Lisa Theresa) (Deceased)* [2007] EWCA Crim 2789. See also A Ashworth, 'Infanticide: whether mens rea of infanticide consists of an intention to kill or cause grievous bodily harm' (2007) 5 *Crim LR* 388.

[86] *R v Kai-Whitewind* [2005] EWCA Crim 1092 [139]. The Law Commission decided against such an amendment to the law: see discussion in section IV.A.

[87] *R v Tunstill* [2018] EWCA Crim 1696.

in section 1(1) to imply use of standard causation principles, which meant that the effect of birth or lactation must at least be a minimal cause of the disturbance in the balance of the mind, but need not be the sole cause.

The meaning of the medical rationale has, however, never been determined by the appeal courts in England and Wales.[88] Often it is assumed that it requires a mental illness linked to the physical effects of childbirth or lactation, such as postnatal depression or psychosis, though in practice the law has been used in situations where there was no mental disorder and to allow for recognition of social circumstances.[89] In section II.A we examine the history of the medical rationale. The aim is to provide a context for any future consideration of the meaning of the medical rationale.

A. Rationalising Infanticide

Recently, the Court of Appeal acknowledged the merciful intentions behind the infanticide law.[90] Certainly, at the time of the enactment/re-enactment of the infanticide statutes of 1922/1938, humanitarian sentiment towards the unwed mother who killed her baby at birth was ingrained in the public and ultimately the criminal justice response to this crime. However, although the history shows that humanitarian sentiment for this offender was an important part of the infanticide reform, this does not mean that legislators primarily sought to achieve mercy through the 1922/1938 laws.[91] As explained, the 1922 and 1938 Infanticide Acts were mainly concerned with the effective administration of justice, particularly ensuring proper and legitimate use of the criminal law and capital punishment, and, specifically in 1938, to avoid reliance on the insanity defence for a category of killer whose 'insanity' was considered temporary. However, problems with the application of the law prior to the enactment of each of these statutes stemmed from public sympathy for the offender, and by facilitating a formal merciful response, the infanticide statute could counteract the negative effects of informal humanitarianism.[92]

Behind the pragmatic criminal justice concerns about the effectiveness and appropriateness of the legal response to maternal infanticide lies the question of

[88] The Canadian Supreme Court recently decided that the equivalent provision in the Canadian law does not require a 'defined mental or psychological condition or mental illness' and 'need not constitute a mental disorder' or amount to 'a significant impairment of [her] reasoning faculties'. The term 'disturbed' was not a legal or medical term and should be given its ordinary grammatical meaning, and so meant 'mentally agitated; mentally unstable; or mental discomposure'. See *R v Borowiec* [2016] 1 SCR 80 [35].

[89] Discussed further in section III.A.

[90] *Tunstill* (n 87).

[91] K Brennan, 'Beyond the Medical Model: A Rationale for Infanticide Legislation' (2007) 58 *NILQ* 505; Brennan, 'A Fine Mixture of Pity and Justice' (n 11).

[92] Ward (n 78); Brennan, 'A Fine Mixture of Pity and Justice' (n 11); Brennan, 'Beyond the Medical Model' (n 91).

why this crime was, in the public imagination, considered less serious than other murders, why there was such public sympathy for this offender and, related to this, how this was then translated into justified differential treatment of this crime in the law. These are questions that remain valid today in debates about the continued meaning, value and appropriateness of the infanticide law. The language of the infanticide statutes, which speak of a 'disturbance in the balance of the mind' and the 'effect of giving birth'/'effect of lactation consequent upon … birth', tends to suggest that compassion for the offender stemmed from an understanding that the crime was the product of mental illness, specifically one related to birth/lactation. However, the history shows that the social context of the crime and the harshness of the criminal law were more important factors in the emergence of humanitarian sentiment for this offender.[93]

At the time of the enactment of the 1922 law, infanticide had for several centuries been perceived as the crime of the unwed mother, being linked to the dire social and economic consequences of unmarried motherhood. This is an important factor in understanding the public and criminal justice response to the crime. When we look at what was said by jurists and legislators who promoted reform of the law of child murder from the mid-1860s onwards, it seems apparent that a number of factors help to explain sympathy for the infanticidal woman who killed her newborn baby.[94] First, she was not thought to have killed as the result of a premediated or deliberated action calculated to rid herself of an unwanted child. Rather, she was usually understood to have acted while in a highly distressed, 'frenzied' state, being governed by intense emotions such as shame, panic and fear in the face of the consequences of giving birth outside of marriage, and at time when she would also have been suffering from the physical and mental impact of an unassisted labour. For example, the Attorney-General Sir John Holker, when introducing to the House of Commons the infanticide provisions included in an 1878 Bill to Establish A Criminal Code, referred to the proposal as an expression of 'mercy' rather than 'logic'.[95] He stated the provision would allow for 'merciful consideration [of] the condition of poor fallen women' who '[consign] to death a creature that can scarcely be said to have lived, in a moment of nervous excitement, perhaps burning shame and intense mental and bodily anguish'.[96]

[93] For examples of literature that explore the history of this law, see: Ward (n 78); Seabourne Davies (nn 57, 58, 66); KJ Kramar, *Unwilling Mothers, Unwanted Babies Infanticide in Canada* (UBC Press 2005); Brennan, 'Beyond the Medical Model' (n 91); Brennan, 'A Fine Mixture of Pity and Justice' (n 11); JA Osborne, 'The Crime of Infanticide: Throwing Out the Baby with the Bath Water' (1987) 6 *Canadian Journal of Family Law* 47; R Lansdowne, 'Infanticide: Psychiatrists in the Plea Bargaining Process' (1990) 16 *Monash University Law Review* 41.

[94] Seabourne Davies (n 58) 320–21. See also Brennan, 'A Fine Mixture of Pity and Justice' (n 11) 799–800. For examples from different legislative attempts to reform the law relating to infanticide, and further examples of evidence given by witnesses before the 1866 Royal Commission on Capital Punishment, which illustrate the points made in the following paragraphs, see Brennan (n 58), chs 6 and 7.

[95] HC Deb 14 May 1878, vol 239, cols 1936–59 at 1948–49.

[96] ibid.

Linked with this was the idea that the woman acted in a moment of temporary madness. Fitzjames Stephen stated in his evidence before the 1866 Commission on Capital Punishment:

> [W]omen in that condition do get the strongest symptoms of what amounts almost to temporary madness, and that they often hardly know what they are about, and will do things that they have no settled or deliberate intention whatever of doing.[97]

This is perhaps the most contentious and complex part of the explanation for humanitarian sentiment towards infanticidal mothers, because of the significance that has been accorded to it in more recent analyses of infanticide law. It is in some ways a valid and natural assumption that the chief reason for sympathy for the infanticidal woman was the view that she was temporarily insane – that she 'must have been mad'. It is usually thought, for example, that this is what the 1922/1938 Acts formally adopted as a rationale for reduced culpability – that the infanticide law recognised puerperal, and later lactational, 'insanity'. This explanation also links with nineteenth-century psychiatric understandings of mental illness after birth and infanticide, and with broader sexist ideologies about women's susceptibility to mental illness, especially linked to their reproductive functions, and more generally to the weak and passive nature of women.[98] The meaning of the 'medical model' of infanticide is discussed in more detail in chapter 6. For now, it suffices to say that one strand of the explanation for humanitarian sentiment for this offender was based on notions of the 'insanities of reproduction' and the sexist attitudes this incorporated. However, it was not necessarily (or consistently) the dominant explanation.

Another aspect to explaining the humanitarian response to the infanticidal woman related to her moral responsibility, in the sense that she was thought to have been placed in an unfair position as a consequence of feckless male sexuality and wider society's failure to support her. In other words, it was considered inequitable to hold her alone to account for the killing of the baby. Double standards of sexuality largely enabled men to avoid responsibility for their 'illegitimate' children, and the 'fallen woman' was often depicted sympathetically in this context as having been seduced and then abandoned to face the harsh social and economic realities of unwed motherhood.[99] Linked with this, there may also have been some understanding of the fact that wider society bore a responsibility for this crime. In his evidence before the 1866 Commission, Osborne observed, for example, that 'mankind generally are so far conscience stricken in this matter that they feel a very natural reluctance to visit on the woman the full penalty of a crime in which themselves have antecedently much to answer for'.[100]

[97] *British Parliamentary Papers* (n 60) 343.
[98] See Loughnan (n 11). For further discussion see Milne and Brennan, ch 6 of this volume.
[99] For example, see evidence given by Fitzjames Stephen before the Royal Commission on Capital Punishment in 1866: *British Parliamentary Papers* (n 60) 343.
[100] ibid 476.

Essentially, sympathy stemmed from a variety of factors, some of which may have been given more importance than others at different times and by different people. It was the product of an interplay between an understanding of the distressing circumstances of the birth and killing, particularly the social context of the woman's giving birth unaided to an 'illegitimate' child; her perceived physical, mental and emotional state in these circumstances, including the notion that she was labouring under a temporary insanity at the time;[101] and her responsibility in a moral sense. Attitudes to the infanticide offender were also clearly imbued with sexist gender norms, which viewed women as susceptible to madness particularly as a consequence of their biological functions, and as weak victims of their circumstances.[102] Underpinning all of this were emerging psychiatric understandings of 'the insanities of reproduction', which also linked insanity to biology.[103] As Loughnan states:

> Beliefs that women's mental conditions were closely related or determined by biology were common to expert medical and psychiatric and lay discourses. … [T]his network of gendered meanings meant that women were constructed as passive subjects … Altogether, a compassionate view of a woman's act of killing her newborn emerged, based on sympathy for her weak physical and moral state and for the physical pain suffered by a woman giving birth without assistance, and on the conception of a 'fallen woman' who was not a fully independent agent.[104]

However, when it came to enacting a law that would offer a merciful response to infanticidal women, there were additional issues to consider. In particular, there was the need to respect the criminal law's requirement for individual responsibility, which meant that despite the fact that the social circumstances of this offence were a key reason for seeking to treat these accused women leniently, the law could not overtly reduce the seriousness of the crime on that basis.[105] Blame for the crime had to reside with the individual, not with wider societal causes, and where this blame was reduced, this also had to be based on her characteristics rather than external factors.[106] Further, although the infanticide legislation was first conceived and enacted at a time when infant life was perhaps held more cheaply than it is now,[107] it seems evident from the history of attempts to legislate for infanticide that there was a hesitancy, at least among some, to reduce the seriousness of this

[101] For example, see Ward (n 78); Loughnan (n 11).

[102] E Showalter, *The Female Malady: Women, Madness and English Culture, 1830–1980* (Penguin Books 1987).

[103] Loughnan (n 11).

[104] ibid 699.

[105] See, eg, Ward (n 78); Lansdowne (n 93) 45–46.

[106] A Norrie, *Crime, Reason and History: A Critical Introduction to Criminal Law*, 3rd edn (Cambridge University Press 2014).

[107] VAR Zelizer, *Pricing the Priceless Child: The Changing Social Value of Children* (Princeton University Press 1994).

crime and thus the deterrent effect of the law: legislators did not want to convey the impression that infant murder was less serious than other killings; women who killed children simply because they were unwanted should not be able to avail themselves of reduced culpability.[108] A final point of note is that in the legal context of the time, the infanticide legislation was a controversial and ground-breaking enactment. Murder was, without exception, a capital crime, unless one of the limited defences available, such as insanity or provocation, applied. And, aside from the provocation defence, there was no other example in the criminal law of partially reducing culpability for murder – diminished responsibility did not make its way into English law until over 30 years later.[109]

Thus, the history behind the 1922 and 1938 Acts highlights a tension: on the one hand, there was the objective to facilitate a lenient option that accepted the prevailing humanitarian sentiment for infanticidal women and thus allow for the effective administration of justice; on the other hand, there was a need to ensure that the deterrent effect of the law was not reduced in the case of infant victims and that individual offenders were held to account according to standard criminal justice norms. Thus, although the history shows that awareness of the social context of the offence was a significant aspect as to why this crime was viewed sympathetically, the 1922 and 1938 Infanticide Acts did not explicitly reference social factors. Instead, the law adopted language that, on the face of it, seems to limit infanticide to situations where the disturbance in the balance of the woman's mind was produced by the effects of birth/lactation.

Interestingly, there are examples in the history of infanticide law reform of attempts to explicitly include social factors as part of the law. For example, two years before the 1938 reform, a bill was presented to the House of Commons, to replace the 1922 Act with a measure that would extend the scope of infanticide to cover any mother who caused the death of her child aged under 8 years while the 'balance of her mind was disturbed' either from the effects of giving birth to that child, or from 'distress and despair arising from solicitude for her child, or extreme poverty, or other causes'.[110] Introducing the Bill, Mr Jagger stated that its purpose was

> merely to legalise what has been the consistent practice for nearly ninety years, and to remove the legal anomaly and legal cruelty involved in sentencing a woman to death

[108] For example, during discussion on the 1938 Bill, Lord Atkin noted '[t]he trouble in the law is, of course, as it has always been, not to weaken the protection that is given to the lives of infant children': HL Deb 22 March 1938, vol 108, col 299. During debates on the 1922 Bill, Lord Carson asserted that the Lords should 'take care … that [they were] not led away by feelings of tender compassion', and that the Bill should not give the impression that the law reduces a woman's crime simply because she had been through the experience of childbirth: HL Deb 25 May 1922, vol 50, col 765. For other examples, see generally Brennan (n 58) chs 6 and 7.

[109] Homicide Act 1957, s 2.

[110] *British Parliamentary Papers*, 1936–37, vol 2, 963 (no 37). See also Seabourne Davies (n 66) 286.

> when it is perfectly well known to everybody, except to the unfortunate prisoner, that there is no intention of that sentence being carried out.[111]

The disturbance surrounding the abdication of King Edward put an end to this effort.[112] During the House of Lords debates on the 1938 Infanticide Bill, Lord Arnold sought to widen the scope of the proposal.[113] He advocated that 'mental disturbance due to distress and despair arising from solicitude for the child and extreme poverty, or either of these' should have been included in the Bill.[114] However, Lord Dawson refused to extend the Bill in this manner, fearing it would make the Government more 'nervous' than it already was.[115]

There are two key points to highlight from this history to serve as a context for understanding and critiquing the current infanticide law. The first is that the purpose of both the 1922 and 1938 Acts was to avoid the 'solemn mockery' of the sentencing to death of women for killing their babies in situations where everyone knew the sentence would invariably be commuted.[116] Linked with this was ensuring conviction for a homicide offence that carried a more suitable lenient punishment than the mandatory death sentence of a murder conviction.[117] Ultimately, both Acts were about respecting the criminal law.

Second, although the infanticide statutes may be read today as providing for a type of insanity defence – something akin to diminished responsibility – that is not necessarily how the crime was understood at the time the 1922/1938 Acts were enacted. For example, Ward has argued that the 1922 Infanticide Act adopted a 'lay' or 'common sense' understanding of a woman's mental state at the time of the killing that took account of the social circumstances.[118] The social context of the crime is crucial to understanding humanitarian sentiment for the infanticidal woman, and whilst it is probably fair to say that legislators did not want to allow for mitigation solely on the basis of social circumstances, it seems equally unlikely that they wanted the law to operate in a way that excluded consideration of the social circumstances that affected her mental state at the time of the killing. There was a balance to be struck between ensuring that women who killed their babies in cold blood simply to be rid of them would not be able to 'get away with murder', whilst also ridding courtrooms of the 'solemn mockery', something that, arguably, called for recognition of the role of social factors in the crime. The debates on

[111] HC Deb 24 November 1936, vol 318, col 235.
[112] Seabourne Davies (n 58) 342.
[113] HL Deb 22 March 1938, vol 108, cols 303–04.
[114] ibid col 304.
[115] ibid cols 308–09.
[116] Seabourne Davies (n 66) 284–85.
[117] See Brennan, 'Beyond the Medical Model' (n 91); Brennan, 'A Fine Mixture of Pity and Justice' (n 11).
[118] Ward (n 78). See Milne and Brennan, ch 6 of this volume, for further discussion.

the 1938 Bill are illustrative of this tension and the fact that, in the end, explicitly allowing for social mitigation was considered simply too controversial and risked the entire legislative endeavour.[119] Lansdowne argues that the emphasis on the woman's mental state was a 'convenient catch all' for other issues, such as poverty and social disgrace due to an illegitimate pregnancy, and that childbirth was blamed because this, unlike social factors, respected criminal norms and because it could be assumed that the physical effects of unassisted childbirth would cause 'considerable shock and distress' and thus affect the balance of the mind.[120] She also notes the possible influence of medical thinking that associated childbirth with insanity.[121] As Osborne asserts, 'the medical rationale was never in vogue or scientifically established. It was simply more conventional, conservative and less contentious than the reasons for the courts' lenient treatment of murdering mothers.'[122]

III. Infanticide Today

Over the course of the twentieth century, the rates of infanticide dropped dramatically. In 1968, 26 women and girls were convicted of infanticide,[123] whereas by the year ending March 2021, no cases of the crime of infanticide were recorded.[124] Between the year ending March 2011 and the year ending March 2021, there were only 10 cases recorded as infanticide.[125] Over the same period, seven women and girls were charged with infanticide,[126] while there were 17 cases of infanticide recorded by the police.[127] It is not possible to say why the 17 recorded cases of infanticide did not result in convictions. It could be that a baby's body was found and the woman who had birthed the child was not identified. It could be she was

[119] See discussion above. See also Brennan, 'Beyond the Medical Model' (n 91).

[120] Lansdowne (n 93) 45–46.

[121] ibid 46.

[122] Osborne (n 93) 58.

[123] Office for National Statistics, 'Crime Statistics, Focus on Violent Crime and Sexual Offences, 2013/14 reference tables' (12 February 2015) at www.ons.gov.uk/peoplepopulationandcommunity/crimeandjustice/compendium/focusonviolentcrimeandsexualoffences/2015-02-12/crimestatisticsfocusonviolentcrimeandsexualoffences201314referencetables (accessed 20 January 2023) Table 2.12.

[124] Office for National Statistics, 'Appendix tables: homicide in England and Wales' (10 February 2022) at www.ons.gov.uk/peoplepopulationandcommunity/crimeandjustice/datasets/appendixtableshomicideinenglandandwales (accessed 20 January 2023) Table 22.

[125] ibid.

[126] ibid Worksheet 25.

[127] Office for National Statistics, 'Year Ending June 2022 edition of this dataset' in *Crime in England and Wales: Appendix tables* (27 October 2022) at www.ons.gov.uk/peoplepopulationandcommunity/crimeandjustice/datasets/crimeinenglandandwalesappendixtables (accessed 20 January 2023) Table A4. It is not possible to look at the historical police data for infanticide, as the records only show 'homicide', rather than splitting the figures into murder, manslaughter and infanticide.

convicted of another offence, homicide or otherwise. It could be she was found not guilty of any offence. Regardless, there is a clear downward trend in infanticide cases in England and Wales during the twentieth century and into the twenty-first century, as illustrated by Figure 1.1.[128]

Figure 1.1 The number of women convicted of infanticide by year, from 1967 to 2020/21

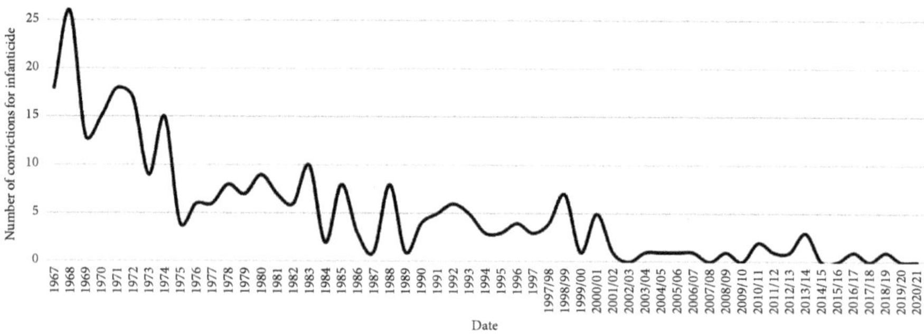

Of course, infanticide can only be committed by women. If we put the infanticide figures into the context of all homicide figures, it is apparent that it is very uncommon for women to commit fatal violence, as illustrated in Table 1.1 (indictment figures) and Table 1.2 (conviction figures).[129]

Table 1.1 Suspects indicted for homicide as an average of the statistics from the years ending March 2011 to March 2021

	Men (numbers)	**Men (percentage)**	**Women (numbers)**	**Women (percentage)**
Indicted for Murder	430	91.49%	40	8.51%
Indicted for Manslaughter	85	88.54%	11	11.46%
Indicted for Infanticide	0	0.00%	0.63	100.00%
Indicted for Homicide (total)	515	90.83%	52	9.17%

[128] Data adapted from Office for National Statistics, 'Crime Statistics, Focus on Violent Crime and Sexual Offences, 2013/14 reference tables' (12 February 2015) at www.ons.gov.uk/peoplepopulationandcommunity/crimeandjustice/compendium/focusonviolentcrimeandsexualoffences/2015-02-12/crimestatisticsfocusonviolentcrimeandsexualoffences201314referencetables (accessed 20 January 2023) Table 2.12; and Office for National Statistics, 'Appendix tables: homicide in England and Wales' (10 February 2022) at www.ons.gov.uk/peoplepopulationandcommunity/crimeandjustice/datasets/appendixtableshomicideinenglandandwales (accessed 20 January 2023) Table 25.

[129] Office for National Statistics, 'Appendix tables: homicide in England and Wales' (10 February 2022) at www.ons.gov.uk/peoplepopulationandcommunity/crimeandjustice/datasets/appendixtableshomicideinenglandandwales (accessed 20 January 2023) Table 25.

Table 1.2 Suspects convicted of homicide as an average of the statistics from the years ending March 2011 to March 2021

	Men (numbers)	Men (percentage)	Women (numbers)	Women (percentage)
Convicted of Murder	265	93.31%	19	6.69%
Convicted of Section 2 Manslaughter	21	84.00%	4	16.00%
Convicted of Other Manslaughter	122	90.37%	13	9.63%
Convicted of Infanticide	0	0.00%	1	100.00%
Convicted of Homicide (total)	408	91.69%	37	8.31%

While reading the chapters in this book, which are of course focused on women's acts of fatal violence towards their infants, it is worth remembering that women commit very little violent crime in general. Women's criminal acts, and particularly their acts of violence, are both qualitatively and quantitatively different from men's.[130] Quantitative differences are apparent from the statistics presented in Table 1.1 and Table 1.2. In terms of qualitative differences in the killing of infants, as we have already outlined, women kill their infants in different circumstances and for different reasons compared to men.[131] Regardless, it is worth pausing to remember that children aged under 1 year suffer the highest rates of homicide compared to any other age group.[132]

A. Contemporary Application of the Infanticide Act

As discussed in this chapter, the wording of the Infanticide Act 1938 could be interpreted to limit the defence/offence to situations where women had mental disturbances caused by the effects of childbirth/lactation. However, past studies that have analysed how the law has been applied show that infanticide has been used in a variety of cases, including situations where the woman had no mental

[130] For example, L Gelsthorpe and S Wright, 'The Context: Women as Lawbreakers' in J Annison, J Brayford and J Deering (eds), *Women and Criminal Justice: From the Corston Report to Transforming Rehabilitation* (Policy Press 2015) 39; Milne and Turton (n 45); C Kruttschnitt and K Carbone-Lopez, 'Moving Beyond the Stereotypes: Women's Subjective Accounts of Their Violent Crime' (2006) 44 *Criminology* 321.

[131] The implication of this difference in relation to the Infanticide Act is discussed in section IV.B.

[132] Office for National Statistics, 'Age' in *Homicide in England and Wales: year ending March 2018* (7 February 2019) at www.ons.gov.uk/peoplepopulationandcommunity/crimeandjustice/articles/homicideinenglandandwales/yearendingmarch2018#which-groups-of-people-are-most-likely-to-be-victims-of-homicide (accessed 20 January 2023).

disorder and/or where her mental disturbance had little or no connection to the physical effects of childbirth/lactation. As Wilczynski notes:

> In theory the wording of the *Infanticide Act* 1938 only allows courts to consider physiological rather than social or psychological causes of the woman's mental imbalance. In practice, however, it would seem that the disturbance need not be solely or even primarily due to childbirth.[133]

Morris and Wilczynski argue that that the infanticide legislation has been 'interpreted very liberally' in England and in other jurisdictions, such as Hong Kong and Australia.[134] They add that it has been used to 'covertly introduce socioeconomic and other factors thought to have led to the child's death'.[135] In their analysis of cases of neonaticide, they highlight that the social factors involved in these killings had to be 'translated into a psychiatric condition' in order to satisfy the medical parameters of the legislation.[136] Similarly, Mackay concludes from a sample of English infanticide cases from the early 1980s that

> the overall impression gained from an examination of the psychiatric reports which were used in support of infanticide leaves little room to doubt that the criteria within the 1938 Act were being used primarily as a legal device for avoiding the mandatory penalty and thus ensure that leniency could be shown in appropriate cases.[137]

The effects of lactation were not mentioned in any of the psychiatric reports he examined. In addition, the requirement relating to the effects of childbirth received little attention by some psychiatrists and, on occasion, 'after prompting by the DPP [Director of Public Prosecutions], was used verbatim as a triggering device for an infanticide charge'.[138]

Similar conclusions have been drawn by scholars who have looked at the application of infanticide laws based on the 1938 model in jurisdictions beyond England and Wales. For example, Lansdowne, in her study of infant homicide between 1976 and 1980 in New South Wales, Australia, found that 'in practice … rigorous adherence to the expressed elements of the offence [of infanticide] is not required'.[139] For example, she found that the prosecution and the judges in these cases did not require that a 'precise connection' be drawn between the birth and the mental disturbance, as long as 'the general description "postnatal" or "puerperal" was applied' to the latter.[140] In a similar study into 35 maternal filicides in Hong

[133] A Wilczynski, *Child Homicide* (Greenwich Medical Media Ltd 1997) 158.

[134] A Morris and A Wilczynski, 'Rocking the Cradle: Mothers Who Kill Their Children' in H Birch (ed), *Moving Targets: Women, Murder, and Representation* (Virago 1993) 207.

[135] ibid 208.

[136] ibid 210. See also d'Orbán (n 38).

[137] RD Mackay, 'The Consequences of Killing Very Young Children' [1993] *Crim LR* 21, 29.

[138] ibid. See also RD Mackay, *Mental Condition Defences in the Criminal Law* (Clarendon Press 1995) 210.

[139] Lansdowne (n 93) 53.

[140] ibid.

Kong between 1971 and May 1985, Chueng found that only six of the 13 women convicted of infanticide could be classified as mentally ill.[141] The remaining seven women 'did not suffer from any abnormality which could be described as mental disorder'.[142] He reached the same conclusion as d'Orban did in his English study covering the period 1970–75,[143] that 'the degree of abnormality in these cases was much less than that required to meet the definition of "abnormality of mind" amounting to diminished responsibility' in Hong Kong.[144] Similarly, in a study of infanticide in Ireland between 1950 and 2015,[145] Brennan found that the infanticide law was applied on the basis of a presumption of mental disturbance, and medical diagnosis of a specific mental disorder, particularly one that was linked to childbirth or lactation, was not required.[146]

Keen-eyed readers might note that the studies mentioned so far are now rather dated, and so do not provide an up-to-date picture of the workings of the infanticide law in the twenty-first century. However, there are few contemporary studies of the application of the Infanticide Act from England and Wales. One of the reasons for this is due to the challenge of researching contemporary criminal cases. As previously outlined, few cases are reported each year, meaning that there are not many opportunities to study the criminal law and justice responses to infanticide. The small number of cases means that methodological approaches to this form of women's offending are limited. Unlike other crimes that are committed more often, it is difficult to complete courtroom ethnographies, as often a case is not reported in the media until the trial has started, or possibly concluded. Other methods of research conducted by scholars could potentially offer insight into contemporary cases, for example Mackay was provided with access to Crown Prosecution case files,[147] Wilczynski reviewed files from the DPP in London,[148] and Cavanagh, Dobash and Dobash reviewed case files of people convicted of murder (866 in total: 786 men and 80 women).[149] However, access to this type of data is incredibly difficult to come by, and so such studies are rare, offering incredibly rich sources of information.

One useful method that can be employed is analysis of court transcripts. Milne did just this in relation to newborn child killing.[150] However, as she outlines in

[141] PTK Cheung, 'Maternal Filicide in Hong Kong, 1971–85' (1986) 26 *Medicine, Science and the Law* 185.

[142] ibid 189–91.

[143] d'Orbán (n 38).

[144] Cheung (n 141) 191, referring to s 3 of the Homicide Ordinance, which was the equivalent to s 2 of the English Homicide Act 1957.

[145] Note that cases involving an infanticide conviction all took place between 1950 and 1974, there being no convictions for infanticide in Ireland from the mid-1970s onwards.

[146] K Brennan, 'Social Norms and the Law in Responding to Infanticide' (2018) 38 *Legal Studies* 480, 493.

[147] Mackay (n 137).

[148] Wilczynski (n 133).

[149] Cavanagh, Dobash and Dobash (n 44).

[150] Milne (n 24).

her study, the process of using court transcripts from England and Wales criminal cases for the purpose of research is long and expensive.[151] The other potential source of data is media reporting of these cases. For example, in his analysis of newspaper reporting of cases of infanticide from 1800 to 2000, Grey has concluded that it is routinely emphasised in reporting that the convicted woman is *also* a victim of tragic circumstances that led to the crime, and thus deserving of sympathetic treatment. Such framing of women who commit infanticide stresses not only their 'normality' prior to the offence but also their 'respectability'.[152]

Undoubtedly, further research into the operation of the Infanticide Act in the twenty-first century is required. However, as this analysis is currently unavailable, the following exploration of the nature of infanticide cases today is based on the observations of the editors, who have both monitored media reporting of cases as they have occurred.[153] Such observations have clear limitations in terms of reliability and validity. However, even a systematic review of every single case of infanticide that occurs would not necessarily result in the production of 'data' that can be considered generalisable. The variations in details of cases, and the 'human' aspect of the criminal justice system, mean that two cases with similar facts may end very differently. For example, factors that affect the outcome of these cases at different points of the criminal process include: the response of the police and how they proceed with an investigation, including if or how they refer a case to the Crown Prosecution Service for charge; whether a prosecutor chooses to charge infanticide or murder; how a jury interpret a woman's behaviour, and whether they consider the prosecution to have successfully disproved the defence of infanticide.[154] The outcome for a woman can be dramatic, as infanticide almost always leads to a non-custodial sentence,[155] whereas a murder conviction results in a life sentence and immediate custody, usually for at least 15 years.

[151] ibid 14.

[152] DJR Grey, '"A Hard-Working and Nice Person"? Respectability, Femininity, and Infanticide in England and Wales, 1800–2000' in S Banwell et al (eds), *The Emerald International Handbook of Feminist Perspectives on Women's Acts of Violence* (Emerald Publishing, 2023) 33.

[153] At the time of writing, Emma Milne is in the process of interviewing legal professionals about their views of the Infanticide Act, a further gap in our knowledge of the criminal law and criminal justice in this area.

[154] We have yet to see a case where a woman has only been charged with infanticide and a jury are asked to determine her guilt of that crime alone. More often than not, if a jury are asked to decide on infanticide, the woman has been charged with murder and is pleading infanticide, or has been charged with murder and infanticide. See Mackay, ch 3 of this volume, who outlines the routes to verdict that juries will be given by a judge if asked to consider infanticide and murder.

[155] The Office for National Statistics report that between April 2010 to March 2011 and April 2020 to March 2021, out of the 10 women convicted of infanticide, only one was imprisoned as part of sentence. Office for National Statistics, 'Appendix tables: homicide in England and Wales' (10 February 2022) at www.ons.gov.uk/peoplepopulationandcommunity/crimeandjustice/datasets/appendixtableshomicideinenglandandwales (accessed 20 January 2023) Worksheet 26. However, it should be noted that the authors are unable to identify this case, and that the nature of the reporting of sentencing statistics means that the imprisonment may have been for a crime concurrently charged, which we are unable to determine. Between 2002 and 2010, no woman convicted of infanticide was imprisoned: Freedom of Information Request to the Ministry of Justice by the authors (Ref: 004-15 FOI 95231).

As we have noted, infanticide cases should be divided into those involving the death of a newborn child and those where the mother has killed her infant aged 1 day and over. In terms of newborn child killing, in recent years, it would appear that it is becoming increasingly difficult for women to make use of the Infanticide Act. For example, since 2019, three women have been convicted of murdering their newborn children.[156] In each case the Crown Prosecution Service proceeded with a murder charge; none of the women was successful in using infanticide as a defence. Other women and girls have successfully made use of infanticide after killing a newborn child. For example, Milne analyses two cases of newborn child infanticide committed by 16 year-old girls: 'Tanya', who was suffering from post-traumatic stress disorder, and 'Fiona', who pleaded guilty to a charge of infanticide after a psychiatrist concluded her complete pregnancy denial meant she acted in panic and shock when she killed the child following birth.[157] In all of these cases, the defence provided evidence of a 'disturbance of the balance of the mind'. The distinction between the cases that resulted in an infanticide conviction, compared to the cases ending in a murder conviction, is that the Crown Prosecution Service accepted a plea of infanticide from the defendant, or, more rarely, charged infanticide rather than murder. The three murder convictions occurred more recently compared to the other cases that resulted in infanticide convictions. It could, perhaps, be observed that there may be a hardening in the approach of the prosecution when it comes to infanticide pleas, with a push towards murder trials, leaving the decision to the jury. Similarly, we might observe that juries appear reluctant to apply the Infanticide Act to newborn child killings.[158] From our monitoring of cases, we conclude that no jury has convicted a woman who killed a newborn child of infanticide in the last 20 years. However, as noted, such observations need to be tempered by the fact that these cases are so rare, and the human aspect of the criminal justice system is such, that a small number of cases

[156] L Roughley, 'Mum who stabbed newborn baby girl to death with scissors is jailed for life – for the second time' *Manchester Evening News* (Manchester, 6 February 2019) at www.manchestereveningnews.co.uk/news/greater-manchester-news/rachel-tunstill-retrial-liverpool-burnley-15789927 (accessed 9 February 2023); C Giordano, 'Mother sealed newborn baby in plastic bags despite signs it was still alive, court hears' *Independent* (London, 8 May 2019) at www.independent.co.uk/news/uk/crime/baby-murder-death-trial-farm-news-leicestershire-hannah-cobley-dead-a8905086.html (accessed 9 February 2023); 'Hythe baby death: Silipa Keresi jailed for woodland murder' *BBC News* (2 December 2021) at www.bbc.co.uk/news/uk-england-hampshire-59509306 (accessed 7 February 2023).

[157] Milne (n 24). See also 'Gintare Suminaite walks free after Bognor baby killing' *BBC News* (30 January 2017) at www.bbc.co.uk/news/uk-england-sussex-38803441 (accessed 9 February 2023); 'Mother guilty of killing baby son' *BBC News* (24 September 2009) at news.bbc.co.uk/1/hi/england/northamptonshire/8272961.stm (accessed 9 February 2023); P Cheston, 'Mother admits burying her newborn baby alive on Tooting Common' *Evening Standard* (London, 7 December 2014) at www.standard.co.uk/news/crime/mother-admits-burying-her-newborn-baby-alive-on-tooting-common-9906124.html (accessed 9 February 2023).

[158] Kramar (n 93) has made similar observations in her study of Canada. See also Loughnan, ch 7 of this volume, who makes similar observations with regard to the use of infanticide laws in Australian jurisdictions.

cannot be said to indicate a pattern in outcomes. Nevertheless, it is significant that while the Infanticide Act was enacted specifically for women who committed newborn child killing, women who commit such form of homicide appear to be finding it increasingly difficult to make use of the statutory leniency the offence/defence provides.

In contrast, women who kill older infants appear to be more readily able to use the Infanticide Act if they can demonstrate some form of mental ill health at the time of the killing.[159] One of the key aspects of infanticide cases involving older infants was that cases never seemed to involve abuse of the child prior to the fatal act by the mother. The infants were considered to be well-looked-after, loved and cared for, and the fatal act by the mother was therefore unexpected and considered unpredictable. In contrast, in cases where prior abuse is known or suspected, the result has generally been a murder conviction,[160] or, where it cannot be proved that the mother or her partner (sometimes the baby's father, sometimes not) killed the child, the offence of causing or allowing the death of a child may be used.[161] However, the recent conviction of Lauren Saint George for infanticide, after her child Lily-Mai sustained a fatal head injury, goes against this trend.[162] Lily-Mai suffered 18 broken ribs and a broken leg, indicating she experienced abuse prior to her death. Social services had been involved with her family to determine if she was safe in her parents' care. Perhaps even more surprising is that the infanticide conviction occurred with the jury finding Saint George not guilty of murder or manslaughter but guilty of infanticide. In sentencing, the judge noted that Saint George suffered from depression and was 'still suffering from the effects of the birth at the time [she] committed the act that caused the death'.[163] There is, of course, nothing that precludes the use of infanticide in cases where prior abuse of the child has occurred. However, the general trend in prosecutions and convictions would

[159] 'Baby-killing mum Natasha Sultan "needed more support"' *BBC News* (22 January 2014) at www.bbc.co.uk/news/uk-england-humber-25842236 (accessed 7 February 2023); 'Amy Black detained indefinitely for killing baby Zoe' *BBC News* (14 May 2014) at www.bbc.co.uk/news/uk-england-nottinghamshire-27415918 (accessed 7 February 2023); S Morris, 'Mother who suffocated baby son to remain in psychiatric unit' *The Guardian* (London, 12 November 2010) at www.theguardian.com/uk/2010/nov/12/mother-smothered-baby-son-court (accessed 7 February 2023); A Dolan, 'Mother smothered baby "after cannabis triggered psychosis"', *The Daily Mail* (London, 8 June 2012) at www.dailymail.co.uk/news/article-2156547/Mother-smothered-baby-cannabis-triggered-psychosis.html (accessed 7 February 2023).

[160] 'Callum Wilson murder: Mother Emma Wilson jailed for life' *BBC News* (24 January 2014) at www.bbc.co.uk/news/uk-england-berkshire-25874635 (accessed 7 February 2023).

[161] D Mercer, 'Amina-Faye Johnson death: Parents jailed after baby died with more than 60 broken bones in "despicable" abuse case' *Sky News* (28 January 2022) at https://news.sky.com/story/parents-of-baby-who-died-with-more-than-60-broken-bones-to-be-sentenced-12525972 (accessed 7 February 2023). For an assessment of the implications of applying 'causing and allowing the death of a child', see S Singh, 'Punishing Mothers for Men's Violence: Failure to Protect Legislation and the Criminalisation of Abused Women' (2021) 29 *Feminist Legal Studies* 181.

[162] 'Lauren Saint George guilty of killing baby girl Lily-Mai' *BBC News* (25 July 2022) at www.bbc.co.uk/news/uk-england-london-62296439 (accessed 7 February 2023).

[163] ibid.

suggest that this is not a favoured outcome, reflecting the research that concludes that women who are able to make use of infanticide are those deemed to be worthy of leniency:[164] generally, child abusers are not categorised in this way.

IV. Contemporary Debates on the Infanticide Law

In this section we provide a brief overview of some of the key debates and issues that have arisen with respect to the Infanticide Act 1938 and laws adopted in other jurisdictions that draw on the 1938 model. These critiques draw on academic literature and also the reports of law reform commissions in different jurisdictions. The purpose of this section is to provide a basis for consideration of the future direction and development of infanticide laws. Some of these issues are tackled directly in chapters in this volume. Others are in need of further investigation to settle the debate.

A. Critiques of the 'Medical Model' – Medicalisation Theory and Contemporary Medical Thinking

One of the key criticisms of the infanticide law is that it 'medicalises' this offence by requiring a bio-psychiatric disorder to the exclusion of consideration of the socio-political causes of the crime.[165] The idea behind this theory of the law is that legislators adopted nineteenth- or early twentieth-century medical theory on the 'insanities of reproduction', which viewed the biological experiences of childbirth and lactation as triggers for mental illness, thus viewing all women as potentially 'mad' due to normal biological processes. However, analysis of the history behind the law brings the medicalisation thesis into question.[166] For example, Ward has argued, based on his historical analysis, that the 1922 Act enshrined a lay or commonsense theory that was partly based on popular sexist perceptions about the impact of birth on a woman's mental balance, but it was not exclusively biological because it also took account of the social circumstances in which the birth took place.[167]

[164] Morris and Wilczynski (n 134); Grey (n 152).

[165] SSM Edwards, *Women on Trial: A Study of the Female Suspect, Defendant, and Offender in the Criminal Law and Criminal Justice System* (Manchester University Press 1984); K O'Donovan, 'The Medicalisation of Infanticide' [1984] *Crim LR* 259. Discussed in more detail in Milne and Brennan, ch 6 of this volume.

[166] See section II, especially section II.A, for discussion history.

[167] Ward (n 78). See also KJ Kramar and WD Watson, 'The Insanities of Reproduction: Medico-Legal Knowledge and the Development of Infanticide Law' (2006) 15 *Social and Legal Studies* 237; K Brennan, '"Traditions of English Liberal Thought": A History of the Enactment of an Infanticide Law in Ireland' (2013) 50 *Irish Jurist* 100; Loughnan (n 11). For further discussion, see Milne and Brennan, ch 6 of this volume.

The infanticide law has also been criticised on the ground that it does not reflect current medical thinking on mental ill health following birth. This critique is premised on the idea that the infanticide law provides for a bio-psychiatric defence that is limited to the physiological effects of childbirth and lactation. Although physiological causes of mental illness related to childbirth have not been completely dismissed by mental-health experts, there is evidence that social and psychological stressors, including poverty, relationship problems, domestic abuse, lack of support from a partner or others, other stressful events such as a bereavement, previous history of mental illness, and difficulty in bonding and adjusting to motherhood, play a much greater causal role in the development of poor mental health following birth, and in conditions such as postnatal depression.[168] In other words, 'childbirth as a life event and the stresses and strains associated with child rearing are more important than the biological events of childbirth and lactation'.[169] Such evidence has been drawn on in discussions of infanticide legislation. For example, the Victorian Law Reform Commission (VLRC), Australia, noted in the mid-2000s that the current formulation of infanticide laws 'distorts the reality of child killing and ignores the complex factors which can lead to the killing of a child'.[170] However, despite the acknowledged problems with the medical basis, one benefit of the mitigation framework that has been cited is the fact that it is widely construed to allow for external stressors that contributed to the accused's mental condition to be taken into account (or at least can be reformulated to make this more apparent) and requires a lower threshold of mental disturbance than that required by diminished responsibility.[171]

One issue that has been considered by different law reform commissions/committees is whether the law should be amended to reflect current medical understandings of mental ill health postpartum, and specifically to take account of social factors. The Law Commission in England and Wales reviewed the Infanticide Act 1938 in its 2006 report *Murder, Manslaughter and Infanticide*. After consulting with medical and legal experts, the Commission concluded there 'is sufficient medical evidence on which to justify the offence/defence of infanticide as it stands'.[172] It recommended that the mitigation framework remain unchanged,

[168] B McSherry, 'The Return of the Raging Hormones Theory: Premenstrual Syndrome, Postpartum Disorders and Criminal Responsibility' (1993) 15 *Sydney Law Review* 292, 293–95; Brennan, 'Beyond the Medical Model' (n 91).

[169] Brennan, 'Beyond the Medical Model' (n 91) 514.

[170] Victorian Law Reform Commission, *Defences to Homicide: Final Report* (2004), para 6.11, at www.lawreform.vic.gov.au/wp-content/uploads/2021/07/VLRC_Defences_to_Homicide_Final_Report-1.pdf (accessed 15 February 2023).

[171] For example, see ibid paras 6.20, 6.22, 6.34–6.35, 6.37. See also New South Wales Law Reform Commission, *Partial Defences to Murder: Provocation and Infanticide* (Report 83, 1997), para 3.24 at www.lawreform.justice.nsw.gov.au/Documents/Publications/Reports/Report-83.pdf (accessed 15 February 2023). For an overview of the literature on how the law has been used, see section III.A.

[172] Law Commission, *Murder, Manslaughter and Infanticide* (Law Com no 304, 2006) para 8.25 at https://s3-eu-west-2.amazonaws.com/lawcom-prod-storage-11jsxou24uy7q/uploads/2015/03/lc304_Murder_Manslaughter_and_Infanticide_Report.pdf (accessed 15 February 2023).

and in particular that it should not be amended to explicitly take account of social factors.[173] Other jurisdictions, however, have amended their infanticide laws based on the 1938 model to reflect current medical thinking. For example, Victoria, following the recommendation of the VLRC, amended its infanticide provision by dropping the reference to lactation and replacing it with reference to 'a disorder consequent on her giving birth to that child'; the legislation was also extended to cover victims up to the age of 2 years.[174]

B. What about Fathers?

Another criticism of the law focuses on the exclusion of fathers and other parents from the ambit of the special leniency offered. The Infanticide Act 1938, and similar laws elsewhere, explicitly link mitigation to childbirth/lactation – experiences that only the biological mother of the infant victim can claim. As the Law Commission noted, it is the link to childbirth/lactation that is key in limiting the infanticide law to the mother.[175] One of the key challenges to the law in terms of how it is currently formulated, however, is that, as discussed, it is generally accepted that the social context of the killing of the infant is crucial: it explains the crime and why (historically at least) the biological mother alone has received leniency.[176] Further, social stressors play an important role in medical understandings of postpartum mental illness.[177] However, fathers and other parents may also struggle with adjustments to parenthood and the burden of childcare, particularly in situations where additional stressors exist.[178] There is also growing awareness of the fact that fathers may too suffer from mental ill health following the birth of a child,[179] and childcare responsibilities are increasingly being shared by men, with some fathers taking up the role of being the main caretaker of their young children. In this context, there is a concern that biological fathers and other parents, especially those who are effectively performing the role of 'mother' by being the main or sole caretaker of a young child, are unfairly treated and indeed

[173] See generally, ibid paras 8.27–8.31. Previously, the Criminal Law Review Committee had recommended that the law be amended to embrace the reality that environmental stresses also play a role in maternal infant killings. They considered that the phrase 'at the time of the act or omission the balance of the woman's mind was disturbed by reason of the effect of giving birth or circumstances consequent upon that birth' would serve to 'more accurately reflect the existing practice of the courts': see Criminal Law Revision Committee, *Offences against the Person* (14th Report, Cmnd 7844, 1980) para 105.

[174] Crimes Act, 1958 (Version 184), s 6, as amended by the Crimes (Homicide) Act, 2005 (Vic), s 5.

[175] Law Commission (n 172) paras 8.27–8.29.

[176] See sections I and II.

[177] See section IV.A.

[178] H Howard, 'The Offence/Defence of Infanticide: A View from Two Perspectives' (2018) 82 *The Journal of Criminal Law* 470; J Mason, 'The Myth of Madness: Murderous Mothers and Maternal Infanticide' (2021) 85 *The Journal of Criminal Law* 441.

[179] HL Stangle, 'Murderous Madonna: Femininity, Violence, and the Myth of Postpartum Mental Disorder in Cases of Maternal Infanticide and Filicide' (2008) 50 *William and Mary Law Review* 669; Mason (n 178).

discriminated against, because the infanticide law provides special lenient treatment for biological mothers only.[180]

Justifications put forward in favour of retaining the sex-specific aspect of this law have tended to focus on the unique relationship between a mother and her baby during the first year of life,[181] on the fact that women do suffer from mental disturbances following childbirth,[182] and on the demands of parenting, which remains overwhelmingly a female role.[183] Another argument that has been advanced in favour of restricting the infanticide law to biological mothers has been the important differences between killings by fathers and mothers. Although not focusing exclusively on the Infanticide Act, Wilczynski, for example, in a sample of English filicide cases from 1984, observed that 'although men and women are committing the same act when they kill their child, the context and the circumstances of that violent act differ markedly'.[184] A particular difference between the maternal/paternal killings was the reasons provided, with the predominantly male motivations (retaliation; jealousy; discipline) being viewed as more reprehensible than the motivations that were predominantly female (namely, altruism; psychotic illness; unwanted child).[185] Wilczynski also highlights that the social stresses that women experience in the context of child homicide differ from those of men and are more closely aligned with the female gender role.[186] She argues that despite social changes that have seen fathers take on more responsibility for childcare, it is still women who carry the bulk of the parenting load with little support, and she concludes:

> If we ignore this fact … and treat the overburdened mother who has cared for her child almost single-handedly since birth in the same way as the father who lashes out after an hour of child-care, we may in fact be entrenching sex inequalities even further.[187]

There is a need for further research to explore the context of fatherhood and/or non-biological maternal infanticide/filicide today, in the third decade of the

[180] For example, see Mason (n 178).

[181] For example, see Victorian Law Reform Commission (n 170) paras 6.23, 6.29; Law Commission (n 172) para 8.36.

[182] For example, see Law Commission (n 172) paras 8.25–8.26; New South Wales Law Reform Commission, *People with Cognitive and Mental Health Impairments in the Criminal Justice System: Criminal Responsibility and Consequences* (Report 138, 2013) para 5.37 at www.lawreform.justice.nsw.gov.au/Documents/Publications/Reports/Report-138.pdf (accessed 15 February 2023).

[183] For example, see New South Wales Law Reform Commission (n 182) para 5.36; Victorian Law Reform Commission (n 170) para 6.36.

[184] Wilczynski (n 133) 64. The sample was not limited to victims aged under 1 year and included 48 cases of a homicide of a child aged under the age of 18 by a parent or parent substitute that had been referred to the DPP by the police in 1984.

[185] ibid ch 3.

[186] A Wilczynski, 'Mad or Bad? Child-Killers, Gender and the Courts' (1997) 37 *The British Journal of Criminology* 419, 430. Her focus in this study was on sentencing across a range of offences rather than the infanticide law per se.

[187] ibid 432.

twenty-first century, and especially to consider the question of whether it is fair to exclude from the infanticide law fathers and other parents who suffer from a similar 'disturbance in the balance of the mind' caused by the impact of parenting a young child in difficult circumstances.[188] In the context of American infanticide, for example, Oberman has recognised that legal reform to allow for a more consistent lenient response to infanticide of children aged over one day[189] should recognise the fact that this crime is 'tied to the culturally-dictated experiences of primary caretaking'.[190] Consequently, she recognises that lenient provision could be extended to anyone, including a father or a grandparent or an adoptive parent, who was 'mothering' in practice, namely being 'permanently in the position of an isolated primary caretaker for a child'.[191]

C. Wider Criminal Justice Principles/Theory

The Infanticide Act 1938 does not require a causal connection between the mental disturbance and the woman's act/omission that caused the death of her child.[192] The law simply requires a temporal connection, in that she was suffering from a disturbance in the balance of her mind at the time she killed her infant.[193] This is recognised as an important difference between the infanticide law and the defence of diminished responsibility, where the law *does* require that offenders' responsibility was impaired in a specific way, such as, for example, by affecting their ability to make sound judgements or exercise self-control.[194] Walker, however, notes that such a literal reading of the English Infanticide Act 1938 is not what the legislature had intended, and that section 1(1) of the statute contains an implicit presumption that the mental disturbance the accused woman experienced was sufficiently connected to her act to reduce her responsibility.[195] The failure of the law to require a causal connection has been criticised. For example, Howard argues that although the lack of a causal connection requirement allows for a more compassionate response to the offender, this 'tips the balance too far away from the harm caused'.[196]

[188] Mason (n 178).
[189] Oberman (n 1). However, she argues for a separate legal response available only to the biological mother in the case of neonaticide.
[190] ibid 88.
[191] ibid.
[192] *Tunstill* (n 87) [32].
[193] Infanticide Act 1938, s 1(1). See Law Commission (n 172) paras 8.40–8.41.
[194] Homicide Act 1957, s 2.
[195] N Walker, *Crime and Insanity in England*, vol 1: *The Historical Perspective* (Edinburgh University Press 1968) 134–35.
[196] Howard (n 178) 478.

Another difficulty of the law that has been highlighted is the 12-month age limit. There has been criticism of the arbitrary nature of the limit, given that women may experience mental disturbances related to childbirth/lactation beyond their baby's first birthday and yet be unable to avail themselves of the special lenient treatment offered by the Infanticide Act if they kill their baby after 12 months have passed. Further, the legislation does not extend to the killing of older children while a mother's mind is disturbed due to the birth of her last-born child,[197] which could lead to her being found guilty of infanticide with respect to the victim aged under 12 months but of another homicide offence, such as manslaughter, with respect to the older child, despite the fact that the killings took place at the same time and in the same circumstances.[198] Oberman has cautioned against age limits, arguing that it is the circumstances of these cases rather than the age of the victim that is important: 'The differences due to the victim's age seem far less significant than one might expect when considering the circumstances giving rise to the crime and the criminal justice system's disposition in these cases.'[199]

D. Status of Infant Life

A further criticism of infanticide is that it is also said that these laws confer a lower status on the life of infants aged under 12 months. Damme, for example, has argued that 'the lower status in which the infant was held by society … has been institutionalized in English laws on infanticide'.[200] Howard also criticises the infanticide law for placing a 'lower value' on the life on the victim.[201] She argues that 'The balance of the current offence/defence of infanticide is tipped far more towards the protection of the vulnerable defendant than the victim.'[202] Contrary to this view, however, it has been noted that since infanticide statutes only provide for lenient treatment in cases where biological mothers kill their infants, no such mercy being extended to fathers and other offenders, they do not confer a lower status on infant life.[203] The VLRC argued that the legislation does not 'condone the killing of babies, but rather recognises the difficulties and complexities which may be present in a woman's relationship with her young child and the kind of factors which can influence maternal child killing'.[204]

[197] Victorian Law Reform Commission (n 170) paras 6.13, 6.38. Osborne (n 93) 55–56, has noted that there is no evidence that the effects of childbirth disappear after 12 months.

[198] See, eg, P Townsend and A Baker, 'Infanticide Law – Primitive and Uncivilised?' (1996) 160 *Justice of the Peace and Local Government Law* 655; Victorian Law Reform Commission (n 170) para 6.13.

[199] Oberman (n 1) 31.

[200] C Damme, 'Infanticide: The Worth of an Infant under Law' (1978) 22 *Medical History* 1, 24.

[201] Howard (n 178) 475.

[202] ibid 480.

[203] PJ Dean, 'Child Homicide and Infanticide in New Zealand' (2004) 27 *International Journal of Law and Psychiatry* 339; Oberman (n 1).

[204] Victorian Law Reform Commission (n 170) para 6.23.

E. The Infanticide Act is Unnecessary in the Current Social and Legal Context

It has also been said that the infanticide law is unnecessary and inappropriate due to the changed social and legal context. For example, Howard argues that although historically this law may have been justified when there was no diminished responsibility defence and when murder was a capital crime, the law is no longer defensible.[205] This position has been challenged by other scholars such as Oberman, and Morris and Wilczynski. These scholars have explored the social context of modern maternal infanticide and have advocated for justifications for special lenient treatment of mothers who kill their children based on the social context of this crime. They draw attention to the particular burdens that mothers carry with respect to parenthood in a patriarchal society, and the lack of support available to them.[206]

The ability of the diminished responsibility defence to cover cases of infanticide has also been highlighted as an argument in favour of abolishing the infanticide law.[207] For example, the Butler Committee (in England and Wales) and the New South Wales Law Reform Commission (NSWLRC) both recommended that the infanticide legislation be abolished on the basis that the partial defence of diminished responsibility could adequately deal with all cases of maternal child killing.[208] The NSWLRC noted that the main advantage of dealing with infanticide as diminished responsibility is that the latter has a wider application than the former and so would not require medical experts to distort their diagnoses.[209] Further, diminished responsibility does not 'single out women on the basis of any notion of their particular vulnerability to mental illness due to their biology'.[210]

Against these arguments in favour of abolishing infanticide and relying exclusively on diminished responsibility it has been argued that the defence of diminished responsibility could not cover all cases currently dealt with by the infanticide legislation, which would put women who would previously have been able to rely on the infanticide law at risk of a murder conviction.[211] There are a number of specific advantages that the offence/defence of infanticide has as against diminished responsibility, such as, for example, the fact that the burden of proof

[205] Howard (n 178) 477.

[206] Oberman (n 1); Morris and Wilczynski (n 134). For further discussion of this point, see Milne and Brennan, ch 6 of this volume.

[207] For example, see Mason (n 178).

[208] For example, see the Committee on Mentally Abnormal Offenders, *Report of the Committee on Mentally Abnormal Offenders* (Cmnd 6244, 1975) paras 19.22–19.26; New South Wales Law Reform Commission (n 171) paras 3.18–3.26.

[209] ibid paras 3.23, 3.30.

[210] ibid para 3.33.

[211] For example, Criminal Law Revision Committee (n 173) 102. See Mackay, ch 3 of this volume.

falls on the prosecution not the defence when infanticide is raised as a defence, and the fact that there is no need to prove a causal connection between the mental disturbance and the killing.[212] Subsuming infanticide under the general defence of diminished responsibility could create problems in relation to sentencing due to the consistently lenient approach to sentencing in infanticide cases.[213]

F. The Debates Continue

Notwithstanding negative assessments of the law, there has been limited criticism of the overall disposition towards taking a lenient approach in appropriate cases. Notably, there has been little real interest in abolishing infanticide. Submissions from medical and criminal justice professionals during the consultation stages of law reform projects across a range of jurisdictions have widely supported maintaining specific infanticide legislation.[214] Overall, despite the fact that this law is rarely used in some jurisdictions, suffers from numerous problems, particularly with respect to the medical rationale and the issue of whether it should be limited to mothers, and may be superfluous in light of diminished responsibility defences, law-reform bodies have tended to favour the retention of this law.[215] Indeed, although the NSWLRC had previously recommended abolishing infanticide and relying instead on the diminished responsibility defence,[216] in a more recent review it reached the opposite conclusion, and infanticide remains part of the law in that jurisdiction.[217]

Justifications by law-reform bodies across a range of jurisdictions for infanticide laws specific to mothers who kill their babies have highlighted the practical advantages of such laws; the undesirable risk of the conviction of women for murder if infanticide were abolished; and the unique nature of this crime.[218] For example, the VLRC agreed with the view that infanticide is a 'distinctive form of human tragedy'.[219] The NSWLRC also recently agreed with this description,

[212] Law Commission (n 172) paras 8.9–8.10.

[213] For example, see Lansdowne (n 93) 59–60. See also D Maier-Katkin and RS Ogle, 'Policy and Disparity: The Punishment of Infanticide in Britain and America' (1997) 21 *International Journal of Comparative and Applied Criminal Justice* 305, 310.

[214] For example, see Victorian Law Reform Commission (n 170) para 6.20; Law Commission (n 172) paras 8.16–8.19.

[215] For example, the Law Commission of England and Wales (n 172); The Victorian Law Reform Commission (n 170); and the New South Wales Law Reform Commission (n 182).

[216] See generally, New South Wales Law Reform Commission (n 171) ch 3.

[217] New South Wales Law Reform Commission (n 182), ch 5. The law was reformed following the recommendations of this report to drop the link to lactation and to extend the provision to include a 'mental health impairment consequent on or exacerbated by her having given birth to that child': see Loughnan, ch 7 of this volume.

[218] See generally Victorian Law Reform Commission (n 170) paras 6.22–6.25; New South Wales Law Reform Commission (n 182) paras 5.35–5.49; Law Commission (n 172) paras 8.3, 8.7–8.12, 8.36–8.38.

[219] Victorian Law Reform Commission (n 170) paras 6.19, 6.22.

noting that the infanticide law allows for 'an appropriate and compassionate criminal law response to the complex and tragic set of circumstances that may result in a mother killing her infant'.[220] The Law Commission in England and Wales, also noting the 'unique' nature of these cases,[221] found that the infanticide law poses few problems in practice and is 'a practicable legal solution to a particular set of circumstances'.[222] One jurisdiction, Western Australia, has recently abolished its infanticide law, following a recommendation by the Law Reform Commission of Western Australia (LRCWA).[223] Despite the fact that the majority of submissions during the consultation stage favoured retention of this law, the LRCWA concluded that lenient treatment of these offenders could be ensured within existing/reformed defence frameworks and sentencing schemes, without the need to rely on a specific offence/defence that was based on the problematic link between childbirth and mental impairment.[224]

Lansdowne has observed that infanticide 'is a crime which for historical, political and emotional reasons has, at least since the eighteenth century, always been treated with leniency'.[225] This tendency is not unique to countries with specific infanticide laws. For example, despite the fact that there is no special infanticide statute at either State or federal level in the United States (US), it seems there is nonetheless a tendency to treat both neonaticide and the killing of older babies as different from other murders.[226] Melmquist, in reference to neonaticide, notes that in comparison with other jurisdictions throughout the world, the failure of the US to give special consideration to this crime is 'striking'.[227] Further, the tendency towards 'exceptionalising' infanticide in the US, coupled with the fact that the law does not make special provision for these cases, leads to problems in terms of disparity and inequality in treatment between cases with similar facts, unpredictability in outcome and a tendency to more punitive disposals in comparisons with other jurisdictions.[228]

V. Structure of the Volume

The contributors of this volume are those who have previously written about the law of infanticide, either in England and Wales or in other legal jurisdictions. As

[220] New South Wales Law Reform Commission (n 182) para 5.49.
[221] Law Commission (n 172) para 8.36.
[222] ibid para 8.3.
[223] See Loughnan, ch 7 of this volume.
[224] Law Reform Commission of Western Australia, *A Review of the Law of Homicide* (Project 97, 2007) 114–17 at www.wa.gov.au/government/publications/project-97-review-of-the-law-of-homicide (accessed 15 February 2023).
[225] Lansdowne (n 93) 60.
[226] Oberman (n 1).
[227] CP Malmquist, 'Infanticide/Neonaticide: The Outlier Situation in the United States' (2013) 18 *Aggression and Violent Behavior* 399.
[228] Oberman (n 1); Oberman and Meyer (n 47); Meyer and Oberman (n 27).

any literature review will demonstrate, there is considerable research considering the phenomenon of infanticide, but very little considering the law of infanticide. And most of the research in England and Wales that focuses on the law, considers the history of the Infanticide Acts and why the offence/defence came about. Contemporary writing on this aspect of homicide law is limited. Therefore, the authors who have contributed to this edited collection are undoubtedly the leading experts in the field.

Part I of the book considers how the Infanticide Act operates in practice. In chapter 2, Rachel Dixon and Tony Ward provide us with an analysis of how infanticide was viewed following the statute's enactment in 1922. They explore the relationship between the offences of murder, manslaughter, infanticide and concealment of birth. Notably through analysis of cases, they consider how an offence that was designed to deal with circumstances that would formerly have constituted murder rather than manslaughter came to be seen as a relatively minor matter that could be dealt with by a non-custodial sentence. Ronnie Mackay also analyses the relationship between infanticide and manslaughter, specifically diminished responsibility. Chapter 3 considers whether and how infanticide may have been impacted by the changes to the diminished responsibility plea that occurred with the passing of the Coroners and Justice Act 2009. As Mackay notes, the reform of diminished responsibility resulted in a new plea that is markedly different from its earlier counterpart. The consequence, Mackay argues, is that if infanticide and diminished responsibility have been pleaded together by a defendant, juries will be presented with a complex and difficult task when attempting to reach a verdict.

Part II of the book focuses on contemporary issues relating to the Infanticide Act. Daniel JR Grey, in chapter 4, provides a newspaper analysis of the representations of infanticidal women from 1922 to date. He finds that the similarity in tone and content is overt and striking over the century. Grey notes that while there are some notable exceptions, whereby women are reported as monstrous, on the whole, such representations are reserved for cases where women are convicted of murder rather than infanticide. Just as was the case in the 1920s, articles about infanticide in the early twenty-first century tend to emphasise the previous good character of the mother and her vulnerability (whether this might be in terms of health, marginalised status or other factors), and suggest that she was suffering from serious mental illness at the time she committed the crime, regardless of whether or not this might fit with accepted medical or legal definitions for mental disturbance. Grey concludes that the overwhelming impression from reviewing such press reportage over a century is of a national ongoing consensus in England and Wales about the 'special' nature of infanticide; the context and experiences of the 'typical' woman charged with the crime; and demonstrates broad agreement with a core cultural script about how it should best be dealt with that emphasises mental-health interventions.

In chapter 5, Helen Howard raises important questions about the assumptions and myths that lie within the Infanticide Act, notably that a woman may seem less blameworthy if she kills her infant aged under 12 months than if she kills an older child; women who kill their infants only do so because of an imbalance of mind due to the effects of childbirth or lactation; and women who kill their infants while suffering from an imbalance of the mind still bear some criminal responsibility, albeit a reduced amount. She offers a useful analysis of the offence/defence of infanticide in the context of Hart's capacity theory and the need to recognise a defendant as a moral agent. In doing so, Howard challenges the continued need for the Infanticide Act in the twenty-first century.

Following from this, in chapter 6 Milne and Brennan offer a defence of the Infanticide Act from a feminist perspective. Noting that the offence/defence has received substantial criticism from feminist scholars for being paternalistic and for pathologising women, they argue that the legislation can, in fact, be justified. They note that a key factor of infanticide is that a significant cause of this form of women's violence comes from the 'gendered harms' that women experience as a consequence of pregnancy and motherhood, and so patriarchal society has a role to play in this crime. Consequently, they conclude that the Infanticide Act can allow for recognition of the role of society in the fatal actions of women, by reducing women's culpability for the killing and so sparing them a prison sentence.

In Part III of the book, we look beyond England and Wales to see how infant killing by mothers has been responded to in other legal jurisdictions. Arlie Loughnan, in chapter 7, provides an analysis of the infanticide provision in the Australian States of New South Wales, Tasmania, Victoria and Western Australia (now abolished). In this chapter, Loughnan first re-examines the parliamentary debates surrounding the introduction of infanticide provisions, and then assesses the operation of the laws by analysing both cases in which infanticide was either charged or pleaded, and cases in which the external element of the offence was made out although the prosecution and defence relied on other homicide provisions and defences. She argues that this assessment shows that the use of infanticide laws is limited and uneven, suggesting that the laws encode a veneer of leniency for all mothers who kill their children but, in practice, are reserved for a small set of cases.

In chapter 8, Lynsey Black and David M Doyle explore the fate of women who were sentenced to death for infant murder in post-independence Ireland prior to the introduction of the Infanticide Act in 1949. They argue that the reluctance to reform the law on infant murder materially shaped the profile of capital cases. Nevertheless, while reform was not 'on the book', the state developed its own approach to cases of this kind, ensuring special accommodation for such women through charging decisions, the swift reprieve of those women sentenced to death and a highly gendered penal landscape, in which women's custody was often delegated to the control of religious sisters rather than prison. Based on extensive archival research, the chapter provides a nuanced understanding of the reform of infanticide law in Ireland and examines the factors that contributed to the belated nature of this reform.

In chapter 9, Maria Kaspersson provides an analysis of infanticide legislation in Sweden, known today as 'child manslaughter'. Child manslaughter covers any mother who kills her newborn child and who is in a 'disturbed state of mind or severe distress on account of giving birth to the child'. Using case studies, Kaspersson illustrates that infanticide in Sweden is understood to occur due to mitigating factors, social or psychological, and to be committed by someone in distress. Therefore, accused women usually receive psychiatric care rather than being sentenced to imprisonment. She concludes the chapter with a consideration of whether infanticidal women should receive greater leniency than other killers.

Finally, in chapter 10, Susan Ayres surveys the legal responses to infanticide in the US. No State has an infanticide law, and so killings of newborn infants and children are typically treated as homicides, and mothers who kill their children are often charged with murder. Prison sentences in the US vary from State to State and trial to trial, but range from six months to life in prison. Ayres argues that these prosecutions represent a punitive response to a complex problem. She specifically notes that the most recent trend, that of authorities using genetic genealogy to solve cold cases, leading to the arrest and prosecution of mothers who gave birth decades ago, is particularly problematic. Ayres takes a feminist vulnerability approach to analyse the social constructions of infanticide and neonaticide cases in the US, and to describe how these social views influence the legal system's treatment of mothers. In doing so, she discusses defences such as psychological denial of pregnancy and insanity, and considers what the future might hold for the disposition of these cases in the US.

References

Books

Beattie, JM, *Crime and the Courts in England, 1660–1800* (Princeton University Press 1986).

Blackstone, W, *Commentaries on the Laws of England*, vol 4 (11th edn, T Cadell 1791).

Coke, E, *The Fourth Part of the Institutes of the Laws of England: Concerning the Jurisdiction of Courts*, 6th edn (Printed by W Rawlins, for Thomas Basset at the George near St Dunstans Church in Fleet-street 1644[1681]).

Edwards, SSM, *Women on Trial: A Study of the Female Suspect, Defendant, and Offender in the Criminal Law and Criminal Justice System* (Manchester University Press 1984).

Farrell, EF, *'A Most Diabolical Deed': Infanticide and Irish Society, 1850–1900* (Manchester University Press 2013).

Hoffer, PC and Hull, NEH, *Murdering Mothers: Infanticide in England and New England, 1558–1803* (New York University Press 1981).

Jackson, M, *New-Born Child Murder: Women, Illegitimacy and the Courts in Eighteenth-Century England* (Manchester University Press 1996).

Kilday, A, *A History of Infanticide in Britain, c 1600 to the Present* (Palgrave Macmillan 2013).

Kramar, KJ, *Unwilling Mothers, Unwanted Babies Infanticide in Canada* (UBC Press 2005).

Mackay, RD, *Mental Condition Defences in the Criminal Law* (Clarendon Press 1995).
Marland, H, *Dangerous Motherhood: Insanity and Childbirth in Victorian Britain* (Palgrave Macmillan 2004).
Meyer, CL and Oberman, M, *Mothers Who Kill Their Children: Understanding the Acts of Moms from Susan Smith to the 'Prom Mom'* (New York University Press 2001).
Milne E, *Criminal Justice Responses to Maternal Filicide: Judging the Failed Mother* (Emerald Publishing Limited 2021).
Norrie, A, *Crime, Reason and History: A Critical Introduction to Criminal Law*, 3rd edn (Cambridge University Press 2014).
Oberman, M and Meyer, CL, *When Mothers Kill: Interviews from Prison* (New York University Press 2008).
Rubinstein, WD, *Britain's Century: A Political and Social History 1815–1905* (Bloomsbury Academic 1998).
Seaman, LCB, *Victorian England: Aspects of English and Imperial History, 1837–1901* (Routledge 1990).
Showalter, E, *The Female Malady: Women, Madness and English Culture, 1830–1980* (Penguin Books 1987).
Smithey, M, *The Cultural and Economic Context of Maternal Infanticide: A Crying Baby and the Inability to Escape* (Emerald Publishing Ltd 2019).
Walker, N, *Crime and Insanity in England*, vol 1: *The Historical Perspective* (Edinburgh University Press 1968).
Wiener, MJ, *Men of Blood: Violence, Manliness and Criminal Justice in Victorian England* (Cambridge University Press 2004).
Wilczynski, A, *Child Homicide* (Greenwich Medical Media Ltd 1997).
Zelizer, VAR, *Pricing the Priceless Child: The Changing Social Value of Children* (Princeton University Press 1994).

Chapters in Edited Volumes

Gelsthorpe, L and Wright, S, 'The Context: Women as Lawbreakers' in Annison, J, Brayford, J and Deering, J (eds), *Women and Criminal Justice: From the Corston Report to Transforming Rehabilitation* (Policy Press 2015) 39.
Grey, DJR, '"A Hard-Working and Nice Person"? Respectability, Femininity, and Infanticide in England and Wales, 1800–2000' in Banwell, S et al (eds), *The Emerald International Handbook of Feminist Perspectives on Women's Acts of Violence* (Emerald Publishing, 2023) 33.
Marland, H, 'Getting Away with Murder?: Puerperal Insanity, Infanticide and the Defence Plea' in Jackson, M (ed), *Infanticide: Historical Perspectives on Child Murder and Concealment* (Ashgate 2002) 168.
Milne, E and Turton, J, 'Understanding Violent Women' in Milne, E et al (eds), *Women and the Criminal Justice System: Failing Victims and Offenders?* (Palgrave Macmillan 2018) 119.
Morris, A and Wilczynski, A, 'Rocking the Cradle: Mothers Who Kill Their Children' in Birch, H (ed), *Moving Targets: Women, Murder, and Representation* (Virago 1993) 198.
Oberman, M, 'A Brief History of Infanticide and the Law' in Spinelli, MG (ed), *Infanticide: Psychosocial and Legal Perspectives on Mothers Who Kill* (American Psychiatric Pub 2003) 3.

Quinn, C, 'Images and Impulses: Representations of Puerperal Insanity and Infanticide in Late Victorian England' in Jackson, M (ed), *Infanticide: Historical Perspectives on Child Murder and Concealment, 1550–2000* (Ashgate 2002) 193.
Rabin, D, 'Bodies of Evidence, States of Mind: Infanticide, Emotion and Sensibility in Eighteenth-Century England' in Jackson, M (ed), *Infanticide: Historic Perspectives on Child Murder and Concealment, 1500–2000* (Ashgate 2002) 73.
Seabourne Davies, D, 'Child-Killing in English Law' in Radzinowicz, L and Turner, JWC (eds), *The Modern Approach to Criminal Law* (Macmillan 1945) 301.
Smout, C, 'Aspects of Sexual Behaviour on Nineteenth Century Scotland' in Laslett, P, Oosterveen, K and Smith, RM, *Bastardy and its Comparative History: Studies in the History of Illegitimacy and Marital Nonconformity in Britain, France, Germany, Sweden, North America, Jamaica and Japan* (Harvard University Press 1980) 192.
Spinelli, MG, 'Neonaticide: A Systematic Investigation of 17 Cases' in Spinelli, MG (ed), Infanticide: Psychosocial and Legal Perspectives on Mothers Who Kill (American Psychiatric Pub 2003) 105.

Journal Articles

Alder, CM and Baker, J, 'Maternal Filicide: More Than One Story to Be Told' (1997) 9 *Women and Criminal Justice* 15.
Amon, S et al, 'Potential Predictors in Neonaticide: The Impact of the Circumstances of Pregnancy' (2012) 15 *Archives of Women's Mental Health* 167.
Ashworth, A, 'Infanticide: whether mens rea of infanticide consists of an intention to kill or cause grievous bodily harm' (2007) 5 *Crim LR* 388.
Beyer, K, McAuliffe Mack, S, and Shelton, JL, 'Investigative Analysis of Neonaticide: An Exploratory Study' (2008) 35 *Criminal Justice and Behavior* 522.
Brennan, K, 'Beyond the Medical Model: A Rationale for Infanticide Legislation' (2007) 58 *NILQ* 505.
——, '"A Fine Mixture of Pity and Justice": The Criminal Justice Response to Infanticide in Ireland, 1922–1949' (2013) 31 *Law and History Review.*
——, '"Traditions of English Liberal Thought": A History of the Enactment of an Infanticide Law in Ireland' (2013) 50 *Irish Jurist* 100.
——, 'Social Norms and the Law in Responding to Infanticide' (2018) 38 *Legal Studies* 480.
——, 'Murderous Mothers and Gentle Judges: Paternalism, Patriarchy, and Infanticide' (2018) 30 *Yale Journal of Law and Feminism* 139.
Bourget, D and Gagné, P, 'Maternal Filicide in Quebec' (2002) 30 *Journal of the American Academy of Psychiatry and the Law Online* 345.
Bourget, D, Grace, J and Whitehurst, L, 'A Review of Maternal and Paternal Filicide' (2007) 35 *Journal of the American Academy of Psychiatry and the Law Online* 74.
Brozovsky, M and Falit, H, 'Neonaticide: Clinical and Psychodynamic Considerations' (1971) 10 *Journal of the American Academy of Child Psychiatry* 673.
Cavanagh, K, Dobash, RE and Dobash, RP, 'The Murder of Children by Fathers in the Context of Child Abuse' (2007) 31 *Child Abuse and Neglect* 731.
Cheung, PTK, 'Maternal Filicide in Hong Kong, 1971–85' (1986) 26 *Medicine, Science and the Law* 185.
Christopher, K, 'Extensive Mothering: Employed Mothers' Constructions of the Good Mother' (2012) 26 *Gender and Society* 73.

Damme, C, 'Infanticide: The Worth of an Infant under Law' (1978) 22 *Medical History* 1.
Dean, PJ, 'Child Homicide and Infanticide in New Zealand' (2004) 27 *International Journal of Law and Psychiatry* 339.
Dobson, V and Sales, BD, 'The Science of Infanticide and Mental Illness' (2000) 6 *Psychology, Public Policy, and Law* 1098.
d'Orbán, PT, 'Women Who Kill Their Children' (1979) 134 *British Journal of Psychiatry* 560.
Ellis-Sloan, K, 'Teenage Mothers, Stigma and Their 'Presentations of Self'' (2014) 19 *Sociological Research Online* 16.
Frederick, A, 'Between Stigma and Mother-Blame: Blind Mothers' Experiences in USA Hospital Postnatal Care' (2015) 37 *Sociology of Health & Illness* 1127.
Geronimus, AT, 'Damned If You Do: Culture, Identity, Privilege, and Teenage Childbearing in the United States' (2003) 57 *Social Science & Medicine* 881.
Hatters Friedman, S, Cavney, J and Resnick, PJ, 'Mothers Who Kill: Evolutionary Underpinnings and Infanticide Law' (2012) 30 *Behavioral Sciences & the Law* 585.
Hatters Friedman, S and Friedman, JB, 'Parents Who Kill Their Children' (2010) 31 *Pediatrics in Review* 10.
Hatters Friedman, S, McCue Horwitz, S and Resnick, PJ, 'Child Murder by Mothers: A Critical Analysis of the Current State of Knowledge and a Research Agenda' (2005) 162 *American Journal of Psychiatry* 1578.
Higginbotham, AR, '"Sin of the Age": Infanticide and Illegitimacy in Victorian London' (1989) 3 *Victorian Studies* 319–37.
Howard, H, 'The Offence/Defence of Infanticide: A View from Two Perspectives' (2018) 82 *The Journal of Criminal Law* 470.
Kaplan, R and Grotowski, T, 'Denied Pregnancy' (1996) 30 *Australian and New Zealand Journal of Psychiatry* 861.
Kramar, KJ and Watson, WD, 'The Insanities of Reproduction: Medico-Legal Knowledge and the Development of Infanticide Law' (2006) 15 *Social and Legal Studies* 237.
Kruttschnitt, C and Carbone-Lopez, K, 'Moving Beyond the Stereotypes: Women's Subjective Accounts of Their Violent Crime' (2006) 44 *Criminology* 321.
Lansdowne, R, 'Infanticide: Psychiatrists in the Plea Bargaining Process' (1990) 16 *Monash University Law Review* 41.
Lewis, CF and Bunce, SC, 'Filicidal Mothers and the Impact of Psychosis on Maternal Filicide' (2003) 31 *Journal of the American Academy of Psychiatry and the Law Online* 459.
Loughnan, A, 'The 'Strange' Case of the Infanticide Doctrine' (2012) 32 *OJLS* 685.
Mackay, RD, 'The Consequences of Killing Very Young Children' [1993] *Crim LR* 21.
Maier-Katkin, D and Ogle, RS, 'Policy and Disparity: The Punishment of Infanticide in Britain and America' (1997) 21 *International Journal of Comparative and Applied Criminal Justice* 305.
Malmquist, CP, 'Infanticide/Neonaticide: The Outlier Situation in the United States' (2013) 18 *Aggression and Violent Behavior* 399.
Mason, J, 'The Myth of Madness: Murderous Mothers and Maternal Infanticide' (2021) 85 *The Journal of Criminal Law* 441.
McSherry, B, 'The Return of the Raging Hormones Theory: Premenstrual Syndrome, Postpartum Disorders and Criminal Responsibility' (1993) 15 *Sydney Law Review* 292.
Milne, E, 'Concealment of Birth: Time to Repeal a 200-Year-Old 'Convenient Stop-Gap'?' (2019) 27 *Feminist Legal Studies* 139.
Oberman, M, 'Mothers Who Kill: Coming to Terms with Modern American Infanticide' (1996) 34 *American Criminal Law Review* 1.

O'Donovan, K, 'The Medicalisation of Infanticide' [1984] *Crim LR* 259.
Osborne, JA, 'The Crime of Infanticide: Throwing Out the Baby with the Bath Water' (1987) 6 *Canadian Journal of Family Law* 47.
Porter, T and Gavin, H, 'Infanticide and Neonaticide: A Review of 40 Years of Research Literature on Incidence and Causes' (2010) 11 *Trauma, Violence & Abuse* 99.
Rapaport, E, 'Mad Women and Desperate Girls: Infanticide and Child Murder in Law and Myth' (2006) 33 *Fordham Urban Law Journal* 527.
Resnick, PJ, 'Child Murder by Parents: A Psychiatric Review of Filicide' (1969) 126 *American Journal of Psychiatry* 325.
——, 'Murder of the Newborn: A Psychiatric Review of Neonaticide' (1970) 126 *American Journal of Psychiatry* 1414.
Seabourne Davies, D, 'Child-Killing in English Law' (1937) 1 *MLR* 203.
——, 'Child-Killing in English Law' (1938) 1 *MLR* 269.
Singh, S, 'Punishing Mothers for Men's Violence: Failure to Protect Legislation and the Criminalisation of Abused Women' (2021) 29 *Feminist Legal Studies* 181.
Stangle, HL, 'Murderous Madonna: Femininity, Violence, and the Myth of Postpartum Mental Disorder in Cases of Maternal Infanticide and Filicide' (2008) 50 *William and Mary Law Review* 669.
Townsend, P and Baker, A, 'Infanticide Law – Primitive and Uncivilised?' (1996) 160 *Justice of the Peace and Local Government Law* 655.
Vellut, N, Cook, JM and Tursz, A, 'Analysis of the Relationship between Neonaticide and Denial of Pregnancy Using Data from Judicial Files' (2012) 36 *Child Abuse and Neglect* 553.
Ward, T, 'The Sad Subject of Infanticide: Law, Medicine and Child Murder, 1860–1938' (1999) 8 *Social and Legal Studies* 163.
Wilczynski, A, 'Mad or Bad? Child-Killers, Gender and the Courts' (1997) 37 *British Journal of Criminology* 419.

Newspaper Articles

Cheston, P, 'Mother admits burying her newborn baby alive on Tooting Common' *Evening Standard* (London, 7 December 2014) at www.standard.co.uk/news/crime/mother-admits-burying-her-newborn-baby-alive-on-tooting-common-9906124.html.
Dolan, A, 'Mother smothered baby "after cannabis triggered psychosis"' *The Daily Mail* (London, 8 June 2012) at www.dailymail.co.uk/news/article-2156547/Mother-smothered-baby-cannabis-triggered-psychosis.html.
Giordano, C, 'Mother sealed newborn baby in plastic bags despite signs it was still alive, court hears' *Independent* (London, 8 May 2019) at www.independent.co.uk/news/uk/crime/baby-murder-death-trial-farm-news-leicestershire-hannah-cobley-dead-a8905086.html.
Morris, S, 'Mother who suffocated baby son to remain in psychiatric unit' *The Guardian* (London, 12 November 2010) at www.theguardian.com/uk/2010/nov/12/mother-smothered-baby-son-court.
'New Infanticide Act: Judge on First Case' *The Times* (London, 31 October 1922) 9.
Roughley, L, 'Mum who stabbed newborn baby girl to death with scissors is jailed for life – for the second time' *Manchester Evening News* (Manchester, 6 February 2019) at www.manchestereveningnews.co.uk/news/greater-manchester-news/rachel-tunstill-retrial-liverpool-burnley-15789927.

Weigel, M, 'The Foul Reign of the Biological Clock' *The Guardian* (London, 10 May 2016) at www.theguardian.com/society/2016/may/10/foul-reign-of-the-biological-clock.

Online Resources

'Amy Black detained indefinitely for killing baby Zoe' *BBC News* (14 May 2014) at www.bbc.co.uk/news/uk-england-nottinghamshire-27415918.

'Baby-killing mum Natasha Sultan "needed more support"' *BBC News* (22 January 2014) at www.bbc.co.uk/news/uk-england-humber-25842236.

'Callum Wilson murder: Mother Emma Wilson jailed for life' *BBC News* (24 January 2014) at www.bbc.co.uk/news/uk-england-berkshire-25874635.

'Gintare Suminaite walks free after Bognor baby killing' *BBC News* (30 January 2017) at www.bbc.co.uk/news/uk-england-sussex-38803441.

'Hythe baby death: Silipa Keresi jailed for woodland murder' *BBC News* (2 December 2021) at www.bbc.co.uk/news/uk-england-hampshire-59509306.

'Lauren Saint George guilty of killing baby girl Lily-Mai' *BBC News* (25 July 2022) at www.bbc.co.uk/news/uk-england-london-62296439.

Mercer, D, 'Amina-Faye Johnson death: Parents jailed after baby died with more than 60 broken bones in "despicable" abuse case' *Sky News* (28 January 2022) at https://news.sky.com/story/parents-of-baby-who-died-with-more-than-60-broken-bones-to-be-sentenced-12525972.

'Mother guilty of killing baby son' *BBC News* (24 September 2009) at http://news.bbc.co.uk/1/hi/england/northamptonshire/8272961.stm.

Office for National Statistics, 'Crime Statistics, Focus on Violent Crime and Sexual Offences, 2013/14 reference tables' (12 February 2015) at www.ons.gov.uk/peoplepopulationandcommunity/crimeandjustice/compendium/focusonviolentcrimeandsexualoffences/2015-02-12/crimestatisticsfocusonviolentcrimeandsexualoffences201314referencetables.

—— 'Age' in *Homicide in England and Wales: year ending March 2018* (7 February 2019) at www.ons.gov.uk/peoplepopulationandcommunity/crimeandjustice/articles/homicideinenglandandwales/yearendingmarch2018#which-groups-of-people-are-most-likely-to-be-victims-of-homicide.

——, 'Appendix tables: homicide in England and Wales' (10 February 2022) at www.ons.gov.uk/peoplepopulationandcommunity/crimeandjustice/datasets/appendixtableshomicideinenglandandwales.

——, 'Year Ending June 2022 edition of this dataset' in *Crime in England and Wales: Appendix* (27 October 2022) at www.ons.gov.uk/peoplepopulationandcommunity/crimeandjustice/datasets/crimeinenglandandwalesappendixtables.

Parliamentary Papers

British Parliamentary Papers, 1866, vol 21.

British Parliamentary Papers, 1936–37, vol 2.

HC Deb 14 May 1878, vol 239, cols 1936–59 at 1948–49.

HL Deb 16 May 1922, vol 50, cols 440–4.

HL Deb 25 May 1922, vol 50, cols 758–62, 765, 767–68.
HC Deb 24 November 1936, vol 318, col 235.
HL Deb 22 March 1938, vol 108, cols 294–95, 299, 303–04.

Reports

Committee on Mentally Abnormal Offenders, *Report of the Committee on Mentally Abnormal Offenders* (Cmnd 6244, 1975).
Criminal Law Revision Committee, *Offences against the Person* (14th Report, Cmnd 7844, 1980).
Law Commission, *Murder, Manslaughter and Infanticide* (Law Com no 304, 2006) at https://s3-eu-west-2.amazonaws.com/lawcom-prod-storage-11jsxou24uy7q/uploads/2015/03/lc304_Murder_Manslaughter_and_Infanticide_Report.pdf.
Law Reform Commission of Western Australia, *A Review of the Law of Homicide* (Project 97, 2007) at www.wa.gov.au/government/publications/project-97-review-of-the-law-of-homicide.
New South Wales Law Reform Commission, *Partial Defences to Murder: Provocation and Infanticide* (Report 83, 1997) at www.lawreform.justice.nsw.gov.au/Documents/Publications/Reports/Report-83.pdf.
——, *People with Cognitive and Mental Health Impairments in the Criminal Justice System: Criminal Responsibility and Consequences* (Report 138, 2013) at www.lawreform.justice.nsw.gov.au/Documents/Publications/Reports/Report-138.pdf.
Victorian Law Reform Commission, *Defences to Homicide: Final Report* (2004) at www.lawreform.vic.gov.au/wp-content/uploads/2021/07/VLRC_Defences_to_Homicide_Final_Report-1.pdf.

Theses

Brennan, K, 'Infanticide Past and Present: Law, History and Culture' (PhD Thesis, University College Dublin 2006).

PART I

The Infanticide Act in Practice

2

Manslaughter, Concealment of Birth and Infanticide, 1900–37

RACHEL DIXON AND TONY WARD

In November 1927, Ethel Garner, a 22-year-old book-keeper, pleaded not guilty to infanticide at Lincoln Assizes. The body of her newborn baby boy had been found in a locked drawer in her wardrobe with a stocking tied tightly around his neck. After Ethel's mother gave evidence for the prosecution, Mr Justice Swift asked defence counsel 'if he might advise his client differently'. The lawyer replied that she might plead guilty to concealment of birth, but not to infanticide.[1] The judge asked:

> [W]hy plead guilty to something involving knowledge when she is charged with something involving absence of knowledge? I should punish much more severely a person who knowingly concealed a birth than a woman who strangled her child while the balance of her mind was disturbed.[2]

Ethel then pleaded guilty to infanticide. The judge told the jury:

> He thought that believing that she might be sent to prison they might have strained their conscience and acquitted her, and therefore he strained his own conscience and all but told her counsel what he intended to do – to bind her over. He might be right or he might be wrong in taking that course – only the girl's future would tell; he did what he thought was right.[3]

Ethel was duly bound over, although the precise nature of the sentence is unclear. Swift J told the jury that 'she would be guarded and properly looked after', which suggests that he had in mind to bind her over with probation,[4] under the Probation of Offenders Act 1907. So far as the local newspaper reports indicate,

[1] 'Collapsed in Dock, Young Book-Keeper Guilty of Infanticide' *Stamford Mercury* (Stamford, 4 November 1927).

[2] 'Lincoln Assizes' *Retford and Worksop Herald* (Retford, 8 November 1927). This appears to be a fuller and more exact quotation than in the *Stamford Mercury* report.

[3] ibid.

[4] L Radzinowicz and JWC Turner, 'Conviction and Probation' (1941) 19 *Canadian Bar Review* 500, 501.

however, he merely bound her over to be of good behaviour, and told her mother to look after her.

Infanticide, as defined in the 1922 Act, was not a crime that implied an absence of knowledge. On the contrary, a woman could be convicted of infanticide, 'notwithstanding that the circumstances were such that but for this Act the offence would have amounted to murder'.[5] It is not easy to imagine how someone could tie a stocking tightly round a baby's neck without knowing what she was doing, so we can see why Swift J had to strain his conscience to justify the sentence in the way that he did, with the suggestion that intentionally concealing the birth by locking the child's body in a drawer was a worse crime than strangling him. Counsel's advice to plead not guilty may have been quite realistic if the medical evidence left room for doubt as to whether the baby had been alive, and fully outside Ethel's body, when the stocking was tied round his neck.[6] As we shall see, similar defences were advanced successfully in other cases.

In this chapter we try to answer the question raised by Ethel Garner's case and others like it: how did an offence that was designed to deal with cases that would formerly have constituted murder rather than manslaughter come to be seen as a relatively minor matter that could be dealt with by a non-custodial sentence? The chapter has two main sections. Section I considers why the 1922 Act took the form it did, setting the parliamentary debates in the context of trials for newborn child murder at the beginning of the twentieth century. It addresses, in more detail than previous accounts,[7] the question why a new lesser offence was chosen in preference to altering the law of manslaughter. Section II, focusing particularly on cases in Lincolnshire (a rural county in the East of England), examines the sentences imposed under the Act, and the reasons given for them by the judges in the context of the cultural factors behind the perceived willingness of jurors and judges to 'strain their consciences' in cases of infanticide. Short concluding section III suggests that we can derive from these factors a reasonably coherent justification for the existence of infanticide as a lesser offence.

I. The Birth of Infanticide as a Separate Offence

The Infanticide Act 1922 began as one of a series of bills that sought to make it easier to convict a woman of the manslaughter of a newborn baby, rather than of either murder or concealment of birth. Had that original Bill been passed, we would now be marking the centenary of an important precursor of diminished

[5] Infanticide Act 1922, s 1(1).

[6] *R v Crutchley* (1837) 7 C & P 814.

[7] T Ward, 'The Sad Subject of Infanticide: Law Medicine and Child Murder, 1860–1948' (1999) 8 *Social & Legal Studies* 163; T Ward, 'Legislating for Human Nature: Legal Responses to Infanticide, 1860–1938' in M Jackson (ed), *Infanticide: Historical Perspectives on Child Murder and Concealment, 1550–2000* (Routledge 2002) 249.

responsibility manslaughter. Instead, the Bill was rewritten to create a new offence of infanticide, by which a woman who would otherwise be guilty of the murder of her newly born child would be liable to the same penalty as for manslaughter, if the offence was committed while 'the balance of her mind was disturbed' as a result of the birth.

The drafting of the Infanticide Act 1922 was mainly the work of Sir Claud Schuster, the Permanent Secretary at the Lord Chancellor's Office. Schuster's political master, Viscount Birkenhead (the barrister and Conservative politician FE Smith), had objected to the original Bill, which was based on one that had been passed by the House of Lords in 1909[8] but had fallen because no time was found for it in the Commons.[9] The Bill provided that where a mother killed her infant child, and 'evidence is given that at the time the offence was committed the woman had not recovered from the effect of giving birth to the child', the jury 'may' convict of manslaughter rather than murder. Birkenhead objected to the Bill several grounds, one of which was that

> an express provision that a jury may return the verdict of manslaughter in these cases might appear to reflect upon the right which they most undoubtedly possess and habitually exercise of returning a verdict of manslaughter in any murder case. The argument upon that point is patent.[10]

To say that juries habitually exercised this power is somewhat of an overstatement, but in the final years of the Old Bailey Sessions Papers (1900–13) there were six manslaughter verdicts in neonaticide cases. Seemingly by chance, they all occurred between 1902 and 1906, so that for that short period Carolyn Conley is correct to say that they outnumbered verdicts of concealment of birth.[11] There were eight verdicts of concealment in Old Bailey murder trials in 1900–13 and five guilty pleas, so over the whole period concealment remained the commonest alternative to a murder conviction.

The legal distinction between murder and manslaughter was not drawn in the same way in the early twentieth century as it is today. The forms of 'murderous malice' set out in the 1929 edition of Kenny's *Outlines of Criminal Law* – the last one completed by Kenny himself – include 'Intention to do an act which is intrinsically likely to kill, though without any purpose of thereby inflicting any hurt whatever'.[12] It also cites, as still representing the law, the case mentioned by Blackstone 'of the harlot, who [abandoned] her child in an orchard, where a kite struck it and killed it',[13] who was convicted of murder and executed.[14]

[8] HL Deb 18 May 1909, vol 1, cols 957–65.

[9] Note by Alexander Maxwell, 13 May 1922, in National Archive, LCO 2/476.

[10] HL Deb 16 May 1922, vol 50, col 440.

[11] CA Conley, *Debauched, Desperate, Deranged: Women Who Killed, London, 1674–1913* (Oxford University Press 2000) 176.

[12] CS Kenny, *Outlines of Criminal Law*, 13th edn (Cambridge University Press 1929) 137.

[13] W Blackstone, *Commentaries on the Law of England*, vol 4 (Clarendon Press 1769) 197.

[14] Kenny (n 12) 127.

In other words, if the mother caused her child's death by what the 1922 Act would call a 'wilful act or omission', and a reasonable person would have foreseen death as a likely result, she was guilty of murder, under a doctrine that was finally abolished only by section 8 of the Criminal Law Act 1967.[15] In all the cases discussed below, therefore, a conviction for murder would have been legally sound, whether or not the mother had any intention or foresight of causing death or serious harm.

On the other hand, as Birkenhead pointed out, a verdict of manslaughter could be returned without any evidence of the mother's physical or mental state. For example, Mildred Cole's baby was found with tape tightly wound round his neck, and the pathologist, Ludwig Freyberger, gave unusually firm evidence that this was a case where the child had been 'shot out' with such force as to tear the umbilical cord, and in these circumstances the hydrostatic test – that is, the fact that baby's lung tissue floated in water – was 'absolutely conclusive' evidence that the child had had a separate existence.[16] There is no record that he was asked anything about Mildred's mental state. Such a question might have elicited a similar reply to the one he gave in another trial a few weeks earlier:

> [A] woman having her first child may, in a way, be affected mentally; there would be pain during the birth, which would be accentuated by depression – child birth is very often followed by a period of partial or total unconsciousness – a woman might not know what was going on around her, or what she was doing herself.[17]

At Mildred Cole's trial, Freyberger was so unyielding when cross-examined about the hydrostatic test that defence counsel may have decided not to risk a question about his client's mental state. The barrister had persuaded the judge to exclude the confession Cole had made to a doctor, and appears to have calculated correctly that he had done enough for the jury to remain unpersuaded that she intended to kill or seriously harm her child, despite the evidence of how tightly she had tied the tape around his neck.

There seems, then, to have been some substance to Birkenhead's objection that the Bill's requirement for evidence that the mother had not recovered from the effects of giving birth would cause confusion, as there was no such requirement in the existing law of manslaughter. As the Bill did not specify *medical* evidence, the requirement might have been satisfied by the defendant's own statement to police. The words of Alice Sergeant, accused of murdering her newborn baby in 1906 by throwing it over a wall, clearly convey a lay understanding of not having recovered from giving birth: 'I was not in my right mind when I did it, I was so frightened, and I did not mean to do it. I was in so much pain.' Sergeant, who protested in court that she had 'put' rather than 'thrown' the child over the wall, was convicted of manslaughter.[18]

[15] See *R v Ward* [1956] 1 QB 35; *Hyam v DPP* [1975] AC 55, 75.
[16] OBP, t19040418-395, 18 April 1904.
[17] Trial of Louisa Lunn, OBP tl19040321-332, 21 March 1904.
[18] OBP, t19061022-40.

A second objection advanced by Birkenhead was that

> the only effect of the Bill, if, indeed, it has any new effect, is to give statutory authority for a jury, in the cases to which the Bill refers, to return a verdict of manslaughter on facts which amount in law to murder – in other words, to return a verdict which is not in accordance with the evidence according to the existing law, which is not altered.[19]

Birkenhead was correct, as Parliamentary Counsel confirmed:[20] by stating that the jury 'may' convict for manslaughter rather than murder, the Bill gave them discretion to return a manslaughter verdict in cases that still legally amounted to murder. This wording reflected the Bill's origin as an amended version of one that would have given the trial judge a discretion to record, rather than pronounce, the sentence of death (making a reprieve virtually automatic).[21] The Bill would not have been entirely without effect, because in a trial such as that of Edith Roberts, whose murder conviction prompted the Bill's introduction,[22] the judge would not have been able to tell the jury that they must not be 'led away by sympathy for a woman':[23] he would have had to make it clear that a verdict of manslaughter would be perfectly proper, even though all the elements of murder had been proved. The fact that the Bill as originally introduced gave the jury this unusual discretion is revealing. The lack of any definition of the partial defence it would have created suggests that reasons why juries might convict of a lesser offence could not be explicitly stated in legislation but the jury could be expected to understand them. Atiyah and Summers have noted the abiding reluctance of English judges to weaken legal prohibitions by 'equitable modifications designed to show mercy or compassion (or even justice) to those who committed prohibited acts in situations of stress or ignorance or lack of cognitive understanding'.[24] Judges and juries could 'stretch out the hand of mercy', but this was not to be explicitly written into law. As Hugh Godley, the Assistant Parliamentary Counsel to the Treasury,[25] put it, the proposed partial defence would introduce 'a point to be considered hitherto unheard of in criminal cases, namely the degree of sympathy which the jury might happen to feel for the accused'.[26]

Birkenhead found the discretion so conferred unacceptably wide. There needed to be something 'to connect the fact that the woman had not recovered from the effect of giving birth to the child with the commission of the offence'.[27] To fill this

[19] HL Deb 16 May 1922, vol 50, col 440.

[20] LCO 2/476, Hugh Godley to Sir Claud Schuster, 19 May 1922.

[21] Child Murder (Record of Sentence of Death) Bill (Committee Stage), HL Deb 18 May 1909, vol 1, cols 957–65.

[22] D Grey, 'Women's Policy Networks and the Infanticide Act 1922' (2010) 21 *Twentieth-Century British History* 441, 445.

[23] 'Hinckley Murder Appeal' *Nottingham Evening Post* (Nottingham, 28 July 1921).

[24] P Atiyah and RS Summers, *Form and Substance in Anglo-American Law* (Clarendon Press 1987) 38. See also M Wiener, *Reconstructing the Criminal* (Cambridge University Press 1990).

[25] 'Hugh John Godley, 2nd Baron Kilbracken' at www.thepeerage.com/p33608.htm.

[26] Hugh Godley, Note in LCO 2/476.

[27] HL Deb 16 May 1922, vol 50, cols 440–41.

gap, Godley proposed that the woman's condition should be such as to 'disturb the balance of her mind'. Schuster adopted the 'balance of the mind' formula when redrafting the Bill, and Sir Archibald Bodkin, the Director of Public Prosecutions, heartily approved of it as a way of encapsulating the non-medical reasons why juries sympathised with infanticidal women. Rather than abstractly considering, as Birkenhead had, 'whether the nature of the ailment from which the woman is suffering is such as to have deflected her will … or her capacity for distinguishing between what is right and what is wrong', Bodkin considered the meaning of the clause in the context of a typical case:

> It is found I should say pretty well in 95% of these cases that the woman, unmarried, possibly a domestic servant or daughter living with other women in the house, has denied her pregnancy in spite of her appearance, makes no preparation, is secret towards all, finds herself just about to begin labour, perhaps struggles to a lavatory … or is in her bedroom alone. The child is born and, to prevent noise, she ties a string or garter around its neck, or inflicts wounds with scissors, or gives it blows on the head or smuggles it with a pillow.[28]

Having set the scene in this way (and in the phrase 'to prevent noise' suggesting how even strangulation or stabbing could be classed as manslaughter), Bodkin told Schuster:

> The phrase 'balance of her mind was then disturbed' seems to me a particularly happy one; no one can doubt what it means when one visualises the scene in the bedroom – the child crying, the woman possibly very inexperienced, a difficult labour, the umbilical cord to be dealt with and, if I may use the homely phrase, 'the breakfast to be got ready as usual in the morning' … so that she, under the stress of circumstances and not being mistress of her actions, does what in cold blood she never would have done.[29]

Bodkin, then, saw the defence as involving a loss of self-control and an act that was out of character.[30] To say that 'no one can doubt what it means' was certainly optimistic; the debate in the House of Commons gives no indication that any MP understood the amendment at all.[31]

It was also Schuster who came up with the proposal for a new offence to be called infanticide rather than manslaughter, in a draft, very close to the final wording of the 1922 Act, which he introduced with the words, 'If one were allowed to express the true object of the Bill I suppose one would say: …' After setting out the wording he added 'I suppose that this is too frank an exposition of what is wanted, to commend itself'. These cryptic remarks do not explain why 'infanticide' rather than manslaughter was chosen, but they once again suggest that the Bill was doing something that criminal legislation did not ordinarily do; although far from

[28] Archibald Bodkin, letter to Sir Claud Schuster, 29 May 1922, in LCO 2/476, 1–2.
[29] ibid, 4–5.
[30] See section III, text to n 78.
[31] See Ward, 'Legislating for Human Nature' (n 7) 264–65.

being 'frank', it was hiding its true purpose behind medical-sounding language. In Bodkin's letter the medical mask is removed, and we find a truly frank description of the Bill as an attempt to give legal form to the sympathy that juries felt for defendants in typical cases.

What Schuster thought might be too frank in the wording of the Bill must have been the phrase 'notwithstanding the fact that but for this Act it would have been [the jury's] duty to return a verdict of murder' – and indeed, the words about the jury's duty, with the implication that for at least the past century juries had been failing in that duty, were dropped from the final wording of the Act ('that the circumstances were such that but for this Act would have amounted to murder'). What the Act in its final form underlines is that infanticide was a serious offence – essentially, murder with mitigating circumstances. How, then, did it come to be seen as an offence that could be considered less serious than concealment of birth?

II. Explaining Judicial Leniency

Cases like Ethel Garner's, with which we began, show the extent of judicial sympathy for infanticidal women, and the assumed sympathy of jurors, arising from the typical circumstances of their crimes.[32] The origins of such sympathetic attitudes can be traced back to at least the eighteenth century, when the infanticidal woman was described as having 'had good reason … to despair of her situation'.[33] Unmarried women faced 'enormous difficulties', deriving from the economic and social implications of unmarried motherhood: the absence of a financial support from the father, the likely loss of employment and the social stigma of being a 'fallen woman' made infanticide appear inevitable in the eyes of some Victorian commentators.[34] The harshness of the new Poor Law of 1834 towards unmarried mothers was implicitly criticised in sympathetic portrayals such as Frances Trollope's novel, *Jessie Phillips*.[35] The sympathy of jurors and judges for the desperate situation of the unmarried woman, pregnant and abandoned by her seducer, was acknowledged even by writers who deplored the resulting leniency.[36]

The conduct of men in infanticide cases became increasingly recognised as a mitigating factor by the courts, as we shall see in several of the cases discussed

[32] K Brennan, '"A Fine Mixture of Pity and Pleasure": The Criminal Justice Response to Infanticide in Ireland, 1922–1949' (2013) 31 *Law and History Review* 793, 799.

[33] RW Malcolmson, 'Infanticide in the Eighteenth Century' in CJ Cockburn (ed), *Crime in England 1550–1800* (Methuen 1977) 187, 192.

[34] AR Higginbotham, '"Sin of the Age:" Infanticide and Illegitimacy in Victorian London' (1989) 32 *Victorian Studies* 319, 321–22.

[35] C Krueger, 'Literary Defenses and Medical Prosecutions: Representing Infanticide in Nineteenth-Century Britain' (1997) 40 *Victorian Studies* 271.

[36] WB Ryan, *Infanticide: Its Law, Prevalence, Prevention and History* (J Churchill 1862); Rev H Humble, 'Infanticide: Its Cause and Cure' in O Shipley (ed), *The Church and the World: Essays on Questions of the Day* (Longmans, Green, Reader & Dyer, 1867) 51.

below. Although the man might not have played a part in the death of the infant, he did play a part in the child's illegitimacy and the mother's economic plight. In a large number of cases, the man would lure the woman into a sexual relationship on the false promise of marriage, seduce her and then, upon the discovery of her pregnancy, abandon her. It was this combination of wicked male intentions and female naivety that became a recurring theme in infanticide cases, and which in turn led to the creation of a wave of sympathy in court.[37]

The trial of Clara Hildebrand epitomised the extent of judicial sympathy towards a woman accused of murdering her newly born infant.[38] She was indicted on 6 March 1905 at the Old Bailey for the wilful murder of her newly born female child: the child had sustained a number of injuries, and medical evidence established that the child died from 'shock caused by injury to the brain and by haemorrhage as a result of those injuries'.[39] The Registered General Practitioner, Patrick McGregor, believed that 'the fractures could have all been done at once with one blow'.[40] An article in the *Barking, East Ham and Ilford Advertiser* reported that defence counsel

> argued that the inquiry was due to accidental causes, and, in the circumstances, the jury were invited to acquit the prisoner.
>
> The jury found the prisoner guilty of manslaughter.
>
> Mr Grantham, said a lady was ready to receive the girl into a Home, subject to his Lordship's sanction. The man who ruined her had refused to do anything for her. He was connected with the theatrical profession at Broadstairs.
>
> Mr Justice Darling: I only wish I could give him part of the punishment [Hear, hear, from the jury].[41]

Despite the palpable sense of sympathy towards Clara and frustration towards the absent father in this exchange, Clara was sentenced to 12 months' imprisonment. This was a longer sentence than women would typically receive under the 1922 Act, as illustrated in the following sample of trials held in Lincolnshire between 1925 and 1937.

During this period, 10 women were charged with infanticide in the county: six of these women were bound over for a sum of between £5 and £10, one woman was acquitted, and two were found not guilty and discharged. One woman was found guilty of concealment of birth and sentenced to six months' imprisonment, while only one of those found guilty of infanticide was imprisoned rather than bound over, and she received four months in the second division, seeming to confirm the idea that infanticide was a lesser offence than concealment. The cases were

[37] Higginbotham (n 34); J McDonagh, *Child Murder and British Culture, 1770–1990* (Cambridge University Press 2003).

[38] OBP, Clara Hildebrand, 6 March 1905, t19050306-276.

[39] ibid.

[40] ibid.

[41] 'Story of a Servants Ruin' *Barking, East Ham and Ilford Advertiser, Upton Park and Dagenham Gazette* (London 11 March 1905) (square brackets original).

reported in both national and provincial newspapers, and whilst they may not provide a comprehensive record of all relevant cases, they do present a general trend.

The first woman to be charged with the new offence of infanticide was Beatrice May Tethers, who appeared at Lincoln City Police Court in October 1924. The body of her newborn child was discovered in an attaché case in her bedroom at the hotel in Lincoln where she worked as a barmaid.[42] A cord had been tied twice around the neck of the infant, and although the knot was not complete, the cord was so tight around the child's neck that it 'was almost invisible in places'.[43] A post-mortem examination indicated that the child had been born alive and that the cause of death was asphyxiation.[44] In spite of this, both the coroner and the magistrates concluded the medical evidence was not sufficiently strong to justify committing the defendant to trial for infanticide.[45] There was, however, evidence that strongly suggested concealment of birth. One of the magistrates described the case as being 'very sad' and continued by stating that 'one thing I regret, is that the father of the child is not beside the girl'.[46]

When Beatrice Tethers pleaded guilty to concealment of birth, the Commissioner of Assize, Mr Hollis Walker, demonstrated a less sympathetic approach towards infanticidal women. He expressed an opinion that, in some cases of concealment of birth,

> there were some features in such cases which aroused sympathy and others which often aroused suspicion. They were so often preceded by knowledge of what was coming yet effort was made to prepare for it. The campaign of secrecy was begun before birth and continued afterwards, causing suspicion that not only was the birth itself concealed, but also the death and the cause of death. Those cases were becoming so frequent that he thought some pronouncement would have to be made were girls coming think that if successful they would all right, and if not, they had only into court, plead guilty and shed a few tears, the Judge would preach little, and they would be let go. If so, it would have to be stopped.[47]

He added, however, that he did not take that view of the prisoner's case and he bound her over so that 'if she behaved herself she would hear no more about it'.[48]

In some cases, there is little doubt that father of the child was guilty not merely of abandoning the mother but of rape. For example, Winifred Barker, a 17-year-old domestic servant from East Keal, was charged with murder, infanticide and concealment of birth in December 1927, at the Lincoln Assizes.[49] Medical evidence

[42] 'Lincoln Barmaid Acquitted of Infanticide' *Lincolnshire Chronicle* (Lincoln, 11 October 1924).
[43] ibid.
[44] ibid.
[45] ibid.
[46] ibid.
[47] 'Concealment of Birth. Commissioner's Comments' *Lincolnshire Echo* (Lincoln, 28 October 1924).
[48] ibid.
[49] 'Boston Girl and Murder Charge' *Lincolnshire Standard and Boston Guardian* (Lincoln, 11 February 1928).

indicated that the child had had a separate existence: there were 'two wounds on the neck and breast of the child, apparently caused by a blade of a safety razor';[50] however, the defendant claimed that the child was already dead when the wounds were inflicted, and medical evidence was unable to establish whether or not this was true. The Grand Jury threw out the charge of murder: Winifred's plea of not guilty to infanticide was accepted by the prosecution, and she pleaded guilty to concealment of birth.[51] Her counsel said that 'the whole thing was not exactly the girl's fault, as a young man at her previous piece of employment had entered her bedroom and forced his attentions upon her'.

Mr Justice Hawke said that

> the fact that the girl had been in prison for a considerable time made his task much easier. He had also seen medical evidence that it was uncertain whether the wounds were inflicted before death or after. Prisoner would be bound over for two years in the sum of £10 and he hoped that her life now would be a happy one.[52]

Some mothers were able to avoid a conviction for infanticide because of the difficulty of proving that the child had had an independent existence and had died as the result of the mother's 'wilful act or omission'. Since a series of cases in the 1830s established that a baby must have lived wholly outside its mother's body for its killing to constitute murder,[53] the difficulty of proving live birth had been a major obstacle to a murder prosecution where the victim was newly born. The Infanticide Act did nothing to address this problem, although one Lincolnshire coroner mistakenly believed that it did. At the inquest on the unnamed child of Alice Bennett in 1929, he suggested that despite medical evidence that a baby found in a parcel under a housekeeper's bed had not had a separate existence, 'he thought the [Infanticide] Act must apply in that case' if the death had been caused by 'any wilful act or commission [*sic*]'.[54] This suggestion was clearly erroneous: it was the Infant Life Preservation Act 1929 that created the felony of child destruction, where a person 'by any wilful act causes a child to die before it has an existence independent of its mother'.[55] There is little case law on the Act, but it seemingly requires the prosecution to prove that the child had *not* been born alive, making it of little use where it could not be proved one way or another

[50] ibid.

[51] The *Lincolnshire Standard* (ibid) reported that she had pleaded guilty to infanticide, but this was corrected by her solicitors in a letter to the editor (18 February 1928).

[52] 'Boston Girl & Murder Charge' *Lincolnshire Standard and Boston Guardian* (Lincoln, 11 February 1928).

[53] We discuss these cases in R Dixon and T Ward, 'Expert Evidence and Uncertainty in English Infanticide Trials, c 1725–1945' in L Bergers et al (eds), *Forensic Cultures in Modern Europe: Expertise and Knowledge Practices* (Manchester University Press 2023) 169.

[54] 'Holbeach Infant's Death' *Lincolnshire Standard and Boston Guardian* (Lincoln, 26 January 1929).

[55] Infant Life Preservation Act 1929, s (1).

whether the baby had had an independent existence; perhaps for this reason, prosecutions of mothers for child destruction appear to have been rare.[56] In Alice Bennett's case, the lack of proof of live birth did not prevent the father's responsibility from becoming an issue. George Lawton, for whom Alice ostensibly worked as a housekeeper, denied that the child was his, to which the coroner responded that 'they were not sitting there as a court of morals … the question was, whether the child was born alive'.[57] The jury returned a verdict of stillbirth, but stated that both Bennett and Lawton were 'deserving of the greatest censure for failing to make proper arrangements for the birth of the child'.[58] The coroner, in his closing statement, told both of them that

> the jury has brought a verdict which allowed them to escape criminal proceedings, but they [the jury] felt that they [Bennett and Lawson] had placed themselves in a serious position and they did not believe the evidence of either of them.[59]

Even where the child was clearly born alive and there were indications of violence, it could be hard to prove that the violence was inflicted before death. For example, an inquest was held April 1932 into the death of the child of Gladys May Barton. The child's body had been discovered in a garden at Corringham, in Lincolnshire.[60] Dr Scorgie, who carried out the post-mortem, described the child as being

> well nourished and there were marks of violence on the body. There was a large compressed fracture of the right side of the head three inches in length and two inches in breadth, while the skull over this area was exposed the scalp having been torn off. There was a lacerated wound of the chest wall one and a half inches long. The legs were in their entirety charred and the skin of the back and abdomen was burned to a much lesser degree. The brain was severely mutilated, but the heart and lungs were normal. The possible cause of death was syncope[61] resulting from haemorrhage. He thought that the wounds on the chest and the fracture of the skull and the burning of the body occurred after death.[62]

The coroner asked whether 'the child must have been alive', to which the doctor replied 'yes probably for an hour'.[63] The coroner then asked if 'there was nothing to

[56] One example is the case of Daisy Bench. The magistrates were not satisfied that her infant was born alive so they committed her for trial for child destruction. At the Assizes she was charged with both child destruction and infanticide, and acquitted of both. See 'Southam Murder Charge Fails' *Rugby Advertiser* (Rugby, 31 July 1931); 'Acquittal of a Southam Mother' *Royal Leamington Spa Courier* (Royal Leamington Spa, 27 November 1931).

[57] 'Inquest on Holbeach Baby: Mother and Man Censured by Jury' *Spalding Guardian* (Spalding, 16 February 1929).

[58] ibid.

[59] ibid.

[60] 'Child's Body in Garden' *Lincolnshire Echo* (Lincoln, 11 April 1932).

[61] 'A Temporary loss of consciousness caused by a fall in blood pressure' at www.oxforddictionaries.com/definition/english/syncope (accessed 1 August 2022).

[62] 'Child's Body in Garden' (n 60).

[63] ibid.

enable [the doctor] to form the opinion there was any wilful act or omission', 'No', replied the doctor.[64] In summing up the coroner stated:

> [T]he cause of death was syncope due to haemorrhage that could not be natural and therefore it must be accidental, there was no evidence said the coroner of murder or manslaughter or of infanticide, because there was no evidence of wilful murder, neglect or omission.[65]

Avoiding a conviction for infanticide, however, did not necessarily result in a lesser degree of punishment where the mother could be convicted of concealment of birth. In June 1925, the child of Ethel Rickell was discovered wrapped and left under a hedge, near Ashby in Lincolnshire. She was indicted for infanticide. Medical tests established that the child had had a separate existence and in the 'opinion of the doctor who carried out the tests, the child died from lack of attention and exposure'.[66] Dr Bellamy said the child was a

> fully developed male, weighing 8lbs and had lived, the cause of death was shock, exposure and general want of attention. He had also seen the accused and her condition was consistent with recently having given birth to a child.[67]

Ethel said she had no memory of what happened in the two hours after she gave birth in a lavatory, and her counsel urged that there had been 'no criminal wilful negligence'; the jury returned a verdict of 'guilty of concealment of birth' and the prisoner was sentenced to six months' imprisonment.'[68]

This was a much more severe sentence than was passed on Rose Emily Taylor, a domestic servant at the Waddington Rectory, in Lincolnshire, whose newborn child was found in the cellar with a piece of cord tied tightly around the child's neck and a fractured skull.[69] Rose pleaded guilty to infanticide and was bound over for the sum of £5 for one year. At the trial at the Lincoln Assizes, her defence counsel, Dr Lindlay, stated that 'what she did on the morning of February 7, she did under great stress of emotion when she could not possibly realise what she was doing'.[70] In this case the child's father had not deserted the defendant, and they were married by the time of the trial. As she pleaded guilty, there was no medical evidence of her mental state, but the defence's explanation must have been accepted by the judge. Inflicting great violence under extreme emotional stress seems to have been seen as less culpable than Rose Rickell's relatively calculated act of wrapping her dead baby in a parcel and hiding it under a hedge.

The Infanticide Act 1922 was limited to the deaths of 'newly born' children, which the Court of Appeal interpreted as meaning no more than one month

[64] ibid.
[65] ibid.
[66] 'Alleged Infanticide' *Lincolnshire Echo* (Lincoln, 18 June 1925).
[67] ibid.
[68] ibid.
[69] 'Infanticide at Waddington' *Lincolnshire Echo* (Lincoln, 6 June 1934).
[70] ibid.

in age.[71] Mothers who killed slightly older infants continued to be sentenced to death, leading to a renewal of calls to end the 'black cap farce' of passing capital sentences that would never be carried out.[72] One case that received national attention was that of Olive Wise, convicted of murdering her 9-month-old infant on Christmas Eve, 1930. The *Lincolnshire Echo* welcomed the Home Secretary's decision to commute the death sentence:

> [T]here is a difference of opinion about the wisdom of retaining capital punishment as part of our criminal code, but there is almost unanimous opinion that infanticide by mothers in circumstances and at a time when they are not fully responsible for their actions, is in a different category, and so seldom is the death sentence carried out that the solemn condemnation has become something of a cruel farce. Nothing must be done that would suggest that the life of a helpless baby is of small account; rather the change must represent the more humane view of the position of the unmarried mother.[73]

An article printed in the *Dundee Courier* describes the sentencing of infanticidal women as

> a legal anomaly and legal cruelty involved in sentencing a woman to death when it was perfectly well known by everyone except the unfortunate prisoner that there was no intention of that sentence being carried out. There had been during the last twelve months ... six cases of this character, and there had been the spectacle of judges slurring over the dreadful words of the sentence and of one judge telling the prisoner that she need take no notice of the sentence about to be passed on her.[74]

III. 'The Partiality of the Law'

This chapter has attempted to shed light on the apparent paradox that a crime designed to cover acts that would otherwise have amounted to murder could be regarded as a less serious offence than concealment of birth, one that, in Mr Justice Swift's words, involved an 'absence of knowledge'. We have seen that two arguments consistently featured in the drafting of the 1922 Act and the sentencing of women under it: first, that the physical and emotional anguish of giving birth in secret was such that a woman was not fully responsible for her actions; and, second, that the responsibility for the situation in which she turned to such desperate measures lay with the father of the child as well as the mother, and it was unfair that the mother alone should face punishment.

[71] *R v O'Donoghue* (1927) 20 Cr App R 132.
[72] 'Commons Bill to Save Death Penalty' *Hull Daily Mail* (Hull, 28 November 1936).
[73] 'The Condemned Mother' *Lincolnshire Echo* (Lincoln, 20 January 1931).
[74] 'When Death Sentence is an Anomaly' *Dundee Courier* (Dundee, 25 November 1936).

There can be no doubt that these arguments reflected gender stereotypes,[75] a 'presumption of female innocence and weakness' that led to a growing divergence in the way male and female killers were treated in the late nineteenth and early twentieth centuries.[76] We should not, however, be too quick to dismiss them as wholly unjustified. The first argument is summed up in Sir Archibald Bodkin's words 'that she, under the stress of circumstances and not being mistress of her actions, does what in cold blood she never would have done'.[77] To be the 'mistress of one's actions' connotes a degree of self-control,[78] or responsiveness to reasons,[79] which is not a prerequisite for legal liability but which arguably is required for more than minimal moral culpability. Thus, as Kenny explained in his *Outlines of Criminal Law*, the infanticidal mother

> is treated as having been in some degree responsible when she did the act, although the balance of her mind is so far disturbed that – like a person who kills under gross provocation – she was not completely mistress of her faculties.[80]

To do 'what in cold blood she never would have done' is to act out of character, in circumstances so exceptional that no inference can fairly be drawn from what one does in those circumstances to any latent predisposition towards violence. Considering that infanticides were typically committed in circumstances where, as Emma Milne puts it, 'a woman's back [was] against the wall' to such an extent that, Milne would argue, we cannot think of her as truly making choices,[81] the idea that such a woman had only a very attenuated degree of responsibility for her acts was not unreasonable, even by twenty-first-century standards.

This brings us to the second argument, that the responsibility for the dire circumstances in which the woman found herself lay largely with the child's father, in a social context where consequences of extra-marital pregnancy fell heavily on the woman involved. This was not so much a feminist argument as an acknowledgement of unease or guilt at the grosser inequities of a patriarchal system; perhaps an implicit questioning of whether the state had the right to punish in such a case,[82] or at any rate to punish severely. Arguably, the compassion the law showed in these circumstances was a kind of 'pressure valve' that

[75] A Loughnan, *Manifest Madness: Mental Incapacity in Criminal Law* (Oxford University Press 2012) ch 8.

[76] MJ Wiener, *Men of Blood: Violence, Manliness and Criminal Justice in Victorian England* (Cambridge University Press 2004) 127.

[77] Bodkin (n 29).

[78] Kenny (n 12) 116 (identifying loss of self-control as a feature common to provocation and infanticide).

[79] JM Fischer and M Ravizza, *Responsibility and Control: A Theory of Moral Responsibility* (Cambridge University Press 1998).

[80] Kenny (n 12) 125.

[81] E Milne *Criminal Justice Responses to Maternal Filicide: Judging the Failed Mother* (Emerald Publishing Ltd 2021) 150.

[82] RA Duff, 'I Might Be Guilty, But You Can't Try Me: Estoppel and Other Bars to Trial' (2003) 1 *Ohio State Journal of Criminal Law* 245, 258.

helped to preserve patriarchy by mitigating some of its harshest consequences.[83] Nevertheless, the case for compassion could easily be given a feminist twist, as it was by the novelist MP Willcocks,[84] writing in *The Woman's Leader* (the successor to the suffragist *Common Cause*) in 1923:

> From the jury, from the crowd, even from the barristers' benches, one can see plain evidence of regret and disgust at the partiality of the law. I have seen, in the West Country, a jury declare a woman not guilty in such a case simply because, as they said afterwards, the man ought to have been there, and, in any case, 'she had suffered enough' … If we value life, as we profess we do, we cannot, as women, continue to allow the burden of the illegitimate child to be borne by the woman alone. … And the driving force for all this must come from the women voters, and especially from the organized women of the Feminist Societies.[85]

It is unclear whether the 'regret and disgust' she mentions were expressed before or after the 1922 Act, which her article surprisingly omits to mention (though she was clearly aware that infanticide was no longer a capital offence). What Willcocks does encapsulate in this article is a convergence of opinion between a conservative legal establishment, public opinion as represented by the jury and feminist demands for justice – demands that, as Daniel Grey has shown, significantly influenced the Infanticide Act.[86] This point is still worth considering as we ponder the future of infanticide law a century later.

References

Archival Sources

LCO 2/476, Hugh Godley to Sir Claud Schuster, 19 May 1922.
Archibald Bodkin, letter to Sir Claud Schuster, 29 May 1922, in LCO 2/476, 1–2.
Note by Alexander Maxwell, 13 May 1922, in National Archive, LCO 2/476.
Hugh Godley, Note in LCO 2/476.

Books

Atiyah, P and Summers, RS, *Form and Substance in Anglo-American Law* (Clarendon Press 1987).

[83] K Brennan, 'Murderous Mothers and Gentle Judges: Paternalism, Patriarchy and Infanticide' (2018) 30 *Yale Journal of Law & Feminism* 139, 184.
[84] See 'Willcocks, MP' in S Kemp, C Mitchell and D Trotter (eds), *The Oxford Companion to Edwardian Fiction* (Oxford University Press, 1997) 418–19.
[85] MP Willcocks, 'Infanticide and Illegitimacy' *The Woman's Leader and The Common Cause* (20 April 1923) 93.
[86] DJR Grey, 'Women's Policy Networks and the Infanticide Act 1922' (2010) 21 *Twentieth Century British History* 441.

Blackstone, W, *Commentaries on the Law of England*, vol 4 (Clarendon Press 1769).
Conley, CA, *Debauched, Desperate, Deranged: Women Who Killed, London, 1674–1913* (Oxford University Press 2000).
Fischer, JM and Ravizza, M, *Responsibility and Control: A Theory of Moral Responsibility* (Cambridge University Press 1998).
Kemp, S, Mitchell, C and Trotter, D (eds), *The Oxford Companion to Edwardian Fiction* (Oxford University Press 1997).
Kenny, CS, *Outlines of Criminal Law*, 13th edn (Cambridge University Press 1929).
Loughnan, A, *Manifest Madness: Mental Incapacity in Criminal Law* (Oxford University Press 2012).
Milne, E, *Criminal Justice Responses to Maternal Filicide: Judging the Failed Mother* (Emerald Publishing Limited 2021).
McDonagh, J, *Child Murder and British Culture, 1720–1990* (Cambridge University Press 2003).
Ryan, WB, *Infanticide: Its Law, Prevalence, Prevention and History* (J Churchill 1862).
Wiener, M, *Reconstructing the Criminal* (Cambridge University Press 1990).
——, *Men of Blood: Violence, Manliness and Criminal Justice in Victorian England* (Cambridge University Press 2004).

Chapters in Edited Volumes

Dixon, R and Ward, T, 'Expert Evidence and Uncertainty in English Infanticide Trials, c 1725–1945' in Bergers, L et al (eds), *Forensic Cultures in Modern Europe: Expertise and Knowledge Practices* (Manchester University Press 2023) 169.
Humble, H, 'Infanticide: Its Cause and Cure' in Shipley, O (ed), *The Church and the World: Essays on Questions of the Day* (Longmans, Green, Reader & Dyer 1867) 51.
Malcolmson, RW, 'Infanticide in the Eighteenth Century' in Cockburn, CJ (ed), *Crime in England 1550–1800* (Methuen 1977) 192.
Ward, T, 'Legislating for Human Nature: Legal Responses to Infanticide, 1860–1938' in Jackson, M (ed), *Infanticide: Historical Perspectives on Child Murder and Concealment, 1550–2000* (Routledge 2002) 249.

Journal Articles

Brennan, K, '"A Fine Mixture of Pity and Pleasure": The Criminal Justice Response to Infanticide in Ireland, 1922–1949' (2013) 31 *Law and History Review* 793.
——, 'Murderous Mothers and Gentle Judges: Paternalism, Patriarchy and Infanticide' (2018) 30 *Yale Journal of Law & Feminism* 139.
Duff, RA, 'I Might Be Guilty, But You Can't Try Me: Estoppel and Other Bars to Trial' (2003) 1 *Ohio State Journal of Criminal Law* 245.
Grey, D, 'Women's Policy Networks and the Infanticide Act 1922' (2010) 21 *Twentieth-Century British History* 441.
Higginbotham, AR, '"Sin of the Age": Infanticide and Illegitimacy in Victorian London' (1989) 32 *Victorian Studies* 319.
Krueger, C.L, 'Literary Defenses and Medical Prosecutions: Representing Infanticide in Nineteenth-Century Britain' (1997) 40 *Victorian Studies* 271.

Radzinowicz, L and Turner, JWC, 'Conviction and Probation' (1941) 19 *Canadian Bar Review* 500.
Ward, T, 'The Sad Subject of Infanticide: Law Medicine and Child Murder, 1860–1948' (1999) 8 *Social & Legal Studies* 163.
Willcocks, MP, 'Infanticide and Illegitimacy' *The Woman's Leader and The Common Cause* (20 April 1923) 93.

Newspaper Articles

[All the articles listed below may be accessed in The British Newspaper Archive, https://britishnewspaperarchive.co.uk.]
'Acquittal of a Southam Mother' *Royal Leamington Spa Courier* (Royal Leamington Spa, 27 November 1931).
'Boston Girl and Murder Charge' *Lincolnshire Standard and Boston Guardian* (Lincoln, 11 February, 1928).
'Child's Body in Garden' *Lincolnshire Echo* (Lincoln, 11 April 1932).
'Collapsed in Dock, Young Book-Keeper Guilty of Infanticide' *Stamford Mercury* (Stamford, 4 November 1927).
'Commons Bill to Save Death Penalty' *Hull Daily Mail* (Hull, 28 November 1936).
'Concealment of Birth. Commissioner's Comments' *Lincolnshire Echo* (Lincoln, 28 October 1924).
'Hinckley Murder Appeal' *Nottingham Evening Post* (Nottingham, 28 July 1921).
'Holbeach Infant's Death' *Lincolnshire Standard and Boston Guardian* (Lincoln, 26 January 1929).
'Inquest on Holbeach Baby: Mother and Man Censured by Jury' *Spalding Guardian* (Spalding, 16 February 1929).
'Lincoln Assizes' *Retford and Worksop Herald* (Retford, 8 November 1927).
'Lincoln Barmaid Acquitted of Infanticide' *Lincolnshire Chronicle* (Lincoln, 11 October 1924).
'Southam Murder Charge Fails' *Rugby Advertiser* (Rugby, 31 July 1931).
'Story of a Servants Ruin' *Barking, East Ham and Ilford Advertiser, Upton Park and Dagenham Gazette* (London, 11 March 1905).
'The Condemned Mother' *Lincolnshire Echo* (Lincoln, 20 January 1931).
'When Death Sentence is an Anomaly' *Dundee Courier* (Dundee, 25 November 1936).

Online Resources

'A Temporary loss of consciousness' at www.oxforddictionaries.com/definition/english/syncope.
'Hugh John Godley, 2nd Baron Kilbracken' at www.thepeerage.com/p33608.htm.

Parliamentary Papers

Child Murder (Record of Sentence of Death) Bill (Committee Stage) HL Deb 18 May 1909, vol 1, cols 957–65.
HL Deb 16 May 1922, vol 50, col 440.

3

Infanticide and Diminished Responsibility – Reviewing the Relationship

RONNIE MACKAY*

When a child under the age of 12 months is unlawfully killed by his or her biological mother, the latter may face a charge of either murder or manslaughter. However, either as an alternative or in addition, she may be charged with the offence of infanticide. Infanticide is governed by the Infanticide Act 1938 ('the 1938 Act'). Section 1(1) provides:

> Where a woman by any wilful act or omission causes the death of her child being a child under the age of twelve months, but at the time of the act or omission the balance of her mind was disturbed by reason of her not having fully recovered from the effect of giving birth to the child or by reason of the effect of lactation consequent upon the birth of the child, then, if the circumstances were such that but for this Act the offence would have amounted to murder or manslaughter, she shall be guilty of felony, to wit of infanticide, and may for such offence be dealt with and punished as if she had been guilty of the offence of manslaughter.[1]

Even if infanticide is not charged as an alternative or in addition to a charge of murder or manslaughter, when it is pleaded as a defence a jury may return a verdict of infanticide to a charge of murder or manslaughter.[2]

* I wish to thank David Hughes (formerly of the Law Commission) for his helpful comments on an earlier draft of this chapter.

[1] Section 57(2)(a) of the Coroners and Justice Act 2009 substituted the word 'if' for the words 'notwithstanding that'. This was in order to reverse *R v Gore (Deceased)* [2007] EWCA Crim 2789, where it was held that s 1(1) applied whenever the requirements of infanticide are made out, regardless of whether the circumstances of the killing would otherwise have amounted to the offence of murder. Section 57(2)(b) inserted the words 'or manslaughter' in order to ensure that s 1(1) can apply where the killing would otherwise have amounted to the offence of manslaughter.

[2] Section 1(2) of the Infanticide Act 1938 provides 'Where upon the trial of a woman for the murder or manslaughter of her child, being a child under the age of twelve months, the jury are of the opinion that she by any wilful act or omission caused its death, but that at the time of the act or omission the balance of her mind was disturbed by reason of her not having fully recovered from the effect of giving birth to the child or by reason of the effect of lactation consequent upon the birth of the child, then the

Subsequent to the enactment of the 1938 Act, section 2(1) of the Homicide Act 1957 introduced the defence of diminished responsibility into the law of England and Wales. Operating as a partial defence to a charge of murder, a successful plea results in a conviction for manslaughter despite the accused (D) having the mens rea for murder. Following the enactment of section 2(1), the partial defence of diminished responsibility was potentially available to biological mothers who killed their child aged under 12 months, thereby opening up the possibility of the deployment of a defence strategy of pleading both infanticide and diminished responsibility to a charge of murder.[3]

When originally enacted, section 2(1) provided that D was to be convicted of manslaughter and not murder if, at the time of the killing, D

> was suffering from such abnormality of mind (whether arising from a condition of arrested or retarded development of mind or any inherent causes or induced by disease or injury) as substantially impaired his mental responsibility for his acts and omissions in doing or being a party to the killing.

Commenting on the then section 2(1), the Law Commission ('the Commission') stated 'it has never been entirely clear whether under the existing law, the abnormality of mind must in some sense "cause" D to kill'.[4] As regards the meaning of 'substantial' impairment, the Commission commented that 'The little case law that there is establishes that the impairment need not be total but it must be more than trivial.'[5]

In its work between 2003–06 on murder, manslaughter and infanticide, the Commission gave detailed consideration as to whether infanticide might be merged with diminished responsibility. This had been recommended in the Butler Report,[6] but it was rejected by the Criminal Law Revision Committee.[7] The Commission initially identified four important differences between the two.[8] First, the different forms of abnormal states of mind in respect of each, namely, 'balance of her mind was disturbed' and 'abnormality of mind'. Second, like diminished responsibility, infanticide is a defence to a charge of murder but, unlike diminished responsibility, it is also an offence in its own right. Third, infanticide

jury may, if the circumstances were such that but for the provisions of this Act they might have returned a verdict of murder or manslaughter, return in lieu thereof a verdict of infanticide.' As with s 1(1), 'if' was substituted for 'notwithstanding that' and the words 'or manslaughter' were inserted (see s 57(3)(a) and (b) of the Coroners and Justice Act 2009).

[3] See section II for further discussion.

[4] *Murder, Manslaughter and Infanticide* (Law Com No 304, 2006) para 5.122.

[5] *Partial Defences to Murder* (Law Commission Consultation Paper No 173, 2003) para 7.69. For discussion of the meaning of 'substantial' impairment prior to the decision of the Supreme Court in *R v Golds* [2016] UKSC 61, [2017] 1 Cr App R 18, see R Mackay and D Hughes, 'Explaining the "Explanation" Requirement in the New Diminished Responsibility Plea' [2021] *Crim LR* 461, 464–66.

[6] *Report of the Committee on Mentally Abnormal Offenders* (Cmnd 6244, 1975) paras 19.26–19.27.

[7] Criminal Law Revision Committee, *Offences Against the Person* (14th Report, Cmnd 7844, 1980) para 103.

[8] *A New Homicide Act for England and Wales? A Consultation Paper* (Law Com Consultation Paper No 177, 2005) paras 9.8–9.13.

does not explicitly require a causal connection between the mental disturbance and the killing.[9] Finally, infanticide is restricted to biological mothers of the child killed, and that child must have been under the age of 12 months at the time of the killing. Subsequently, the Commission identified a further difference. Where infanticide is raised as a defence, the burden of proof is on the prosecution to disprove the defence beyond reasonable doubt, whereas with diminished responsibility the burden of proof is on D to discharge on the balance of probabilities.[10]

The Commission concluded that infanticide should not be subsumed within diminished responsibility[11] and recommended that it should be retained without amendment.[12] This was accepted by the Government.[13]

In contrast, the Commission recommended the adoption of a new definition of diminished responsibility.[14] Subsequently, Parliament enacted the substance of the Commission's recommendation. Section 52 of the Coroners and Justice Act 2009 provided that the following should be substituted for section 2(1) of the Homicide Act 1957:

> (1) A person (D) who kills or is a party to the killing of another is not to be convicted of murder if D was suffering from an abnormality of mental functioning which—
>
> (a) arose from a recognised medical condition,
> (b) substantially impaired D's ability to do one or more of the things mentioned in subsection (1A), and
> (c) provides an explanation for D's acts and omissions in doing or being a party to the killing.
>
> (1A) Those things are—
>
> (a) to understand the nature of D's conduct;
> (b) to form a rational judgment;
> (c) to exercise self-control.[15]
>
> (1B) For the purposes of subsection (1)(c), an abnormality of mental functioning provides an explanation for D's conduct if it causes, or is a significant contributory factor in causing, D to carry out that conduct.

Section 2(1)(c) reflected the Commission's view that an explanation requirement was essential to ensure that the diminished responsibility plea should succeed only if there was 'an appropriate connection (that is, one that grounds a case for mitigation of the offence) between the abnormality of mental functioning … and

[9] Thereby implying that the diminished responsibility defence as originally enacted did require a causal connection between D's abnormality of mind and the killing. However, see *Murder, Manslaughter and Infanticide* (n 4) para 5.122 and the associated text.

[10] ibid para 8.9.

[11] ibid paras 8.35–8.39.

[12] ibid para 9.27. The Commission reported before the decision in *Gore* (n 1).

[13] Subject to the amendments to the 1938 Act effected by s 57(2) and (3) of the Coroners and Justice Act 2009 – see n 1.

[14] *Murder, Manslaughter and Infanticide* (n 4) para 9.20.

[15] I subsequently refer to these as 'the three abilities'.

the killing'.[16] However, section 2(1B) went further in stipulating that, in order to provide an explanation, the abnormality of mental functioning must either cause or be a significant contributory factor in causing D to kill the victim. The Commission had not insisted that there should be a causal connection.[17]

The Government's position was that reformulation of section 2(1) was 'really just a clarification of the way that the defence works'[18] and that 'we do not expect any significant shifts in the number or types of cases which benefit from the partial defence of diminished responsibility'.[19] In fact, the reformed plea was radically different from and more exacting than the previous definition.[20]

In making its recommendations, the Commission did not consider what effect, if any, they might have on the relationship between infanticide and diminished responsibility. Given the legislative response to the recommendations, it might be thought that although the operation of the diminished responsibility plea would be impacted,[21] the operation of infanticide would remain unaffected.[22] However, as discussed in section II, this does not appear to be the case. There is evidence that, for reasons that are not readily identifiable, the Crown Prosecution Service has become less amenable either to charging infanticide or to accepting a plea of infanticide to a charge of murder/manslaughter.

This raises the prospect, despite appearing counter-intuitive given the now more exacting defence of diminished responsibility, of the increasing choice of defendants to adopt a defence strategy of pleading both infanticide and diminished responsibility. In this chapter I will argue that the current regime for directing juries in such cases can and should be improved. I do so in the light of my empirical studies into both pleas together with recent litigation.

I. The Empirical Studies

I have conducted two empirical studies that have dealt with infanticide and diminished responsibility, both of which were conducted prior to the enactment

[16] *Murder, Manslaughter and Infanticide* (n 4) para 5.124.

[17] For detailed discussion of s 2(1B), see Mackay and Hughes (n 5) 466–77.

[18] Maria Eagle MP, Coroners and Justice Bill, Public Bill Committee, 3 February 2009.

[19] Ministry of Justice, Impact Assessment, Coroners and Justice Bill: homicide clauses, 14 January 2009.

[20] See R Mackay and B Mitchell, 'The New Diminished Responsibility Plea in Operation: Some Initial Findings [2017] *Crim LR* 18; and R Mackay, 'What's happening with the reformed diminished responsibility plea?' (2021) 72 *NILQ* 224.

[21] Particularly in the light of *Golds* (n 5) [29], where the Supreme Court held that 'in the context of diminished responsibility an impairment of consequence or weight is what is required to reduce murder to manslaughter, and not *any* impairment which is greater than merely trivial' (emphasis added).

[22] Particularly in the light of *R v Tunstill* [2018] EWCA Crim 1696, where the Court of Appeal (at [31]) *expanded* the ambit of infanticide by holding that 'by reason of' in s 1(1) of the 1938 Act did not mean 'solely by reason of'. For further discussion of *Tunstill*, see section II.A.

of the reformed diminished responsibility plea. The first study examined the files of 36 females who had killed one of their children under the age of 12 months.[23] These cases led to 15 infanticide convictions and 13 cases where it was decided not to proceed with a prosecution owing to lack of evidence, or where it was felt not to be in the public interest. In the remaining eight cases it was unclear what the final outcome had been in four cases, while convictions were returned for manslaughter (one case) or cruelty offences in two cases and one case of concealment of birth.

In respect of the infanticide convictions, 10 were the result of initial charges under the 1938 Act. In the remaining five cases, murder was charged in all except one case where manslaughter was the charge. All these defendants eventually were charged with and permitted to plead guilty to infanticide. Further, although there was a small number of cases where the medical evidence supported both pleas, it was clear that this study lent

> no support to the fact that diminished responsibility [was] either being widely used in cases which might otherwise be infanticide or that [as it then stood] the 1957 Act would safely cover all cases which [then] fell within the 1938 Act.[24]

My second empirical study, commissioned by the Commission as part of its work on *Murder, Manslaughter and Infanticide*, contained two parts – the first dealing with infanticide cases and the second relating to diminished responsibility cases.[25] In respect of the sample of 49 infanticide convictions, it was found that although the vast majority of defendants (75.5 per cent) were initially charged with murder, after pre-trial negotiations that altered dramatically to 63.3 per cent facing charges of infanticide and 36.7 per cent charges of murder with a second count of infanticide added. There was no jury trial in all but two of the cases, where both defendants maintained a not-guilty plea.[26] Infanticide verdicts were returned in all cases except one, who was convicted of a separate count of common law manslaughter. Of the 67 psychiatric reports, 43 (64.2 per cent) favoured infanticide, while 23 (34.3 per cent) made no mention of infanticide. In addition, 26 of the reports (38.9 per cent) favoured diminished responsibility rather than or as an alternative to infanticide, while 39 (58.1 per cent) made no mention of diminished responsibility.

In relation to the second part of this study, there was a sample of 35 cases of diminished responsibility manslaughter convictions of biological mothers who had killed their children aged 3 years and under, all of which, except one,[27] were section 2 pleas accepted by the prosecution. In respect of infanticide, only nine

[23] RD Mackay, 'The Consequences of Killing Very Young Children' [1993] *Crim LR* 21.

[24] ibid 30.

[25] See RD Mackay, 'Infanticide and Related Diminished Responsibility Manslaughters: An Empirical Study' in *Murder, Manslaughter and Infanticide* (n 4) Appendix D.

[26] Both cases are discussed in nn 77 and 78 of this chapter.

[27] In one case (no 26) the accused was ultimately found unfit to plead.

defendants had killed a child under the age of 12 months. These cases gave rise to 12 reports, eight in favour of infanticide and four being of the view that the accused's condition did not fall within the 1938 Act. The eight reports favouring infanticide also supported a plea of diminished responsibility, as did the four reports that rejected infanticide. It seems likely, therefore, that as all the reports in question favoured a plea of diminished responsibility, this was why the prosecution accepted such a plea.

Although it is difficult to draw any firm conclusions from this study about any overlap between infanticide and diminished responsibility, what is apparent is the lack of contested cases. Thus, in all 84 cases from both samples, with the exception of the two cases where both defendants maintained a not-guilty plea, there was no jury trial. However, in my empirical study for the Commission into diminished responsibility, again conducted prior to the enactment of the reformed diminished responsibility plea, in a sample of 157 defendants where this plea was identified as a defence that was raised, 36 (22.9 per cent) were contested.[28] Of those 157 cases, only two of the accused might have qualified for infanticide as biological mothers of victims under 12 months of age. In both cases, the prosecution accepted a plea of diminished responsibility. In neither of these cases was diminished responsibility pleaded in conjunction with infanticide.[29]

Consequently, these empirical studies lend no evidence to suggest that pleading both infanticide and diminished responsibility was a defence strategy prior to the enactment of the new diminished responsibility plea. However, it must be pointed out that each of these empirical studies primarily concerned cases where the accused had been convicted of infanticide or diminished responsibility manslaughter, and so did not identify cases of murder prosecutions, where the accused was convicted of murder despite pleading both infanticide and diminished responsibility. In short, it is possible that this existed as a defence strategy before the enactment of the new section 2 of the Homicide Act 1957.

The following section will discuss the implications of this emerging defence strategy, followed by a review of three recent cases where it is clear that both pleas were relevant in the proceedings.

II. Pleading Both Infanticide and Diminished Responsibility

As mentioned in section I, the Commission made it clear in its Report, *Murder, Manslaughter and Infanticide* that infanticide should remain essentially unaltered.[30] One of the reasons given was that '[a]t present, there are so few cases of infanticide

[28] See RD Mackay, 'The Diminished Responsibility Plea in Operation' in *Partial Defences to Murder* (n 5) Appendix B, para 20 and Table 10a.

[29] See cases 61 and 80, ibid 165 and 167 respectively.

[30] *Murder, Manslaughter and Infanticide* (n 4) para 9.27.

that it does not seem worth countenancing the perhaps unforeseeable changes that would result from an insistence that such cases be dealt with under section 2'.[31] In making this remark, the Commission might perhaps have given some consideration to 'the perhaps unforeseeable changes that would result from an insistence' on its part that section 2 of the Homicide Act 1957 should be reformed in a manner that would make it very different from the original. In that connection, it is clear from the three cases discussed in section II.A that pleading both infanticide and diminished responsibility to a charge of murder is currently being deployed as a defence strategy.

In cases where the defence have medical evidence supporting both infanticide and diminished responsibility but the prosecution have evidence to the contrary, infanticide will not be charged and a plea of diminished responsibility manslaughter will not be accepted. It is then that a full jury trial will proceed on a charge of murder. Because the medical evidence for the defence supports both pleas, the defence will understandably adopt a strategy that permits both infanticide and diminished responsibility to go to the jury.

At this stage, it may be worth contrasting the defence strategy of pleading both infanticide and diminished responsibility with that of pleading loss of control (formerly provocation) and diminished responsibility in combination. The latter was not uncommon as a defence strategy before provocation was replaced by 'loss of control'.[32] Indeed, it did seem that the then combination of the two pleas resulted in juries blending the requirements of both and returning a verdict of manslaughter on both grounds.[33] While the replacement of provocation with 'loss of control' together with a reformed diminished responsibility plea means that the two are now more separate and distinct, this has not prevented both from being pleaded together. Nor has it prevented a verdict of manslaughter from being returned on both grounds, as was made clear by the Court of Appeal in *R v Caddick*,[34] an appeal against a sentence of eight years, eight months' imprisonment imposed upon the appellant 'for manslaughter by reason of both diminished responsibility and loss of control',[35] where it is stated:

> The indicated basis of plea had been on grounds of diminished responsibility. This was on the basis that at the time of the killing the appellant was suffering from an abnormality of the mind arising from a recognised medical condition, namely post-traumatic stress disorder (PTSD), which resulted in outbursts of temper.
>
> The court in sentencing, however, indicated that the appellant, through his counsel and his defence case statement, had put forward the other partial defence, namely that of loss of control. Having had regard to the opinions of the psychiatrists as to the

[31] See a *New Homicide Act for England and Wales* (n 8) para 9.94.
[32] See ss 54–56 of the Coroners and Justice Act 2009.
[33] See RD Mackay, 'Pleading Provocation and Diminished Responsibility Together' [1988] *Crim LR* 411, 423.
[34] *R v Caddick* [2018] EWCA Crim 865.
[35] ibid [1].

> impact on the appellant's loss of control of his mental state and abnormality of mental functioning at the time the court accepted that the appellant should be sentenced on this basis also.[36]

However, such a combined verdict cannot be returned when infanticide and diminished responsibility are pleaded together. This is because, unlike 'loss of control' and diminished responsibility, infanticide is not a form of voluntary manslaughter but is instead an offence/defence in its own right. This in turn means that when infanticide and diminished responsibility are pleaded together, only a single verdict based on one or the other can be returned by a jury. What impact this might have on a jury's deliberations in such cases is difficult to assess. However, the new and stricter requirements to be proved by the accused in diminished responsibility could be relevant here, as is noted in section II.B.

It seems clear (see *R v Martins* in section II.A) that because with infanticide the burden of proof remains on the Crown,[37] the jury will be asked to consider this plea first. If the jury reject infanticide, only then will they go on to consider whether the accused has proved all the requirements for diminished responsibility. In principle, because the two pleas are separate and distinct, a jury should be able to treat them as such. However, although one can never know how a jury set about their decision making, there might be a concern that in cases where the jury are asked to consider both pleas, with medical and other evidence both in support of and against each, it may be difficult to treat each plea as distinct. Certainly, there remains some degree of overlap between the two pleas, which is one of the reasons why psychiatrists in their reports frequently conclude that the accused's medical condition at the time of the offence lends support to both pleas being satisfied. This occurred in some cases under the old section 2, which by reason of its wording was more closely aligned with infanticide,[38] but is also apparent under the new section 2 despite its stricter requirements.[39] For example, the 1938 Act requires that 'the balance of her mind was disturbed', which is more than likely to qualify as 'an abnormality of mental functioning' under the reformed section 2.[40] In addition, any diagnosed disorder that resulted in the accused's mental disturbance is also likely to be regarded as a 'recognised medical condition' for the purposes of diminished responsibility. We are then left with the other novel requirements, namely, the three abilities and the 'explanation' factor under section 2, which have to be considered by the jury in their decision making. This overlap between the two

[36] ibid [9] and [11].

[37] See *Murder, Manslaughter and Infanticide* (n 4) para 8.9; *R v Claudia Martins* (Bristol Crown Court, 14 April 2015).

[38] This seems to be borne out by the empirical studies discussed in section: see Mackay (n 25) 206, Table 15b.

[39] See Coroners and Justice Act 2009, s 52, reproduced in the text following n 14 of this chapter.

[40] Particularly because, in order to establish that the accused's mind was 'disturbed', English law currently seems to require evidence of a psychiatric disorder – see n 79 for the position in Canadian law.

pleas was considered by the Court of Appeal in *Tunstill*,[41] which is now reviewed together with two other relevant cases.

A. Three Recent Cases

In *Tunstill*,[42] the accused killed her newly born child by stabbing her 14 times with a pair of scissors. Two psychiatric reports prepared for the defence supported a defence of diminished responsibility. One of the reports considered that the appellant was suffering from paranoid schizophrenia, the other that the appellant was suffering from severe depression with psychotic symptoms at the material time. A psychiatric report for the prosecution considered that there was no evidence of psychotic symptoms prior to the offence other than the appellant's subsequent self-report. In addition, both psychiatrists for the defence supported infanticide, while the prosecution expert did not. The trial judge withdrew infanticide from the jury and they convicted the accused of murder, having rejected the alternative plea of diminished responsibility. The Court of Appeal allowed the accused's appeal, ruling that the trial judge had been wrong to conclude that because the 'mother's post-birth condition was not due only to the effects of having given birth, but in part based on a pre-birth mental condition, the conditions for infanticide were not made out'.[43] In doing so the Court concluded:

> In the circumstances, we are persuaded that the judge should not have withdrawn infanticide from the jury. There was evidence fit for the jury's consideration. It is not for this court to assess the likelihood of its success. Dr Barlow's evidence was to the contrary, but the issue for us is whether a jury should have had this alternative option to consider. We think it should have had that opportunity. In the circumstances, therefore, the conviction for murder is unsafe and the verdict is quashed. In our judgment, the interests of justice require a re-trial and we so order.[44]

In arriving at this conclusion Treacey LJ remarked:

> We are conscious that the purpose of the Infanticide Act was to ameliorate the potential harshness of the law of murder by recognising that in a period after birth a mother's balance of mind may be affected. Whilst at the time of the introduction of this provision the diminished responsibility provisions introduced by the Homicide Act 1957 did not exist, it is nonetheless clear that the intention behind the legislation was to be merciful. Since the passing of the Homicide Act, Parliament has not withdrawn the infanticide provisions and, as observed above, has extended them to the crime of manslaughter. It seems to us that to interpret Judge LJ's dictum as to 'other circumstances'[45] as applying

[41] *Tunstill* (n 22).
[42] ibid.
[43] ibid [26].
[44] ibid [36].
[45] ibid [15], where the full dictum is cited as follows: 'At paragraph 134 of *Kai-Whitewind* [2005] 2 Cr App R 31 Judge LJ had said in obiter observations: "Under s 1(2) provision is made for infanticide to be an alternative verdict available to the jury trying a mother for murder of her infant child. It does

> to a situation such as the present one is unnecessarily harsh and runs counter to the intent of the legislation.[46]

In addition, his Lordship remarked:

> The judge ruled that there was evidence capable of supporting a defence of diminished responsibility. That issue was left to the jury and its verdict shows that it concluded that the partial defence to murder was not made out. The burden of proving that defence lay with the appellant. In the case of infanticide, the burden lay with the Crown to negative infanticide as an alternative verdict to murder. *It is to be noted that the conditions for demonstrating diminished responsibility and infanticide laid down by statute are in very different terms and include very different approaches to a defendant's mental state at the relevant time.*[47]

Despite the sympathetic approach contained in this judgment, it is of interest to note that when the accused was retried, although both infanticide and diminished responsibility were left to the jury, she was convicted of murder. In his discussion of the case, leading counsel for the appellant states:

> After the Court of Appeal overturned Rachel Tunstill's conviction for murder in July 2018 she was retried before King J at Liverpool Crown Court in December 2018. The trial lasted seven weeks during which the jury heard evidence from seven psychiatrists and psychologists. The issues of diminished responsibility and infanticide were left to the jury. Rachel Tunstill was subsequently convicted of murder.[48]

So the jury, in returning a unanimous verdict of murder, rejected both infanticide and diminished responsibility, about which more will be said later.

In the second case, *R v Cobley*,[49] where the accused killed her newly born child who died from multiple injuries, the Court of Appeal refused to allow an application to admit fresh medical evidence and upheld the accused's murder conviction. During the trial, no medical defence was pleaded because the defence psychiatrist, who had initially opined that the defendant's condition 'met the criteria for a defence of infanticide and/or diminished responsibility',[50] altered his opinion after hearing the accused give evidence, and 'informed the defence team that he no longer believed that her mental functioning had been sufficiently disturbed as to explain her actions'.[51]

however require evidence that the 'balance of her mind was disturbed' either because the mother has not recovered from giving birth to the child, or the effect of lactation on her. No other circumstances are relevant.'".

[46] ibid [30].

[47] ibid [13] (emphasis added).

[48] Simon Kealey QC, 'Disentangling the balance of the mind: infanticide reconsidered' (10 September 2019) at www.newparkcourt.co.uk/wp-content/uploads/2019/09/Criminal-Briefing-Simon-Kealey-QC.pdf. See also 'Rachel Tunstill, 28, stabbed Mia Kelly to death' *Liverpool Echo* (Liverpool, 7 February 2019) at www.liverpoolecho.co.uk/news/uk-world-news/mother-jailed-life-murdering-newborn-15791762.

[49] *R v Cobley* [2021] EWCA Crim 954.

[50] ibid [20].

[51] ibid [21].

In *Cobley*, the fresh medical evidence the accused wished to adduce consisted of the opinions of two consultant psychiatrists. Both confined their opinion to whether the accused satisfied the criteria for the diminished responsibility defence. Their opinions did not address infanticide. Presumably, it was for this reason that the Court of Appeal considered the application solely in relation to diminished responsibility. The Court concluded that it was 'not a case where the contemporaneous empirical evidence reveals there to be a robust case for the defence of diminished responsibility'.[52] It is difficult to understand why the new medical evidence did not address infanticide. Perhaps the most likely explanation is that the experts did not consider that the accused satisfied the criteria for the defence.

It is of interest to note the manner in which Macur LJ dismisses the fresh evidence introduced by the applicant to support diminished responsibility, saying:

> Assuming, in the applicant's favour, that the jury would have found that, on the balance of probabilities, there was at the time of the killing an abnormality of mental functioning which arose from a recognised medical condition, the issue of whether the defendant had a substantial impairment of ability to understand/form rational judgment/exercise control and whether it is a cause or explanation for the killing is not so readily resolved. This, we consider, would necessarily be adjudged against the empirical evidence of the time, and not the applicant's retrospective reports upon which Dr di Lustro and Dr Rampling's opinions are based.[53]

As a result, and having regard to the opinion of Dr Kennedy for the respondent, who in the Court's view showed that

> the applicant's different account of her personal history given to him in January 2021 … even if accepted in its entirety, would not have substantially affected her ability to exercise a rational judgement or to exercise self-control particularly if the act consisted of considerable violence …[54]

the Court ruled that it was not 'necessary or expedient in the interests of justice to admit this fresh evidence for the conviction is not undermined by this prospective evidence'.[55] However, what is troubling is that one would have thought that, having conceded that 'substantial impairment', etc are issues 'not so readily resolved', these then are matters for a jury, especially in the light of the Supreme Court's decision in *Golds*.[56]

The third and final case, although it did not result in an appeal, is interesting because of the verdict. In *R v Claudia Martins*,[57] the accused, who suffered

[52] ibid [67].
[53] ibid [52].
[54] ibid [61].
[55] ibid [68].
[56] *Golds* (n 5).
[57] Martins unpublished transcript (n 37). See 'Claudia Martins convicted of the manslaughter of her newborn baby girl' *Daily Mail Online* (16 May 2015) at www.dilymail.co.uk/news/article-3042275/Mother-five-33-suffocated-newborn-daughter-stuffing-toilet-paper-throat-hid-body-suitcase-spared-jail.htm.

from an intellectual disability, gave birth alone, and three days later the deceased victim was found in a suitcase with toilet paper stuffed in her mouth. Martins was tried for murder and convicted of diminished responsibility manslaughter, for which she was sentenced to a community order for two years with a supervision requirement. During the trial, the defence pleaded both infanticide and diminished responsibility.

In the course of his direction to the jury, Teare J said:

> It is quite clear that Claudia had a pathological denial of the pregnancy. This could be considered a disturbance of the balance of her mind. In such a condition, giving birth would have led to a state of panic and an absence of clear or rational thinking, and this may explain her actions.

In respect of diminished responsibility, he told the jury:

> The argument could be put forward that her low IQ and her pathological denial of pregnancy led to an abnormality of mental functioning that impaired her ability to make rational judgments about her pregnancy, what to do about the pregnancy and how to deal with and prepare for the forthcoming birth. Therefore, once she goes into labour and the baby arrives, she goes into a state of extreme panic and perhaps continues in a state of denial about the existence of the baby.

So it is clear that both pleas were left to the jury, after which they rejected infanticide but found in favour of diminished responsibility, which is interesting given the different requirements and burdens of proof with respect to the two pleas. In his sentencing remarks, Teare J said that the accused's actions were 'wholly out of character' and that her 'intellectual disability' had probably contributed to her condition. He added, 'Having regard to the fact that you suffered from an abnormality of mental function this does not require a custodial sentence.'[58] Indeed, the community order seems more than likely to have been the sentence the defendant would have been given if an infanticide verdict had been returned.

In summary, in none of the three cases discussed above was infanticide successful, with murder convictions returned in two and diminished responsibility manslaughter in one. In each of the three cases, the prosecution charged murder and a jury trial followed. While it is clear, as is discussed in section II.B, that the stricter requirements under the reformed section 2 make it more demanding for the accused to plead diminished responsibility successfully, by contrast there have been no changes to the 1938 Act that make it more difficult to plead successfully.[59] So it remains unclear why juries are rejecting an infanticide plea, although it may be to do with the evidence that is used in its support, together with its interrelationship with diminished responsibility, to which I now turn.

[58] See *BBC News* (16 April 2015) at www.bbc.co.uk/news/uk-england-bristol-32337828.

[59] However, the dictum of Judge LJ in *Kai-Whitewind* [2005] 2 Cr App R 31 [34], that 'no other circumstances are relevant', may, prior to *Tunstill* (n 22), have had some impact in this connection. See n 45 of this chapter.

B. Discussion

When the accused is tried for murder and pleads both infanticide and diminished responsibility, it is clear that both pleas are optional.[60] This means that the accused must decide whether or not to enter either or both pleas. In some cases, she will choose not to do so. In that case she risks a murder conviction, without the jury being able to consider any medical defence that might otherwise have been available. This may happen when the accused considers that she is not guilty of causing the death of her child, and includes cases where the accused is charged with both murder and infanticide, as occurred in *R v Silipa Keresi*.[61] In that case, the accused left her newborn son to die in woodland in the New Forest. She denied both charges and was convicted of murder. Addressing the jury, defence counsel said that, at the time of the pregnancy, Keresi suffered 'acute stress' from her circumstances; these stresses led her to be in denial about the pregnancy and caused her mind to be 'disturbed'.[62] In sentencing, the judge said 'The abandonment of Maliki was an act of desperation by a vulnerable woman, facing challenging circumstances. The emotional effect of your giving birth outdoors and unaccompanied was profound.'[63] The defendant was sentenced to life imprisonment, with a minimum term of nine years. This contrasts with the sentence for infanticide, which is more often than not non-custodial.

A case like *Keresi* clearly demonstrates the importance of ensuring that when the prosecution charge murder and infanticide, the accused pleads guilty to infanticide;[64] or when only murder is charged, infanticide and diminished responsibility are pleaded if both are supported by expert evidence. However, using the two pleas as a defence strategy poses problems. As discussed, although infanticide and diminished responsibility are separate pleas and should be considered as

[60] *R v Campbell* (1987) 84 Cr App R 255, 260, where it is stated 'However, section 2(2) of the Homicide Act 1957 provides that "it shall be for the defence to prove" diminished responsibility. It seems to us that those words not only dictate which party shoulders the burden of proof once the issue is raised, but also leave it to the defence to decide whether the issue should be raised at all.' This provision remains unaltered by the reformed s 2. As for infanticide, although the burden of proof is on the prosecution, whether the accused chooses to run the plea 'at all' is also entirely a matter for the defence.

[61] I am grateful to Emma Milne for drawing my attention to this case.

[62] See 'Woman accused of murdering baby in Hythe stands trial in Winchester' *Southern Daily Echo* (Southampton, 22 November 2021) at www.dailyecho.co.uk/news/19733319.woman-accused-murdering-baby-hythe-stands-trial-winchester/.

[63] See 'Hythe mum Silipa Keresi jailed for life for murdering her newborn' *New Milton Advertiser and Lymington Times* (New Milton, 2 December 2021) at www.advertiserandtimes.co.uk/news/hythe-mum-silipa-keresi-jailed-for-life-for-murdering-her-ne-9228858/.

[64] As mentioned, the accused may consider she is not guilty, in which case she runs the risk of a murder conviction. However, this is up to the jury, and in *R v Babita Ria* (Winchester Crown Court, 20 May 2021), where the prosecution charged both murder and infanticide to which the accused pleaded not guilty, the jury, after deliberating for over 15 hours, returned a verdict under the 1938 Act for which she received a two-year community order. See 'Baby M mother is found guilty of infanticide but not guilty of murder' *Hampshire Live* (20 May 2021) at www.hampshirelive.news/news/hampshire-news/baby-m-murder-verdict-live-5438173.

such, there is an interrelationship between the two. As a result, a jury may find it difficult to keep the two pleas entirely separate when considering both.

This difficulty may be exacerbated by the psychiatric reports. For example, in *Cobley*, the defence psychiatrist's opinion up until the conclusion of the applicant's evidence is referred to by the Court of Appeal as follows:

> On balance he considered that there was evidence of an acute stress reaction which had disturbed the balance of her mind and her ability to think logically. This was related to pregnancy and the birth. It would impact her ability to form a rational judgment and was a possible explanation for her actions and met the criteria for a defence of infanticide and/or diminished responsibility.[65]

But what is of note is the way that the expert refers to disturbance of the accused's mind – relevant to infanticide – but then proceeds to state that this 'would impact her ability to form a rational judgment and was a possible explanation for her actions'. These are ingredients of the diminished responsibility defence, but are not and never have been requirements in relation to infanticide. Indeed, if any support is needed that no causal link[66] is required between the mental disturbance and the accused's actions, this is to be found in *Tunstill*, where Treacey LJ stated that 'there is no required causal link between the disturbance of balance of mind and the act or omission causing death'.[67]

Of course, one can only speculate here. However, having heard expert evidence that conflates the requirements of the two pleas, there is a danger that the jury may find it very difficult to consider each plea completely separately. This difficulty may not be entirely obviated by the directions they will have received, which require the jury to consider infanticide first, and only if they reject such a verdict to then consider diminished responsibility.

However, a further difficulty concerns the reformed diminished responsibility plea, which is stricter than the original.[68] Not only is the new section 2 more psychiatrically focused,[69] but it also requires the accused to prove a substantial impairment of ability to understand/form rational judgement/exercise self-control, which in turn provides an explanation for the killing. In that connection, whether the impairment is 'substantial' requires a higher level of impairment than was formerly the case, and the three abilities,[70] at least one of which must be

[65] *Cobley* (n 49) [20].

[66] For the purposes of diminished responsibility, the 'explanation' requirement is expressed in term of causation, see s 2(1B) of the Homicide Act 1957.

[67] *Tunstill* (n 22) [32].

[68] For discussion, see Mackay (n 20).

[69] See *R v Brennan* [2014] EWCA Crim 2387 [49], where Davis LJ states 'The new wording gives significantly more scope to the importance of expert psychiatric evidence.' See also *Golds* (n 5) [38], where Lord Hughes remarks '[M]edical evidence (nearly always forensic psychiatric evidence) has always been a practical necessity where the issue is diminished responsibility. If anything, the 2009 changes to the law have emphasised this necessity by tying the partial defence more clearly to a recognised medical condition …'.

[70] For discussion, see R Mackay, 'The Impairment Factors in the New Diminished Responsibility Plea' [2018] *Crim LR* 462.

proved, are new, as is the 'explanation' requirement,[71] which must be 'a cause, or a significant contributory factor in causing' the killing.[72] In short, once a diminished responsibility plea is left to a jury, the accused now has a more difficult task to prove all of the plea's requirements.

Such empirical evidence as there is tentatively suggests that the prosecution accept fewer diminished responsibility pleas than they did under the original plea, leading to more jury trials for murder and more murder convictions.[73] While one must treat the empirical evidence with caution, there is an argument that the novel requirements contained in the reformed section 2 have impacted not only on the prosecution's acceptance of the plea but also on the jury's decision making once a plea comes before them. In relation to the former, it is possible that this could be a reason why the prosecution might be more reluctant to accept a diminished responsibility plea in cases where a mother kills her child under the age of 12 months.

However, even if that were so, this would not explain cases where the prosecution refuse either to charge infanticide or to accept a plea of infanticide. Instead, the explanation must surely be that such a decision will depend on the expert evidence available to the prosecution, together with what the Court of Appeal in *Cobley* referred to as 'the contemporaneous empirical evidence'.[74] Once such a decision is taken to refuse to accept both pleas, the empirical evidence again tentatively suggests that a diminished responsibility plea is more than likely to be rejected by a jury.[75]

In the past, contested infanticide pleas were extremely rare. In my empirical research, there were only two such cases where both defendants maintained a not-guilty plea that necessitated a full jury trial.[76] In the first case, the prosecution charged the accused with murder but later added a count of infanticide, which was considered by the jury first. As a result, the jury convicted the accused of infanticide and a not-guilty verdict was returned on the murder charge.[77] In the second case, the prosecution withdrew a murder charge because of the accused's mental disorder. She then pleaded not guilty to both infanticide and common law manslaughter. A full trial followed, and the jury rejected infanticide but convicted the accused of common law manslaughter. Interestingly, two psychiatric reports favoured infanticide but considered there was no abnormality of mind within the old section 2 of the Homicide Act.[78]

[71] For discussion, see Mackay and Hughes (n 5).
[72] See text following n 14, where s 2 is reproduced in full.
[73] See Mackay and Mitchell (n 20) 35.
[74] *Cobley* (n 49) [67].
[75] Mackay and Mitchell (n 20) 27. It should be pointed out that this empirical study related to cases decided before *Golds* (n 5), where the Supreme Court established a more stringent test regarding 'substantial' impairment.
[76] Mackay (n 29) 200.
[77] ibid 217, case 30.
[78] ibid 218, case 34.

However, there is now some evidence to suggest that contested infanticide cases are becoming more common, as is demonstrated by the recent cases of *Tunstill*, *Martins* and *Keresi*. From these cases, it would appear that juries are rejecting the infanticide plea despite, as noted below, its being easier to prove than diminished responsibility.

Again, one must assume that juries are rejecting infanticide in the light of the conflicting expert and other contemporaneous empirical evidence. However, the burden is on the Crown to prove that the partial defence of infanticide does not apply. So, to obtain a conviction for murder, the Crown must prove that there is no reasonable doubt that the accused did not kill the child 'by reason of her mind being disturbed'.

This, together with the fact that such a plea does not explicitly require that the accused suffered from any mental disorder but only that 'the balance of her mind was disturbed[79] by reason of her not having fully recovered from the effects of giving birth to the child', ought to mean that a jury in principle should be able to find that the requirements for infanticide are easily satisfied. So why might a jury reject infanticide but return a diminished responsibility verdict, as they did in Claudia Martins' trial? Again, one can only speculate here. In sentencing the defendant for diminished responsibility manslaughter, Teare J said:

> The explanation for your conduct is you were suffering from an abnormality of mental functioning which substantially impaired your judgement.
>
> This arose from a medical condition known as a pathological denial of pregnancy which continued despite the obvious presence of a baby.
>
> The giving of birth didn't bring the denial to an end and you continued to deny the pregnancy to your family, friends and medical personnel. It was a great shock to you and induced in you a state of panic.

[79] This important point has yet to be tested in the English courts. At present, infanticide in English law seems to require expert evidence of a psychiatric disorder. This is supported by my empirical study for the Law Commission, see Mackay (n 25) 201. However, the Supreme Court of Canada in *R v Borowiec* [2016] 1 SCR 80 [35], ruled that '[t]he disturbance need not constitute a defined mental or psychological condition or a mental illness'. In arriving at this decision, Cromwell J, discussing the legislative history of infanticide, noted at [32] that 'It was also expressed in debates that, as the UK statute, the provision was intended to apply to cases "where there is not the degree of mental derangement amounting to insanity" and that "[i]t does not go as far as the rule in Macnaughton's case [which sets out a legal test for insanity]": House of Commons Debates, at p 5185 (Hon JL Ilsley, then Minister of Justice). It was also noted that the provision would capture "a slightly deranged, distressed mother" who would otherwise be guilty of murder: p 5187.' See also *Cagimaira v State* [2020] 1 LRC 391 [44], where, in adopting a similar approach, the Court of Appeal of Fiji stated, 'To prove that the balance of a woman's mind is disturbed by reason of her not having recovered fully from the effect of giving birth to a child and especially 30 minutes after child birth is not arduous, as proving that the accused at the time of causing death was in "such a state of abnormality of mind (whether arising from a condition of arrested or retarded development of mind or inherent causes or induced by disease or injury) as substantially to impair" his capacity to understand, to control or to know what he is doing. The former condition is something within the knowledge of many while the latter needs some form of medical evidence.'

> Your actions of killing the baby were a manifestation of your irrational condition and your actions were wholly out of character.[80]

Such a condition seems also to have formed the basis of the accused's infanticide plea, which the jury rejected, perhaps on the basis that her condition, although a 'mental disturbance', was not sufficiently connected to 'giving birth to the child'. Alternatively, might a jury, having been given diminished responsibility manslaughter as an alternative verdict in the same decision-making process, consider infanticide overly lenient[81] and so prefer a section 2 verdict?[82]

The complex interrelationship between the pleas of infanticide and diminished responsibility is a cause for concern. When both pleas are pleaded together, juries may encounter difficulty not only in fully comprehending and keeping separate each plea, but also, when deciding what verdict to return, in assessing which verdict most accurately reflects what they perceive to be the culpability of the accused. How can this concern be best addressed? A possible way forward will be considered in section III.

III. Concluding Remarks

The pleading of infanticide and diminished responsibility together in answer to a charge of murder poses problems. Each plea has its own requirements, a different burden of proof, and a separate and distinctive verdict. As a result, there is some likelihood that a jury will find it difficult to reach a decision when charged with reaching a verdict in such a case. The reasons for such difficulty have been discussed in section II, and an important question is whether the problems a jury may encounter in such a case might be due, at least in part, to the current procedure, which requires the jury to consider both pleas at the same time. In short, at present, the judge will direct the jury to consider both infanticide and diminished responsibility in that order, and, having done so, ask them to retire to consider their verdict. Might there be a better way to approach this matter?

[80] Unpublished transcript.

[81] A jury will not be informed about possible sentencing options as the disposal on conviction is not something for the jury's consideration; see *Edgington* [2013] EWCA Crim 2185. However, when both pleas are left to a jury, they will, when considering both, presumably have a view on the different labels attached to infanticide and manslaughter under s 2.

[82] It has been argued that a possible shift in social norms may have produced a disinclination to charge infanticide or to return a verdict of infanticide. For the position in Canada, see KJ Kramar *Unwilling Mothers, Unwanted Babies: Infanticide in Canada* (UBC Press 2005). This is despite the ruling of the Supreme Court of Canada in *Borowiec* (n 79). For possible confirmation of this, discussing the case of Jeanene Rosa Moar, see 'Infanticide expert puzzled to see Winnipeg mother charged with manslaughter in newborn's death' *CBC News* (12 June 2022) at www.cbc.ca/news/canada/manitoba/jeanene-rosa-moar-infanticide-manslaughter-experts-1.6485231. For a similar argument relating to Ireland, see K Brennan, 'Social norms and the law in responding to infanticide' (2018) 38 *Legal Studies* 480, 497–99.

The first thing to consider is whether this problem is a unique one. Is this the only type of case where a jury are asked to consider two separate defences that lead to two different verdicts? The answer is that it is not unique, as there is a second type of case that arises in which a jury in a murder prosecution are asked to consider both insanity and diminished responsibility. This may arise in two situations. The first is where section 6 of the Criminal Procedure (Insanity) Act 1964 is used. Section 6 provides that where the accused pleads insanity or diminished responsibility, 'the court shall allow the prosecution to adduce or elicit evidence tending to prove the other of those contentions'.[83] This means that when the accused pleads insanity, and the Crown has evidence that supports a section 2 plea, it may argue for a manslaughter verdict.[84]

The second situation is where the defence have expert evidence that supports both insanity and diminished responsibility and decide to plead both. Two cases illustrate this. First, in *R v Lewis-Ranwell*, the prosecution, in refusing to accept that the accused was legally insane at the time of the killings, argued that he bore some responsibility for his offences and so favoured a section 2 plea, as did the defence as an alternative to insanity. The jury were asked to consider both verdicts and returned one of 'not guilty by reason of insanity'.[85] In the second case, *R v Jack Ralph*, again, the prosecution, in answer to the accused's plea of insanity, argued that manslaughter by reason of diminished responsibility was the appropriate verdict, which was also put forward by the defence as an alternative. According to the press report:

> The Jury unanimously found that defendant was not insane, convicting him of two counts of manslaughter by reason of diminished responsibility and one count of attempted murder. Due to the unusual nature of the case, trial judge Mrs Justice Cheema-Grubb herself asked the jury of seven women and five men for their verdicts. On the counts of murder, they were asked whether they found him not guilty by reason of insanity or guilty of manslaughter on the grounds of diminished responsibility. All the verdicts were unanimous and returned within two hours of the jury retiring.[86]

[83] Section 6 of the Criminal Procedure (Insanity) Act 1964 provides: 'Where on a trial for murder the accused contends – (a) that at the time of the alleged offence he was insane so as not to be responsible according to law for his actions; or (b) that at that time he was suffering from such abnormality of mental functioning as is specified in subsection (1) of section 2 of the Homicide Act 1957 (diminished responsibility), the court shall allow the prosecution to adduce or elicit evidence tending to prove the other of those contentions, and may give directions as to the stage of the proceedings at which the prosecution may adduce such evidence.'

[84] This also applies in the case where the accused pleads diminished responsibility and the Crown has evidence that supports insanity. Again, the jury will be left with two different verdicts.

[85] *R v Lewis-Ranwell* (Exeter Crown Court, 2 December 2019). See press account in 'Exeter triple killer found not guilty of murder by reason of insanity' *Cornwall Live* (2 December 2019) at www.cornwalllive.com/news/exeter-triple-killer-found-not-3600789. For details of the civil litigation that followed, see *Lewis-Ranwell v G4S Health Services (UK) Ltd* [2022] 3 WLR 677.

[86] *R v Jack Ralph* (Maidstone Crown Court, 19 March 2019). See *Kentlive* Press Report of the cases of 19 March 2019 at www.kentlive.news/news/kent-news/frenzied-chef-who-killed-mum-2663419. See the sentencing remarks of Cheena-Grubb J at www.judiciary.uk/wp-content/uploads/2019/03/sentencing-remarks-r-v-ralph.pdf.

What both of these cases show is that the jury were asked to consider two separate defences, namely insanity and diminished responsibility, giving rise to two different verdicts, that is, 'not guilty by reason of insanity' or 'guilty of manslaughter by reason of diminished responsibility'. The differences between this type of case and that where infanticide and section 2 are pleaded together are that, first, in the former type of case, one of the pleas, namely diminished responsibility, is accepted by the prosecution. However, this does not detract from the fact that in both types of case the jury are confronted by a complex and difficult task in trying to reach a verdict, where two pleas with different requirements have to be evaluated in order to decide which of the separate verdicts should be returned. This is also true of the section 6 type of case, where only the insanity defence is pleaded by the defence, which the prosecution counter by favouring diminished responsibility. Here again, the jury face the same difficulty in having to reach a verdict where both pleas have to be considered at the same time.

The second difference is that in cases where both infanticide and section 2 are left to the jury, they have to grapple with the added complication of having to consider different offences, namely infanticide and manslaughter, which is not the case where both insanity and diminished responsibility are pleaded together or where section 6 is used, as in such cases, if either plea is successful, a jury can only return a verdict of not guilty of murder by reason of insanity or not guilty of murder but guilty of manslaughter by reason of diminished responsibility.

Might there be a way to make a jury's task less difficult in cases of this type? A possible solution might be as follows. Concentrating on infanticide and diminished responsibility, which are the subject matter of this chapter, at present the jury retire, having been directed in relation to both infanticide and diminished responsibility. Would it not be preferable for the judge initially to direct the jury solely in relation to infanticide? The jury would have to consider whether it was sure that the prosecution had proved that one or more of the elements of infanticide were lacking.

If the jury were not sure, they would return a verdict of infanticide and, *without any consideration of diminished responsibility*, the trial would proceed to sentencing. If the jury were sure that one or more of the elements of infanticide were lacking, having previously been told by the judge that they would receive further directions, the jury would return to court to be directed in relation to diminished responsibility. The jury would then determine whether the accused had proved all the ingredients of the defence on a balance of probabilities. If of the view that she had, they would return a verdict of manslaughter. If of the view that she had not, the jury would return a verdict of murder. Of course, it would depend very much on the evidence in each case. But if a jury, for example, considered that the prosecution had not made them sure that the balance of D's mind was not disturbed at the time of the killing, they would return an infanticide verdict. If, on the other hand, the jury were so satisfied, they would be required to retire again to consider diminished responsibility separately, and would only return a murder verdict if the defence failed to prove on a balance of probabilities one or more of the ingredients contained in section 2.

The advantages of this approach are two-fold. First, at present, on retiring, a jury will have had directions in relation to two defences, each with its own verdict, specific requirements, and with different burdens and standards of proof. This against a background of what might be quite complex psychiatric evidence. This would not be the case under the procedure being proposed.

Second, it would result in juries being less susceptible to labelling considerations. At present, a jury will retire having been directed that, if they reject infanticide, they should consider manslaughter by virtue of diminished responsibility. There is a danger that the jury's verdict may be unconsciously influenced by the view they take as to whether the more appropriate label for the killing perpetrated by the accused is infanticide or manslaughter. If the latter, the temptation to return that verdict may be difficult to resist, resulting in the plea of infanticide not being considered solely on its merits. This would not happen if the jury were initially directed solely in relation to infanticide. The jury will have been told no more than that if they reject the infanticide defence, they will be further directed in relation to another potential defence. The jury will not know the ingredients of that defence and what verdict, if successful, will result. The jury will consider the infanticide plea purely on its merits.

Currently, so far as is known, no judicial procedure has been adopted for splitting the timing of the verdicts to be considered by the jury in the way being suggested. However, if such an approach were to be thought to be of possible help to juries, then the suggestion being made could be considered by the Judicial College, which is the body responsible for training judges in England and Wales.[87]

At present, the relationship between the two pleas is problematic. Infanticide is ill-understood, and the reforms contained in the diminished responsibility plea make the latter more difficult to plead successfully. Taken together, a combination of the two pleas is likely to pose considerable difficulties for a jury. Infanticide is justified as a separate offence/defence as being a compassionate response to a particular problem. In the light of the stricter requirements contained in the new section 2, infanticide is, in my view, not only needed now more than ever but should also, when both pleas are pleaded together, be evaluated separately by the jury through the adoption of the type of split procedure discussed above. Such a procedure would not work any injustice to either the prosecution or the defence, but it would assist the jury in arriving at an appropriate verdict.

[87] At present the *Crown Court Compendium*, pt 1 (June 2022) has a section at (para 19-2 (A)) entitled 'Infanticide and Diminished Responsibility', which discusses *Tunstill* (n 22). There is no other mention of the 1938 Act, no Practice Direction and no reference to the fact that in practice this defence is sometimes raised in conjunction with diminished responsibility.

References

Books

Kramar, KJ, *Unwilling Mothers, Unwanted Babies: Infanticide in Canada* (UBC Press, 2005).

Journal Articles

Brennan, K, 'Social norms and the law in responding to infanticide' (2018) 38 *Legal Studies* 480.

Mackay, R, 'The Impairment Factors in the New Diminished Responsibility Plea' [2018] *Crim LR* 462.

——, 'What's happening with the reformed diminished responsibility plea?' (2021) 72 *NILQ* 224.

Mackay, RD, 'Pleading Provocation and Diminished Responsibility Together' [1988] *Crim LR* 411.

——, 'The Consequences of Killing Very Young Children' [1993] *Crim LR* 21.

Mackay, R and Hughes, D, 'Explaining the 'Explanation' Requirement in the New Diminished Responsibility Plea' [2021] *Crim LR* 461.

Mackay, R and Mitchell, B, 'The New Diminished Responsibility Plea in Operation: Some Initial Findings [2017] *Crim LR* 18.

Newspaper Articles

'Hythe mum Silipa Keresi jailed for life for murdering her newborn' *New Milton Advertiser and Lymington Times* (New Milton, 2 December 2021) at www.advertiserandtimes.co.uk/news/hythe-mum-silipa-keresi-jailed-for-life-for-" www.advertiserandtimes.co.uk/news/hythe-mum-silipa-keresi-jailed-for-life-for-murdering-her-ne-9228858/.

'Rachel Tunstill, 28, stabbed Mia Kelly to death' *Liverpool Echo* (Liverpool, 7 February 2019) at www.liverpoolecho.co.uk/news/uk-world-news/mother-jailed-life-murdering-newborn-15791762.

'Woman accused of murdering baby in Hythe stands trial in Winchester' *Southern Daily Echo* (Southampton, 22 November 2021) at www.dailyecho.co.uk/news/19733319.woman-accused-murdering-baby-hythe-stands-trial-winchester/.

Online Resources

'Claudia Martins convicted of the manslaughter of her newborn baby girl' *Daily Mail Online* (16 May 2015) at www.dailymail.co.uk/news/article-3042275/Mother-five-33-suffocated-newborn-daughter-stuffing-toilet-paper-throat-hid-body-suitcase-spared-jail.htm.

'Claudia Martins given community order for killing newborn' *BBC News* (16 April 2015) at www.bbc.co.uk/news/uk-england-bristol-32337828.

Simon Kealey QC, 'Disentangling the balance of the mind: infanticide reconsidered' (10 September 2019) at www.newparkcourt.co.uk/wp-content/uploads/2019/09/Criminal-Briefing-Simon-Kealey-QC.pdf.
'Exeter triple killer found not guilty of murder by reason of insanity' *Cornwall Live* (2 December 2019) at www.cornwalllive.com/news/exeter-triple-killer-found-not-3600789.
'Jack Ralph has been convicted of a terrifying knife attack in his neighbours home' *Kentlive* (19 March 2019) at www.kentlive.news/news/kent-news/frenzied-chef-who-killed-mum-2663419.
'REGINA – JACK RALPH Sentencing Remarks of Mrs Justice Cheema-Grubb DBE' (19 March 2019) at www.judiciary.uk/wp-content/uploads/2019/03/sentencing-remarks-r-v-ralph.pdf.
'Baby M mother is found guilty of infanticide but not guilty of murder' *Hampshire Live* (20 May 2021) at www.hampshirelive.news/news/hampshire-news/a-tragedy-involved-timeline-baby-5702372.
'Infanticide expert puzzled to see Winnipeg mother charged with manslaughter in newborn's death' *CBC News* (12 June 2022) at www.cbc.ca/news/canada/manitoba/jeanene-rosa-moar-infanticide-manslaughter-experts-1.6485231.
Crown Court Compendium, pt 1 (June 2022) at www.judiciary.uk/guidance-and-resources/crown-court-compendium/.

Parliamentary Papers

Coroners and Justice Bill, Public Bill Committee, 3 February 2009.
Ministry of Justice, Impact Assessment, Coroners and Justice Bill: homicide clauses, 14 January 2009.

Reports

Criminal Law Revision Committee, *Offences Against the Person* (14th Report, Cmnd 7844, 1980).
Law Commission, *Partial Defences to Murder* (Law Commission Consultation Paper No 173, 2003).
——, *A New Homicide Act for England and Wales? A Consultation Paper* (Law Com Consultation Paper No 177, 2005).
——, *Murder, Manslaughter and Infanticide* (Law Com No 304, 2006).
Mackay, RD, 'The Diminished Responsibility Plea in Operation' in *Partial Defences to Murder* (Law Com No 290, 2004) Appendix B.
——, 'Infanticide and Related Diminished Responsibility Manslaughters: An Empirical Study' in *Murder, Manslaughter and Infanticide* (Law Com No 304, 2006) Appendix D.
Report of the Committee on Mentally Abnormal Offenders (Cmnd 6244, 1975).

PART II

Understandings, Misunderstanding and Questions of Principle

4

'Sometimes the Worst Happens': Newspaper Reportage of Infanticide and the Law in England and Wales Since 1922

DANIEL JR GREY

In February 1965, Peggy Edwards, a prominent county councillor for the Liberal Party in Derbyshire who had a longstanding commitment to social justice issues, wrote a column for the women's page of *The Guardian*.[1] Her article began with a vivid description of visiting a friend in hospital who became acutely distressed and seriously ill a week after giving birth, convinced she was at risk of killing the baby: as Edwards arrived at the maternity ward, she was greeted with 'quite desperate sobbing, which … turned to a crescendo of screams'.[2] Alleging that postpartum mental illness was all too common, the article was intended to draw reader's attention to what Edwards described as the ongoing deficiencies in the treatment of infanticide cases that came before the courts, arguing vehemently that 'some alteration in the law on these cases is long overdue'.[3] In her opinion, the Infanticide Act 1938 was by now seriously outdated, and this represented a positive danger to vulnerable women and their infants rather than a just solution to the problem of these distressing cases.[4] As Sarah Crook has demonstrated, maternal distress was an increasingly influential topic in post-war Britain, and could be deployed in the service of a variety of different personal and professional agendas. While it does not seem to have led to any lasting interventions or triggered significant interest in the subject, Edwards' article is fascinating not only when seen as part of the broad

[1] For an example of Edwards' wide-ranging concerns, see recorded footage of her speech at the Liberal Party conference at Dundee in September 1985 on homelessness: Media Archive for Central England, 'Central News East: 18.09.1985: Liberal Party Conference – Homeless Version 2'.

[2] P Edwards, 'Infanticide' *The Guardian* (London, 26 February 1965) 10.

[3] ibid.

[4] See Infanticide Act 1922 and the amending Infanticide Act 1938 that remains in force as of 2022. Following the Coroners and Justice Act 2009, infanticide has also become a defence to charges of manslaughter as well as murder.

range of interventions Crook describes, but also in its own right as an example of how a national broadsheet represented actual or potential infanticide cases during this period.[5]

Across the course of the twentieth century, the press has arguably remained the most significant forum for understandings of infanticide and how the crime should best be dealt with by the criminal justice system in England and Wales.[6] Usually, this has been through reports that focus on the circumstances of individual cases that bring these to public attention.[7] Prior to the First World War, debates regarding the crime in the press, as in Parliament or other forums such as medical and legal journals, had often concentrated on whether there was any real need for a specific Infanticide Act to be passed that would separate these offences out from being treated as any other case of murder, or whether the existing informal policy by the Home Office of reviewing all capital cases following a conviction was sufficient.[8] Opinions remained divided as late as the early 1920s between a substantial minority who believed that women accused of infanticide were treated too leniently by the courts, and a majority who believed that existing systems were inadequate if not positively cruel and risked frequent miscarriages of justice.[9] The only point of agreement between supporters of these two broad factions – which could not be easily divided along lines of gender, class, faith, region, political alignment or profession – was a unifying conviction that infanticide was a 'special' crime deserving of particular attention and responses.[10] However, following the relatively abrupt passage of the Infanticide Act 1922, the

[5] S Crook, 'The Uses of Maternal Distress in British Society, c 1948–1979' (PhD thesis, Queen Mary University of London 2017).

[6] Newspapers played a central role in shaping attitudes towards gender, sexuality and crime in England and Wales during the period covered by this chapter. See key context in A Oram, *Her Husband was a Woman! Women's Gender-Crossing in Modern British Popular Culture* (Routledge 2007); A Bingham, *Family Newspapers?: Sex, Private Life, and the British Popular Press 1918–1978* (Oxford University Press 2009); A Davies, *City of Gangs: Glasgow and the Rise of the British Gangster* (Hodder & Stoughton 2013); J Rowbotham, K Stevenson and S Pegg, *Crime News in Modern Britain: Press Reporting and Responsibility, 1820–2010* (Palgrave Macmillan 2013); A Bingham and M Conboy, *Tabloid Century: The Popular Press in Britain, 1896 to the Present* (Peter Lang 2015); J Butler, 'Representations of Paternal Child Killers in the English National Press, 1900 to 1939' (PhD thesis, University of Liverpool 2018).

[7] In Scotland, 'infanticide' does not exist as a separate criminal offence but was and is still dealt with as murder or culpable homicide; in Northern Ireland, between 1922 and 1938 the English Act was held to apply, but the offence is now dealt with under the Infanticide Act (Northern Ireland) 1939, a statute almost identical to the (English) 1938 Act.

[8] ML Arnot, 'Understanding Women Committing Newborn Child Murder in Victorian England' in S D'Cruze (ed), *Everyday Violence in Britain, 1850–1950: Gender & Class* (Longman 2000) 55; T Ward, 'Legislating for human nature: Legal responses to infanticide, 1860–1938' in M Jackson (ed), *Infanticide: Historical Perspectives on Child Murder and Concealment, 1550–2000* (Ashgate 2002) 249; A-M Kilday, *A History of Infanticide in Britain, c.1600 to the Present* (Palgrave Macmillan 2013).

[9] SA Smith, *'Out of Sight, out of Mind': Infanticide, Baby Farming and Abortion in South and West Wales, 1870–1922* (Rowanvale Books Ltd 2021); DJR Grey, 'Discourses of Infanticide in England, 1880–1922' (PhD thesis, Roehampton University 2008).

[10] DJR Grey, 'Parenting, Infanticide, and the State in England and Wales, 1870–1950' in H Barron and C Siebrecht (eds), *Parenting and the State in Britain and Europe, 1870–1950: Raising the Nation* (Palgrave Macmillan 2017) 41, 79–83.

focus for inter-war commentators shifted entirely on to whether the law was fit for purpose or needed further amendment. Since the 1950s, a further element has been introduced to this discussion: the question of whether the Infanticide Act should simply be abolished outright, with critics arguing that the statute is based on medical, legal and cultural understandings of motherhood that are at best outdated and at worst actively harmful.[11] Central to these ongoing conversations, which have been resurrected at several points without ever securing a resolution, is the enduring representation in England and Wales of the infanticidal woman as a criminal who does not fit neatly into more established (and often overtly misogynistic) tropes of female offenders,[12] and where they have often been depicted as a tragic rather than malevolent figure. While not wishing to suggest that the current media, judicial and cultural treatment of infanticide cases in either England or Wales simply replicates that of earlier periods, and with due acknowledgement of the historical specificity of such cases tried since the turn of the millennium,[13] the legacy of these precedents and attitudes remains extremely powerful. By examining the reportage of such cases in the press – both the broadsheets and the tabloids – over the course of a century, the enduring power of this legacy comes into stark focus.

I. Drawing and Re-Drawing the Line: The First 50 Years of the Infanticide Act (1922–72)

Reports of suspicious infant deaths, sometimes simply the mention of discovery of an unknown infant's body in a town or countryside with no further identification possible, sometimes where there was a clear link to a suspect, were a routine feature of the nineteenth- and early twentieth-century press across England, Wales and Ireland.[14] In those instances where there were sufficient grounds for an indictment and criminal trial, the reportage of both local and national newspapers in these regions was liable to follow such stories all the way to the assize court, potentially generating very substantial coverage of a case. While it is almost impossible to reconstruct the decision-making process that led (invariably anonymous) individual reporters to pursue writing about particular events beyond

[11] See especially Brennan and Milne, ch 1 in this volume.

[12] L Seal, *Women, Murder and Femininity: Gender Representations of Women Who Kill* (Palgrave Macmillan 2010).

[13] E Milne, *Criminal Justice Responses to Maternal Filicide: Judging the Failed Mother* (Emerald Publishing Limited 2021).

[14] E Farrell, *'A most diabolical deed': Infanticide and Irish society, 1850–1900* (Manchester University Press 2013); Grey (n 9); Smith (n 9). In Scotland, '[t]rials of new-born child murder rarely made the pages of newspapers beyond a few lines outlining the accused, the verdict and the sentence': see T Siddons, 'Suspected New-born Child Murder and Concealment of Pregnancy in Scotland, c 1812–c 1930' (PhD thesis, University of Edinburgh 2014) 20, fn 83.

the generic assumption of 'newsworthiness', any homicide was almost guaranteed to generate substantial interest from the reading public, and consequently to improve sales: it was therefore logical for Victorian and Edwardian journalists to try to provide as much detail in their articles as was possible regarding these crimes.[15] Infanticide trials were thus likely to be a reasonably familiar narrative for English and Welsh newspaper readers to come across in this period, even if remarkably few such cases ended in conviction on the capital charge, and the small number that did so were still liable to be reported very sympathetically.[16] For instance, when 22-year-old laundress Alice Cleaver was convicted for the murder of her 3-month-old son at the Central Criminal Court in 1909, the *Daily Mail* and *Daily Telegraph* were each careful to note that both the judge and the jury emphatically recommended her to mercy despite the legal requirement to pass sentence of death: outraged readers who had been following the trial nonetheless wrote in to the *Daily Mail* demanding that the law be changed.[17]

By 1922, however, the context of infanticide reporting in England and Wales had changed somewhat. The pattern of explicitly sympathetic reporting, and a willingness by commentators to suggest a degree of (usually temporary) mental disturbance in the woman charged that did not necessarily correspond with either legal or medical definitions of criminal insanity, were both still firmly present in such articles, representing a cultural consensus that dated back to at least 1860 if not before.[18] Yet despite the feverish concern exhibited by a range of conservative commentators – including journalists – during the 1920s and 1930s about the dangers posed by the 'modern woman' in the wake of the Great War, infanticide remained entirely absent from such debates.[19] Moreover, while crime reporting remained a staple of inter-war newspapers, as part of broader formatting changes to the press, such as the standardised inclusion of photographs across

[15] J Flanders, *The Invention of Murder: How the Victorians revelled in death and detection and created modern crime* (HarperPress 2011); CBA Wilson, 'Mad, sad, or bad?: newspaper and judicial representations of men who killed children in Victorian England, 1860–1900' (PhD thesis, University of Essex 2012); Rowbotham, Stevenson and Pegg (n 6); A Smalley, 'Representations of Crime, Justice, and Punishment in the Popular Press: A Study of the *Illustrated Police News*, 1864–1938' (PhD thesis, Open University 2017).

[16] DJR Grey, '"Agonised Weeping": Representing Femininity, Emotion and Infanticide in Edwardian Newspapers' (2015) 21 *Media History* 468.

[17] 'Murder Trial Pathos' *Daily Mail* (London, 10 March 1909) 4; 'Death-Sentence Scene' *Daily Telegraph* (London, 10 March 1909) 14. See also letters to editor in 'Girl Mother's Ordeal' *Daily Mail* (London, 12 March 1909) 8 and 'The Cleaver Case' *Daily Mail* (London, 15 March 1909) 10, and further details in Grey (n 16).

[18] DJR Grey, '"The Agony of Despair": Pain and the Cultural Script of Infanticide in England and Wales, 1860–1960' in R Boddice (ed), *Pain and Emotion in Modern History* (Palgrave Macmillan 2014) 204. This overlapped with – yet was also distinct from – other discourses that might be applied to women who killed their children: see AC Pedley, *Mothers, Criminal Insanity and the Asylum in Victorian England: Cure, Redemption and Rehabilitation* (Bloomsbury 2023).

[19] On inter-war debates over the 'modern woman', see B Melman, *Women and the Popular Imagination in the Twenties* (Macmillan 1988); L Bland, *Modern Women on Trial: Sexual Transgression in the Age of the Flapper* (Manchester University Press 2013); C Wildman, *Urban Redevelopment and Modernity in Liverpool and Manchester, 1918–1939* (Bloomsbury 2016).

the tabloids, articles about crime not only tended to be shorter than they had been before 1914, but also invariably focused on the most sensational cases.[20] Even in specialist publications like the *Illustrated Police News*, there was a reduction in the space allocated to crime reporting, which likewise followed the broad media turn away from accounts of 'everyday crime' to briefer and more sensationalised articles.[21]

It is likely that, regarding infanticide, this impact on crime reporting was compounded by the passage of the new Act, and an assumption that this had removed the longstanding controversy surrounding the fact that murder convictions mandated an automatic death sentence, which in these cases was almost guaranteed to be commuted to penal servitude.[22] While the 1922 Act was based in large measure on an unsuccessful Bill from 1909 that had been derailed by the constitutional crisis that erupted around the Liberal Party's 'People's Budget' between 1909 and 1911, its rapid resurrection and passage was the result of concerted organisation and lobbying by several influential women activists, among them the wife of the Prime Minister, Margaret Lloyd George, whose personal and professional connections included the highest levels of the new Labour Government.[23] Their interest in changing this law resulted from the extensive local and national press coverage given to the June 1921 trial and conviction of Edith Mary Roberts, a 21-year-old factory worker from Hinkley, for the murder of her newborn child.[24] As Nicola Goc has demonstrated, Roberts' local newspaper, the *Leicester Mercury*, ran an extensive campaign on her behalf, even as it simultaneously published other sensationalised and gruesome stories of infanticide in the East Midlands.[25] In contrast to these other stories, Roberts' conviction at the Leicester Assizes and subsequent, unsuccessful attempt to appeal against her sentence (both reported in detail) were represented as a self-evident miscarriage of justice and tapped into a wellspring of popular sympathy.[26] A demonstration calling for her immediate release attracted over 500 protestors, and included speeches to the crowd from serving magistrates who shared their view of the case as unjust.[27] However, the extensive coverage bestowed on Roberts' case was unusual, even if the sympathetic tone of the reportage was not. Much less attention was given to the case of Emma

[20] Bingham (n 6); Bingham and Conboy (n 6); Butler (n 6).

[21] Smalley (n 15).

[22] See context in A Ballinger, *Dead Woman Walking: Executed Women in England and Wales, 1900–55* (Ashgate 2000); and L Seal, *Capital Punishment in Twentieth-Century Britain: Audience, Justice, Memory* (Routledge 2014).

[23] DJR Grey, 'Women's policy networks and the Infanticide Act 1922' (2010) 21 *Twentieth Century British History* 441.

[24] The National Archives (hereinafter 'TNA') ASSI 11/43. See 7 June 1921 (unpaginated); TNA ASSI 12/115. *R v Roberts*; TNA ASSI 13/51. *R v Roberts*; TNA HO 144/1749/419784.

[25] N Goc, *Women, Infanticide and the Press, 1822–1922: News narratives in England and Australia* (Ashgate 2013) 145–69.

[26] Roberts was released after serving just 12 months. See TNA HO 144/1749/419784. Note on file 6 June 1922.

[27] 'Standing Alone in Her Agony' *Leicester Mercury* (Leicester, 19 July 1921) 5.

Temple, a 19-year-old domestic servant, who was the first woman tried under the new Act in October 1922.[28] This was partly due to the fact that Temple pleaded guilty to infanticide at the Lincoln Assizes rather than going through a full trial for murder, meaning that publishable details of the case were confined to a few local press reports of preliminary hearings (although these were quite extensive) before the magistrates who committed her for trial at the assizes.[29] However, part of the reason is also the likelihood that the press – and, significantly, the judge who heard the case – seems to have assumed that this law would henceforth mean the controversies of previous decades related to infanticide would be avoided. Both *The Times* and the *Pall Mall Gazette*, along with several provincial newspapers from across England and Wales, ran short articles that quoted from Mr Justice Lush's sentencing of Temple to just four months' imprisonment, including his observation that this 'most wise and humane piece of legislation' now avoided a murder trial and thus the possibility of a capital conviction, something he believed could only be an improvement on previous years.[30]

In fact, the deliberately vague definition of 'newly born', which had been decided on by politicians and civil servants in the wording of the Infanticide Act 1922 as a way to bypass the interminable wrangling over where the fairest age limit lay, continued to be a source of problems.[31] In the first place, not all judges were as enamoured of the new law as Mr Justice Lush: the Recorder of the Central Criminal Court, Sir Ernest Wild, complained to the Grand Jury in January 1925 that he considered the Act to be 'beneficent but badly drafted', believing that a Grand Jury could not find for infanticide if a Bill had already been presented for murder.[32] Following Wild's instructions that one of the four women charged with killing their children should definitely have been charged with infanticide rather than murder, the Grand Jury rejected that indictment and instead charged the defendant under the 1922 Act.[33] Conversely, in October 1929, Mr Justice Humphreys complained at the opening of the Liverpool Assizes that juries had become far too willing to immediately conclude a potential case fell within the auspices of the Act, which he believed was not only dangerous but went against the spirit of the legislation.[34]

Neither Wild nor Humphreys was unique, even if many (perhaps most?) commentators approved of the 1922 Act. High-profile cases such as that of Mary O'Donoghue in 1927 had underscored these ongoing differences in opinion, not

[28] TNA ASSI 11/43. See 30 October 1922 (unpaginated); TNA ASSI 12/119; TNA ASSI 13/52.

[29] 'Tattershall Sensation' *Skegness Standard* (Skegness, 27 September 1922) 8; 'Tattershall Murder Charge' *Lincolnshire Standard and Boston Guardian* (Lincoln, 30 September 1922) 12; 'Tattershall Murder Charge' *Skegness Standard* (Skegness, 4 October 1922) 6.

[30] 'New Infanticide Act' *The Times* (London, 31 October 1922) 9; 'Humaner [*sic*] Law', *Pall Mall Gazette* (London, 31 October 1922) 12.

[31] Grey (n 23).

[32] 'The Infanticide Act' *The Times* (London, 14 January 1925) 16.

[33] ibid.

[34] 'Judge on charges of infanticide' *The Times* (London, 30 October 1929) 5.

only within the judiciary but beyond it, about what could, or should, count as 'infanticide'.[35] O'Donoghue, a 24-year-old waitress, had become pregnant while on a visit home to her family in County Kerry, and immediately returned from Ireland to work in London, moving jobs twice in 10 weeks before being discovered by a colleague while in labour.[36] When released from St Pancras Infirmary, O'Donoghue secured lodgings on Euston Road and found a new job as a cook nearby; but when she asked her landlady to look after the baby she was told this was impossible, and she did not have the funds to pay for foster care or to purchase food.[37] Shortly after bathing and dressing him on the morning the new job started, O'Donoghue strangled her son and hid his body under the bed before leaving for work.[38] Medical witnesses disagreed during the trial over whether her mental state could amount to not being criminally responsible, though agreeing she had been suffering from depression, but attempts to mount an insanity defence were ultimately unsuccessful and she was found guilty of John O'Donoghue's murder.[39] Although her death sentence was commuted by the Home Office to penal servitude for life within 24 hours, in accordance with the strong recommendation of both the judge and the jury, O'Donoghue's lawyers appealed on the grounds that she should instead have been convicted for infanticide. The Court of Appeal demurred, ruling that her conviction must be upheld since a child of 35 days old could not possible count as 'newly born' and was thus too old fall within the confines of the Infanticide Act.[40] Indeed, Mr Justice Avory took the opportunity, as part of upholding the conviction, to clarify a misunderstanding included in the appeal (and that had been reproduced in at least one law textbook during the 1920s), which erroneously believed he had ruled that a case in 1924 involving a 3-week-old baby came under the Act.[41] The ruling was widely reported across provincial newspapers as well as in the national press and in the law reports, and it is worth noting that – very unusually in infanticide cases – sufficient interest had been generated by O'Donoghue's trial for both the *Daily Mail* and the *Evening News* to later run short articles in March 1929 to alert their readers to the fact that she was about to be released from prison on licence.[42]

[35] TNA CRIM 1/414; TNA MEPO 3/1630; *R v O'Donoghue* (1927) 28 Cox CC 461; *R v O'Donoghue* (1928) 20 Cr App R 132; 'A Case for Mercy' *Daily News* (London, 14 October 1927) 10; 'Strangled Baby. Sentence of Death on Waitress' *News of the World* (London, 16 October 1927) 5; 'Court of Criminal Appeal' *The Times* (London, 8 November 1927) 5; 'Tragedy of a Mother' *Daily Herald* (London, 8 November 1927) 7.

[36] For essential context, see J Redmond, 'In the family way and away from the family: examining the evidence in Irish unmarried mothers in Britain, 1920s–40s' in E Farrell (ed), *'She said she was in the family way': Pregnancy and infancy in the Irish past* (Institute of Historical Research 2012) 163.

[37] 'Death Sentence on Waitress' *The People* (London, 16 October 1927) 4.

[38] TNA CRIM 1/414. Statement made under caution of Mary O'Donoghue, 24 September 1927.

[39] 'A Case for Mercy' *Daily News* (London, 14 October 1927) 10.

[40] *R v O'Donoghue* (1927) (n 35); *R v O'Donoghue* (1928) (n 35); Court of Criminal Appeal' *The Times* (London, 8 November 1927) 5.

[41] 'What IS A "Newly Born" Child?' *The Times* (London, 22 November 1927) 5.

[42] 'Infanticide Trial Sequel' *Daily Mail* (London, 19 March 1929) 7; *Evening News* (London, 19 March 1929).

Similar confusion and concern were generated by the 1936 case of Brenda Hale, a middle-class, 24-year-old farmer's wife from Welwyn in Hertfordshire, described as a devoted wife and mother.[43] Both the consultant who attended Hale at and after both of her confinements, and the governor of Holloway Prison (who in his other role as medical officer had assessed her mental state while she was being held on remand) were in agreement that Hale had been suffering from puerperal insanity after the birth of each of her children, a diagnosis roughly equivalent to contemporary postnatal depression or psychosis.[44] Although very few nineteenth-century sufferers had harmed themselves or their children, as Hilary Marland has observed, the condition – accounting for 10 per cent of women's asylum admissions – had long been closely associated with infanticide.[45] In many respects, the new Infanticide Act 1922 and its wording formally enshrined this perceived link between puerperal insanity and child homicide. During a short period one morning, when she and her younger child were left alone, Hale cut the baby's throat and her own with a razor. As with Mary O'Donoghue, albeit for different reasons, this was a case where – even by the standards of infanticide trials – sympathy was both explicit and unanimous in the press and in the courtroom. Since her son had been 3 weeks old when he died, in the wake of O'Donoghue's trial it seemed dubious whether the jury would be allowed to convict for infanticide rather than murder, despite the testimony for the defence of Lord Dawson of Penn, the president of the Royal College of Physicians, that most doctors would agree 'newly born' to include infants up to a month old even if the 1922 Act did not set a specific date.[46] Instead, without leaving the witness box to confer, the jury immediately announced that she was 'not guilty of murder but guilty of the act charged, for which she was not responsible in law', seemingly because they believed the wording of the normal 'guilty but insane' verdict to imply culpability.[47]

The jury's decision and apparently unique verdict prompted the presiding judge, Mr Justice Humphreys, to include in his summing up the hope that Parliament might intervene to set a specific time limit for what constituted a 'newly born child' under the framework of the 1922 Act.[48] Taking up the suggestion, Lord Dawson consulted with other medical colleagues to draft and introduce what became the Infanticide Act 1938, eventually replacing the 'newly born' requirement entirely

[43] TNA CRIM 1/850; TNA DPP 2/357; '"Devoted Mother" Hears First Mercy Verdict' *Daily Mirror* (London, 22 July 1936) 17; 'Infanticide' *The Times* (London, 22 July 1936) 13; 'New Verdict in Mother's Trial for Murder' *Daily Telegraph* (London, 22 July 1936) 9; 'Not Responsible in Law' *Illustrated Police News* (London, 30 July 1936) 6.

[44] TNA CRIM 1/850. See deposition of Charles Harold Medlock; TNA DPP 2/357. Report of JCM Matheson, 13 July 1936.

[45] H Marland, *Dangerous Motherhood: Insanity and Childbirth in Victorian Britain* (Palgrave Macmillan 2004).

[46] 'Not Responsible in Law' *Illustrated Police News* (London, 30 July 1936) 6.

[47] 'New Verdict in Mother's Trial for Murder' *Daily Telegraph* (London, 22 July 1936) 9.

[48] 'Spared Hearing Verdict of Murder' *Daily Herald* (London, 22 July 1936) 9.

with a period of 12 months after the woman had given birth, and including specific reference to the balance of her mind's being left disturbed by lactation as well as parturition itself: the Bill passed without opposition.[49]

The line having thus been re-drawn for what might or might not count as 'infanticide' in law, there it remained, despite periodic concerns that the 1938 Act was not fit for purpose or that potentially 'deserving' cases might still be excluded.[50] Newspaper articles on infanticide cases both during and well after the Second World War continued to regularly emphasise the vulnerable and tragic (but also potentially recoverable) position of the women involved. For instance, Marian Collins, the 27-year-old wife of a schoolteacher from Newport, was charged with killing her 10-week-old son Geoffrey in September 1959.[51] A short report of her trial in the *Western Mail* simultaneously emphasised Collins' physical and mental fragility in the period shortly before the crime – suggesting her health had been permanently damaged by influenza and that she was still recovering from the shock of witnessing a severe traffic accident – as well as alluding to her happy marriage, noting that her husband had returned home on the day of Geoffrey's death in his lunch hour to help with feeding the baby.[52] At a period of changing attitudes towards 'good fatherhood', this would have stood out for readers and the court as an example of particularly involved and supportive paternal care.[53] Nothing about this situation fit with the 'traditional' stereotype of a single young woman left penniless and abandoned by an uncaring lover to deal with the shame and pain of an illegitimate pregnancy, driven to madness as a result, but this short article nonetheless portrayed Collins as deserving of deep sympathy and a tragic victim of circumstances. Convicted at the Monmouthshire Assizes of infanticide, Collins was told by the judge that 'you are in need of help and treatment rather than punishment' and placed on probation for two years, subject to the condition that she became a voluntary patient at a psychiatric hospital.[54]

II. Continuity and Controversy (1973–2004)

It was possible that either the introduction in England and Wales of the Homicide Act 1957, which introduced to English law the concept of 'diminished responsibility' as a partial defence for murder, or the abolition in 1968 of capital punishment might have also led to a reconsideration of whether the Infanticide Act 1938 was

[49] Ward (n 8).
[50] Grey (n 10).
[51] 'Mother who killed her baby son "needs help"' *Western Mail* (Cardiff, 4 November 1959) 10.
[52] ibid.
[53] L King, *Family Men: Fatherhood and Masculinity in Britain, 1914–1960* (Oxford University Press 2015).
[54] 'Mother who killed her baby son "needs help"' (n 51).

still warranted.[55] After all, assertions that the circumstances of the crime meant that infanticide should be an offence punishable by imprisonment rather than the death penalty, and that such cases did not necessarily correspond with existing 'insanity' definitions, were longstanding complaints, and these had actively fuelled demands for a change in the law over several decades before 1922.[56] Yet for many people, the Act still clearly served a distinct purpose, something underlined by very similar laws being passed in Ireland, Canada and several States in Australia during the post-war years that were explicitly and closely modelled on the English Act.[57]

Tellingly, the Report of the Royal Commission on Capital Punishment in 1953 specifically recommended leaving the Infanticide Act untouched by any further reforms.[58] Even those commentators who suggested in the 1970s that it might be possible to amend or abolish the Infanticide Act did so cautiously, and such suggestions, such as those by the Butler Committee on Mentally Abnormal Offenders (1975) or by the Criminal Law Revision Committee (1980), were in practice either rejected outright or ignored.[59] The Royal College of Psychiatrists, reporting the findings of its Working Group on Infanticide in 1978 as part of preparation for the Criminal Law Committee hearings, in fact was careful to explain that although its members were uncomfortable with aspects of the Infanticide Act 1938 (especially the references to lactation), unless the most sweeping reforms suggested by the Butler Committee were adopted – thus removing the need for it entirely – then it was essential that the Act be retained, subject to minor amendments that would if anything slightly *increase* the number of potential cases it could deal with.[60]

Just as had been true of the early and mid-twentieth century, cases from the 1970s through to the 2000s could be and often were reported – even just briefly in terse summaries of fewer than a hundred words – with clear sympathy by the authorities that was implicitly or explicitly echoed by the press, as demonstrated by a short report from the *Lynn Advertiser* in January 1973. In an article of less than 60 words and on the front page of this issue of the local paper, it recorded that 19-year-old Louise Woodward, who had given birth to her baby while at an allotment, had pleaded guilty to infanticide at Norwich Crown Court.[61] Sentencing her

[55] Homicide Act 1957. The concept of 'diminished responsibility' had been introduced much earlier in Scotland, first outlined during the 1867 trial of Alexander Dingwall for the murder of his wife: Dingwall was instead convicted of culpable homicide. See *HM Advocate v Dingwall* (1867) 5 Irvine 466.

[56] J Gregory, *Mercy and British Culture, 1760–1960* (Bloomsbury 2021) 139.

[57] See, eg, KJ Kramer, *Unwilling Mothers, Unwanted Babies: Infanticide in Canada* (UBC Press 2005); KM Brennan, '"Traditions of English Liberal Thought": A History of the Enactment of an Infanticide Law in Ireland' (2013) 50 *Irish Jurist* 100; KM Brennan, 'Murderous Mothers & Gentle Judges: Paternalism, Patriarchy, and Infanticide' (2018) 30 *Yale Journal of Law and Feminism* 140; A Loughnan, *Self, Others and the State: Relations of Criminal Responsibility* (Cambridge University Press 2020) 165–92.

[58] Home Office, *Report of the Royal Commission on Capital Punishment* (Cmd 8932, 1953) 961.

[59] Crook (n 5) 219.

[60] R Bluglass, 'Infanticide' (1978) 2 *Bulletin of the Royal College of Psychiatrists* 139.

[61] 'Girl put on probation' *Lynn Advertiser* (Norfolk, 16 January 1973) 1.

to two years' probation, Mr Justice Melford abjured her to 'Go away and make the most of these unhappy circumstances.'[62] The outcome in this case was not unusual but should be seen as part of a pattern of lenient judicial treatment that was increasingly standardised over the course of the late twentieth century: no woman convicted of infanticide in England and Wales between 1979 and 1988 seems to have received a custodial sentence.[63] This was a fact specifically referenced by the Court of Appeal in 1989 when reviewing the case of 17-year-old Joan Sainsbury, who had been sentenced to 12 months' detention in a young offender's institution after pleading guilty to infanticide.[64] Sainsbury had become pregnant at 14 and had given birth in 'squalid conditions' and without assistance at the flat of her boyfriend, Lee Clarke, who had similarly confessed to the manslaughter of their son. A short article about Clarke's conviction in *The Times* noted that the couple had intended to abandon the baby at a hospital in Bath, but 'could not afford the bus fare and were afraid of being seen'.[65] In amending Sainsbury's sentence to a probation order, the Court specifically argued that '[t]he sentencer was wrong to say that the welfare of society demanded a custodial sentence; the mitigating factors were overwhelming'.[66]

Despite the very substantial legislative, social, cultural, economic and political changes – particularly those that impacted specifically on women's lives, such as the enactment of laws against sex discrimination, the expansion of reproductive rights, and the increase in educational and work opportunities – in England and Wales from the mid-1970s onwards, infanticide trials and their representation were still strongly influenced by attitudes and precedents that had been established much earlier in the twentieth century. Although abortion had been legalised in England, Scotland and Wales since 1967, and contraception and birth-control advice were finally incorporated and made available to all (regardless of age or marital status) from 1974 onwards, these important changes do not seem to have significantly impacted on the ways that infanticide was either reported in the news or dealt with by the courts, even though both of these developments had – at least in theory – significantly reduced the likelihood of unwanted pregnancies being carried to term, and thus could have been interpreted as making such cases less deserving of sympathy than they had been in previous decades.[67] Just as Karen Brennan has demonstrated with regard to Ireland, shared social norms and ideas

[62] ibid.

[63] A Loughnan, *Manifest Madness: Mental Incapacity in Criminal Law* (Oxford University Press 2012) 224.

[64] *R v Sainsbury* (1989) 11 Cr App R (S) 533.

[65] 'Man threw newborn into river' *The Times* (London, 15 November 1989) 4.

[66] *Sainsbury* (n 64).

[67] Abortion Act 1967. On the tensions between abortion law and current healthcare practice, see S Sheldon, 'British Abortion Law: Speaking from the Past to Govern the Future' (2016) 79 *MLR* 283. Birth control was intended for married couples only until the passage of the National Health Service (Family Planning) Act 1967 expanded access for women. See C Rusterholz, *Women's Medicine: Sex, family planning and British female doctors in transnational perspective, 1920–70* (Manchester University Press 2020).

about what represents the most 'just' outcome in suspected infanticide cases have remained central to determining processes and outcomes in England and Wales.[68] It is difficult to determine exactly when probation orders (often accompanied by the requirement for psychiatric treatment) started to displace prison sentences in infanticide cases, but this process had certainly been underway by the late 1940s.[69] The 13th updated edition of the influential forensic medicine textbook *Glaister's Medical Jurisprudence and Toxicology*, published in 1973, continued to devote relatively substantial space (specifically a 26-page chapter) to setting out the complicated case law and tests necessary to interpret in suspected infanticide cases, arguing that this remained one of the most difficult questions for a medical witness to resolve.[70]

Crucially, a series of cases in the mid- and late 1990s also meant that concerns about infanticide and the most fair and appropriate way to deal with these offences were suddenly the subject of high-profile news coverage in England and Wales, even though none of these cases were prosecuted under the Infanticide Act but as other types of homicide – indeed, one of these trials actually took place in the United States (US), though it involved a British defendant. Although these events ran in parallel to stories or trials that were dealt with under the 1938 Act, they are nonetheless mentioned here because all of them received voluminous coverage in the British press and, in the American case, several newspaper articles revolved around the legal differences between how infanticide cases were dealt with in the two jurisdictions. In 1994, Caroline Beale, a 30-year-old civil servant living in London, was arrested at JFK Airport in New York when attempting to board a flight back to the United Kingdom (UK) with her partner and friends: the dead body of a baby girl was discovered hidden in a plastic bag carried underneath her coat.[71] She had told nobody that she was pregnant, claiming that the baby had been stillborn when she gave birth in her hotel bathroom while her partner slept and hiding the body in the plastic bag she then carried with her. The New York authorities, however, argued that the baby had been born alive before dying from suffocation, and that the concealment of her pregnancy and even delivery from friends and family strongly suggested premeditation.[72] Charged with second-degree murder, Beale spent 14 months held on remand at Riker's Island prison before a full psychiatric report was completed, and later entered a plea bargain that required her to confess to her daughter's manslaughter as a condition of being released.[73] On returning to England, Beale resumed her job in the Department of Health and was attending the Maudsley Hospital for ongoing mental health treatment.[74]

[68] K Brennan, 'Social norms and the law in responding to infanticide' (2018) 38 *Legal Studies* 480.

[69] Grey (n 18).

[70] E Rentoul and H Smith, *Glaister's Medical Jurisprudence and Toxicology*, 13th edn (Churchill Livingstone 1973) 399–424.

[71] J Wheelwright, 'A moment as mother' *The Guardian* (London, 13 May 1995) A13 and 16.

[72] R Mead, 'The Imaginary Infant', *New York Magazine* (New York, 18 December 1995) 36.

[73] C Laurence, 'So just why did it take them so long?' *Daily Telegraph* (London, 8 March 1996) 13.

[74] C Davies, 'I just knew I had to bring my dead baby back home' *Daily Telegraph* (London, 19 August 1997) 11.

As Julie Wheelwright has suggested, '[t]he media … remains fascinated with the macabre details and the haunting question of motive in such cases'.[75] Transatlantic coverage of Beale's case over these three years was extensive, and in the British press (both broadsheet and tabloid) overtly sympathetic, as exemplified by one *Daily Mail* headline: 'The Torturing of Caroline Beale'.[76] It is revealing that the *Daily Mail*, a right-wing tabloid that has traditionally tended to emphasise sensationalised reporting and – in cases relating to crime – the need for severe punishment of offenders, chose instead to focus in its substantial coverage on elements of the case that portrayed Beale as a victim of her circumstances and as being treated with inappropriate harshness. Much turned on the fact that had Beale's situation occurred in England, she would have been charged under the Infanticide Act; but the US was (and remains) unusual, in that there are no equivalent laws to separate this offence from other types of homicide.[77] Practically no British commentators considered this to be an improvement on the English and Welsh process, the notable exception being the journalist Yvonne Roberts, who suggested in the *Sunday Telegraph* that, unlike the Infanticide Act's problematic constructions of womanhood, 'American rules are clearer, unmuddled by prejudices or unproven beliefs about biological destiny'.[78] Reporting could thus often take an overtly nationalistic line that implied such controversies would never occur in the British criminal justice system. Indeed, not only criticisms of the American approach by the British media, but also comments by Caroline Beale's father complaining that her treatment was 'barbaric' provoked the sentencing judge in her case, Robert Hanophy, to issue an emphatic defence of the US system that explicitly criticised the 1938 Act:

> I believe that any law that grants a blanket exemption from prosecution or punishment to those people who kill their children when their children are under the age of one is a law that is primitive and uncivilised. Granting parents a law to kill their children harkens to uncivilised times. I say to our friends in Britain, God bless America.[79]

New York State's Commission on Judicial Conduct later reprimanded Hanophy, arguing that in making these remarks, along with other sharply critical comments on the political situation in Northern Ireland at the same time, he had overstepped the bounds of his role.[80] Responding directly to Hanophy's assessment in an article for *The Times*, British law lecturer Gary Slapper argued that in fact, denying infanticide its status as a 'special' defence or charge 'is to wish to return to principles of law regarded here as intolerably primitive in the 1920s'.[81]

[75] J Wheelwright, '"Nothing in between": modern cases of infanticide' in Jackson (ed) (n 8) 271.
[76] F Hardy and G Gordon, 'The Torturing of Caroline Beale' *Daily Mail* (London, 19 May 1995) 30–31.
[77] M Spinelli, 'Infanticide and American criminal justice (1980–2018)' (2018) 22 *Archives of Women's Mental Health* 173.
[78] Y Roberts, 'The case for the American prosecution' *Sunday Telegraph* (London, 10 March 1996) 5.
[79] G Slapper, 'Mothers and madness' *The Times* (London, 19 March 1996) 33.
[80] J Bone, 'US judge rebuked for attack on Britain' *The Times* (London, 12 April 1997) 19.
[81] Slapper (n 79).

Reading the extensive newspaper reports of Beale's case (only some of which can be touched on here) strongly suggests that the public and the media in England and Wales emphatically shared that view. This can only have been reinforced by a high-profile series of controversies between 1999 and 2005, in which four women – Donna Anthony, Sally Clark, Angela Cannings and Trupti Patel – were accused of the murder of their children, partly on the basis of evidence given by influential paediatrician Sir Roy Meadow, who believed repeated instances of Sudden Infant Death Syndrome (SIDS) within the same household were in themselves suspicious: his arguments were widely reported in the media and, as Victoria Bates has shown, likely helped shape the overall landscape of child protection at the time.[82] Patel was acquitted at her trial, while Clark, Cannings and Anthony all had their murder convictions overturned on appeal as unsafe.[83] Between the seventeenth and mid-twentieth centuries, medical jurisprudence had routinely demonstrated what Rachel Dixon has described as 'positive uncertainty' regarding infanticide: an acknowledgement that forensic science struggled to provide definitive answers in cases of suspicious infant death and that offered the courts a degree of flexibility in how they approached individual cases.[84] The discrediting of Meadow, and the substantial media coverage of these four women's experiences, emphatically reinscribed this uncertainty for the general public as well as for the medical and legal professions in early twenty-first-century England and Wales.[85]

III. 'The Mitigation in This Case … is Overwhelming': Consensus Maintained (2005–22)

Although the cases of Clark, Cannings, Patel and Anthony had involved charges of murder rather than infanticide, they definitively shaped how newspaper readers responded to stories of suspected baby killing – indeed, journalist Cassandra Jardine explicitly drew this connection in a 2008 article for *The Telegraph* that focused on concerns about the case of Chaha'oh Niyol Kai-Whitewind, who had been convicted some years earlier of the murder of her 12-week-old son

[82] V Bates, 'Three is Murder: The Rise and Fall of Munchausen Syndrome by Proxy Experts' (2019) 104 *History* 189.

[83] J Revill and G Hinscliff, 'Call for an end to cot death court anguish: As Trupti Patel is cleared of killing her babies, experts urge overhaul of way bereaved mothers are treated' *The Guardian* (London, 15 June 2003) 8; *R v Clark (Sally)* [2003] EWCA Crim 1020, [2003] 4 WLUK 399; *R v Cannings (Angela)* [2004] EWCA Crim 1, [2004] 1 WLR 2607; *R v Anthony (Donna)* [2005] EWCA Crim 952, [2005] 4 WLUK 144.

[84] R Dixon, *Infanticide: Expert Evidence and Testimony in Child Murder Cases, 1688–1955* (Routledge 2022).

[85] G Slapper, 'Mothers, madness and medieval justice' *The Times* (London, 4 February 2003) 3 [s 2].

Bidziil, the youngest of her three children.[86] There had been no attempt to mount a defence of infanticide in this case: instead, Kai-Whitewind had vehemently denied suffocating her son, insisting his death had been from natural (unexplained) causes and refusing to give evidence during her trial at Birmingham Crown Court in 2003.[87] Medical experts called to give evidence had disagreed about what conclusions could be drawn regarding his death, but Kai-Whitewind had said to a health visitor she was depressed and, though she had resisted terminating the pregnancy, had told people previously that he had been conceived when she was raped, as well as that she had struggled to bond with him.[88] While rejecting her appeal against the sentence, on the grounds that there had been sufficient evidence available to the jury beyond that provided by medical witnesses to ensure that the conviction was safe, the judges argued that this case highlighted deficiencies in the Infanticide Act on two key points.[89] The first of these was the question of whether the wording of the Act should be reformed to take into account 'circumstances subsequent to the birth, but connected with it, such as the stresses imposed on a mother by the absence of natural bonding with her baby'.[90] The second concern was that it could not be applied to a woman who refused to accept that she had killed her child and so would not cooperate in providing evidence that the balance of her mind had been disturbed at the time.[91] When the Law Commission reviewed the existing laws on unlawful killing the following year, including the Infanticide Act, it directly addressed the points that had been raised by the Court of Appeal.[92] Although noting the issues posed by the 1938 Act (not least of which, the outdated language and potentially essentialist tropes about madness and motherhood it contains), the Commission agreed that this should be retained, albeit subject to rewording to remove references to 'lactation' and to expand the time period allowable from 12 months to two years after giving birth.[93] While these proposals were not taken up by the Government, these recommendations underline the ongoing importance of the Act and the general consensus that approved of it, even if some newspapers ran actively misleading headlines about the appeal judgment in *Kai-Whitewind* that implied that critics (including senior judges) were advocating its abolition rather than its amendment and expansion.[94]

[86] C Jardine, 'Has Sally Clark's case changed attitudes to infant death?' *The Telegraph* (London, 11 March 2008) at www.telegraph.co.uk/news/uknews/1581407/Has-Sally-Clarks-case-changed-attitudes-to-infant-death.html (accessed 5 August 2022).

[87] O Bowcott, 'Mother loses murder appeal' *The Guardian* (London, 4 May 2005) at www.theguardian.com/uk/2005/may/04/ukcrime.children (accessed 5 August 2022).

[88] *R v Kai-Whitewind (Chahaòh Niyol)* [2005] EWCA Crim 1092, [2005] 2 Cr App R 31, [2006] Crim LR 348.

[89] 'Jury to decide dispute between experts' *The Times* (London, 11 May 2005) 57.

[90] ibid.

[91] ibid.

[92] Law Commission, *Murder, Manslaughter and Infanticide* (Law Com No 304, 2006).

[93] ibid.

[94] M Frith, 'Scrap outdated infanticide law, say judges' *The Independent* (London, 4 May 2005) at www.independent.co.uk/news/uk/crime/scrap-outdated-infanticide-law-say-judges-5345949.html (accessed 9 August 2022).

This consensus and the significant sympathy shown to the accused have remained key features of newspaper articles about infanticide published in England and Wales since 2006. This can even be the case where extreme violence was used towards the baby, a situation that can lead to awkward and contradictory shifts in tone and overall message within the confines of a single article as the reportage veers between gruesome and distressing details on the one hand, and depictions of the guilty mother as vulnerable, tragic and mentally unwell on the other. The press coverage of the case of 24-year-old care worker Babita Rai in Hampshire, which was reported across both national and local newspapers, is a particularly striking example of this paradox.[95] Rai had been six months pregnant when she arrived in the UK in 2017 from Nepal, a migrant with poor English and desperate to conceal her condition from her family she was joining in England, who held traditional Nepalese views stigmatising sex and motherhood outside marriage.[96] Giving birth in a local park in Aldershot at night in May 2017, Rai inflicted catastrophic head injuries on the baby almost immediately after giving birth, and hid the body in the undergrowth where it was discovered some days later: despite an extensive police investigation to try and locate the child's mother, she was not identified and arrested until March 2020.[97] Nonetheless, Mr Justice Johnson argued, when passing judgment, that 'the mitigation in this case, as in many cases of its type, is overwhelming', sentencing her to a two-year community order, including 30 days of rehabilitation activity with mental-health professionals.[98] In addition to the suggestion that Rai was suffering from Post-Traumatic Stress Disorder (PTSD), reportage also touched on the implications of the global COVID-19 pandemic for the progress of the case, suggesting that the delay this may have caused and the additional COVID restrictions imposed on prisoners, especially combined with factors such as Rai's limited English proficiency and migrant status, had rendered her experience of time spent on remand an especially gruelling ordeal.[99] Despite

[95] M Robinson, 'Nepalese care worker, 24, who gave birth to secret baby girl in darkness behind a Hampshire park tree, killed her by crushing her skull and abandoned the body is spared jail after court heard she felt "intolerable' shame at being an unwed mother' *Daily Mail* (London, 26 July 2021) at www.dailymail.co.uk/news/article-9826239/Care-worker-mother-24-spared-jail-killing-newborn-crushing-skull.html (accessed 8 August 2022).

[96] PR Regmi, PP Simkhada and ER van Teijlingen, '"Boys Remain Prestigious, Girls Become Prostitutes": Socio-Cultural Context of Relationships and Sex among Young People in Nepal' (2010) 2 *Global Journal of Health Science* 60.

[97] K-A Mills, 'Young mum accused of murdering newborn daughter after hiding pregnancy from colleagues' *Daily Mirror* (London, 5 May 2021) at www.mirror.co.uk/news/uk-news/young-mum-murdered-newborn-daughter-24042959 (accessed 8 August 2022).

[98] C Hayhurst, 'Woman handed community order for infanticide of newborn daughter' *Evening Standard* (London, 26 July 2021) at www.standard.co.uk/news/uk/hampshire-aldershot-none-winchester-crown-court-hampshire-police-b947683.html (accessed 30 July 2021).

[99] E Menendez, 'Woman who killed secret baby after giving birth in park spared jail' *Metro* (London, 26 July 2021) at https://metro.co.uk/2021/07/26/woman-who-killed-secret-baby-after-giving-birth-in-park-spared-jail-14990537/ (accessed 30 July 2021). Research suggests this is indeed liable to have been experienced by prisoners as a harsher environment than 'normal' prison: see M Maycock, '"Covid-19 has caused a dramatic change to prison life". Analysing the impacts of the Covid-19 pandemic on the pains of imprisonment in the Scottish Prison Estate' (2022) 62 *The British Journal of Criminology* 218.

the obvious potential for articles to focus negatively on the violence of the crime or implicit and explicitly racist depictions of Rai's status as a migrant woman of colour (features of the case that might always have been targeted but have arguably become even more likely in the British media since 2016, in the wake of often explicitly anti-migrant sentiments galvanised by the controversial vote to leave the European Union), newspaper discussions of her case followed standard, primarily sympathetic, patterns regarding infanticide.[100]

The descriptions of Rai's case in the press, and the response to it by judge and jury, sit in stark contrast to recent instances where the plea of infanticide has been rejected and the woman on trial has instead been convicted of murder. In 2017, Rachel Tunstill secretly gave birth at her flat in Burnley and stabbed her newborn daughter to death, claiming to her partner and medics that she had suffered a miscarriage. The baby's body was later discovered wrapped in a bag and hidden in a bin.[101] Convicted of murder and sentenced to 20 years' imprisonment, the Court of Appeal ruled that Tunstill was entitled to a retrial, as the judge had refused to allow the jury to consider whether she was entitled to the partial defence of infanticide.[102] At the subsequent retrial in 2019, however, the jury at Liverpool Crown Court rejected this, and she was again convicted of murder. Despite the acknowledgement that she had been 'suffering from some degree of mental disorder' at the time of the crime, both the press and the judge's summing up emphasised her apparent lack of remorse.[103]

IV. Conclusions

In July 2022, it was reported that 25-year-old Lauren St George had been convicted of infanticide at the Old Bailey.[104] Her 10-day-old daughter, Lily-Mai, born

[100] E Połońska-Kimunguyi, 'Echoes of Empire: racism and historical amnesia in the British media coverage of migration' (2022) 9 *Humanities and Social Science Communications* at https://doi.org/10.1057/s41599-021-01020-4 (accessed 10 August 2022).

[101] Tanveer Mann, 'Mother, 26, stabbed newborn to death because she thought she would harm her career' *Metro* (London, 8 June 2017) at https://metro.co.uk/2017/06/08/mother-26-stabbed-newborn-to-death-because-she-thought-she-would-harm-her-career-6694738/ (accessed 3 January 2023).

[102] *R v Tunstill* [2018] EWCA Crim 1696, [2018] 2 Cr App R 31.

[103] L Roughley, 'Mum who stabbed newborn baby girl to death with scissors is jailed for life – for the second time' *Manchester Evening News* (Manchester, 6 February 2019) at https://www.manchestereveningnews.co.uk/news/greater-manchester-news/rachel-tunstill-retrial-liverpool-burnley-15789927 (accessed 3 January 2023).

[104] *R v St George* (Central Criminal Court, 25 July 2022); J Beal, '"Suffering mother" convicted of killing her baby' *The Times* (London, 26 July 2022) 12; K Terry, 'Mother, 25, found guilty of shaking her 10-week-old baby girl to death after she was discharged from hospital against doctors' advice will not be sent to prison so she can "rebuild her life"' *Daily Mail* (London, 25 July 2022) at www.dailymail.co.uk/news/article-11046629/Mother-guilty-death-baby-daughter-shaking-10-week-old-violent-attack.html (accessed 7 August 2022); 'Depressed mum spared jail for killing daughter' *Western Mail* (Cardiff, 26 July 2022) 10; J Beal, 'Baby-killer mother spared jail' *The Times* (London, 10 September 2022), 37.

prematurely, had died in 2018 from multiple injuries caused after being released to the care of her parents. Both hospital staff and social services had raised safeguarding concerns about the baby's welfare, and shortly before her death a legal gateway meeting had been requested to review next steps. The jury deliberated for several hours before finding St George guilty of infanticide.[105] In his summing up, Mr Justice Spencer thanked the jury for the sensitive way in which they had dealt with such a distressing case. He told S George that he believed she had 'suffered and continued to suffer', and that this would be taken into account when later passing sentence, which would be a suspended one.[106] Spencer was also careful to note that verdicts of infanticide traditionally emphasised sympathy for tragic circumstances over the prospect of punishment.[107]

Comparing newspaper articles on infanticide written in England and Wales in the early 1920s with those written in the 2020s, even given the significant changes over time to the medium in format and style (not the least of which being the jump from print to smartphone screen accessibility), and accounting for the respective genre conventions of tabloid and broadsheet, the similarity in tone and often content is nonetheless overt and striking. Despite the very substantial differences between these two periods, a century apart – not least the dramatic shifts in the cultural, legal, economic, social, medical and political contexts – the small number of women charged with infanticide in England and Wales in the early twenty-first century are described in extremely (perhaps even disturbingly?) similar ways to defendants from preceding decades.[108] While debates have continued at periodic intervals since the Second World War over whether the Infanticide Act 1938 should be retained or not, especially in light of the fact that its quasi-medical language was already increasingly out of step with scientific understanding in the inter-war years, women accused of killing their infants are usually still seen by the press, the criminal justice system and the general public as a 'special' type of criminal. Although some individual cases of infant homicide stand out for their representation in the media as being monstrous rather than deserving of sympathy, these remain very much an exception rather than the general rule, and are usually those cases in which the charge of infanticide has been rejected by the jury and the mother has instead been convicted of murder. Instead, just as was the case in the 1920s, articles about infanticide in the early twenty-first century tend to emphasise the previous good character of the mother and her vulnerability (whether in terms of health, marginalised status or other factors), and suggest that

[105] The presiding judge directed the jury to dismiss charges of murder and manslaughter against her partner, 25-year-old Darren Hurrell, arguing there was no evidence of his involvement in Lily-Mai's death.

[106] *R v St George* (n 104). Mr Justice Spencer as quoted in *The Times* (London, 26 July 2022) 12.

[107] ibid.

[108] As Brennan and Milne note in ch 1 of this volume, the use of infanticide as a charge seems to be reducing in England and Wales.

she was suffering from serious mental illness at the time she committed the crime, regardless of whether or not this might fit with accepted medical or legal definitions for mental disturbance.

While the term 'respectability' has fallen out of favour since the 1970s, the fundamental attributes and accompanying social judgements that this description formerly encompassed, and the strong likelihood that women in England and Wales charged with or found guilty of infanticide will still be interpreted by the press, the courts and the general public as fitting positively into this framework, have not gone away. In cases where there does not seem to have been any obvious sign of violence directed towards the baby, both historical and contemporary newspaper articles were and are likely to note the difficulty of determining the cause of death in infants, and question whether the death might be from natural causes or an accident rather than resulting from the action (or inaction) of the mother. Arguably, in the wake of the quashing of Angela Cannings' and Sally Clark's convictions, lingering public awareness of these as miscarriages of justice and the resulting furore over contested medical expertise, concerns about the possibility of physicians 'getting it wrong' have perhaps become even *more* likely to be raised since 2002 than they were in previous decades, as they are now an integral part of the public perception of these cases rather than confined to debates between lawyers and physicians.

The overwhelming impression from reviewing such press reportage over a century is of a national ongoing consensus in England and Wales about the 'special' nature of infanticide; the context and experiences of the 'typical' woman charged with the crime; and demonstrates broad agreement with a core cultural script about how it should best be dealt with that emphasises mental-health interventions. Such newspaper articles and their influence on public understandings of infanticide were, and are, double-edged, inherently riven with contradictory ideas. Some of these aspects are potentially beneficial for the women written about, but others rely on conformity with 'good girl' narratives, implicit or sometimes explicit sexism and a troubling biological essentialism, as well as denial of agency. For this reason, it is crucial to remain alert to the enduring power and legacy of earlier twentieth-century representations when reading about contemporary infanticide cases. As the cultural critics Rosalind Gill and Katie Toms have powerfully concluded in their study of the visibility of feminism in the British media, 'There may be a "feminist zeitgeist" yet the tenacity of anti-feminist ideas remains striking, even in this new moment, and postfeminism, sexism and misogyny are also trending now'.[109]

[109] R Gill and K Toms, 'Trending Now: Feminism, Postfeminism, Sexism and Misogyny' in C Carter, L Steiner and S Allan (eds) *Journalism, Gender and Power* (Routledge, 2019) 112.

References

Archival Sources

Media Archive for Central England, 'Central News East: 18.09.1985: Liberal Party Conference – Homeless Version 2'
The National Archives (TNA) ASSI 11/43
TNA ASSI 12/115
TNA ASSI 12/119
TNA ASSI 13/51
TNA ASSI 13/52
TNA CRIM 1/414
TNA CRIM 1/850
TNA DPP 2/357
TNA HO 144/1749/419784
TNA MEPO 3/1630

Books

Ballinger, A, *Dead Woman Walking: Executed Women in England and Wales, 1900–55* (Ashgate 2000).
Bingham, A, *Family Newspapers?: Sex, Private Life, and the British Popular Press 1918–1978* (Oxford University Press 2009).
Bingham, A and Conboy, M, *Tabloid Century: The Popular Press in Britain, 1896 to the Present* (Peter Lang 2015).
Bland, L, *Modern Women on Trial: Sexual Transgression in the Age of the Flapper* (Manchester University Press 2013).
Davies, A, *City of Gangs: Glasgow and the Rise of the British Gangster* (London 2013).
Dixon, R, *Infanticide: Expert Evidence and Testimony in Child Murder Cases, 1688–1955* (Routledge 2022).
Farrell, E, *'A most diabolical deed': Infanticide and Irish society, 1850–1900* (Manchester University Press 2013).
Flanders, J, *The Invention of Murder: How the Victorians revelled in death and detection and created modern crime* (HarperPress 2011).
Goc, N, *Women, Infanticide and the Press, 1822–1922: News narratives in England and Australia* (Ashgate 2013).
Gregory, J, *Mercy and British Culture, 1760–1960* (Bloomsbury 2021).
Kilday, AM, *A History of Infanticide in Britain, c 1600 to the Present* (Palgrave Macmillan 2013).
King, L, *Family Men: Fatherhood and Masculinity in Britain, 1914–1960* (Oxford University Press 2015).
Kramer, KJ, *Unwilling Mothers, Unwanted Babies: Infanticide in Canada* (UBC Press 2005).
Loughnan, A, *Manifest Madness: Mental Incapacity in Criminal Law* (Oxford University Press 2012).

——, *Self, Others and the State: Relations of Criminal Responsibility* (Cambridge University Press 2020).

Marland, H, *Dangerous Motherhood: Insanity and Childbirth in Victorian Britain* (Palgrave Macmillan 2004).

Melman, B, *Women and the Popular Imagination in the Twenties* (Macmillan 1988).

Milne, E, *Criminal Justice Responses to Maternal Filicide: Judging the Failed Mother* (Emerald Publishing Limited 2021).

Oram, A, *Her Husband was a Woman! Women's Gender-Crossing in Modern British Popular Culture* (Routledge 2007).

Pedley, AC, *Mothers, Criminal Insanity and the Asylum in Victorian England: Cure, Redemption and Rehabilitation* (Bloomsbury 2023).

Rentoul, E and Smith, H, *Glaister's Medical Jurisprudence and Toxicology*, 13th edn (Churchill Livingstone 1973).

Rowbotham, J, Stevenson, K and Pegg, S, *Crime News in Modern Britain: Press Reporting and Responsibility, 1820–2010* (Basingstoke 2013).

Rusterholz, C, *Women's Medicine: Sex, family planning and British female doctors in transnational perspective, 1920–70* (Manchester University Press 2020).

Seal, L, *Women, Murder and Femininity: Gender Representations of Women Who Kill* (Palgrave Macmillan 2010).

——, *Capital Punishment in Twentieth-Century Britain: Audience, Justice, Memory* (Routledge 2014).

Smith, SA, *'Out of Sight, out of Mind': Infanticide, Baby Farming and Abortion in South and West Wales, 1870–1922* (Rowanvale Books Ltd 2021).

Wildman, C, *Urban Redevelopment and Modernity in Liverpool and Manchester, 1918–1939* (Bloomsbury 2016).

Chapters in Edited Volumes

Arnot, ML, 'Understanding Women Committing Newborn Child Murder in Victorian England' in D'Cruze, S (ed), *Everyday Violence in Britain, 1850–1950: Gender & Class* (Longman 2000) 55.

Gill, R and Toms, K, 'Trending Now: Feminism, Postfeminism, Sexism and Misogyny' in Carter, C, Steiner, L and Allan, S (eds), *Journalism, Gender and Power* (Routledge, 2019) 112.

Grey, DJR, '"The Agony of Despair": Pain and the Cultural Script of Infanticide in England and Wales, 1860–1960' in Boddice, R (ed), *Pain and Emotion in Modern History* (Palgrave Macmillan 2014) 204.

——, 'Parenting, Infanticide, and the State in England and Wales, 1870–1950' in Barron, H and Siebrecht, C (eds), *Parenting and the State in Britain and Europe, 1870–1950: Raising the Nation* (Palgrave Macmillan 2017) 41.

Redmond, J, 'In the family way and away from the family: examining the evidence in Irish unmarried mothers in Britain, 1920s–40s' in Farrell, E (ed), *'She said she was in the family way': Pregnancy and infancy in the Irish past* (Institute of Historical Research 2012) 163.

Ward, T, 'Legislating for Human Nature: Legal Responses to Infanticide, 1860–1938' in Jackson, M (ed), *Infanticide: Historical Perspectives on Child Murder and Concealment, 1550–2000* (Ashgate 2002) 249.

Wheelwright, J, '"Nothing in Between": Modern Cases of Infanticide' in Jackson, M (ed), *Infanticide: Historical Perspectives on Child Murder and Concealment, 1550–2000* (Ashgate 2002) 271.

Journal Articles

Bates, V, 'Three is Murder: The Rise and Fall of Munchausen Syndrome by Proxy Experts' (2019) 104 *History* 189.

Bluglass, R, 'Infanticide' (1978) 2 *Bulletin of the Royal College of Psychiatrists* 139.

Brennan, KM, '"Traditions of English Liberal Thought": A History of the Enactment of an Infanticide Law in Ireland' (2013) 50 *Irish Jurist* 100.

Brennan, K, 'Social Norms and the Law in Responding to Infanticide' (2018) 38 *Legal Studies* 480.

Brennan, KM, 'Murderous Mothers & Gentle Judges: Paternalism, Patriarchy, and Infanticide' (2018) 30 *Yale Journal of Law and Feminism* 140.

Grey, DJR, 'Women's Policy Networks and the Infanticide Act 1922' (2010) 21 *Twentieth Century British History* 441.

——, '"Agonised Weeping": Representing Femininity, Emotion and Infanticide in Edwardian Newspapers' (2015) 21 *Media History* 468.

Połońska-Kimunguyi, E, 'Echoes of Empire: Racism and Historical Amnesia in the British Media Coverage of Migration' (2022) 9 *Humanities and Social Science Communications* at doi.org/10.1057/s41599-021-01020-4 (accessed 10 August 2022).

Regmi, PR, Simkhada, PP and van Teijlingen, ER, '"Boys Remain Prestigious, Girls Become Prostitutes": Socio-Cultural Context of Relationships and Sex among Young People in Nepal' (2010) 2 *Global Journal of Health Science* 60.

Sheldon, S, 'British Abortion Law: Speaking from the Past to Govern the Future' (2016) 79 *MLR* 283.

Spinelli, M, 'Infanticide and American Criminal Justice (1980–2018)' (2018) 22 *Archives of Women's Mental Health* 173.

Newspaper Articles

'A Case for Mercy' *Daily News* (London, 14 October 1927) 10.

Beal, J, '"Suffering mother" convicted of killing her baby' *The Times* (London, 26 July 2022) 12.

—— 'Baby-killer mother spared jail', *The Times* (London, 10 September 2022) 37.

Bone, J, 'US judge rebuked for attack on Britain' *The Times* (London, 12 April 1997) 19.

Bowcott, O, 'Mother loses murder appeal' *The Guardian* (London, 4 May 2005) at www.theguardian.com/uk/2005/may/04/ukcrime.children (accessed 5 August 2022).

'Court of Criminal Appeal' *The Times* (London, 8 November 1927) 5.

Davies, C, 'I just knew I had to bring my dead baby back home' *Daily Telegraph* (London, 19 August 1997) 11.

'Death-Sentence Scene' *Daily Telegraph* (London, 10 March 1909) 14.

'Death Sentence on Waitress' *The People* (London, 16 October 1927) 4.

'Depressed mum spared jail for killing daughter' *Western Mail* (Cardiff, 26 July 2022) 10.

'"Devoted Mother" Hears First Mercy Verdict' *Daily Mirror* (London, 22 July 1936) 17.

Edwards, P, 'Infanticide' *The Guardian* (London, 26 February 1965) 10.
Evening News (London, 19 March 1929).
Frith, M, 'Scrap outdated infanticide law, say judges' *The Independent* (London, 4 May 2005) at www.independent.co.uk/news/uk/crime/scrap-outdated-infanticide-law-say-judges-5345949.html (accessed 9 August 2022).
'Girl Mother's Ordeal' *Daily Mail* (London, 12 March 1909) 8.
'Girl put on probation' *Lynn Advertiser* (Norfolk, 16 January 1973) 1.
Hardy, F and Gordon, G, 'The Torturing of Caroline Beale' *Daily Mail* (London, 19 May 1995).
Hayhurst, C, 'Woman handed community order for infanticide of newborn daughter' *Evening Standard* (London, 26 July 2021) at www.standard.co.uk/news/uk/hampshire-aldershot-none-winchester-crown-court-hampshire-police-b947683.html (accessed 30 July 2021).
'Humaner [*sic*] Law' *Pall Mall Gazette* (London, 31 October 1922) 12.
'Infanticide' *The Times* (London, 22 July 1936) 13.
'Infanticide Trial Sequel' *Daily Mail* (London, 19 March 1929) 7.
Jardine, C, 'Has Sally Clark's case changed attitudes to infant death?' *The Telegraph* (London, 11 March 2008) at www.telegraph.co.uk/news/uknews/1581407/Has-Sally-Clarks-case-changed-attitudes-to-infant-death.html (accessed 5 August 2022).
'Judge on charges of infanticide' *The Times* (London, 30 October 1929) 5.
'Jury to decide dispute between experts' *The Times* (London, 11 May 2005) 57.
Laurence, C, 'So just why did it take them so long?' *Daily Telegraph* (London, 8 March 1996) 13.
'Man threw newborn into river' *The Times* (London, 15 November 1989) 4.
Mann, T, 'Mother, 26, stabbed newborn to death because she thought she would harm her career' *Metro* (London, 8 June 2017) at https://metro.co.uk/2017/06/08/mother-26-stabbed-newborn-to-death-because-she-thought-she-would-harm-her-career-6694738/ (accessed 3 January 2023).
Maycock, M, '"Covid-19 has caused a dramatic change to prison life". Analysing the impacts of the Covid-19 pandemic on the pains of imprisonment in the Scottish Prison Estate' (2022) 62 *The British Journal of Criminology* 218.
Mead, R, 'The Imaginary Infant' *New York Magazine* (New York, 18 December 1995) 36.
Menendez, E, 'Woman who killed secret baby after giving birth in park spared jail' *Metro* (London, 26 July 2021) at https://metro.co.uk/2021/07/26/woman-who-killed-secret-baby-after-giving-birth-in-park-spared-jail-14990537/ (accessed 30 July 2021).
Mills, KA, 'Young mum accused of murdering newborn daughter after hiding pregnancy from colleagues' *Daily Mirror* (London, 5 May 2021) at www.mirror.co.uk/news/uk-news/young-mum-murdered-newborn-daughter-24042959 (accessed 8 August 2022).
'Mother who killed her baby son "needs help"' *Western Mail* (Cardiff, 4 November 1959) 10.
'Murder Trial Pathos' *Daily Mail* (London, 10 March 1909) 4.
'New Infanticide Act' *The Times* (London, 31 October 1922) 9.
'New Verdict in Mother's Trial for Murder' *Daily Telegraph* (London, 22 July 1936) 9.
'Not Responsible in Law', *Illustrated Police News* (London, 30 July 1936) 6.
Revill, J and Hinscliff, G, 'Call for an end to cot death court anguish: As Trupti Patel is cleared of killing her babies, experts urge overhaul of way bereaved mothers are treated' *The Guardian* (London, 15 June 2003) 8.
Roberts, Y, 'The case for the American prosecution' *Sunday Telegraph* (London, 10 March 1996) 5.

Robinson, M, 'Nepalese care worker, 24, who gave birth to secret baby girl in darkness behind a Hampshire park tree, killed her by crushing her skull and abandoned the body is spared jail after court heard she felt "intolerable" shame at being an unwed mother' *Daily Mail* (London, 26 July 2021) at https://www.dailymail.co.uk/news/article-9826239/Care-worker-mother-24-spared-jail-killing-newborn-crushing-skull.html (accessed 8 August 2022).
Roughley, L, 'Mum who stabbed newborn baby girl to death with scissors is jailed for life – for the second time' *Manchester Evening News* (Manchester, 6 February 2019) at www.manchestereveningnews.co.uk/news/greater-manchester-news/rachel-tunstill-retrial-liverpool-burnley-15789927 (accessed 3 January 2023).
Slapper, G, 'Mothers and madness' *The Times* (London, 19 March 1996) 33.
——, 'Mothers, madness and medieval justice' *The Times* (London, 4 February 2003) 3 [s 2].
'Strangled Baby. Sentence of Death on Waitress' *News of the World* (London, 16 October 1927) 5.
'Spared Hearing Verdict of Murder' *Daily Herald* (London, 22 July 1936) 9.
'Standing Alone in Her Agony' *Leicester Mercury* (Leicester, 19 July 1921) 5.
'Tattershall Murder Charge' *Skegness Standard* (Skegness, 4 October 1922) 6.
'Tattershall Sensation' *Skegness Standard* (Skegness, 27 September 1922) 8.
'Tattershall Murder Charge' *Lincolnshire Standard and Boston Guardian* (Lincoln, 30 September 1922) 12.
Terry, K, 'Mother, 25, found guilty of shaking her 10-week-old baby girl to death after she was discharged from hospital against doctors' advice will not be sent to prison so she can "rebuild her life"' *Daily Mail* (London, 25 July 2022) at www.dailymail.co.uk/news/article-11046629/Mother-guilty-death-baby-daughter-shaking-10-week-old-violent-attack.html (accessed 7 August 2022).
'The Cleaver Case' *Daily Mail* (London, 15 March 1909) 10.
'The Infanticide Act' *The Times* (London, 14 January 1925) 16.
'Tragedy of a Mother' *Daily Herald* (London, 8 November 1927) 7.
'What IS A "Newly Born" Child?' *The Times* (London, 22 November 1927) 5.
Wheelwright, J, 'A moment as mother' *The Guardian* (London, 13 May 1995) A13 and 16.

Parliamentary Papers

Home Office, *Report of the Royal Commission on Capital Punishment* (Cmd 8932, 1953).

Reports

Law Commission, *Murder, Manslaughter and Infanticide* (Law Com No 304, 2006).

Theses

Butler, J, 'Representations of Paternal Child Killers in the English National Press, 1900 to 1939' (PhD thesis, University of Liverpool 2018).

Crook, S, 'The Uses of Maternal Distress in British Society, c 1948–1979' (PhD thesis, Queen Mary University of London 2017).
Grey, DJR, 'Discourses of Infanticide in England, 1880–1922' (PhD thesis, Roehampton University 2008).
Siddons, T, 'Suspected New-born Child Murder and Concealment of Pregnancy in Scotland, c 1812–c 1930' (PhD thesis, University of Edinburgh 2014).
Smalley, A, 'Representations of Crime, Justice, and Punishment in the Popular Press: A Study of the *Illustrated Police News*, 1864–1938' (PhD thesis, Open University 2017).
Wilson, CBA, 'Mad, Sad, or Bad?: Newspaper and Judicial Representations of Men who Killed Children in Victorian England, 1860–1900' (PhD thesis, University of Essex 2012).

5

Myths and Moral Agency: A Principled Approach to Infanticide Law

HELEN HOWARD

Sometimes described as a 'type of speech'[1] and often understood to be an ancient story, a myth tends to be grounded in history and acts as an uncontested assumption, 'a commonly believed but false idea'.[2] Since the statutory offence/defence of infanticide was introduced in 1922 to circumvent the death penalty, many false ideas have arisen. Some of these myths are pertinent to the culpability of the defendant, and will be more closely examined in this chapter. They include: a woman might be perceived as less blameworthy if she kills her infant[3] under 12 months than if she kills an older child; women who kill their infants do so because of an imbalance of mind due to the effects of childbirth or lactation; and women who kill their infants while suffering from an imbalance of the mind still bear some criminal responsibility, albeit a reduced amount. These myths are examined in the context of principles of culpability, highlighting the need for legal theory to underpin any principled development of the law.

Throughout this chapter, it is asserted that theory, and the search for legal principles, should underpin any reform of the law so that it can develop in a principled manner. The Law Commission shares the view that theoretical principles relating to responsibility should underpin any principled development of the law,[4] stating that the 'concept of responsibility is a philosophical question'[5] and, accordingly, concepts of culpability should 'inform our proposals for reform'.[6] These concepts are necessary in order to determine when an individual should be held blameworthy and, consequently, criminally responsible.

[1] R Barthes, *Mythologies*, tr A Lavers (Farrar, Straus & Giroux 1972) 108.
[2] https://dictionary.cambridge.org/dictionary/english/myth (accessed on 24/2/22).
[3] For the purpose of this chapter, a child under 12 months will be termed an 'infant'.
[4] Law Commission, *Criminal Liability: Insanity and Automatism: A Discussion Paper* (23 July 2013).
[5] ibid A.4.
[6] ibid.

The development of legal theory in the nineteenth century began 'a search for legal concepts, legal rules and legal principles that the whole of mankind would share'.[7] While Lacey establishes that 'only by the 1950s has the question of individual, let alone subjective, responsibility *as a question of agency and of individual fairness* become the primary focus for criminal law commentaries',[8] it is apparent that, even during the late nineteenth century, the concept of 'manifest criminality'[9] was being replaced by a belief that 'crime was – at least in some cases – the product of either social environment or physical pathology'[10] and, thus, experienced subjectively. Consequently, 'the legitimacy of harsh, uniform punishments became more and more questionable'.[11]

The image of an unmarried mother at the turn of the twentieth century epitomises the types of defendant perceived 'as victims of mental incapacity or social deprivation and hence as proper objects not so much of punishment as of medical or welfare-oriented intervention'.[12] The social circumstances that, at the turn of the twentieth century, might have driven a pregnant single woman to kill her infant, present her as needing protection and pity rather than punishment. Thus, when infanticide legislation was introduced in 1922, it was 'chiefly a product of social factors rather than the result of a morbid personality',[13] reflecting a social, humanitarian and pragmatic[14] need to protect the impoverished 'fallen woman'[15] from the death penalty. The two overwhelming reasons for recognising the need to provide such a defence stemmed from the social stigma of having a child outside of marriage, compounded by the severe poverty that might ensue.[16] Amidst this backdrop of pity and protection, it is unsurprising that the offence/defence of infanticide was introduced.

Equally conceivable, given the pragmatic and 'compassionate'[17] reasons for the introduction of the offence/defence of infanticide, is the lack of any principled underpinning surrounding the introduction of the Infanticide Act 1922. An offence/defence that demands lenience due to 'social norms'[18] while allowing for

[7] M Van Hoecke, *Methodologies of Legal Research: Which Kind of Method for What Kind of Discipline?* (Bloomsbury Publishing 2013) 2.

[8] N Lacey, 'In Search of the Responsible Subject: History, Philosophy and Social Sciences in Criminal Law Theory' (2001) 64(3) *MLR* 350, 360.

[9] G Fletcher, *Rethinking Criminal Law* (Little, Brown 1978) 116. Fletcher's pattern of manifest criminality states that criminal behaviour will be objectively recognisable.

[10] Lacey (n 8) 365.

[11] ibid.

[12] ibid.

[13] T Ward, 'The Sad Subject of Infanticide: Law, Medicine and Child Murder 1860–1938' (1999) 8 *Social and Legal Studies* 163, 166.

[14] K Brennan, '"A Fine Mixture of Pity and Justice": The Criminal Justice Response to Infanticide in Ireland, 1922–1949' (2013) 31 *Law and History Review* 793, 800.

[15] Ward (n 13) 165.

[16] Brennan (n 14) 799.

[17] K Brennan, 'Social Norms and the Law in Responding to Infanticide' (2018) 38(3) *Legal Studies* 480, 496.

[18] ibid.

inculpation, as well as exculpation, on pseudo-medicalised grounds is a bewildering tangle of concepts that bear no relationship to the reality of the tragic circumstances under which women kill their infants. As with all defences, an examination of the proper attribution of criminal responsibility, and the circumstances under which moral agency is established, should be paramount prior to any reform. Realistically, the offence/defence of infanticide falls far below the list of priorities for legal reform, insanity and unfitness to plead requiring more urgent attention, rendering this theoretical discussion largely hypothetical but still relevant. Despite being rarely used in the twenty-first century,[19] the offence of infanticide is still charged and the defence is still employed by a small number of female defendants.[20] Advocates for the defence[21] assert that it is still needed, but the suggestion in this chapter will be that it is no longer relevant in its current form. The close association between 'illegitimacy, concealment and murder'[22] is no longer apposite, nor are the '[i]ntolerant attitudes toward female sexual misconduct'.[23] Nevertheless, given that the defence continues to be used in the courts, theoretical discussions relating to the proper attribution of blame are still crucial to the direction in which it develops.

In addressing the defendant's level of culpability, two competing theories of moral agency will be examined. These theories suggest that culpability is established either where the defendant has the capacity to choose and a fair opportunity to conform her conduct to the law,[24] or where her conduct demonstrates bad character.[25] A woman who kills her infant might 'lack the capacity to choose due to the "effects of childbirth" and, consequently, ought not to be viewed as a moral agent'.[26] Alternatively, her conduct might not be viewed as attributable to bad character[27] and, for this reason, she should not be seen as a moral agent. Where moral agency is lacking, a full defence should be applied. In the absence of moral agency, a partial defence, such as that provided by the defence of infanticide, is inappropriate. A partial defence should arise only where the woman is a moral agent, and therefore criminally responsible, but where there are factors that reduce her level of culpability.[28]

The competing theories of culpability are examined in section I of this chapter in the context of a mother who kills her infant. Subsequently, some of the surrounding myths that accompany the partial *defence* of infanticide will be

[19] E Milne, *Criminal Justice Responses to Maternal Filicide: Judging the Failed Mother* (Emerald Publishing Limited 2021) 911.

[20] ibid.

[21] See, eg, research undertaken by Karen Brennan, Emma Milne and Tony Ward.

[22] K Brennan, '"Traditions of English liberal thought": a history of the enactment of an infanticide law in Ireland' (2013) 50 *Irish Jurist* 100, 106.

[23] Brennan (n 14) 809.

[24] HLA Hart, *Punishment and Responsibility* (Oxford University Press 1968) 160, 181.

[25] MD Bayles, 'Hume on Blame and Excuse' (1976) 2 *Hume Studies* 17.

[26] H Howard, 'The offence/defence of infanticide: A view from two perspectives' (2018) 82 *Journal of Criminal Law* 470, 479.

[27] Law Commission (n 4) A.25.

[28] Howard (n 26) 478.

considered. Although problematic to separate, for the purpose of this chapter, infanticide is described as a *defence*; its inculpatory function is only considered tangentially where it cannot be kept distinct. In section II, is asserted that applying a distinction in culpability is inappropriate when a woman kills her infant as well as her older children in the same circumstances, although admittedly such circumstances are rare.[29] Further, in section III, that in depriving a woman of moral agency, or in seeking to reduce the level of her culpability, 'a link should be required to a recognised medical condition'.[30] Finally, in section IV the inappropriate attribution of partial responsibility is addressed and, within this, the need to recognise in certain circumstances that a mother who kills her infant ought to bear no criminal responsibility whatsoever.

I. The Proper Attribution of Criminal Responsibility

It is usual to expect serious *mala in se* crimes, including infanticide, to be linked with moral blame.[31] As one of the most 'disquieting' offences,[32] when we find a woman guilty of infanticide, or any other *mala in se* offence, we are expressing a moral criticism.[33] Thus, holding her criminally responsible for this offence should only be on the basis of proven culpability meriting moral blame and punishment. According to both leading theories of culpability, she should not be blamed for carrying out the killing if, at the time of the offence, she was not morally responsible. As is discussed below, in some circumstances, a successfully pleaded defence of infanticide to a charge of murder should negate a woman's criminal responsibility entirely, undermining any moral judgement to be made against her.

Lacey states 'At the start of the twenty-first century, it is generally agreed among theorists of criminal responsibility in England (as indeed in other common law systems) that responsibility for crime is founded in a certain set of capacities.'[34] These capacities lead to the attribution of criminal responsibility and recognition of the defendant as a moral agent in one of two ways. The first, choice/capacity theory, requires the defendant to make a choice, while possessing an intellectual

[29] RD Mackay, 'Infanticide and Diminished Responsibility Manslaughter: An Empirical Study' in Law Commission, *Murder, Manslaughter and Infanticide* (Law Com No 304, 2006) Appendix D, D.44: eldest child also suffered neck injuries but survived; D.125: four children were killed, with one under 12 months. Infanticide was considered in respect of the youngest but diminished responsibility was applied for all.

[30] Howard (n 26) 479.

[31] P Arenella, 'Convicting the Morally Blameless: Reassessing the Relationship Between Legal and Moral Accountability' (1992) 39 *UCLA Law Review* 1511, 1513.

[32] RS Ogle and D Maier-Katkin, 'A Rationale for Infanticide Laws' (1993) *Criminal Law Review* 903, 903.

[33] SH Kadish, *Blame and Punishment* (MacMillan Publishing, 1987) 87.

[34] N Lacey, 'Responsibility and Modernity in Criminal Law' (2001) 9 *Journal of Political Philosophy* 249, 255. Referred to by the Law Commission (n 4) A.8: '[T]here is a consensus amongst writers on the subject that lack of capacity of some kind justifies treating some people as non-responsible.'

knowledge of rules, a capacity to understand their content, in order to be a moral agent.[35] There is no additional requirement that the defendant have any sense of moral obligation towards others. The second, character theory, requires an individual to possess an understanding of the concept of morality and a sense of moral obligation as well as a knowledge of rules in order to be regarded as a moral agent.[36] Each of these will be considered in turn.

The choice/capacity theorists' claim is that the defendant's capacity to choose to act reprehensibly explains why she should be seen as blameworthy.[37] When she freely chooses to act in such a way, having the opportunity to do otherwise, then she ought to be blamed. Choice theorists are prepared to attribute blame without reference to the defendant's goals, desires, values and emotions that motivate her choice.[38] According to choice theory, a teenage mother who conceals her pregnancy, gives birth in secret and kills her infant to avoid discovery, might still have chosen to kill, regardless of how hard the choice not to kill might have been. Capacity theory, propounded by Hart, is the leading version of choice theory and asserts that, without capacity and fair opportunity, a defendant cannot make a free choice to conform her conduct to the law.[39] While Hart's capacity theory is a version of choice theory, given that it attributes criminal responsibility for the defendant's choices, some academics[40] prefer these two theories to be treated distinctly, so as not to 'dilute … the focus on actual choice'.[41] Henceforth, 'capacity theory' is the term adopted in this chapter.

Within capacity theory, a moral agent is an individual who chooses to act in a particular way, having the capacity and fair opportunity to avoid doing otherwise.[42] Setting out the reasoning for these requirements, Hart states:

> [A] primary vindication of the principle of responsibility could rest on the simple idea that unless a man has the capacity and a fair opportunity or chance to adjust his behaviour to the law its penalties ought not to be applied to him.[43]

Thus, a teenage mother who hides her pregnancy and gives birth alone might lack capacity to choose due to the physical and mental shock of giving birth, or because of dissociative amnesia brought on by concealment of the pregnancy.[44] However,

[35] Hart (n 24) 160.

[36] See C Crosby, 'Culpability, Kingston, and the Law Commission' (2010) 74 *Journal of Criminal Law* 434 for a detailed analysis of the competing character theory. See also Law Commission (n 4) A.33–A.38 for an exposition of a pure version choice theory (in the absence of capacity).

[37] Hart (n 24) 182.

[38] P Arenella, 'Character, Choice and Moral Agency: the relevance of character to our moral culpability judgments' in EF Paul, FD Miller and J Paul (eds), *Crime, Culpability, and Remedy* (Basil Blackwell 1990) 65.

[39] Hart (n 24) 182.

[40] J Horder, 'Criminal Culpability: The Possibility of a General Theory' (1993) 12 *Law and Philosophy* 193 at 198–99. Cited by Crosby (n 36) 437.

[41] Crosby (n 36) 437.

[42] Hart (n 24) 160.

[43] ibid 181.

[44] Milne (n 19) 20–21.

the stigma and economic desperation experienced by an unmarried mother in England and Wales in the early twentieth century are, arguably, no longer relevant to the twenty-first century;[45] more babies are now born outside of marriage or civil partnership than are born within such relationships.[46] In this respect, it is unlikely that economic desperation would provide a sufficient reason for a lack of capacity or fair opportunity to conform to the law.

The ability to develop morally is not addressed within capacity theory; a woman need only have sufficient capacity to choose her actions. Such capacity might only involve her possessing an understanding that a *mala in se* offence is legally wrong, but without a deeper understanding as to *why* it is morally wrong. For example, according to capacity theory, in order to be considered a moral agent, a mother who kills her infant must have the capacity to choose this course of action and the fair opportunity to avoid doing so. If she is experiencing post-traumatic shock, following a concealed delivery, she might not have the necessary capacity and should not be held, even partially, criminally responsible. If she retains the capacity, but kills her newborn baby, thinking that, in her opinion, he or she is no different from a foetus, according to capacity theory, she will be held responsible despite lacking a deeper moral insight. This is perhaps the most substantial criticism against capacity theory, namely, its failure to take account of characteristics that enable a person to be a moral agent. Arenella insists that only character theory is able to explain moral responsiveness[47] and that moral agency requires at least some capacity for moral insight.[48] If a capacity to appreciate the morality of her actions cannot be explained without reference to the defendant's character, in the latter example, the mother's actions must fail to demonstrate bad character traits so that she might avoid being described a moral agent and thus avoid any criminal responsibility. If she does not see a baby as being different from a foetus, her lack of moral insight, according to character theory, might mean that she should not be viewed as a moral agent. It is submitted that this explanation is inelegant and will be rejected in favour of capacity theory, however the possibility of character theory will first be considered.

Character theory focuses on acts that are 'constitutive of undesirable character traits'.[49] The Law Commission sets out a 'modern version'[50] of character theory described by Tadros:

> An agent is responsible for an action … insofar as that action reflects on the agent qua agent. In relation to action performed for a reason, [the action will only reflect

[45] 'More babies born out of wedlock or civil partnerships "for first time on record"' *The Independent* (London, 9 August 2022) at www.independent.co.uk/news/uk/office-for-national-statistics-wales-england-harry-benson-nhs-b2141556.html (accessed 2 September 2022).

[46] ibid.

[47] Arenella (n 38) 59–61.

[48] ibid.

[49] Crosby (n 36) 453.

[50] Law Commission (n 4) A.19, citing V Tadros, *Criminal Responsibility* (Oxford University Press 2005) 44.

> on the agent qua agent] insofar as the desire that motivated the action is appropriately connected to the system of values of the agent … and that value of the agent is accepted [by the agent] in the light of the agent's system of values.

The central tenet of character theory is that a defendant's character causes her to carry out blameworthy conduct. The defendant's character is the primary object for her responsibility[51] and, therefore, her culpability. This theory of blame originates in Aristotle,[52] was adopted by Hume[53] and developed by Bayles,[54] one of the most influential character theorists. In his view, it is the moral quality of the defendant's character as exemplified by her conduct for which she should be blamed. A defendant should be blamed for those of her acts that demonstrate undesirable character traits,[55] while her actions are merely evidence of her undesirable character traits.[56] Blame is not attributed to a wrongful act, rather to a wrongful actor. In focusing on punishing the actor for bad character traits, this theory allows for a moral agent to have an ability to be self-critical, and to develop morally.[57]

While character theory can explain that mental disorder does not reflect an actor's character, it 'is limited as an explanation of why mental disorder should exculpate a person'.[58] Crosby's explanation assists in this regard:

> As the mentally disordered individual is incapable of engaging in a critical discussion of his conduct or his underlying motives for acting, such a person cannot be held morally responsible or criminally liable as this is reserved only for rational agents.[59]

Consequently, a woman who kills her infant while in a state of severe depression or psychosis, ought not to be held culpable as she is incapable of 'engaging in a critical discussion' of her behaviour and reasons for acting. A woman who has concealed her pregnancy and given birth in secret might similarly lack this ability, due to the trauma of delivery or being in a state of dissociative amnesia, but this will not necessarily be the case. It would be wrong to assume that all women who give birth under such, undeniably, difficult circumstances are incapable of engaging in a discussion of their behaviour. To make this presumption is to deny moral agency to all women during traumatic deliveries.

Despite the merits of only inculpating those who are able to engage in a moral conversation, the flaws of character theory are too significant to disregard. A theory that punishes for bad character traits must be capable of defining which

[51] MS Moore, *Law and Psychiatry* (Cambridge University Press 1984) 29.

[52] Aristotle, *Nichomachean Ethics*, tr T Irwin (Hackett Publishing 1985) bk III, ch 5.

[53] Bayles (n 25) 17.

[54] ibid.

[55] MD Bayles, 'Character, Purpose, and Criminal Responsibility' (1982) 1 *Law and Philosophy* 5, 7.

[56] Moore confines the relationship between action and character to the former's being evidence of the latter. Statements about causal relations or behaviour that is in character open up the possibility of greater criticism: Moore (n 51) 47–48.

[57] SH Pillsbury, 'The Meaning of Deserved Punishment: An Essay on Choice, Character and Responsibility' (1992) 67 *Indiana Law Journal* 719, 734.

[58] Law Commission (n 4) A.25.

[59] Crosby (n 36) 454.

particular character traits should be punishable. Duff describes character traits as 'stable patterns of thought, emotion, and action'.[60] In the chaotic circumstances of a concealed pregnancy and secret delivery, a character theorist might struggle to identify such 'stable patterns of thought', in which case culpability could not be established. Clearly, only bad character traits should be punishable, but a theory that punishes these must also recognise the extent to which a woman might be unable to address these traits, as well as the extent to which her character can change over time. Thus,

> character-based theory of responsibility … assumes a fixed sense of a person's character. Even if it is accepted that a fifty-year-old does have a character settled in all relevant respects, which is disputable, it is even less certain that an eleven-year-old's character is fixed.[61]

Out-of-character behaviour further challenges the scope of character theory. If an actor of previous good character commits a *mala in se* offence, there are two possibilities. First, she should not be punished for her actions because they do not represent her bad character, in which case she should be entitled to a defence; or, second, she only appeared to be of good character and possessed previously hidden bad character traits.[62] Neither of these possibilities satisfactorily explains the attribution or removal of criminal responsibility, and this remains one of the weakest aspects of the theory.[63] A woman who kills her infant, having never previously shown any criminal tendencies,[64] might be seen as having acted out of character. In a character-based defence she could claim that her actions were the product of her condition or the circumstances in which she found herself, where her particular condition or circumstances could not be linked to her character. As repeat infanticide is rare,[65] there is an argument that a character-based defence might be appropriate. The flaw here might be that she has not previously been a mother and that her out-of-character behaviour might have occurred due to unfavourable social circumstances, failure to bond with the infant or sheer exhaustion, none of which should allow for a defence. Furthermore, all out-of-character behaviour is uncharacteristic of an individual's personality the first time it is performed, but such behaviour might still be deserving of blame.

On balance, any theory of culpability requiring an understanding of morality would result in a radical increase in exemptions from criminal liability. Many

[60] A Duff, *Criminal Attempts* (Clarendon Press, 1996) 178.

[61] Law Commission (n 4) A.23, citing J Horder, *Excusing Crime* (Oxford University Press 2004) 122–23.

[62] Crosby (n 36) 460.

[63] Law Commission (n 4) A.21.

[64] Most women who commit infanticide have no previous convictions. Rarely, a history of similar offending is uncovered. See Mackay (n 29) D.47, in which a mother killed her infant daughter, following two earlier suspicious deaths of her daughters.

[65] ibid.

people lack a deep engagement with morality and do not care about the interests of people outside of their 'circle of care'.[66] Given that capacity theory does not require that a moral agent be capable of any moral engagement, Hart's theory is the preferred approach in this chapter. His view that 'no one should be punished who could not help doing what [s]he did'[67] is endorsed. The contention here will be that a loss of capacity should be linked to a mental condition. A loss of fair opportunity seems inappropriate when considering whether a mother should receive a defence for killing her infant. In the same way that social deprivation ought not to be an exculpatory factor – since not all individuals coming from the same level of deprivation will go on to offend – the social circumstances surrounding a concealed pregnancy, in the absence of a traumatic delivery and associated mental condition, ought not to exculpate. The following sections will consider the need for capacity theory to underpin some of the myths perpetuated by the defence of infanticide.

II. Myth 1: In England and Wales, a Woman Might be Perceived as Less Blameworthy if She Kills Her Infant under 12 Months than if She Kills an Older Child

One view regarding the status of infants is that, without denying 'the humanness of the … newborn child', they have no past, are unable to speak or contribute to society and, as such, they 'cannot be considered to be the equivalent in terms of the intellectual, moral, or social and cultural value of the woman whose body they are within or have just been expelled from'.[68] This stance, made in the context of a newborn infant's being given an arguably greater value than the mother's 'ability to protect herself from harm',[69] seemingly contradicts the legal position that 'the law must stand firm recognising that its highest duty is to protect the freedom and lives of those that live under it',[70] and denies the widely accepted view that all lives are equal.[71] In this context, it might be posited that the infanticide defence in England and Wales creates a false perception that, at the very least, a newborn infant, and arguably an older infant of less than 12 months, lacks the same status as a child of one year or older.

While it is uncommon for a woman to kill a child aged over a year, in Mackay's empirical research for the Law Commission, of 35 diminished responsibility

[66] I Haji, 'On Psychopaths and Culpability' (1998) 17 *Law and Philosophy* 117, 122–25.

[67] Hart (n 24) 39.

[68] Milne (n 19) 156–57.

[69] ibid.

[70] *R v Howe* [1987] AC 417, 444, per Lord Griffiths.

[71] A Lodge, 'Domestic Abuse, Suicide and Liability for Manslaughter: in Pursuit of Justice for Victims' (2020) 84 *Journal of Criminal Law* 273, 276.

convictions of women who killed their children, 28 of the victims were over 12 months.[72] The possibility therefore exists that a mother of two who kills her infant at the same time and in the same manner as her older child, might receive a far more lenient charge of infanticide in respect of her infant while she could only be charged with murder in respect of the older one. A defence of diminished responsibility[73] in respect of the older child might reduce her conviction to voluntary manslaughter, and in sentencing a judge would have the discretion to reflect the same level of culpability in respect of both children, but this disregards the fact that differences in terms of labelling and proof are attached to identical acts. In respect of the younger child, the mother need only demonstrate that at the time of the killing 'the balance of her mind was disturbed by reason of her not having fully recovered from the effect of giving birth to the child or by reason of the effect of lactation consequent upon the birth of the child'.[74] By contrast, in respect of the older child, she would have to show that she was suffering from an abnormality of mental functioning, arising from a recognised medical condition,[75] that substantially impaired her ability to understand the nature of her conduct or to form a rational judgement or to exercise self-control,[76] and that one of these impairments provides an explanation for the killing.[77]

Not only does this disparity apply to the woman's defences, it also demonstrates an unacceptable attitude towards the value of an infant as compared with a child aged over 12 months. In 1922 this distinction might have been understandable, given the high infant mortality rate;[78] in the twenty-first century, it is no longer defensible and clearly demonstrates that the 'lower status in which the infant was held by society … has been institutionalized in English laws on infanticide'.[79]

From a purely theoretical stance, the myth that a woman might be perceived as less blameworthy if she were to kill her infant aged under 12 months than if she were to kill an older child is possibly the easiest to challenge. If a woman is not a moral agent in respect of her infant, there is no reason why she should be a moral agent in respect of an older child. Equally, if she is a moral agent but deserving of reduced culpability, the same reduction and the same level of culpability should be applicable in respect of both children. While it is conceded that there might be a difference between one woman who kills her infant and another woman who kills her teenage daughter, it is impossible to draw such a distinction between the woman who, hypothetically, kills two of her children at the same time and in the same manner. It would be an untruth to suggest that the woman's state of mind differed in relation to the two victims.

[72] Mackay (n 29) Table 5C. Sample was for time period 1990–2003 in relation to children killed under the age of 4: D.88.

[73] Homicide Act 1957, s 2, as amended by Coroners and Justice Act 2009, s 52(1).

[74] Infanticide Act 1938, s 1(2).

[75] For further details, see the discussion of *Borowiec* in section III.A.

[76] Coroners and Justice Act 2009, s 52(1A).

[77] See Mackay, ch 3 of this volume.

[78] R Bluglass, 'Infanticide' (1978) 2(8) *Bulletin of the Royal College of Psychiatrists* 139, 141 at doi:10.1192/S0140078900003060 (accessed on 8 April 2022).

[79] C Damme, 'Infanticide: The Worth of an Infant under Law' (1978) 22 *Medical History* 1, 24.

An alternative view is that the different treatment in respect of the infant does not necessarily mean the law takes that killing less seriously, only that it recognises that there may be circumstances involving this victim that lower the woman's responsibility so much that she deserves a different response.[80] It can also be the case, historically, that 'Far from denying women's legal responsibility, the acts were intended to hold women criminally responsible for actions for which they would previously have been either exculpated or found insane.'[81]

While the above, historically, might have been the case, by continuing in the twenty-first century to accept infanticide as a defence in respect of a defined category of victim, a myth is perpetuated: killing an infant is not as serious as killing an older child. While the sentencing might be comparable in respect of both children, reflecting an equivalent level of moral agency and culpability, the message conveyed to society in terms of fair labelling is that killing an infant, while still amounting to a homicide offence, need not be seen as comparable to either murder or manslaughter.

III. Myth 2: Women Who Kill their Infants Only Do So Because of an Imbalance of Mind Due to the Effects of Childbirth/Lactation

Wilczynski and Morris suggest that 'half of the women who plead guilty to or are convicted of infanticide are not suffering from any identifiable mental disorder at all',[82] a view echoed by Meyer and Oberman[83] and Ward.[84] Consequently, it may be argued that the defence of infanticide is not, in reality, a mental condition defence. This view will be explored and rejected, before examining the falsehood that the effects of childbirth and lactation are the only reasons for a woman to kill her infant.

A. Infanticide as a Mental Condition Defence

The 'legal invention'[85] of infanticide as a medicalised defence disguises the fact that it owes more to its existence as a social/situational defence than a medicalised/mental condition defence. Even 100 years ago, rather than overtly allowing

[80] With thanks to Karen Brennan for challenging me to consider this alternative.

[81] Ward (n 13) 176.

[82] A Wilczynski and A Morris, 'Parents Who Kill Their Children' [1993] *Crim LR* 31, 35.

[83] C Meyer and M Oberman, *Mothers Who Kill Their Children: Inside the Minds of Moms From Susan Smith to the 'Prom Mom'* (New York University Press, 2001) 32.

[84] Ward (n 13) 170.

[85] K Brennan, 'Beyond the Medical Model: a Rationale for Infanticide Legislation' (2007) 58 *NILQ* 505, 533.

a social defence, the Infanticide Act 1922 'enslav[ed] psychiatric concepts'[86] in order 'to fit the needs of the law'.[87] The outcome of this enslavement was to create an 'apparently psychiatric defence for precisely the category of mothers who were least likely to be considered insane'.[88]

At the turn of the twentieth century, links were being made to 'lactational insanity or exhaustion psychosis',[89] but no such link was made between 'puerperal mental disturbance and newborn infanticide'.[90] Other commentators assert the true position of the defence is a recognition of 'principally emotional and economic hardship, heredity and obstetric complications'.[91] Even today, the defence of infanticide is at times accepted where there is evidence of 'emotional disturbance'[92] falling short of mental illness. Similarly, in 2016, the Supreme Court of Canada was of the view that, in the context of infanticide, a disturbed mind should not be restricted to 'a substantial psychological problem'[93] and 'need not constitute a defined mental or psychological condition or a mental illness'.[94]

Historically, there was clearly a case for an emotional/social defence, but Kramer and Watson[95] urge that 'caution should be exercised before the medicalization interpretation is rejected wholesale'.[96] In their view:

> The mere fact that a bio-psychiatric interpretation of the causation of infanticide is written into documents as culturally significant as the English Acts, especially given that biological psychiatric thinking has gained extraordinary dominance within medical psychiatry in the last few decades, may be of some social significance.[97]

Despite the historical origins of infanticide, arguably the defence can and should move with the times and be interpreted in line with medical psychiatry. It seems wrong in the twenty-first century to allow infanticide as an emotional/social defence for one of the most serious crimes. The assertion here is that Wakeling JA, the dissenting judge in *Borowiec*, took a more apposite view: a woman's mind would only be disturbed if

> her psychological health was substantially compromised because she recently gave birth and she had a newborn to care for and, as a result, her ability to make rational decisions promoting the best interests of her child was substantially impaired.[98]

[86] Ward (n 13) 174.
[87] ibid.
[88] ibid 170.
[89] Brennan (n 22) 125.
[90] ibid.
[91] KJ Kramar and WD Watson, 'The Insanities of Reproduction: Medico-Legal Knowledge and the Development of Infanticide Law' (2006) 15 *Social & Legal Studies* 237, 250.
[92] RD Mackay, 'The Consequences of Killing Very Young Children' [1993] *Crim LR* 21, 29.
[93] *R v Borowiec* [2016] 1 SCR 80 [35].
[94] ibid.
[95] Kramer and Watson (n 91) 251.
[96] ibid.
[97] ibid.
[98] *Borowiec* (n 93) [10].

There is a compelling reason today to take a medicalised view of the infanticide defence, regardless of its original function, given that social conditions have evolved significantly away from the dire economic hardship and social stigma of Victorian times. Mackay, in his empirical study,[99] identified a range of primary diagnoses in respect of women who killed their children, including postnatal depression (in 14 cases), depression (7), puerperal psychosis (6) and dissociative disorder (5), to name only a few. In constructing infanticide in the twenty-first century as a mental condition defence, and applying a principled approach to this area, the capacity required for a woman to be a moral agent should only be found lacking where there is a mental disorder. The cases identified above are likely to satisfy this requirement. Similarly, in Milne's work on neonaticide, some of the women under consideration suffered from severe depression,[100] dissociative amnesia,[101] 'underlying mental health conditions … exacerbated by the birth',[102] and 'mental and physical shock'.[103] Both Mackay and Milne, however, point to women who killed either where information was not available,[104] or where there was no mention of a mental disorder.[105] Undeniably, this is problematic, as the requirement of a mental disorder in order to satisfy a newly reformed infanticide defence might result in more women being convicted of murder or voluntary manslaughter. Additionally, requiring a link to a mental disorder might bring the defence of infanticide too close to that of diminished responsibility, eliminating the need for the infanticide defence. In the author's view, echoing the recommendations of the Butler Committee,[106] this ideal solution is considered in brief below.

The central question, if the defence is to be retained, should be whether social factors falling short of a mental disorder ought to form a defence for these women. Some criminal defences are situational, and there is an argument for including infanticide in such a category. Duress, for example, relies on threats overpowering the will of the defendant[107] and is clearly not a medicalised defence, but significantly it is not available as a defence to murder.[108] Loss of control[109] is possibly the closest comparable defence. Like infanticide, it recognises some criminal responsibility alongside a reduced amount of culpability.[110] However, loss of control requires a qualifying trigger[111] and has moved on since a crying baby could be a factor that

[99] Mackay (n 29) D23.
[100] Milne (n 19) 20.
[101] ibid 21.
[102] ibid.
[103] ibid 22.
[104] Mackay (n 29) D23.
[105] Milne (n 19) 24.
[106] Home Office, *Report of the Committee on Mentally Abnormal Offenders* (Cmnd 6244, 1975) para 19.27, although not the view of the Law Commission in 2009: Law Commission, *Murder, Manslaughter and Infanticide* (Law Com CP No 304, 2006) para 9.106.
[107] *R v Graham* (1981) 74 Cr App R 235.
[108] *R v Howe* [1987] AC 417.
[109] Coroners and Justice Act 2009, ss 54–56.
[110] ibid s 54(7).
[111] ibid s 54(1)(b).

causes a defendant to lose control.[112] Despite the historical social reasons for its introduction and its current contemporary use, the infanticide defence should be narrowly limited to medical rather than social conditions or, better still, be abolished in favour of diminished responsibility.

B. Effects of Childbirth/Lactation and Pre-Existing Conditions

While the Court of Appeal in *Kai-Whitewind*[113] determined that, besides the effects of childbirth or lactation, 'no other circumstances are relevant'[114] in determining the woman's mental state, a wider view was taken in the more recent case of *Tunstill*.[115] Here, the Court of Appeal held[116] that the effects of childbirth or lactation need not be the sole cause of the woman's imbalance so long as they were the substantial cause. This decision is a welcome approach, especially given that there is no direct medical or psychological evidence that women kill their infants due to the effects of childbirth and lactation.[117]

The prevalence of psychiatric conditions in mothers shortly after giving birth is nevertheless undeniable.[118] Spinelli notes that in failing to provide a specific diagnostic classification for postpartum psychosis,[119] there is a danger that a psychiatrist will not recognise the 'unpredictability'[120] of the condition, potentially putting both the infant's and the mother's lives at risk. It is astonishing that postpartum psychosis should lack a unique classification under DSM-V in the twenty-first century.[121] Infanticide remains a defence of 'constructive madness', creating a myth that ignores the fact 'that science has not found a connection between mental illness and lactation'.[122] The need for a link between a recognised medical condition and the killing will be addressed in more detail in section III.C.

[112] *R v Doughty* (1986) 83 Cr App R 319.

[113] *R v Kai-Whitewind* [2005] EWCA Crim 1092.

[114] ibid [134].

[115] *R v Tunstill* [2018] EWCA Crim 1696.

[116] ibid [31].

[117] Ogle and Maier-Katkin (n 32) 905.

[118] MG Spinelli, 'Maternal Infanticide Associated With Mental Illness: Prevention and the Promise of Saved Lives' (2004) 161 *American Journal of Psychiatry* 1548, 1552.

[119] ibid 1551.

[120] ibid.

[121] *Diagnostic and Statistical Manual of Mental Disorders*, 5th edn (American Psychological Association 2013) ('DSM-V'). Spinelli continues to advocate for a unique classification for postpartum psychosis within DSM-V: MG Spinelli, 'Postpartum Psychosis: a Diagnosis for the DSMV' *Archives of Women's Mental Health* (8 September 2021) at https://pubmed.ncbi.nlm.nih.gov/34494144/ (accessed 21 April 2022). Although there is a code for this condition under ICD10, the condition falls within the generic category of psychoses: see at https://icd.codes/icd10cm.F53 (accessed 21 April 2022).

[122] E Rapaport, 'Mad Women and Desperate Girls: Infanticide and Child Murder in Law and Myth' (2006) 33 *Fordham Urban Law Journal* 527, 555.

C. Causal Link/Diagnostic Threshold

The lack of an identifiable medical condition is compounded by the absence of a causal link,[123] and raises the presumption that the killing is attributable to the effects of childbirth or lactation by virtue of 'a mere temporal connection between the mental disturbance and the actus reus'.[124] The Law Commission views this state of affairs 'pragmatically',[125] commenting that 'Medical experts consulted were of the view that the Act generally works well.'[126]

However, the 'implicit assumption'[127] that the mental disturbance caused the killing is incorrect. Described as 'the largest documented contemporary sample of American women who have killed their children',[128] Meyer and Oberman[129] classify five types of infanticide. The first category refers to killing as a result of 'an ignored pregnancy',[130] and involves neonaticide, generally committed by 'juveniles'. The second category is 'abuse-related', that is, killing during a 'physical assault' and often as a form of 'discipline'.[131] 'Neglect' forms the third category either by omission to feed/provide adequate care, or by commission, such as shaking or 'putting something over the child's head'.[132] The fourth category involves 'assisted/coerced' killing,[133] while the final category is described as 'purposeful' and where 'the mother acted alone',[134] and might occur with or without mental illness. Despite being an American study, and the fact that the research was conducted on the news database NEXIS, what is evident from these categories is not all women who kill their infants are 'mad'. The infanticide defence, in describing a woman's balance of mind as being disturbed, partially exculpates for the wrong reasons. The lack of any principled underpinning results in a defence that is unable to accurately describe the reasons for either partially inculpating or exculpating a woman who kills her infant.

Commenting on the proper attribution of responsibility, Gardner suggests that 'if I am suffering from a delusional mental illness, my responsibility is only absent in respect of the actions which are explained by the delusions'.[135] The absence of a causal connection within the infanticide defence contradicts the expectation that a defendant's mental condition should explain her actions in order to allow for an excuse. While a mother might lack moral agency, or might kill for reasons

[123] Ogle and Maier-Katkin (n 32) 903.
[124] A Loughnan, 'The Strange Case of the Infanticide Doctrine' (2012) 32 *OJLS* 685, 702.
[125] Law Commission (n 106) para 8.41.
[126] ibid.
[127] Loughnan (n 124) 703.
[128] Spinelli (n 118) 1550.
[129] Meyer and Oberman (n 83).
[130] ibid 36.
[131] ibid 37.
[132] ibid.
[133] ibid.
[134] ibid 38.
[135] J Gardner, 'The Mark of Responsibility' (2003) 23(2) *OJLS* 157, 161.

other than childbirth and lactation, the Infanticide Acts inaccurately describe the conditions under which culpability should be allocated. As already discussed, situational circumstances ought not to be sufficient reason to describe a woman as lacking moral agency. Rather, a link should be made to a medical condition and, if the condition is sufficiently serious to deprive her of capacity to conform her conduct to the law, it is inappropriate to attribute even partial responsibility to her. The recognised medical condition is necessary to provide evidence for the defendant's lack of moral agency, or reduced culpability, and to achieve consistency between the mental condition defences. The benefit in retaining infanticide as a defence might then only be in terms of fair labelling to reflect the nature of the woman's conduct and the unique set of circumstances in which she found herself.

It is inaccurate to portray all cases of infanticide as representative of the effects of childbirth or lactation. If the offence/defence is to survive, we should be prepared to call it what it is. A woman ought not to be able to plead a full or partial defence in the absence of proof of any recognised medical condition. There should also be a causal link between her actions and that condition. A causal link exists for the current insanity defence, in the form of defect of reason attributable to a disease of the mind. The Law Commission[136] has recognised the need for a causal link in relation to a reformed insanity defence, recommending a connection to a recognised medical condition. The same link exists within the partial defence of diminished responsibility.[137]

The criminal law provides the opportunity for a defendant to take part in a moral conversation with the state.[138] This conversation should be viewed not only as an obligation owed by the defendant to the state, but as a right or privilege afforded to the defendant. The absence of a diagnostic threshold, in the form of a recognised medical condition, obfuscates the conversation. The woman must say 'I was mad because I had given birth' or 'because I was breastfeeding'. The absence of a causal link to the killing removes the privilege afforded to other defendants. The woman must say 'I was mad and I killed', rather than 'I killed because I was mad'. In the twenty-first century, this Victorian view of women who kill is incorrect. It would be preferable for the explanation to be 'I killed because I was suffering from a condition that partially or wholly deprived me of capacity.'

The criminal justice system should allow a defendant to 'acknowledge their wrongdoing and … to move forward in their lives'.[139] This can only occur where the woman shows, as Gardner describes, 'response-ability, an ability to respond'.[140] A trial that provides 'a psychologically informative and persuasive view of the mother and of her delusional certainty' will 'give them a voice that can be heard

[136] Law Commission (n 4) A.101.

[137] Coroners and Justice Act 2009, s 52(1A). It is conceded that the causal link might need only to be more than merely trivial, reflecting the decision in *R v Golds* [2016] UKSC 61.

[138] A Duff, 'Fitness to Plead and Fair Trials: (1) A Challenge' [1994] *Crim LR* 419, 420.

[139] N Lacey and H Pickard, 'To Blame or to Forgive? Reconciling Punishment and Forgiveness in Criminal Justice' (2015) 35 *OJLS* 665, 695.

[140] Gardner (n 135)161.

with greater compassion and justice'.[141] Spinelli asserts that 'defendants with mental illness who face the criminal justice system have the right to a defense based on scientific fact. Such a defense is essential for equal representation under the law'.[142] It is unfortunate that 'few psychiatric standards exist for this area'.[143]

In an ideal world, the myth that women who kill their infants only do so because of an imbalance of mind due to the effects of childbirth/lactation should not be necessary. This pretence should be replaced by a principled underpinning to the infanticide law, allowing for a clearly defined mental condition defence to women who demonstrate a lack of moral agency due to a recognised medical condition. A defence of not criminally responsible by reason of recognised medical condition (RMC defence), proposed by the Law Commission[144] to replace the insanity defence, would eradicate the need for a partial defence of infanticide. It would allow those women who are not moral agents and who do not bear any criminal responsibility to receive treatment and no stigma of conviction or punishment. In an ideal world, medical advancements would categorise and describe genuine mental disorders experienced after childbirth without implicitly labelling all women as nurturing or mad. Until then, pragmatism must abrogate principles. In truth, the offence/defence of infanticide was introduced to address socio-economic needs, but these reasons are 'disguised'[145] by a pseudo-medical defence. As Brennan rightly states, 'an express recognition of the socio-economic explanation for infanticide would have been impossible'.[146] Equally impossible might be the recognition that some women who kill their infants should bear no criminal responsibility at all.

IV. Myth 3: Women who Kill their Infants While Suffering from an Imbalance of the Mind Still Bear Some Criminal Responsibility, Albeit a Reduced Amount

Finally, the 'half-way house'[147] of partial responsibility must be addressed. In relation to the diminished responsibility defence, the Law Commission[148] has recognised that responsibility 'cannot either be enhanced or diminished. It is capacity or culpability that can be enhanced or diminished'.[149] This contention

[141] S Ayres, 'Newfound Religion: Mothers, God, and Infanticide' (2006) 33 *Fordham Urban Law Journal* 335, 356.
[142] Spinelli (n 118)1555.
[143] ibid 1552.
[144] Law Commission (n 4) chs 3 and 4.
[145] Brennan (n 22) 136.
[146] ibid.
[147] Loughnan (n 124) 705.
[148] Law Commission, *A New Homicide Act for England and Wales* (Law Com CP No 177, 2005).
[149] ibid para 6.36.

is equally applicable to the defence of infanticide. Of particular concern here is neonaticide, the killing of a baby within 24 hours of delivery, which can cause in new mothers, who have concealed their pregnancy and given birth alone, a state of dissociation or 'depersonalization'.[150] This 'unique form of killing'[151] is worthy of separate consideration from other types of infanticide. The woman who conceals a pregnancy and goes through giving birth alone is substantially different from the mother who, for example, kills her 10-month-old infant. Women who kill in these circumstances are often 'not in control of their actions due to dissociative psychosis or hallucinations. Such psychotic breaks are understood to be brought on by the experience of the solo birth.'[152] To shoehorn neonaticide into the same classification as other types of infanticide, and to afford them the same (partial) defence, fails to recognise the particular vulnerability of these women.[153] Given that infants of one week and younger 'are at greatest risk from their mothers',[154] perhaps this is where the line for an infanticide or neonaticide defence should be drawn, if it is to be retained. The particular vulnerability of some women so soon after delivery, who might be experiencing dissociation due to a concealed pregnancy and traumatic secret delivery, should allow for a full, rather than partial, defence due to their complete lack of moral agency.

It is impossible to imagine the state of desperation experienced in these circumstances. A lower level of culpability seems inappropriate here, but the *M'Naghten* Rules,[155] outdated and ineffective at the best of times, are unlikely to afford an insanity defence to a mother who knew that she was killing a human being and knew that this is against the law. As Spinelli states,[156] 'we in psychiatry continue fruitless attempts to adapt our contemporary scientific knowledge to antiquated legislation. We endeavor to fit our current "square peg" into the obsolete "round hole" of the law.' A psychotic mother who 'suffers prominent cognitive impairment and is not thinking rationally'[157] ought not to be viewed as a moral agent, nor should she be even partially criminally responsible if she kills her infant.

Punishment of a woman who is not a moral agent is 'wasteful' and causes suffering 'to the accused who is punished in circumstances where it could do no good'.[158] Expanding on Hart's capacity theory, Lacey describes the capacities required for the attribution of responsibility, namely, 'capacities for knowledge, awareness, reflection, deliberation, and choice',[159] and points out that this

> conception of criminal responsibility therefore makes a strong assumption about what it is that we are responsible for: we are responsible not for our selves, for who we are, or

[150] Spinelli (n 118) 1550.
[151] K Brennan and E Milne, 'Infanticide: Guarding against Harshness' (2019) 169 *New Law Journal* 13.
[152] ibid 14.
[153] ibid.
[154] Rapaport (n 122) 536.
[155] *R v M'Naghten* (1843) 10 Cl & Fin 200.
[156] Spinelli (n 118) 1552.
[157] Ayres (n 141) 351.
[158] ibid 41.
[159] Lacey (n 8) 255.

> for our social status, but ... for the specific acts which we (choose to) do or (in limited circumstances) refrain from doing.[160]

If we are responsible for our acts, there does not need to be any inquiry into what traits of character drove us to behave in a particular way. In defining capacity, the Law Commission summarised 'discussions of capacity come back to the same two fundamental capacities: of rationality, and of control over one's actions'.[161] Either of these capacities might be absent in a woman who kills her infant. In respect of control, it is submitted that an absence of control should only be relevant in establishing a lack of moral agency where it is so severe as to render the defendant irrational.[162] Any lesser degree of compulsion is too difficult to measure reliably.[163] In respect of the minimum level of rationality for moral agency, Morse's definition of 'the sensibleness of the actor's goals and the logic of the means chosen to achieve them'[164] seems apposite. By way of example, a mother who suffers from puerperal psychosis and kills, believing her infant to be possessed by evil forces, might act logically according to her false beliefs, but her goal would not be viewed as sensible. A mother who kills while suffering from dissociative amnesia or mental trauma might not even be described as having a 'goal', let alone employing logical means towards achieving it. Given that the partial defence of diminished responsibility[165] and proposals for the reform of the insanity defence[166] both contain references to rationality, and rationality is crucial for moral agency, the same requirement should be applied to any reformed defence of infanticide, if the defence is to be retained and to survive another century. The absence of any direct reference to rationality within the infanticide defence compounds the obsolescence of this defence.

Employing the Law Commission's RMC defence (see section III.C), it is likely that many of the conditions experienced by women who kill their infants would fall within its remit. For example, puerperal psychosis is recognised in paragraph F53

[160] ibid.

[161] Law Commission (n 4) A.40, citing N Lacey, 'Psychologising Jekyll, Demonising Hyde: The Strange Case of Criminal Responsibility' (2010) 4 *Criminal Law and Philosophy* 109, 117, and SJ Morse, 'Excusing the Crazy: The Insanity Defence Reconsidered' (1985) 58 *Southern California Law Review* 777, 783.

[162] SJ Morse, 'Crazy Behavior, Morals and Science: An Analysis of Mental Health Law' (1978) 51 *Southern California Law Review* 527, 584.

[163] H Howard, 'Reform of the Insanity Defence: Theoretical Issues for Consideration' (2003) 67 *Journal of Criminal Law* 51, 57–58; Morse (n 162) 584.

[164] Morse (n 161) 783.

[165] Coroners and Justice Act 2009, s 52(1) inserts into s 2 of the Homicide Act 1957: '(1) A person ("D") who kills or is a party to the killing of another is not to be convicted of murder if D was suffering from an abnormality of mental functioning which: (a) arose from a recognised medical condition, (b) substantially impaired D's ability to do one or more of the things mentioned in subsection (1A) [(b) to form a rational judgment] and (c) provides an explanation for D's acts and omissions in doing or being a party to the killing.'

[166] Law Commission (n 4) para 4.160: the defendant must wholly lack capacity, inter alia, '(i) rationally to form a judgment' about the relevant conduct, 'as a result of a qualifying recognised medical condition'.

of the *International Classification of Diseases*,[167] while dissociate amnesia falls within F44. The RMC defence would allow for the removal of criminal responsibility from women who do not deserve to be punished for their actions; moreover, it would be unlikely to carry the same stigma as either the current insanity defence or the infanticide offence/defence.

For those women who ought not to be completely absolved of criminal responsibility, in order to address the distinction between responsibility and culpability, some definitions are needed. As with the diminished responsibility defence, partial criminal responsibility in relation to infanticide is a misnomer.[168] A distinction can be drawn between the terms 'responsibility' and 'culpability'. Responsibility implies attribution for the act. For *mala in se* crimes, such as infanticide, criminal responsibility requires an additional element of moral blameworthiness/culpability,[169] and within moral blameworthiness, there is the presupposition that D is a rational moral agent.[170] In the absence of moral agency there can be no culpability; without culpability there should be no criminal responsibility.'[171]

Thus, a woman who kills her infant will be 'responsible' for her act, but to be '*criminally* responsible', she must be a rational moral agent. If she is not a rational moral agent, she should not be held criminally responsible. It is inappropriate and unjust to punish, even to a lesser degree, mothers who kill their infants when they are not rational moral agents. Where a mother lacks the capacity to choose not to kill her infant, attributing partial criminal responsibility seems wholly inappropriate. In this context, neonaticide should be treated as distinct from the killing of older infants and should lead to a complete defence, ideally employing a reformed RMC defence. In respect of women who kill older infants, where the mother is a moral agent but deserving of a reduced amount of blame, diminished responsibility should be used in order to avoid the mandatory life sentence for murder, but only where the woman is suffering from a recognised medical condition. If infanticide is to be retained, it should similarly allow for the avoidance of the mandatory life sentence but its purpose, as distinct from diminished responsibility, might only be to allow for fair labelling.

It is likely, despite strong arguments to the contrary,[172] that most women who kill their infants should be deemed moral agents, given that a minimal capacity

[167] World Health Organization, *ICD-10: International Statistical Classification of Diseases and Related Health Problems* (10th rev, 2nd edn, World Health Organization 2004) at https://apps.who.int/iris/handle/10665/42980 (accessed 13 September 2022).

[168] H Howard, 'Diminished Responsibility, Culpability and Moral Agency' in B Livings, A Reed and N Wake (eds), *Mental Condition Defences and the Criminal Justice System: Perspectives from Law and Medicine* (Cambridge Scholars Publishing 2015) 320.

[169] Arenella (n 31) 1513.

[170] Moore (n 51) 244.

[171] Howard (n 168) 321.

[172] Milne (n 19) 151: 'To truly have agency, to truly have choice, to truly be "free" to make a decision as to how to respond to a pregnancy, and to then be judged fairly and equally as a "reasonable (wo)man"

should suffice for moral agency. The question then should be how their *culpability*, not their criminal responsibility, is reduced by their mental condition. The best response might be that reduced culpability is applicable where D's mental condition affects the capacity 'limb' of capacity theory. While an individual who wholly lacks capacity should have the insanity defence available to her, or ideally a reformed version of it,[173] reduced capacity should lead to reduced culpability in respect of any infanticide defence. Where a minimum level of rationality is established, and the woman is a moral agent, the *potential* exists for her to be held criminally responsible. Given the range of mental disorders that can be suffered by a woman after giving birth, as with diminished responsibility,[174] it is clear that there is a sliding scale of rationality that, above a minimum threshold, reduces her level of culpability.[175] For example, a severely depressed mother who kills her infant, believing that life is futile, will not be as rational as the ordinary individual, but might be sufficiently rational to be treated as a moral agent. It is in these circumstances that a partial defence might be justified, but not because her criminal responsibility is reduced; rather, her culpability is diminished. In these circumstances, the woman must say 'I am responsible, but I deserve less blame.' Allowing a woman in these tragic circumstances to take responsibility for her actions grants her the dignity and equality of being treated as a moral agent. Denying her moral agency in these circumstances further highlights a misogynistic approach towards the perception and treatment of women within the criminal justice system, a system already 'saturated by misogynistic ideas about women, embodying the control and regulation of women's bodies, sexuality, and motherhood'.[176]

V. Conclusion

The offence/defence of infanticide is out of place among other mental condition defences, but if it is to survive, it should fall within this category of defences. The omission of a causal link to a recognised medical condition creates a presumption of constructive madness among women who have recently given birth, and also artificially creates a medicalised defence for women who have killed for reasons other than their mental condition. This archaic attitude patronises women and devalues the life of an infant. Diminished responsibility contains

requires an overhaul of the system. None of this is possible while women live within the grip and under the weight of patriarchy.'

[173] Law Commission (n 4) para 4.160.

[174] Howard (n 168) 330.

[175] ibid 330–31. Morse has suggested that there will be degrees of rationality along a continuum: S Morse, 'Diminished Capacity' in S Shute, J Gardner and J Horder (eds), *Action and Value in Criminal Law* (Clarendon Press, 1993) 239, 248–49.

[176] Milne (n 19) 6.

a link to a recognised medical condition[177] and, it is respectfully submitted, ought to apply to women who kill their infants. Even the universally unfair insanity defence requires a causal link to a 'disease of the mind',[178] although a reformed insanity defence would be the preferred approach.[179] Admittedly, accurate psychiatric diagnoses are difficult to achieve for new mothers, but this should not prevent the medical and legal disciplines from aspiring to achieve more accurate diagnoses and correctly defined, principled rather than unpredictable defences.

Applying a distinction in labelling and culpability to a woman who kills her infant at the same time and in the same manner as her older child is inappropriate. Applying a principled approach to the attribution of blame, it would be wrong to offer a defence of infanticide in respect of the infant alongside a voluntary manslaughter conviction in respect of the older child, and untrue to suggest that the woman's mental state differed in relation to both victims.

We might not wish to acknowledge that women kill their infants for reasons other than mental instability, but acceptance of this unpalatable fact is necessary. Some mothers who kill their infants are not mentally disturbed. To claim otherwise is to overlook the particular vulnerability of infants and to perpetuate the myth that all mothers are mad.

If a woman lacks the capacity and fair opportunity to choose to do anything other than kill her infant, a partial defence is wholly inappropriate. An absence of moral agency should result in an absence of criminal responsibility. In an ideal world, the defence would fall within a newly reformed insanity defence. This should be particularly applicable in tragic cases of neonaticide, where a woman has concealed or denied a pregnancy and given birth alone. However, in the absence of a recognised medical condition, she should be convicted of murder. The tragedy here is the existence of the mandatory life sentence, which ties the hands of the court when recognition of different levels of culpability is crucial to a just outcome.

The defence of infanticide does not stem from a principled theoretical underpinning but is the product of a social problem[180] of unplanned parenthood, social stigma and financial ruin that existed over 100 years ago and was introduced to avoid the death penalty for murder. Times have changed. The stigma of childbirth outside of marriage has diminished substantially[181] in today's society. The value of an infant's life is significantly greater than it once was. The Infanticide Act 1922 introduced a defence for a woman who killed her infant, without the need for her to demonstrate any kind of medical condition, nor even that the killing was caused by her disturbed state of mind, and this position is untenable. This 'compassionate' defence perpetuates too many myths to survive another century in its current form.

[177] Homicide Act 1957, s 2, as amended by s 52(1) of the Coroners and Justice Act 2009.
[178] *M'Naghten* (n 155).
[179] Law Commission (n 4) para 4.160.
[180] Brennan and Milne (n 151) 14.
[181] Although not entirely.

References

Books

Aristotle, *Nichomachean Ethics*, tr T Irwin (Hackett Publishing 1985).
Barthes, R, *Mythologies*, tr A Lavers (Farrar, Straus & Giroux 1972).
Blackstone, *Commentaries on the Laws of England 1765–69* (University of Chicago Press 1979).
Duff, A, *Criminal Attempts* (Clarendon Press 1996).
Fletcher, G, *Rethinking Criminal Law* (Little, Brown 1978).
Hart, HLA, *Punishment and Responsibility* (Oxford University Press 1968) 160.
Horder, J, *Excusing Crime* (Oxford University Press 2004).
Kadish, SH, *Blame and Punishment* (MacMillan Publishing 1987).
Meyer, C and Oberman, M, *Mothers Who Kill Their Children: Inside the Minds of Moms From Susan Smith to the 'Prom Mom'* (New York University Press 2001).
Milne, E, *Criminal Justice Responses to Maternal Filicide: Judging the Failed Mother* (Emerald Publishing Ltd 2021).
Moore, MS, *Law and Psychiatry* (Cambridge University Press 1984).
Stephen, JF, *A History of the Criminal Law of England* (Macmillan 1883).
Tadros, V, *Criminal Responsibility* (Oxford University Press 2005).
Van Hoecke, M, *Methodologies of Legal Research: Which Kind of Method for What Kind of Discipline?* (Bloomsbury Publishing 2013).
Williams, G, *Criminal Law: The General Part*, 2nd edn (Stevens and Sons 1961).

Chapters in Edited Volumes

Arenella, P, 'Character, Choice and Moral Agency: the relevance of character to our moral culpability judgments' in Paul, EF, Miller, FD and Paul, J (eds), *Crime, Culpability, and Remedy* (Basil Blackwell, 1990).
Howard, H, 'Diminished Responsibility, Culpability and Moral Agency' in Livings, B, Reed, A and Wake, N (eds), *Mental Condition Defences and the Criminal Justice System: Perspectives from Law and Medicine* (Cambridge Scholars Publishing 2015) 320.
Morse, 'Diminished Capacity' in S Shute, J Gardner and J Horder (eds), Action and Value in Criminal Law (Clarendon Press 1993).

Journal Articles

Arenella, P, 'Convicting the Morally Blameless: Reassessing the Relationship Between Legal and Moral Accountability' (1992) 39 *UCLA Law Review* 1511.
Ayres, S, 'Newfound Religion: Mothers, God, and Infanticide' (2006) *33 Fordham Urban Law Journal* 335.
Bayles, MD, 'Hume on Blame and Excuse' (1976) 2 *Hume Studies* 17.
——, 'Character, Purpose, and Criminal Responsibility' (1982) 1 *Law and Philosophy* 5.
Bluglass, R, 'Infanticide' (1978) 2(8) *Bulletin of the Royal College of Psychiatrists* 139 at doi:10.1192/S0140078900003060 (accessed on 8 April 2022).

Brennan, K, 'Beyond the Medical Model: a Rationale for Infanticide Legislation' (2007) 58 *NILQ* 505.
——, '"A Fine Mixture of Pity and Justice": The Criminal Justice Response to Infanticide in Ireland, 1922–1949' (2013) 31 *Law and History Review* 793.
——, '"Traditions of English liberal thought": a history of the enactment of an infanticide law in Ireland' (2013) 50 *Irish Jurist* 100.
——, 'Social Norms and the Law in Responding to Infanticide' (2018) 38(3) *Legal Studies* 480.
Brennan, K and Milne, E, 'Infanticide: Guarding against Harshness' (2019) 169 *New Law Journal* 13.
Crosby, C, 'Culpability, Kingston, and the Law Commission' (2010) 74 *Journal of Criminal Law* 434.
Damme, C, 'Infanticide: The Worth of an Infant under Law' (1978) 22 *Medical History* 1.
Duff, A, 'Fitness to Plead and Fair Trials: (1) A Challenge' [1994] *Crim LR* 419.
Gardner, J, 'The Mark of Responsibility' (2003) 23(2) *OJLS* 157.
Haji, I, 'On Psychopaths and Culpability' (1998) 17 *Law and Philosophy* 117.
Horder, J, 'Criminal Culpability: The Possibility of a General Theory' (1993) 12 *Law and Philosophy* 193.
Howard, H, 'Reform of the Insanity Defence: Theoretical Issues for Consideration' (2003) 67 *Journal of Criminal Law* 51.
——, 'The Offence/Defence of Infanticide: A View from Two Perspectives' (2018) 82 *Journal of Criminal Law* 470.
Kramar KJ and Watson, WD, 'The Insanities of Reproduction: Medico-Legal Knowledge and the Development of Infanticide Law' (2006) 15 *Social & Legal Studies* 237.
Lacey, N, 'In Search of the Responsible Subject: History, Philosophy and Social Sciences in Criminal Law Theory' (2001) 64(3) *MLR* 350.
——, 'Responsibility and Modernity in Criminal Law' (2001) *9 Journal of Political Philosophy* 249.
——, 'Psychologising Jekyll, Demonising Hyde: The Strange Case of Criminal Responsibility' (2010) 4 *Criminal Law and Philosophy* 109.
Lacey, N and Pickard, H, 'To Blame or to Forgive? Reconciling Punishment and Forgiveness in Criminal Justice' (2015) 35 *OJLS* 665.
Laird, K, 'Case Comment: Infanticide: R v Tunstill (Rachel Julie) Court of Appeal (Criminal Division)' [2019] 2 *Crim LR* 163.
Lodge, A, 'Domestic Abuse, Suicide and Liability for Manslaughter: In Pursuit of Justice for Victims' (2020) 84 *Journal of Criminal Law* 27.
Loughnan, A, 'The Strange Case of the Infanticide Doctrine' (2012) 32 *OJLS* 685.
Mackay, RD, 'The Consequences of Killing Very Young Children' [1993] *Crim LR* 21.
Morse, SJ, 'Crazy Behavior, Morals and Science: An Analysis of Mental Health Law' (1978) 51 *Southern California Law Review* 527.
——, 'Excusing the Crazy: The Insanity Defence Reconsidered' (1985) 58 *Southern California Law Review* 777.
Ogle, RS and Maier-Katkin, D, 'A Rationale for Infanticide Laws' [1993] *Crim LR* 903.
Pillsbury, SH, 'The Meaning of Deserved Punishment: An Essay on Choice, Character and Responsibility' (1992) 67 *Indiana Law Journal* 719.
Pincoffs, EL, 'Legal Responsibility and Moral Character' (1973) 19 *Wayne Law Review* 905.
Rapaport, E, 'Mad Women and Desperate Girls: Infanticide and Child Murder in Law and Myth' (2006) *33 Fordham Urban Law Journal* 527.

Spinelli, MG, 'Maternal Infanticide Associated with Mental Illness: Prevention and the Promise of Saved Lives' (2004) 161 *American Journal of Psychiatry* 1548.
Thomas, M, 'Infanticide and Pre-Existing Mental Conditions' (2018) 82 *Journal of Criminal Law* 366.
Ward, T, 'The Sad Subject of Infanticide: Law, Medicine and Child Murder, 1860–1938' (1999) 8 *Social and Legal Studies* 163.
Wilczynski, A and Morris, A, 'Parents Who Kill Their Children' [1993] *Crim LR* 31.

Newspaper Articles

'More babies born out of wedlock or civil partnerships 'for first time on record'' *The Independent* (London, 9 August 2022) at www.independent.co.uk/news/uk/office-for-national-statistics-wales-england-harry-benson-nhs-b2141556.html (accessed 2 September 2022).

Online Resources

Spinelli, MG, 'Postpartum Psychosis: A Diagnosis for the DSMV', *Archives of Women's Mental Health* (8 September 2021) at https://pubmed.ncbi.nlm.nih.gov/34494144/.
World Health Organization, *ICD-10: International Statistical Classification of Diseases and Related Health Problems* (10th rev, 2nd edn, World Health Organization 2004) at https://apps.who.int/iris/handle/10665/42980 (accessed 13 September 2022).

Reports

Law Commission, *A New Homicide Act for England and Wales* (Law Com CP No 177, 2005).
Law Commission, *Murder, Manslaughter and Infanticide* (Law Com CP No 304, 2006).
Law Commission, *Criminal Liability: Insanity and Automatism: A Discussion Paper* (23 July 2013).
Mackay, RD, 'Infanticide and Diminished Responsibility Manslaughter: An Empirical Study' in Law Commission, *Murder, Manslaughter and Infanticide* (Law Com No 304, 2006) Appendix D.

6

The Infanticide Act 1938 as a Means to Provide Justice for Women against the Hardships and Harms of Pregnancy and Motherhood?

EMMA MILNE AND KAREN BRENNAN

One of the main criticisms of the English and Welsh infanticide laws, and laws in other jurisdictions that adopt a similar model, comes from feminist analyses that argue that the Infanticide Acts of 1922/38 enshrine bio-deterministic explanations for infanticide,[1] embody problematic sexist gender constructions[2] and are paternalistic.[3] Feminist critiques do not necessarily fault the notion of providing for different and more lenient treatment for this crime, though some feminists may do so, but the fact that the legislation, in their view, ignores the structural causes of infanticide and bases lenience on sexist notions of biological difference and 'mad'/'sad' stereotypes of women offenders.

In this chapter we offer a feminist argument in favour of the infanticide law. First, we explore feminist critiques of the infanticide law and the challenges that have previously been made to these conceptions of infanticide. Second, we advance a feminist argument in favour of the Infanticide Act 1938. Our feminist argument draws on West's concept of gendered harms, demonstrating how pregnancy, childbirth and mothering in contemporary Western society all produce 'gendered harms', not as a consequence of these events in themselves but due to how they are experienced in a patriarchal, capitalist, racist and heteronormative

[1] SSM Edwards, *Women on Trial: A Study of the Female Suspect, Defendant, and Offender in the Criminal Law and Criminal Justice System* (Manchester University Press 1984).

[2] S Weare, 'Bad, Mad or Sad? Legal Language, Narratives, and Identity Constructions of Women Who Kill Their Children in England and Wales' (2016) 30 *International Journal for the Semiotics of Law* 201.

[3] K Brennan, 'Murderous Mothers and Gentle Judges: Paternalism, Patriarchy, and Infanticide' (2018) 30 *Yale Journal of Law and Feminism* 139.

society. In particular, we consider the impact of the patriarchal ideology of 'the myths of motherhood' on all mothers and the role this plays in infanticide cases. Understanding infanticide through the lens of gendered harm leads us to consider the masculine and patriarchal nature of the criminal law and, in particular, its failure to take account of women's experiences. We argue that the infanticide law, though imperfect, is a pragmatic[4] means of recognising women's experiences and the harms that they suffer as a consequence of pregnancy, childbirth and mothering in the twenty-first century.

I. Sex, Gender and the Infanticide Law

Infanticide is the only criminal offence and defence where one of the factors in determining criminal responsibility is the sex and biological experience of the offender.[5] The law provides for lenient treatment of women on the basis that at the time of the killing, 'the balance of her mind was disturbed by reason of her not having fully recovered from the effect of giving birth to the child or by reason of the effect of lactation consequent upon the birth of the child'.[6] Infanticide is therefore defined according to the sex and reproductive function of the offender, who must be the biological mother of the victim aged under 12 months, and the mitigation provided for is based on having given birth or lactating. The infanticide law is usually understood as providing for a medical defence based on the *biological* effect of childbirth/lactation and as requiring a mental disorder, though in practice this is not necessarily how the law is used,[7] nor was it the aim of Parliament when enacting the law.[8] While the law is based on sex, gender is also a significant factor in our understanding of the law and how it is applied. As we outline in this chapter, social expectations for the division of childcare labour and how women are expected to parent their children also play an important role in the crime and the law.[9]

The gendered/sex-based aspects of the infanticide law are often perceived as controversial, and consequently form the basis for one of the key arguments for seeking abolition of the offence/defence. Although, as Daniel Grey has shown,

[4] MJ Radin, 'The Pragmatist and the Feminist' (1989) 63 *Southern California Law Review* 1699; M Oberman, 'Mothers Who Kill: Coming to Terms with Modern American Infanticide' (1996) 34 *American Criminal Law Review* 1, 84.

[5] While rape offered another example, this is no longer the case, as a surgically constructed penis '(in particular, through gender reassignment surgery)' would fulfil the element of intentional penetration of a vagina, anus or mouth with a penis, Sexual Offences Act 2003, s 79(3).

[6] Infanticide Act 1938, s 1.

[7] PT d'Orbán, 'Women Who Kill Their Children' (1979) 134 *British Journal of Psychiatry* 560; RD Mackay, 'The Consequences of Killing Very Young Children' [1993] *Crim LR* 21; A Morris and A Wilczynski, 'Parents Who Kill Their Children' [1993] *Crim LR* 31.

[8] See discussion below and also ch 1 of this volume, where the history of the law is discussed in more detail.

[9] See discussion in section II.

feminist campaigning played an important part in the enactment of the 1922 Infanticide Act,[10] over the last 40 years (at least) feminists have criticised infanticide statutes for enshrining stereotypical bio-psychiatric sexist notions that women are vulnerable to madness due to their normal reproductive functions.[11] The law has also been subjected to feminist criticism for embedding sexist gender constructions – the 'sad' and 'mad' tropes.[12]

Feminists first critiqued the infanticide law on the ground that it medicalises the crime by enshrining a bio-psychiatric explanation of maternal infanticide that ignores the structural causes of the offence. For example, Katherine O'Donovan argued that the 1938 Act 'makes explicit the medicalisation of the crime':

> As the wording makes clear, it is to the process of giving birth, the effect of this on the mother's body, and the hormonal and other processes that are involved in lactation that the statute refers. The idea behind this is that physical processes, whether they are called chemistry or hysteria, can influence behaviour in such a way as to reduce criminal responsibility.[13]

Medicalisation is considered problematic because it explains female criminality on the basis of sex difference, specifically the physiological experiences of childbirth and lactation, blaming 'raging hormones' and ignoring the social, political and economic causes of infanticide.[14] In particular, it is said that the infanticide law masks the real reasons for women's violence against their young children – their position and role in the family, particularly with respect to the burden of child-caring responsibilities.[15] As Edwards states, 'Women are punished for society's failure, a reality which becomes translated into one of a pathological dimension.'[16]

Linked with this is the need to explain a crime that is so unthinkable in our culture and so at odds with our cultural expectations of mothers as self-sacrificing, entirely child-focused, selfless, patient, nurturing, gentle and loving.[17] Blaming 'raging hormones' not only avoids uncomfortable confrontation about the role of social and political factors in the death of infants at the hands of their mothers, it also eludes recognition of the fact that our cultural ideals of motherhood are just that – ideals, which are often difficult, if not impossible, to meet.[18] Thus, rather than countenance that the reality for many women in how they experience motherhood, particularly in contexts of social and economic stresses, is very different

[10] DJR Grey, 'Women's Policy Networks and the Infanticide Act 1922' (2010) 21 *Twentieth Century British History* 441.

[11] See, eg, Edwards (n 1); K O'Donovan, 'The Medicalisation of Infanticide' [1984] *Crim LR* 259; S Weare, '"The Mad", "the Bad", "the Victim": Gendered Constructions of Women Who Kill within the Criminal Justice System' (2013) 2 *Laws* 337.

[12] Outlined below.

[13] O'Donovan (n 11) 262.

[14] Edwards (n 1) 99.

[15] See, eg, ibid 96–100.

[16] ibid 97.

[17] For further discussion of the expectations of idealised motherhood, see discussion in section II.

[18] Such perceptions of motherhood are discussed in section II.

from idealised expectations, and that 'normal' mothers can act violently in the face of such stresses, it is said that the infanticide law seeks a pathological explanation, so negating the woman's agency.[19] The consequence of the infanticide offence/defence, so the argument concludes, is that women's actions are viewed as irrational and 'mad' outbursts of violence, instead of rational, if desperate, responses to the often intolerable nature of child rearing.[20] Wilczynski notes that the 'medicalization' of maternal filicide 'promotes the view that *all* women are "natural" mothers, and helps reconcile society's view that motherhood is constantly and innately fulfilling and joyful, with the stark reality that many women do not actually experience it this way'.[21]

There are two responses to the above medicalisation critique. First, although this approach to the law assumes that the infanticide statutes explicitly adopted nineteenth-century medical thinking that linked the 'insanities of reproduction' with the physiological impact of birth on the mother's mind, historical analysis of the background to this legislation shows this to be a false assumption.[22] Indeed, critiques of the law from the medicalisation perspective place undue emphasis on the idea that nineteenth- and early twentieth-century medical thinking was, first, purely biologically focused in its approach and, second, a significant influence on the infanticide reform, such that legislators simply lifted these theories and made them part of the law. The history behind this law tells a different story. Although it would not be fair to say that sexist medical thinking played no part in the enactment of the English and Welsh infanticide statutes,[23] these theories were much less important than has been credited.[24] In fact other factors, particularly popular lay understandings of this crime that took account of the distressing social circumstances involved and did not explain infanticide in a purely biological sense, as well criminal justice concerns and norms,[25] played a more important role.

For example, Ward refutes the medicalisation theory, arguing that these laws embody a lay understanding of the crime that is not purely biological in nature. He argues that the 1922 Act enshrined a lay or commonsense theory to explain, and mitigate, infanticide, and that medical theory played no part in the adoption of

[19] Discussed further below.

[20] See generally, A Morris and A Wilczynski, 'Rocking the Cradle: Mothers Who Kill Their Children' in H Birch (ed), *Moving Targets: Women, Murder, and Representation* (Virago 1993) 216; A Wilczynski, 'Mad or Bad? Child-Killers, Gender and the Courts' (1997) 37 *British Journal of Criminology* 419, 425–26; A Wilczynski, *Child Homicide* (Greenwich Medical Media Ltd 1997) 124.

[21] Wilczynski, 'Mad or Bad?' (n 20) 425; Wilczynski, *Child Homicide* (n 20) 124.

[22] See discussion in ch 1 of this volume.

[23] A Loughnan, 'The "Strange" Case of the Infanticide Doctrine' (2012) 32 *OJLS* 685.

[24] T Ward, 'The Sad Subject of Infanticide: Law, Medicine and Child Murder, 1860–1938' (1999) 8 *Social & Legal Studies* 163; KJ Kramar and WD Watson, 'The Insanities of Reproduction: Medico-Legal Knowledge and the Development of Infanticide Law' (2006) 15 *Social & Legal Studies* 237. See also, for the Irish experience: K Brennan, '"Traditions of English Liberal Thought": A History of the Enactment of an Infanticide Law in Ireland' (2013) 50 *Irish Jurist* 100, and KJ Kramar, *Unwilling Mothers, Unwanted Babies Infanticide in Canada* (UBC Press 2005), for the Canadian experience.

[25] Ward (n 24); Kramar and Watson (n 24).

this law. Whilst this lay rationale did have a biological element, being based partly on popular sexist perceptions about the impact of birth on a woman's mental balance, it also took account of the social circumstances in which the birth took place.[26] Further, although he recognises that medical thinking played a greater part in the 1938 statute, this was only because it suited the legislative agenda by providing a justification for extending the law to cover women who killed older babies. Loughnan also emphasises the importance of lay thinking in the history of this law and in how the infanticide doctrine developed, as well as the 'porous boundary between women's mental state and their circumstances' in these non-expert understandings that 'result[ed] in a long-lasting legal construction of [infanticide offenders] … as over-determined and hyper-contextualized'.[27] However, she identifies a 'close connection' between lay and medical knowledge about postpartum mental illness, in that scientific expertise 'formed a firm under layer for the lenient practices that would be formalised in the infanticide doctrine'.[28] She also highlights the importance of nineteenth-century sexist gender constructions in both expert and non-expert knowledge, which viewed women as passive subjects and saw their mental conditions as being 'closely related or determined by biology'.[29]

Kramar and Watson took up up Ward's anti-medicalisation argument, finding further support for it through an exploration of the contemporary medical literature on postpartum mental disturbances. They found that the literature rarely explained mental disturbances in women postpartum as being due to either one cause or another (ie biological or social). Rather, 'the interplay between mind/body and social context seemed obvious to experts in mental science'.[30] However, although Kramar and Watson 'broadly support' Ward's conclusions about the 1922/1938 infanticide laws as not being as bio-psychiatric or sexist, as had been thought by those supporting the medicalisation thesis, they do not fully reject the medicalisation theory. They argue that although legislators, lawyers and psychiatrists may not have intended to adopt a bio-psychiatric explanation, the fact that such an explanation 'was written into documents as culturally significant as the English Acts … may be of social significance'.[31] Medicalisation theorists have interpreted the infanticide statutes as embodying a bio-psychiatric theory, and this, in their view, means that 'some quantum of "medicalization" can be said to have occurred'.[32]

Ultimately, as explained in chapter 1 of this volume, the reasons for the enactment and re-enactment of the infanticide law were pragmatic, and the medical rationale was never the *raison d'être* of the law but the means through which legislators were able to achieve a more lenient response to this offender.[33] The importance

[26] For further discussion, see ch 1 of this volume.
[27] Loughnan (n 23) 698.
[28] ibid 699.
[29] ibid.
[30] Kramar and Watson (n 24) 250.
[31] ibid 251.
[32] ibid 252.
[33] K Brennan, 'Beyond the Medical Model: A Rationale for Infanticide Legislation' (2007) 58 *NILQ* 505. See also ch 1 of this volume.

of the medical rationale was that it contained a justification for treating women who killed their babies differently from, and more leniently than, other killers, while respecting the criminal law's usual requirement for individual responsibility.[34] However, as these accounts of the history of the law show, the supposed medical theory embodied in the law was, in reality, a lay theory that understood the role of social causes in the crime, albeit that it was also imbued with sexist ideas about the connection between childbirth and 'madness'. Thus, the medicalisation argument is significantly undermined by these historical accounts of the foundations of the infanticide law. This is not to say that the medicalisation theory has no merit, because, as Kramar and Watson point out, the fact that the law has been read in this way – that is, as providing for a bio-psychiatric defence – means something.[35] Indeed, if this is how the law is widely understood and applied now[36] then, irrespective of what Parliament may have intended or meant by the law when it was enacted, this would arguably validate the feminist medicalisation theory. Further, although the lay conception of the infanticide mitigation did recognise the social causes of this crime, it is fair to say that this was not necessarily without sexist undertones, in that popular perceptions about the impact of childbirth on a woman's mental state arguably did play a part, albeit that this was not directly informed by medical thinking and was not exclusively biological in focus – the social circumstances of this crime were an important part of how it was understood.

Finally, it is worth pointing out that although the medicalisation theory assumes that the language of the statute provides for a bio-psychiatric mitigation (a mental *illness* caused by the *physiological* effects of childbirth/lactation), the meaning of the relevant phrase (or phrases) contained in the Infanticide Act 1938 – 'the balance of her mind was disturbed by reason of her not having fully recovered from the effect of giving birth to the child or by reason of the effect of lactation consequent upon the birth of the child' – has never been considered by the courts. The English appeal courts may well, should an opportunity arise, interpret the language of the law in the way that feminist medicalisation adherents and others view it – as bio-psychiatric. However, it is at least arguable that such an interpretation is not a foregone conclusion. Indeed, the Canadian Supreme Court recently held that the infanticide provision does not require a defined mental or psychological condition or mental illness:[37] parliamentary intention was for a 'broad and flexible legal standard which will serve the ends of justice in the particular circumstances of these difficult cases'.[38] Although the Court said nothing about what is meant by the effects of birth or lactation, it seems clear that the Canadian provision does not require a psychiatric condition. This suggests that the medicalisation argument may be based on a misconception of what the law means.

[34] Discussed in section II.B in further detail.
[35] Kramar and Watson (n 24).
[36] See discussion in ch 1 of this volume.
[37] *R v Borowiec* [2016] 1 SCR 80.
[38] ibid [2].

There is a second challenge to the feminist medicalisation thesis relating to how the law has been used. Studies have shown that the infanticide law has been applied more generously than the language of the legislation appears to allow according to the medicalisation interpretation: notably, that any sign of emotional distress is perceived as justification for use of the infanticide offence/defence.[39] Interestingly, studies indicate that the way the law has been used, at least in the later decades of the twentieth century,[40] reflects the lay interpretation of infanticide that Ward and others have argued the legislation adopted, one that takes account of social factors and which does not require a medical diagnosis of a mental disorder.[41] Thus, even if it could be said that the wording of the statute sets infanticide up as bio-psychiatric offence/defence, in practice the law has not always medicalised this group of offenders to the extent critics have suggested. However, while the application of the law may lessen the force of the medicalisation argument, it does not wholly deal with feminist concerns about this law. In particular, if the infanticide law is being used to give special, lenient treatment to mothers who are *not* mentally ill then this may nonetheless be considered problematic, even if social factors are in reality being considered, because these offenders are officially being labelled as 'mad'. In other words, while those involved in these cases may understand that the mitigation is something very different from what is suggested by the medicalisation thesis and may be taking account of the social factors that caused this crime, the message being sent with an infanticide conviction is that the mother was 'mad' because this is what the law ostensibly says.

The labelling of the offender as 'mad' via an infanticide conviction leads us to the issue of gender construction theory and a second feminist critique of the infanticide law. The construction of women offenders as 'mad', 'bad' or 'sad' is something feminists have identified as a tendency within the criminal justice system generally.[42] Weare, in her analysis of the way in which women's agency and responsibility are denied in the criminal justice system through psychiatric understandings of their crimes, identifies the infanticide law as a 'clear example' of the trend to pathologise women's offending, highlighting how women are labelled as 'mad' under this law, despite not having a diagnosis of puerperal psychosis or

[39] Morris and Wilczynski (n 7); d'Orbán (n 7); Mackay (n 7). See also discussion in ch 1 of this volume.

[40] There is some evidence that a stricter approach may be emerging, particularly in cases of newborn child killing. For example, since 2019, three women have been convicted of murdering their newborn children. In each case the Crown Prosecution Service proceeded with a murder charge. Historically, the trend appears to be that the prosecution would accept a plea of infanticide.

[41] Morris and Wilczynski (n 7); d'Orbán (n 7); Mackay (n 7). See ch 1 of this volume for discussion.

[42] For example, see A Ballinger, 'Masculinity in the Dock: Legal Responses to Male Violence and Female Retaliation in England and Wales, 1900–1965' (2007) 16 *Social & Legal Studies* 459; A Ballinger, *Gender, Truth and State Power: Capitalising on Punishment* (Routledge 2016); B Morrissey, *When Women Kill: Questions of Agency and Subjectivity* (Routledge 2003); E Milne and J Turton, 'Understanding Violent Women' in E Milne et al (eds), *Women and the Criminal Justice System: Failing Victims and Offenders?* (Palgrave Macmillan 2018) 119; Morris and Wilczynski (n 20); Wilczynski, 'Mad or Bad?' (n 20).

indeed any mental disorder (Weare appears to assume that the statute requires a diagnosis of puerperal psychosis).[43] Furthermore, it can also be said that the infanticide law enshrines the 'sad' construction of the female offender – the view that she is a pathetic victim of her circumstances – when it is used in cases where there is no mental disorder and yet lenient treatment is provided because of the social circumstances of the offence. Ward, for example, argues that the Infanticide Acts recognises the 'sad' construct of the legal subject – the 'social casualty driven by overwhelming stress'.[44]

Although individual women who kill their infants benefit from the lenience offered by these sexist constructions of madness and sadness – notably, it is incredibly rare for a woman convicted of infanticide to be sentenced to immediate custody[45] – feminists are critical because of the ramifications of such approaches for women more generally. First, it is said that the construction of women who offend along these gendered lines 'reproduces and reinforces' wider societal constructions of women as passive objects who are subject to their circumstances, which harm all women in terms of how they are understood.[46] Second, these constructions are perceived to serve to deny the offender's agency – she is either mad or a vulnerable victim of her circumstances, and in neither case is she understood to have made a rational choice to commit the crime in the face of overwhelming inequalities.[47] While the woman is held individually accountable for her action through the application of the criminal law, it is not the woman as a moral agent who is to blame, but rather her 'madness' or 'sadness' that has caused her criminalised behaviour. The consequence is that ultimately the structural causes of the offence, such as the role of different intersecting inequalities, are not recognised and so remain unchallenged.[48] As Ballinger argues:

> [L]eniency … [comes] at a price, particularly when it [is] the end result of replacing agentic, rational explanations with pathological excuses … In particular, it undermine[s] the structural causes of infanticide and child murder such as gross gender inequality and the wider social and economic circumstances which [flow] from that inequality.[49]

[43] Weare (n 11) 344–45.

[44] Ward (n 24) 176.

[45] The Office for National Statistics reports that between April 2010 to March 2011 and April 2020 to March 2021, out of the 10 women convicted of infanticide, only one was imprisoned as part of her sentence. Office for National Statistics, 'Appendix Tables: Homicide in England and Wales' (10 February 2022) at www.ons.gov.uk/peoplepopulationandcommunity/crimeandjustice/datasets/appendixtableshomicideinenglandandwales (accessed 20 January 2023) Worksheet 26. However, it should be noted that the authors are unable to identify this case, and that the nature of the reporting of sentencing statistics means that the imprisonment may have been for a crime concurrently charged, which we are unable to determine. Between 2002 and 2010, no woman convicted of infanticide was imprisoned: Freedom of Information Request to the Ministry of Justice by the authors (ref 004-15 FOI 95231).

[46] For example, see Ballinger, 'Masculinity in the Dock' (n 42) 475–78; Ballinger, *Gender, Truth and State Power* (n 42) 74. See generally, Morrissey (n 42) 1–29.

[47] See generally, Morrissey (n 42) 1–29; Ballinger, *Gender, Truth and State Power* (n 42) 57, 74.

[48] Ballinger, *Gender, Truth and State Power* (n 42) 53–74; Morrissey (n 42) 19.

[49] Ballinger, *Gender, Truth and State Power* (n 42) 57.

As Brennan has previously argued, however, the 'mad'/'sad' construction of the infanticide offender must be read in the context of wider criminal law doctrine.[50] Our modern criminal law is based on the Enlightenment idea of the rational and free individual (typically male) who chooses to break the law, and whose criminality is always decontexualised: the criminal law never understands offending in its wider socio-economic or political context; it always blames the individual.[51] Indeed, even when mental condition defences such as insanity are used to mitigate a crime by focusing on the offender's lack of rationality, these defences focus on individual pathology rather than wider social conditions, something we see reflected in the infanticide law.[52] Thus, although it is not ideal that women who kill their babies may be viewed as mad or sad (or a mixture of both) and hence as non-agentic/irrational, eradicating these constructions would not result in recognition of the structural causes of this crime or leniency on that basis; in fact, without these constructions it would be impossible to provide for lenient convictions and harsher punishment would be more likely to result.[53] In other words, some degree of agency denial is arguably needed in order to justify lenient disposals in the context of how our current criminal law allocates and understands criminal responsibility.[54] Assuming we do not want harsher outcomes for offending women, these sad/mad gender constructions therefore constitute a 'necessary evil'.[55] Indeed, as we have noted above, the purpose of the ostensible medical rationale of the infanticide law was to ensure that the law's requirement for individualised responsibility was respected – otherwise, reform would have been impossible.[56] The issue of the masculinity of the criminal law and the problems it poses in terms of recognising women's experiences will be discussed further below in section II.B.

Although we may now read the infanticide law as a clear example of the construction of women offenders as mad/sad and thus non-agentic, the socio-legal history of the law suggests a more nuanced interpretation. Ward considers the enactment of the 1922 infanticide statute not as a denial of the legal status and agency of the woman who killed her baby, but as an effort to 'limit the disruption that … humanitarian sentiments caused to legal ascriptions of responsibility by *reasserting* the woman's status as a legal subject', stating '[f]ar from denying the woman's legal responsibility, the [1922 and 1938] acts were intended to hold women criminally responsible for actions for which they would previously have been either exculpated or found insane'.[57] He argues that infanticide 'constitutes a remarkable and perhaps unique exception' in terms of how the criminal law normally constructs

[50] Brennan (n 3) 176–78.

[51] A Norrie, *Crime, Reason and History: A Critical Introduction to Criminal Law*, 3rd edn (Cambridge University Press 2014). Discussed further in section II.B.

[52] ibid.

[53] Brennan (n 3).

[54] ibid.

[55] ibid.

[56] Ward (n 24); JA Osborne, 'The Crime of Infanticide: Throwing out the Baby with the Bathwater' (1987) 6 *Canadian Journal of Family Law* 47.

[57] Ward (n 24) 176.

subjects. The woman who kills her baby is neither an '"abstract legal subject" who sits outside any social or emotional context', nor is she 'an insane non-subject'.[58] He concludes that the law's construction of the infanticide offender is that she is 'sad', but, unlike in feminist critiques of such approaches, he does not view this as meaning that the woman's responsibility – or agency – is wholly abrogated.[59]

Ward's analysis of the history of this law and the intentions of parliamentarians when enacting/re-enacting the infanticide laws thus enables a different understanding of the mad/sad construct the law has been claimed to embody. One of the key problems with the law on maternal child murder before the enactment of the 1922 Act was that public sympathy for this offender, which was based on an understanding of the circumstances of sadness and madness in which she killed her child, made it impossible to effectively bring her to justice.[60] Consequently, one of the purposes of the 1922 statute was to hold women who killed their babies accountable before the law for a crime that reflected the seriousness of the conduct and her culpability by 'channelling' compassion into an appropriate conviction and sentence that reflected the seriousness of her crime.[61]

Further, the infanticide law does not acquit a woman of the crime of killing her baby; it reduces her criminal responsibility. Thus, although the law may embody the idea that circumstances of sadness/madness were involved in the killing of the child, and that the woman's culpability should be reduced on that basis, it does not abstract her agency from this. In fact, it seems more accurate to say that the infanticide statute treads the line between a wholly agentic and wholly non-agentic explanation for this crime, one where it is recognised that the offender is guilty of a homicide offence, which involved a *wilful* act or omission that caused death, and where her responsibility is reduced, but not eradicated, on the basis of a reduction in, but not elimination of, her rationality. In this light, it could be said that the law recognises the nuances of her agency: she 'wilfully' killed her child by an act or omission, but at a time whilst the 'balance of her mind was disturbed'. This reading of the law also reflects the reality of the experiences of women who cause the death of an infant, as outlined by Milne in her study of suspected newborn child murders. Milne disputes that the debate should be understood as a dichotomy:

> It is not that women either have agency and therefore made a decision to end the life of the [child], or that their actions or inactions occurred as a consequence of wider factors and so they had no option and thus lacked agency; the debate cannot be that simple. When a woman's back is against the wall and she can see only bad options … we cannot think of this as her having 'choices'. And to do so would be to lose sight of the concept of what it means to 'choose'.[62]

[58] ibid.
[59] ibid.
[60] See ch 1 of this volume.
[61] K Brennan, '"A Fine Mixture of Pity and Justice": The Criminal Justice Response to Infanticide in Ireland, 1922–1949' (2013) 31 *Law and History Review* 793.
[62] E Milne, *Criminal Justice Responses to Maternal Filicide: Judging the Failed Mother* (Emerald Publishing Limited 2021) 150.

The feminist medicalisation and gender construction critiques are not necessarily critical of the fact that women who kill their babies receive lenient treatment under the law, because it is understood that the circumstances in which infanticide occurs often do merit a more lenient disposal than could be achieved through other criminal law doctrines.[63] Ultimately what both critiques are concerned with is the fact that the law provides for lenient treatment without explicitly recognising the socio-political causes of infanticide and the sexist message that is then conveyed by medicalising the woman or constructing her as a passive actor driven by circumstances of sadness/madness. Whilst it is regrettable that the law does not explicitly recognise the socio-political causes of infanticide and, arguably, the *real* reasons for lenient treatment of this offender, in the context of wider criminal law principles it would be impossible to allow for a lenient response without employing notions of 'madness'. However, if, as is often argued by proponents of abolition of infanticide,[64] we were to rely on the defence of diminished responsibility to capture cases that have traditionally been covered by infanticide, we would find that it would not be possible to meet the more exacting requirements for that defence, a point that is even more apposite following the 2009 reform of homicide laws in England and Wales, which tightened the conditions for diminished responsibility.[65] Research shows that the infanticide doctrine has in the past, at least, operated more generously than that of diminished responsibility.[66] Notably, unlike the defence of diminished responsibility, a mental disorder has not always been required for infanticide, and neither does the law require a causal link between the accused's mental state and her criminal conduct – a temporal link suffices.[67] Ultimately, while some infanticide cases may be captured by diminished responsibility, many would not be. Thus, although the law does not do what we as feminists would like it to (to explicitly base lenient treatment on the structural causes of the crime), it is better than the alternative, which is arguably more murder convictions and higher sentences in cases where this outcome is not deserved.

In this section we have provided a critical overview of feminist debates on the infanticide law. We argue that although feminist criticisms of the law are not without merit, consideration of the history of this law, how it has been employed in practice, the role of criminal law norms and how the law is currently understood/interpreted by those who use it, offer important challenges to the feminist medicalisation and gender construction critiques. We have also highlighted the importance of the infanticide statute in terms of ensuring lenient treatment for mothers who kill their babies where the circumstances call for a lenient response. In section II we address the infanticide law from a different angle. Rather than looking at why

[63] See ch 1 of this volume for discussion of the circumstances of this crime.

[64] For example, see J Mason, 'The Myth of Madness: Murderous Mothers and Maternal Infanticide' (2021) 85 *The Journal of Criminal Law* 441.

[65] See Mackay (n 7); Mackay, ch 3 of this volume.

[66] See research by d'Orbán (n 7); Mackay (n 7).

[67] N Walker, *Crime and Insanity in England*, vol 1: *The Historical Perspective* (Edinburgh University Press 1968) 134–35.

the infanticide law is considered problematic from a feminist standpoint, we offer a feminist argument in favour of the infanticide law. This argument does not engage in a doctrinal analysis of what the law says or should, from a feminist viewpoint, say. The argument we make is a theoretical one that seeks to provide a feminist justification for the principle behind this law, namely, lenient and different treatment of women who cause the death of their infants. Drawing on West's theory of 'gendered harm' and linking in with feminist critiques of the criminal law as being masculinist in character and focus, we put forward a justification for the infanticide law that argues for special lenient treatment of this offender due to the harms she suffers as a consequence of giving birth and mothering in a patriarchal society, and the inability of the criminal law as it currently stands to address this offence from a feminist stance.

II. Infanticide and Gendered Harms

To justify special lenient treatment for women who kill infants, and thus that supporting the existence of the Infanticide Act 1938 can be and is feminist, we will make two arguments. First, that the phenomenon of infanticide, that is maternal filicide of infants, is a product of society, which is patriarchal and thus prioritises the needs and desires of men to the detriment of women. Consequently, we can understand infanticide as a consequence of one of the 'gendered harms' experienced by women. When viewed in this way, we can also see that responsibility for the crime of infanticide does not fall solely at the feet of the mother but is also shared by wider society.[68] Second, the law, and, specifically for this chapter, the criminal law, is masculine in nature, so prioritises the needs of men to the disadvantage of women. In this legal context, maternal filicide of infants – a crime that exists predominantly due to the oppression of women – is treated by the criminal law and criminal justice as similar to other homicides, which are mostly committed by men. Without the Infanticide Act, women who kill their babies in circumstances where they deserve a lenient response due to the gendered harm they have experienced will find themselves facing a murder conviction, and thus a mandatory life sentence.

The arguments we outline here offer the basis for a feminist argument in support of the principle encapsulated by the Infanticide Act, namely, the possibility of lenient and different treatment of women who kill their babies. We do not pretend that what we present here is a fully developed justification for the retention of this law, nor are we uncritical of the current legislation and how it is applied. However, the chapter does aim to suggest that despite the criticisms of the infanticide law that have been made by feminists, it can be supported on feminist

[68] See, Brennan (n 3) for an analysis of this in Ireland in mid- to late 20th century. See also Oberman (n 4).

grounds. What we provide is a theoretical argument in support of this law; consequently, we do not engage with the doctrinal aspects of the Infanticide Act as it currently stands. However, our argument is premised on the points we made in the previous section: the current infanticide law does not necessarily incorporate a bio-psychiatric defence, and is capable (based on evidence from how it has previously been used) of applying in a way that takes account of the social context of the crime and without the necessity for a psychiatric diagnosis.

A. Infanticide and Patriarchy

One of the key aspects of maternal filicide of infants is that it is a crime that is largely a produce of patriarchy. In chapter 1 of this volume, we outlined the substantial research that has explored the nature of cases of maternal filicide of newborn children and older infants, and the motivations and causes of this form of parental homicide. What is apparent from the analysis of cases of infant killing by women is that the social, economic and cultural contexts are key factors that not only explain why women end the life of their infants, but also can be seen as significant causes of women's fatal acts towards their newborn children and older infants. An important factor in explaining infanticide is the experience of pregnancy, birth and motherhood in a patriarchal society, and the gendered harms that pregnant women and mothers consequently experience. In this section, we begin by examining the social construction of 'good' motherhood and the impact this has upon how women behave and societal expectations of women's behaviour. These social constructions of motherhood can be observed to play a role in infanticide cases.

Motherhood and pregnancy are laden with cultural ideals and expectations of the 'good' mother, which have an impact on how women behave and how they are expected to behave. The ideals against which women are held in terms of when they mother a child or become pregnant can be summarised in feminist literature as the 'myths of motherhood'.[69] Mothering is presented as 'natural' and 'instinctive', rather than cultural, political, economic and historical.[70] The pervasive message of the myths is that to be a woman is to be a mother, and motherhood and mothering are natural, universal and unchanging for all women. Furthermore, the myths draw on the perception that women are inherently caring, nurturing and self-sacrificing, and that such behaviours originate from biology and a woman's ability to birth children.[71] Consequently, the myths set unachievable standards of perfection for women who are mothers, while also

[69] For a full analysis of the myths of motherhood, see Milne (n 62).

[70] SB Hrdy, *Mother Nature: A History of Mothers, Infants, and Natural Selection* (Ballantine Books 2000).

[71] A Oakley, *Woman's Work: The Housewife, Past and Present* (Pantheon 1974); SJ Douglas and MW Michaels, *The Mommy Myth: The Idealization of Motherhood and How It Has Undermined All Women* (Free Press 2005).

constructing and maintaining a popular belief that all women should want to be mothers and that motherhood is the true destiny for women to fulfil. The ideal woman is the 'good' mother who dedicates her life to the health, happiness and well-being of her children, at the expense of all else. The myths of motherhood also impact women before they give birth to a child, and even before they become pregnant.[72] Popular narratives surrounding pregnancy promote that idea that being a 'good' pregnant woman is to put the foetus first and sacrifice your own life for the betterment of the unborn child.[73]

While the myths have a clear impact on how women are expected to mother children, many feminists argue that it is not the act of mothering or being pregnant that is inherently problematic, recognising that mothering can be and is fulfilling for many women.[74] Instead, it is how the biological activities of becoming pregnant and the physical labour of caring for a child are culturally organised and given meaning.[75] The framing of motherhood in ways that result in the oppression and subjugation of women has led feminist scholars to identify that patriarchy is the underlying cause of the myths of motherhood.[76] The myths hold merit due to the ideologies that shape popular thoughts and beliefs of mothering. The dominant ideology in a society represents that society's dominant group: white, heterosexual, middle- and upper-class men. The consequence is that the myths are not just sexist, they are also racist, classist, homophobic, ableist and based on Western standpoints. The ideal 'good' mother is the white, middle-class, married, heterosexual, able-bodied woman who has the exclusive responsibility for mothering her biological children, focusing her time and activities solely on their care and well-being, or doing everything she can to care for and protect her foetus or infant.[77] One of the consequences of this is that such women have far greater resources to mitigate the hardships and difficulties of motherhood. Furthermore, as they fit more closely to the ideals of motherhood, if they do behave in a way

[72] S Bordo, *Unbearable Weight: Feminism, Western Culture, and the Body* (University of California Press 2003); D Lupton, 'Risk and the Ontology of Pregnant Embodiment' in D Lupton (ed), *Risk and Sociocultural Theory: New Directions and Perspectives* (Cambridge University Press 1999) 59; E Martin, *The Woman in the Body: A Cultural Analysis of Reproduction* (Beacon Press 1987).

[73] D Lupton, '"The Best Thing for the Baby": Mothers' Concepts and Experiences Related to Promoting Their Infants' Health and Development' (2011) 13 *Health, Risk & Society* 637; R Gregg, *Pregnancy in a High-Tech Age: Paradoxes of Choice* (New York University Press 1995); C Brooks-Gardner, 'Pregnant Women as Social Problem' in DR Loseke and J Best (eds), *Social Problems: Constructionist Readings* (Aldine de Gruyter 2003) 188.

[74] A Rich, *Of Woman Born: Motherhood as Experience and Institution* (Norton 1986).

[75] T Arendell, 'Conceiving and Investigating Motherhood: The Decade's Scholarship' (2000) 62 *Journal of Marriage and Family* 1192.

[76] S Hays, *The Cultural Contradictions of Motherhood* (Yale University Press 1996); Rich (n 74).

[77] EN Glenn, 'Social Construction of Mothering' in EN Glenn, G Chang and LR Forcey (eds), *Mothering: Ideology, Experience, and Agency* (Routledge 1994) 1; R Solinger, 'Race and "Value": Black and White Illegitimate Babies, 1945–1965' in Glenn, Chang and Forcey (eds) (this footnote) 287; J Flavin, *Our Bodies, Our Crimes: The Policing of Women's Reproduction in America* (New York University Press 2009).

contrary to the myths of motherhood then society is much more likely to demonstrate leniency towards them.[78]

One of the key harms experienced by women due to the myths of motherhood is that, as the responsibility for childbearing and childrearing is overwhelmingly situated with women, it is women who shoulder the greatest share of the labour and burden of pregnancy and motherhood.[79] Further specific harms connected with pregnancy and motherhood may be identified. The focus here is not upon the existence of a pregnancy per se, or the act of mothering a child as the harm, but on the context that surrounds women and dictates their behaviour, and on how society responds to them when they become pregnant and while mothering. The harms of pregnancy and motherhood are social, cultural and economic. While not universal, and not felt to the same extent by all women, we are able to identify these harms when looking at women's experiences. For many women, having children increases their levels of poverty, notably for those women who are supported by state welfare.[80] Women also face significant impact on their earning potential and career progression options after they have a child.[81] Thus we can see a number of palpable costs for women due to pregnancy and motherhood, and this is without considering the physical labour and bodily harm of pregnancy and childbirth, nor the social and cultural controls that society places on women, dictating cultural standards of who should be mothers, when they should be mothers and how they should behave as mothers, often shaming those who do not conform.[82] Furthermore, as the myths saturate society and social and cultural interaction,[83] the harms of motherhood are masked and women who fail to conform to the myths

[78] For example, Morris and Wilczynski give two examples of the application of the Infanticide Act – the middle-class woman is able to make use of the offence/defence, the working-class woman is not: Morris and Wilczynski, 'Rocking the Cradle' (n 20). Discussion of this aspect of the application of infanticide legislation is beyond the scope of this chapter but remains important, and is connected to the myths of motherhood we discuss here.

[79] Diva Dhar, *Women's Unpaid Care Work Has Been Unmeasured and Undervalued for Too Long*, 2020).

[80] For example, in the UK women only receive the child element of child tax credit for their first two children, excluding all future children, a change to welfare brought in by the Conservative Government in 2017: HM Revenue & Customs, 'Guidance: Child Tax Credit: Support for a Maximum of 2 Children' (2020) at www.gov.uk/guidance/child-tax-credit-exceptions-to-the-2-child-limit (accessed 28 August 2020). The policy has plunged women and children into further poverty: A Bawden, 'Two-child benefits cap cuts support for over 1 million children during pandemic' *The Guardian* (London, 15 July 2021) at www.theguardian.com/society/2021/jul/15/two-child-benefits-cap-cuts-support-for-over-1-million-children-during-pandemic (accessed 11 February 2022).

[81] Understanding Society, *How Women's Employment Changes after Having a Child* (2019) at www.understandingsociety.ac.uk/2019/10/22/how-womens-employment-changes-after-having-a-child (accessed 1 September 2020); Fawcett Society, *Parents, Work and Care: Striking the Balance* (2016) at www.fawcettsociety.org.uk/parents-work-and-care-striking-the-balance (accessed 1 September 2020).

[82] Milne (n 62) 94.

[83] DD Johnston and DH Swanson, 'Invisible Mothers: A Content Analysis of Motherhood Ideologies and Myths in Magazines' (2003) 49 *Sex Roles* 21; A Dally, *Inventing Motherhood: The Consequences of an Ideal* (Burnett 1982); EA Kaplan, *Motherhood and Representation: The Mother in Popular Culture and Melodrama* (Routledge 1992); JR Gillis, *A World of Their Own Making: A History of Myth and Ritual in Family Life* (Oxford University Press 1997).

of motherhood are presented as inherently unnatural and bad. The construction of individual women as either 'good' or 'bad' mothers has led scholars to theorise a particular form of oppression of women: 'mother-blame'.[84] Feelings of unhappiness or dissatisfaction that women may feel as mothers are attributed to the failings of the individual woman rather than of the system: a good mother is a happy and contented mother, able to cope with the hardships of motherhood.

Applying this theory to cases of infanticide offers an illustration of how the patriarchal construction and expectations of motherhood are core factors in the conduct of women who kill their infants. As the nature of newborn child killing and the killing of older infants are distinct, we will present examples of each form of infant killing separately. As outlined in chapter 1, newborn child killing follows a crisis pregnancy. Using the theory of the myths of motherhood, we can identify social causes of the crisis that results from the pregnancy, such as experiencing violence and abuse from a partner or other family members, poverty, shame connected to an 'unauthorised' pregnancy.[85] For example, Silipa Keresi, who discovered she was pregnant at 26 weeks of gestation, did not seek medical care for her pregnancy and walked into woods near her place of residence after going into labour. She delivered alone in the middle of the night and then left the baby unattended; the little boy died soon after.[86] At the time she became pregnant, she was living in one hotel room with her abusive and violent husband and their two children, unable to work due to her immigration status and so living in poverty, facing the prospect of being forcibly returned to her country of origin, having been a UK resident for a number of years due to her husband's position in the British Army. In this social context, it is perhaps not surprising that Keresi did not put the needs and well-being of her foetus before her own. And yet the myths of motherhood identify Keresi's failing as 'bad' motherhood and as the individual fault of the pregnant woman. Little to no relief and support are provided for women in situations such as Keresi's; note that nothing was done by society and the state to support her existing children, let alone her unborn child. Rather than providing the support she needed to live in a safe environment, away from violence and abuse and the fear of her husband's discovering she was pregnant, with the economic support she required, she was simply expected, in line with the

[84] PJ Caplan and I Hall-McCorquodale, 'Mother-Blaming in Major Clinical Journals' (1985) 55 *American Journal of Orthopsychiatry* 345; D Jackson and J Mannix, 'Giving Voice to the Burden of Blame: A Feminist Study of Mothers' Experiences of Mother Blaming' (2004) 10 *International Journal of Nursing Practice* 150; AI Garey and T Arendell, 'Children, Work, and Family: Some Thoughts on "Mother-Blame"' in R Hertz and NL Marshall (eds), *Working Families the Transformation of the American Home* (University of California Press 2001) 189; PJ Caplan, 'Mother-Blaming' in M Ladd-Taylor and L Umansky (eds), *'Bad' Mothers: The Politics of Blame in Twentieth-Century America* (New York University Press 1998) 127.

[85] Milne (n 62).

[86] 'Hythe Baby Death: Silipa Keresi was Stressed and Desperate, Court Hears' *BBC News* (22 November 2021) at www.bbc.co.uk/news/uk-england-hampshire-59375040 (accessed 7 February 2023). Note that infanticide was presented by the defence in this case but rejected by the jury. Keresi was convicted of murder and imprisoned for a minimum of nine years:, 'Hythe Baby Death: Silipa Keresi Jailed for Woodland Murder' *BBC News* (2 December 2021) at www.bbc.co.uk/news/uk-england-hampshire-59509306 (accessed 7 February 2023).

myths of motherhood, to prioritise the needs of the unborn child, regardless of the personal cost. The burden of pregnancy in such contexts is felt by women alone.

'Crisis' is also an apt word to describe the context that surrounds cases of maternal filicide of older infants. For example, Natasha Sultan killed her 5-week-old baby, a 'much-wanted child', by inflicting blunt trauma to her child's head.[87] Prior to the violent incident, Sultan had presented to her GP with symptoms that were diagnosed as post-natal depression and sleep deprivation. Sultan was prescribed anti-depressants, but did not take the full dose, as she reported that the need for the medication made her feel like a bad mother (a 'good' mother is a happy and contented mother, able to cope with the hardships of motherhood). Sultan's partner worked nights and so she was often alone with the child, receiving little support with the labour of childcare.[88] Sultan's case provides a further example of the hardships of motherhood, which arguably led to her violent act, being the product of the context in which women are required to mother. As noted above, the burden and harms of parenting overwhelmingly fall on women, and the 'failure' for not mothering well enough, according to the standards of the myths of motherhood, results in the blaming of individual women. The lack of social support provided for Sultan, from either the state or her community, can be identified as creating the context in which she found herself when she inflicted violence on her child – alone, sleep deprived, with no help in sight.

The two cases offer examples of typical cases of infant killings by mothers. Other examples exist, of course, but it is beyond the scope of this chapter to present an analysis of every such case. Other scholars have similarly noted the importance of the role of the gendered context of pregnancy and mothering in contemporary Western society in infanticide cases. Langer, for example, in her review of 86 infanticide cases across five jurisdictions,[89] highlights the contribution that ideals of motherhood make to the development of postpartum mental ill-health and the crime of infanticide.[90] She emphasises in particular the impact of the internalisation of idealised expectations of good motherhood by mothers, and how experiences of shame and denial, when the reality of motherhood fails to meet these expectations, contribute to postpartum depression and ultimately infanticide.

Similarly, Oberman in her American study explains infanticide as a 'gendered phenomenon'.[91] In particular she highlights the role of the biological and socio-cultural context of pregnancy and childbirth in neonaticide, the killing of an

[87] 'Baby-Killing Mum Natasha Sultan "Needed More Support"' *BBC News* (22 January 2014) at www.bbc.co.uk/news/uk-england-humber-25842236 (accessed 7 February 2023).

[88] Sultan was convicted of infanticide, after her guilty plea was accepted by the Crown Prosecution Service.

[89] Australia, New Zealand, UK, Canada and the US.

[90] R Langer, '"Mother of Sorrows": Post-Partum Mental Disorder and the Law across Five Jurisdictions' (2012) 19 *Psychiatry, Psychology and Law* 358, 374–79. See also M Smithey, *The Cultural and Economic Context of Maternal Infanticide: A Crying Baby and the Inability to Escape* (Emerald 2019); R Lansdowne, 'Infanticide: Psychiatrists in the Plea Bargaining Process' (1990) 16 *Monash University Law Review* 41, 60–62; Morris and Wilczynski, 'Rocking the Cradle' (n 20) 216.

[91] Oberman (n 4).

infant within 24 hours of birth. In cases involving older children, she identifies society's allocation of caretaking duties to mothers as a core explanation for maternal infanticide.[92] It is the experience of motherhood in terms of how women are expected to mother and the challenges of mothering in contemporary society that she identifies as crucial to understanding this crime. Notably, she attributes infanticide (of children older than one day) to the division of labour between parents and society's 'fervent commitment to the notion that is normal and healthy for mothers to care for their babies in isolation in the home in the early months and years of their babies' lives'.[93] In an effort to explain the ambivalent public and criminal justice response to this crime in the USA, where there is no specific infanticide law and where women who kill their children have no special defence, she states:

> Our ambivalence in punishing these women comes not so much from our sensitivity to issue of diminished capacity as from our awareness that the mothers had precious few options. At the time they killed their children, all of these women were emotionally, intellectually, socially, and/or financially unable to cope with the demands of motherhood in isolation – motherhood as it is structured in modern American society.[94]

The key point we have highlighted in this section is that due to the ways women are expected to mother under patriarchy – the myths of motherhood – women who kill their infants come to the situation where the death of the child by their hand is, to a lesser or greater extent, a product of the context in which the women are pregnant and/or mothers. To make this point is not to remove all agency from women who cause the death of their infants but to acknowledge the reality of these killings. Of course, not all women who face difficulties mothering their children will cause their deaths. As we have already noted, differing levels of resources to which women have access, and the operation of the myths inconsistently and prejudicially, mean that certain groups of women will be impacted more readily. Our purpose in highlighting the harms of motherhood and pregnancy as significant causes of infanticide is not to say that no woman would ever be responsible for killing her child but to illustrate that wider society – specifically patriarchy – has a hand in these tragic outcomes for infants, and for their mothers who cause their deaths.

B. Gendered Harm of Maternal Infant Filicide and the Law

As outlined in section II.A, through a feminist lens the patriarchal construction of motherhood and mothering can be identified as a significant cause in maternal infant killing. Feminist legal scholars argue that the criminal law only sees some harms – the harms of men – as *true* harms that need to be criminalised. To recognise the disadvantages experienced by women in law, feminist legal

[92] ibid.
[93] ibid 65.
[94] ibid 68.

scholars use the concept of 'gendered harm'. The term is used to acknowledge the harms experienced by women because they *are* women.[95] These harms are based both on the reality of women's sex, but also on the way in which women are expected to live their lives because of gender norms. Mother-blame and the impact of the myths of motherhood upon women are clear examples of gendered harms. The significance of gendered harm for feminist legal scholars is that these are harms that the state and the law often fail to recognise and respond to in the way that harms perceived and experienced by men are addressed. For example, sexual harassment and rape,[96] intimate partner violence and abuse,[97] and unwanted pregnancy[98] are harms predominantly, or entirely, experienced by women, and so men have struggled, and continue to struggle, to be able to see and appreciate the consequences of such harms. As West argues, the law is based on the values and fears of men – the harms they see and experience – rather on than the values and fears of women.[99] Thus, experiences of women, the harms they face, are either negated or not fully recognised by the law.[100] There is not one singular experience of being a woman, and thus the harms are not universal.[101] Nevertheless, West's analysis makes for a useful tool to understand the maleness and patriarchal nature of the Rule of Law. One clear example of this is the difficulties women have found in making use of the partial defence of loss of control in instances where they kill an abusive partner. The partial defence was originally designed for men to use when they killed their adulterous wives in a fit of anger.[102] While attempts were made to change the law in 2009, so making it easier for women to successfully plead the defence, and harder for men to employ when they kill partners who have been unfaithful,[103] women still find it incredibly difficult to make use of this defence, and feminist scholars argue that gender biases against women and lack of comprehension of the reality of intimate partner violence and abuse are the key reasons for this continued gendered injustice.[104]

[95] J Conaghan, 'Gendered Harms and the Law of Tort: Remedying (Sexual) Harassment' (1996) 16 *OJLS* 407; R West, *Caring for Justice* (New York University Press 1997); A Howe, '"Social Injury" Revisited: Towards a Feminist Theory of Social Justice' (1987) 15 *International Journal of the Sociology of Law* 423; R Graycar and J Morgan, *The Hidden Gender of Law*, 2nd edn (Federation Press 2002).

[96] Conaghan (n 95).

[97] A Carline and PW Easteal, *Shades of Grey: Domestic and Sexual Violence against Women: Law Reform and Society* (Routledge 2014).

[98] R West, 'Jurisprudence and Gender' (1988) 55 *University of Chicago Law Review* 1.

[99] ibid.

[100] See also W Chan and GS Rigakos, 'Risk, Crime and Gender' (2002) 42 *British Journal of Criminology* 743.

[101] AP Harris, 'Race and Essentialism in Feminist Legal Theory' (1990) 42 *Stanford Law Review* 581.

[102] *R v Mawgridge* (1707) Kel 119.

[103] Coroners and Justice Act 2009; Ministry of Justice, *Murder, Manslaughter and Infanticide: Proposals for Reform of the Law* (Law Com CP No 19, 2008); Law Commission, *Murder, Manslaughter and Infanticide* (Law Com No 304, 2006).

[104] SSM Edwards, 'Anger and Fear as Justifiable Preludes for Loss of Self-Control' (2010) 74 *The Journal of Criminal Law* 223; K Fitz-Gibbon, *Homicide Law Reform, Gender and the Provocation Defence: A Comparative Perspective* (Palgrave Macmillan 2014); A Wu, 'Going Full Circle: Gender and the "Loss of Control" Defence under the Coroners and Justice Act 2009' (2019) 1 *Rule of Law Journal* 46.

The gendered harms of pregnancy and motherhood can be connected to women's acts of violence against their children, an argument made by both authors in separate work. Brennan, in her analysis of infanticide cases in Ireland during the twentieth century, argues that women's decisions to conceal their pregnancies and then kill their newborn children can be seen as a consequence of the gendered harms of pregnancy and motherhood.[105] Within Irish society over this period, women lacked reproductive autonomy, including access to contraception and abortion; there were substantial negative responses to women who became pregnant outside of marriage, with unmarried pregnant women forced into Magdalene Laundries and mother and baby homes; and there was a lack of economic, cultural and social support to raise children. This lack of reproductive autonomy and the harm it caused to women can be seen to directly lead to the taking of steps by women to rid themselves of a pregnancy and/or newborn child:

> [P]atriarchal norms and values, which were embedded in various legal provisions and in the Irish state's approach to unmarried mothers, cause harm to women … [I]t is possible to see that the harm caused to the baby by its mother was a consequence of the 'gendered harms' caused to her by patriarchy, and the state's adoption of patriarchal values in its laws and policies.[106]

Milne builds on Brennan's work, in her analysis of 15 criminal cases of women suspected of causing the death of a late-term foetus or newborn child from England and Wales, heard in the courts between 2010 and 2019.[107] Milne argues that while it cannot be said for certain that the women in these cases did not want the pregnancy to exist, it is apparent that they conceptualised their pregnancies as 'unauthorised' by society and/or the environment in which they lived. Such perceptions existed for a host of reasons, including due to fear of reactions from their partners and/or family members, fear of losing other children to social care, and the trauma of sexual violence. The unauthorised nature of these pregnancies can be directly connected to gendered harms outlined above – society makes it very clear to women when they can or should be pregnant. Consider, for example, the social panics over both 'teen' pregnancies[108] and 'geriatric' mothers.[109] Thus, even today, we can see that women do not have reproductive autonomy to determine when and whether they should be pregnant and to act accordingly. As with Brennan's study, Milne argues that we can directly attribute women's decisions to illegally end the pregnancy in the later stages of gestation, or to conceal/deny a pregnancy, give birth alone, and then not take steps to prevent the death of the child, or to actively kill the newborn, to the gendered harms of pregnancy and motherhood.

[105] Brennan (n 3).

[106] ibid 186.

[107] Milne (n 62).

[108] Public Health England, 'Guidance: Teenage Pregnancy Prevention Framework' (2018) at www.gov.uk/government/publications/teenage-pregnancy-prevention-framework (accessed 28 August 2020).

[109] National Health Service, 'Pregnancy Warning for Older Women' (2009) at www.nhs.uk/news/pregnancy-and-child/pregnancy-warning-for-older-women/ (accessed 28 August 2020).

However, as already noted, the principle of criminal law doctrine is that unless a mental impairment can be proved, defendants are considered rational and free individuals, and judged for their conduct accordingly. The current operation of the criminal law means it can only see an individual as responsible for their actions, and criminality is always decontextualised.[110] However, as countless feminist legal scholars have pointed out, this construction of the criminal law means that the realities of crime for women are negated and hidden. As Naffine argues:

> The persons of criminal law, in their various guises, are typically portrayed as being without a sex, as simply human beings. They are also treated as beings whom the law respects equally. The sex of the person is not meant to matter or even count. Blame and protection of the person is not meant to depend on their sex … the persons of criminal law were and are still men and … this has undermined the claims of criminal law and lawyers that theirs is a principled institution concerned equally with the wrongdoing and welfare of all.[111]

The nature of the criminal law and its application, due to the maleness and patriarchal nature of the Rule of Law, is that the acts of women who kill an infant are seen to be individual. The killing, and possibly the context of the killing, is understood and perceived to be her fault alone. There is little to no ability of the criminal law to perceive that society may play a role in the death of the infant due to the gendered harms of motherhood and pregnancy, and so to consider that the accused woman should not shoulder all the criminal sanction of the conduct.[112] If we look at Keresi and Sultan's cases, for example, we can clearly see that they are both responsible for the death of the infant.[113] The maleness of the Rule of Law means that they are also considered culpable, as the focus is on their individual conduct and state of mind at the time of the fatal act or omission. Consequently, the 'harm' of patriarchy in cases of infanticide is exacerbated by the legal system and criminal law, under which rules a woman who kills an infant will be judged. The legal response is to hold her alone accountable and to decline to recognise the contribution of patriarchy to this crime.

The nature of most cases of maternal filicide of an infant is that, if the offence/defence of infanticide did not exist, or if it were to continue to be narrowly interpreted as a medical defence similar to diminished responsibility,[114] women generally would have no defence to a charge of murder, which carries a life sentence and usually a minimum term of imprisonment of 15 years. The question we are raising in this chapter is whether this is a *just* outcome to these cases, considering the role patriarchal society has in the death of the child. If society were to operate in a way that alleviates the pain and difficulties of pregnancy

[110] Norrie (n 51).
[111] N Naffine, *Criminal Law and the Man Problem* (Hart Publishing 2019) 2.
[112] Brennan (n 3); Milne (n 62); Morris and Wilczynski, 'Rocking the Cradle' (n 20); Oberman (n 4).
[113] Although it should be noted that Keresi denied responsibility, a denial the jury rejected when convicting her.
[114] See ch 1 and Ronnie Mackay's analysis in ch 3 of this volume.

and motherhood, so minimising or eradicating the gendered harms, and with it the myths of motherhood, then we might be in a position to turn to the woman who kills her infant and consider her alone to be responsible and thus deserving of the punishment of the criminal law for her act of homicide. In a truly equal society, where women are not disadvantaged, perhaps a murder conviction and life sentence might be appropriate. However, while both the operation of society and the law are orientated towards men, we would query the fairness of holding women alone culpable.

Ideally, society is moving towards the end of patriarchal rule, resulting in actual fairness and equality for women. Such an endpoint nevertheless seems a distant prospect, so, while we wait for that, we need to consider the legal outcomes for women such as Keresi and Sultan. How cases of maternal filicide of infants conclude, we are arguing, is where the offence/defence of infanticide plays a crucial part. If we assess the legal response to women who kill infants from a feminist perspective, as we are proposing here, then the level of culpability of women such as Keresi and Sultan changes. No longer are they the only culpable party in the death of the child. We could argue that women who kill infants continue to be responsible, but culpability is now also situated with society as a whole, either entirely or in part, due to the social causes of the fatal behaviour of the women – the gendered harms of pregnancy and motherhood.

If the criminal law were to take a feminist approach to these cases then one outcome could be that women would simply not be prosecuted for their actions. Such an outcome would be unpalatable for many, as it fails to acknowledge the taking of a life and indicating that a wrong was done. Furthermore, such an approach risks implying that children's lives do not matter, an approach inconsistent with the UN Convention on the Rights of the Child.[115] The core benefit of an infanticide offence is that it is a homicide offence, and so a conviction for infanticide means that the unlawful killing of a child, and the wrongness of that action/inaction by a woman, is acknowledged. But what is also acknowledged is that the woman has reduced culpability for the death of the child, hence the lower sentence received for infanticide compared to murder. Furthermore, if the infanticide law is utilised as we are proposing, the limited culpability is not based on the 'madness' or 'sadness' of the woman, as feminists have criticised, but is an acknowledgement that society has a role in the death of this child due to the ways it expects women to mother their children.[116]

If the criminal law were feminist, or at least not masculine, in the way it constructed criminal culpability, it might be possible to achieve reduced culpability

[115] Unicef UK, 'How We Protect Children's Rights' (nd) at www.unicef.org.uk/what-we-do/un-convention-child-rights/ (accessed 11 October 2020).

[116] We do not have the space to elaborate on this point here, but it is important to highlight that further research is needed to consider how the law could and should be interpreted, particularly considering the history of the Infanticide Act and Parliament's intentions when enacting it in 1922 and re-enacting it in 1938.

for maternal infanticide in a way that explicitly acknowledges in the law the role of patriarchy – the gendered harm of pregnancy and motherhood – in the crime. However, as it stands, accepting this arguably imperfect infanticide offence/defence is a pragmatic way to achieve justice in these cases. The ideal situation is that society will change, patriarchy will be overturned and women will be equal to men, so ending the myths of motherhood and the harms to women. However, while we fight for that outcome, which is currently nowhere in sight, an infanticide offence/defence can provide justice for women.

III. Conclusion

Michelle Oberman argues that there are 'dangers inherent in [an] unarticulated impulse to exceptionalize infanticide'.[117] Arguably, the reasons for a merciful response to infanticide were understood by wider society when the law was first enacted in 1922: specifically, there was awareness of the difficult socio-economic circumstances that surrounded cases of newborn child killing, and that these factors contextualised the woman's actions of secret and unassisted childbirth, leading to the infant's death. However, a century later the reasons for lenience have either been forgotten or are no longer considered relevant in a much-changed social, political and legal context.[118] Mason, for example, criticises the 2006 Law Commission Report that supported retention of the infanticide law, because, as he phrases it, the Commission rested its conclusion 'on the mere assumption that infanticidal mothers are deserving of lenient treatment'.[119] He claims that those who favour the infanticide law

> rarely … attempt to justify special treatment for mothers. When they do, they inevitably fall into the trap of relying on the social stresses associated with the crime. However, any attempt to isolate the types of social circumstances that should impact on criminal responsibility is ultimately an arbitrary exercise.[120]

We are in need, therefore, of a contemporary justification for the retention of the infanticide law, one that explains why (at least some) mothers who kill their babies 'deserve' special, lenient treatment in the law. A justification for leniency must go beyond merely pointing to the difficult social circumstances that contribute to this crime, as arguably most crime involves socio-economic factors that could serve to mitigate.[121] In this vein, our argument here does just that: it goes beyond just blaming social circumstances by recognising that

[117] Oberman (n 4) 49.
[118] See, eg, Howard, ch 5 of this volume.
[119] Mason (n 64).
[120] ibid 454.
[121] Though it should be noted that in a situation where murder is the offence, there is arguably a reason to treat the offence differently from other crimes because of the need to avoid the mandatory life sentence.

structural – patriarchal – factors are at play in this crime; by reconsidering how responsibility should be allocated/spread/understood in cases of maternal infanticide in light of the contribution of patriarchy to the crime; and by recognising that the current masculinist criminal law is unable to accommodate such a reallocation. Taking account of all of the above, we argue that it is possible, as feminists, to justify a special infanticide law. We make this argument while recognising that the law is not perfect as it stands, notably due to how it is generally understood and interpreted by the courts at present.

There are a number of issues relating to the infanticide law that we have not addressed in this chapter, due both to space and our specific focus here: the experiences of women. Our argument is that a law that grants special treatment for mothers who kill their biological children is defensible, in principle, on the grounds of the gendered harms women experience through pregnancy, childbirth and mothering. We also support an interpretation of the Infanticide Act 1938 that explicitly takes account of structural factors that form part of the explanation for this crime – the harms the offending women experienced in a patriarchal, class-based, racist, heteronormative world. We recognise that there is more work to be done in terms of how the Infanticide Act 1938 as it currently stands should be interpreted and applied in order to achieve recognition of the structural causes of the crime in a way that ensures consistency and fairness. There is also a question of what is achievable in this respect given the criminal law's masculinist individualistic approach to assigning responsibility. Further, there is the need to ensure that the law is interpreted without recourse to gendered judgements of the accused women. As we have alluded to in this chapter, the application of the current law poses significant problems, specifically as it too draws on the myths of motherhood to determine which women are 'worthy' of leniency.[122] Consequently, further research into the role, scope and purpose of the Infanticide Act is needed, so that we can ensure a justifiable leniency is available to all who deserve it. Linked with this is the question of whether the law should be reformed to explicitly take account of the structural causes of infanticide, and specifically whether this is achievable in the context of wider (masculinist) criminal law theory and doctrine. The pragmatic answer to this question may be that there is little to be gained from such a legislative reform, which would undoubtedly be controversial, and that working with the existing law provides a more realistic prospect of realising justice in these cases.

Another issue to consider is the question of whether fathers and other parents are discriminated against if a separate offence/defence, which is exclusively available to biological mothers only, is retained. Fathers have taken on a greater share of the load of parenting in more recent years, and there is also growing recognition of the impact of fatherhood on men's mental well-being. There is also a need to consider the issue of the law's response where the non-biological mother

[122] Morris and Wilczynski, 'Rocking the Cradle' (n 20).

(eg, in the case of a same-sex relationship/parenting, or adoptive mothers) kills the child. Finally, the harms experienced as a result of pregnancy/childbirth/mothering do not end once a child turns 12 months old, and so a question also arises about whether the 12-month age limit of the infanticide legislation may need reconsideration.[123]

References

Books

Ballinger, A, Gender, *Truth and State Power: Capitalising on Punishment* (Routledge 2016).

Bordo, S, *Unbearable Weight: Feminism, Western Culture, and the Body* (University of California Press 2003).

Carline, A and Easteal, PW, *Shades of Grey: Domestic and Sexual Violence against Women: Law Reform and Society* (Routledge 2014).

Dally, A, *Inventing Motherhood: The Consequences of an Ideal* (Burnett 1982).

Douglas, SJ and Michaels, MW, *The Mommy Myth: The Idealization of Motherhood and How It Has Undermined All Women* (Free Press 2005).

Edwards, SSM, *Women On Trial: A Study of the Female Suspect, Defendant, and Offender in the Criminal Law and Criminal Justice System* (Manchester University Press 1984).

Fitz-Gibbon, K, *Homicide Law Reform, Gender and the Provocation Defence: A Comparative Perspective* (Palgrave Macmillan 2014).

Flavin, J, *Our Bodies, Our Crimes: The Policing of Women's Reproduction in America* (New York University Press 2009).

Gillis, JR, *A World of Their Own Making: A History of Myth and Ritual in Family Life* (Oxford University Press 1997).

Graycar, R and Morgan, J, *The Hidden Gender of Law*, 2nd edn (Federation Press 2002).

Gregg, R, *Pregnancy in a High-Tech Age: Paradoxes of Choice* (New York University Press 1995).

Hays, S, *The Cultural Contradictions of Motherhood* (Yale University Press 1996).

Hrdy, SB, *Mother Nature: A History of Mothers, Infants, and Natural Selection* (Ballantine Books 2000).

Kaplan, EA, *Motherhood and Representation: The Mother in Popular Culture and Melodrama* (Routledge 1992).

Kramar, KJ, *Unwilling Mothers, Unwanted Babies Infanticide in Canada* (UBC Press 2005).

Martin, E, *The Woman in the Body: A Cultural Analysis of Reproduction* (Beacon Press 1987).

Milne, E, *Criminal Justice Responses to Maternal Filicide: Judging the Failed Mother* (Emerald Publishing Ltd 2021).

Morrissey, B, *When Women Kill: Questions of Agency and Subjectivity* (Routledge 2003).

Naffine, N, *Criminal Law and the Man Problem* (Hart Publishing 2019).

Norrie, A, *Crime, Reason and History: A Critical Introduction to Criminal Law*, 3rd edn (Cambridge University Press 2014).

[123] See ch 1 of this volume for a more detailed discussion of these points.

Oakley, A, *Woman's Work: The Housewife, Past and Present* (Pantheon 1974).
Rich, A, *Of Woman Born: Motherhood as Experience and Institution* (Norton 1986).
Smithey, M, *The Cultural and Economic Context of Maternal Infanticide: A Crying Baby and the Inability to Escape* (Emerald Publishing Ltd 2019).
Walker, N, *Crime and Insanity in England*, vol 1: *The Historical Perspective* (Edinburgh University Press 1968).
West, R, *Caring for Justice* (New York University Press 1997).
Wilczynski, A, *Child Homicide* (Greenwich Medical Media Ltd 1997).

Chapters in Edited Volumes

Brooks-Gardner, C, 'Pregnant Women as Social Problem' in Loseke, DR and Best, J (eds), *Social Problems: Constructionist Readings* (Aldine de Gruyter 2003) 188.
Caplan, PJ, 'Mother-Blaming' in Ladd-Taylor, M and Umansky, L (eds), *'Bad' Mothers: The Politics of Blame in Twentieth-Century America* (New York University Press 1998) 127.
Garey, AI and Arendell, T, 'Children, Work, and Family: Some Thoughts on "Mother-Blame"' in Hertz, R and Marshall, NL (eds), *Working Families the Transformation of the American Home* (University of California Press 2001) 293.
Glenn, EN, 'Social Construction of Mothering' in Glenn, EN, Chang, G and Forcey, LR (eds), *Mothering: Ideology, Experience, and Agency* (Routledge 1994) 1.
Lupton, D, 'Risk and the Ontology of Pregnant Embodiment' in Lupton D (ed), *Risk and Sociocultural Theory: New Directions and Perspectives* (Cambridge University Press 1999) 59.
Milne, E and Turton, J, 'Understanding Violent Women' in Milne, E et al (eds), *Women and the Criminal Justice System: Failing Victims and Offenders?* (Palgrave Macmillan 2018) 119.
Morris, A and Wilczynski, A, 'Rocking the Cradle: Mothers Who Kill their Children' in Birch, H (ed), *Moving Targets: Women, Murder, and Representation* (Virago 1993) 198.
Solinger, R, 'Race and "Value": Black and White Illegitimate Babies, 1945–1965' in Glenn, EN, Chang, G and Forcey, LR (eds), *Mothering: Ideology, Experience, and Agency* (Routledge 1994) 287.

Journal Articles

Arendell, T, 'Conceiving and Investigating Motherhood: The Decade's Scholarship' (2000) 62 *Journal of Marriage and Family* 1192.
Ballinger A, 'Masculinity in the Dock: Legal Responses To Male Violence and Female Retaliation in England and Wales, 1900–1965' (2007) 16 *Social & Legal Studies* 459.
Brennan, K, 'Beyond the Medical Model: A Rationale for Infanticide Legislation' (2007) 58 *NILQ* 505.
——, '"A Fine Mixture of Pity and Justice": The Criminal Justice Response to Infanticide in Ireland, 1922–1949' (2013) 31 *Law and History Review* 793.
——, '"Traditions of English Liberal Thought": A History of the Enactment of an Infanticide Law in Ireland' (2013) 50 *Irish Jurist* 100.

——, 'Murderous Mothers and Gentle Judges: Paternalism, Patriarchy, and Infanticide' (2018) 30 *Yale Journal of Law and Feminism* 139.
Caplan, PJ and Hall-McCorquodale, I, 'Mother-Blaming in Major Clinical Journals' (1985) 55 *American Journal of Orthopsychiatry* 345.
Chan, W and Rigakos, GS, 'Risk, Crime and Gender' (2002) 42 *British Journal of Criminology* 743.
Conaghan, J, 'Gendered Harms and the Law of Tort: Remedying (Sexual) Harassment' (1996) 16 *OJLS* 407.
d'Orbán, PT, 'Women Who Kill Their Children' (1979) 134 *British Journal of Psychiatry* 560.
Edwards, SSM, 'Anger and Fear as Justifiable Preludes for Loss of Self-Control' (2010) 74 *The Journal of Criminal Law* 223.
Grey, DJR, 'Women's Policy Networks and the Infanticide Act 1922' (2010) 21 *Twentieth Century British History* 441.
Harris, AP, 'Race and Essentialism in Feminist Legal Theory' (1990) 42 *Stanford Law Review* 581.
Howe, A, '"Social injury" Revisited: Towards a Feminist Theory of Social Justice' (1987) 15 *International Journal of the Sociology of Law* 423.
Jackson, D and Mannix, J, 'Giving Voice to The Burden of Blame: A Feminist Study of Mothers' Experiences of Mother Blaming' (2004) 10 *International Journal of Nursing Practice* 150.
Johnston, DD and Swanson, DH, 'Invisible Mothers: A Content Analysis of Motherhood Ideologies and Myths in Magazines' (2003) 49 *Sex Roles* 21.
Kramar, KJ and Watson, WD, 'The Insanities of Reproduction: Medico-legal Knowledge and the Development of Infanticide Law' (2006) 15 *Social & Legal Studies* 237.
Langer, R, '"Mother of Sorrows": Post-Partum Mental Disorder and the Law Across Five Jurisdictions' (2012) 19 *Psychiatry Psychol Law* 358.
Lansdowne, R, 'Infanticide: Psychiatrists in the Plea Bargaining Process' (1990) 16 *Monash University Law Review* 41.
Loughnan, A, 'The "Strange" Case of the Infanticide Doctrine' (2012) 32 *OJLS* 685.
Lupton, D, '"The Best Thing for the Baby": Mothers' Concepts and Experiences Related to Promoting their Infants' Health and Development' (2011) 13 *Health, Risk & Society* 637.
Mackay, RD, 'The Consequences of Killing Very Young Children' [1993] *Crim LR* 21.
Mason, J, 'The Myth of Madness: Murderous Mothers and Maternal Infanticide' (2021) 85 *The Journal of Criminal Law* 441.
Morris, A and Wilczynski, A, 'Parents Who Kill their Children' [1993] *Crim LR* 31.
O'Donovan, K, 'The Medicalisation of Infanticide' [1984] *Crim LR* 259.
Oberman, M, 'Mothers Who Kill: Coming to Terms with Modern American Infanticide' (1996) 34 *American Criminal Law Review* 1.
Osborne, JA, 'The Crime of Infanticide: Throwing Out the Baby with the Bathwater' (1987) 6 *Canadian Journal of Family Law* 47.
Radin, MJ, 'The Pragmatist and the Feminist' (1989) 63 *Southern California Law Review* 1699.
Ward, T, 'The Sad Subject of Infanticide: Law, Medicine and Child Murder, 1860–1938' (1999) 8 *Social & Legal Studies* 163.
Weare, S, '"The Mad", "The Bad", "The Victim": Gendered Constructions of Women Who Kill within the Criminal Justice System' (2013) 2 *Laws* 337.
——, 'Bad, Mad or Sad? Legal Language, Narratives, and Identity Constructions of Women Who Kill their Children in England and Wales' (2016) 30 *International Journal for the Semiotics of Law* 201.

West, R, 'Jurisprudence and Gender' (1988) 55 *University of Chicago Law Review* 1.
Wilczynski, A, 'Mad or Bad? Child-killers, Gender and the Courts' (1997) 37 *British Journal of Criminology* 419.
Wu, A, 'Going Full Circle: Gender and the "Loss of Control" Defence under the Coroners and Justice Act 2009' (2019) 1 *Rule of Law Journal* 46.

Newspaper Articles

Bawden, A, 'Two-child benefits cap cuts support for over 1 million children during pandemic' *The Guardian* (London, 15 July 2021) at www.theguardian.com/society/2021/jul/15/two-child-benefits-cap-cuts-support-for-over-1-million-children-during-pandemic (accessed 11 February 2022).

Online Resources

'Baby-Killing Mum Natasha Sultan "Needed More Support"' *BBC News* (22 January 2014) at www.bbc.co.uk/news/uk-england-humber-25842236> accessed 7 February 2023.
'Hythe Baby Death: Silipa Keresi was Stressed and Desperate, Court Hears' *BBC News* (22 November 2021) at www.bbc.co.uk/news/uk-england-hampshire-59375040 (accessed 7 February 2023).
'Hythe Baby Death: Silipa Keresi Jailed for Woodland Murder' *BBC News* (2 December 2021) at www.bbc.co.uk/news/uk-england-hampshire-59509306 (accessed 7 February 2023).
HM Revenue & Customs, 'Guidance: Child Tax Credit: support for a maximum of 2 children' 2020) at www.gov.uk/guidance/child-tax-credit-exceptions-to-the-2-child-limit (accessed 28 August 2020).
Office for National Statistics, 'Appendix Tables: Homicide in England and Wales' (10 February 2022) at www.ons.gov.uk/peoplepopulationandcommunity/crimeandjustice/datasets/appendixtableshomicideinenglandandwales (accessed 20 January 2023) Worksheet 26.
National Health Service, 'Pregnancy warning for older women' (2009) at www.nhs.uk/news/pregnancy-and-child/pregnancy-warning-for-older-women/ (accessed 28 August 2020).
Public Health England, 'Guidance: Teenage pregnancy prevention framework' (2018) at www.gov.uk/government/publications/teenage-pregnancy-prevention-framework (accessed 28 August 2020).
Understanding Society, 'How women's employment changes after having a child' (2019) at www.understandingsociety.ac.uk/2019/10/22/how-womens-employment-changes-after-having-a-child (accessed 1 September 2020).
Unicef UK, 'How We Protect Children's Rights' (nd) at www.unicef.org.uk/what-we-do/un-convention-child-rights/ (accessed 11 October 2020).

Reports

Fawcett Society, *Parents, Work and Care: Striking the Balance* (2016).
Law Commission, *Murder, Manslaughter and Infanticide* (Law Com No 304, 2006).
Ministry of Justice, *Murder, Manslaughter and Infanticide: Proposals for Reform of the Law* (Law Com CP No 19, 2008).

PART III

Criminal Justice Responses to Infanticide beyond England and Wales

7

The Use and Non-Use of Infanticide Provisions in Australian Criminal Laws

ARLIE LOUGHNAN*

In recent years, the public profile of infanticide in Australia has been dominated by the extensive media coverage given to two contrasting cases, one from New South Wales (NSW) and one from Victoria. In the first case, in 2010, a 35-year-old woman from Sydney, Keli Lane, was charged with having murdered her newborn daughter, Tegan, in 1996.[1] No body was found, and Lane consistently claimed that, after discharging herself from the hospital, she gave the baby to its father, a man the police were never able to locate. Lane's pregnancy with Tegan was the fourth of five pregnancies, with the first two resulting in terminations and Lane putting the third and fifth babies up for adoption.[2] Each of these pregnancies had been concealed from family and friends, with Lane, an elite water polo player who had represented Australia at the Olympics, continuing to train and teach sport over the periods. There was no evidence of psychiatric disorder (as is a default requirement for infanticide, as I discuss in this chapter), and Lane was convicted of the murder of Tegan and sentenced to 18 years' imprisonment with a non-parole period of 13 years and 5 months.[3] In 2013 and 2014, citing insufficient evidence for conviction, Lane appealed to the NSW Court of Criminal Appeal and then the High Court of Australia, but both appeals were denied.[4]

* I would like to thank the editors for inviting me to contribute to this collection, and Hae Soo Park and Kimberley Hammerton for excellent research assistance.

[1] See *R v Lane* [2011] NSWSC 289. Lane's case was the subject of a three-part television documentary, *Exposed: The Case of Keli Lane*, which aired on the ABC in 2018: see at iview.abc.net.au/show/exposed-the-case-of-keli-lane.

[2] Lane was charged with Tegan's murder following investigations by social workers handling the adoption of her fifth baby: see for discussion *R v Guode* (2020) 267 CLR 141. Evidence of Lane's other pregnancies was admitted at her murder trial because she was also charged with perjury regarding statements she had made to the coronial inquest into Tegan's disappearance. Lane subsequently carried a sixth baby to term and gave birth to a girl in 2001.

[3] See *R v Lane* [2011] NSWSC 289.

[4] *Lane v R* (2013) 241 A Crim R 321, [2013] NSWCCA 317; *Lane v The Queen* [2014] HCATrans 171.

In the second case, in 2015, Akon Guode, a 35-year-old refugee from South Sudan with a history of sexual abuse and depression, drove her car, with four of her seven children inside it, into Lake Gladman in Wyndham Vale, Victoria. Three of the children, 4-year-old twins and a 16-month-old boy, Bol, drowned. The eldest child, who was 5 years old at the time, survived. Guode pleaded guilty to one count of infanticide, two charges of murder and one charge of attempted murder.[5] She was sentenced to a prison term of 26 years and 6 months with a non-parole period of 20 years. For the offence of infanticide specifically, she received a sentence of 12 months' imprisonment. Following an appeal to Victorian Court of Appeal, in 2020, Guode's sentence was found to be manifestly excessive and was reduced to 18 years with a non-parole period of 14 years, a sentence that was upheld following a prosecution appeal to the High Court.[6] Although infanticide carries with it a maximum term of five years' imprisonment, until Guode's case, no woman had been sentenced to a term of imprisonment for infanticide in Victoria.

While only one of these two cases involves the offence/defence of infanticide, each involves the external element of the offence/defence, the act of killing a very young child by its mother. I suggest it is necessary to consider both these sorts of cases together to develop a holistic understanding of infanticide in Australian criminal law. It is only when taken together that a comprehensive picture of infanticide emerges. As I argue based on my analysis of Australian cases across the decades since the introduction of the laws, there has been a decline in social and legal tolerance of the act of infanticide in Australia in the current era, and this is reflected in an increased punitiveness in individual cases. In Guode's case, although expert psychiatric evidence of 'disturbance of mind' was accepted, and the judgments make multiple references to the need to show the defendant mercy, she received a custodial sentence for the infanticide offence.[7] Keli Lane – a young woman who had concealed her pregnancy and was found to have killed her newborn baby – is arguably the archetypal infanticide defendant.[8] But the absence of psychiatric evidence that would have provided support for the 'disturbance of mind' element of infanticide meant the offence/defence was not available.[9] Despite

[5] *R v Guode* [2017] VSC 713.

[6] *Guode v The Queen* [2018] VSCA 205 and *The Queen v Guode* [2020] HCA 8 (18 March 2020) respectively.

[7] On references to mercy, see N Antolak-Saper, 'The Role of Mercy in Infanticide' (2023) 35 *Current Issues in Criminal Justice* 65.

[8] Research in other jurisdictions indicates that certain cases – which feature the youth of the defendant, and the killing of a newborn in circumstances of extreme distress or isolation – are likely to attract leniency: see for discussion E Milne, *Criminal Justice Responses to Maternal Filicide: Judging the Failed Mother* (Emerald Publishing Ltd 2021). These were the features of *R v Hutty* [1953] VLR 338, referred to in n 33 of this chapter.

[9] The trial judge's failure to direct the jury that infanticide was available as an alternative to the charge of murder was initially one of the grounds of appeal in Lane's case: see *Lane v The Queen* [2013] NSWCCA 317 [31]. This ground was dropped during the course of the trial.

the absence of the baby's body, and more than a decade after the killing, the Crown proceeded with a prosecution for murder. Given the relevance of both of these types of case – in which infanticide was either charged or pleaded, or a woman was alleged to have killed her very young child – to the picture of infanticide in Australia, they are incorporated into the study presented here.

In this chapter, I re-examine the enactment of Australian criminal laws on infanticide in the mid-century period and assess their operation in the decades since then. Infanticide provisions have been enacted in four jurisdictions in Australia and utilised in only a handful of cases. In assessing the operation of the laws, I consider those cases in which infanticide has been either charged or pleaded, and also those cases in which the external element of the offence was satisfied, that is, where the facts of the case involve a mother killing a biological child under the requisite age (although there may be no admission of guilt or any psychiatric evidence, and prosecution and defence rely on homicide provisions other than infanticide). This approach makes it possible to draw some broad comparisons between those cases in which infanticide is raised and those in which it is not. Recognising that a number of relevant decisions are unreported, in my analysis I also draw on media reports of infanticide cases. While my analysis is qualitative rather than quantitative, I have attempted to gather all relevant cases in my datasets.[10] My assessment reveals that the legal reliance on infanticide provisions is limited and uneven, with prosecutors tending to rely on charges of murder and manslaughter instead, and defence counsel raising other defences.

This chapter makes two main arguments. First, in relation to the enactment of infanticide laws in Australia, as legislative change was not preceded by high-profile cases or high levels of public or political concern, I suggest that the inclusion of infanticide provisions in the laws of several States was a matter of keeping the law up to date and in good working order, that is, good legal housekeeping (rather than, say, a response to a perceived gap in the law). Second, in relation to the operation of the laws, I suggest that the use of infanticide provisions is limited and uneven, with infanticide rarely charged and only slightly more frequently pleaded by the defence. In the current era, reflecting increased access to abortion services, and a highly moralised climate around childrearing, there is decreased social and legal tolerance for the act of infanticide, which is reflected in increased punitiveness in individual cases. But, as I discuss, infanticide provisions remain on the books in three States and have been expanded in one of these, testifying to the contradictory status of infanticide in the current era: the laws encode a veneer of leniency for all mothers who kill their children, but in practice they are reserved for a small set of cases.

[10] Four Australian jurisdictions have or have had infanticide laws: NSW, Victoria, Western Australia and Tasmania. I searched for relevant cases in major case-law databases, and national and State media from each of these jurisdictions, for the period since enactment of the laws (in 1951, 1949, 1986 and 1934, respectively) to the present. I acknowledge that there may be some gaps in my data, particularly in relation to older cases.

I. The Enactment of Infanticide Laws in Australia

As is well known, infanticide entered the statute books in England and Wales in the early twentieth century, although the creation of a specific infanticide provision had first been proposed in the 1880s, and there had long been significant public and political debate about the appropriate legal response to women who killed their newborn children.[11] Although it is now regarded as a merciful amendment to the law, against a backdrop in which the death penalties for women convicted of the murders of their young children were not typically carried out, infanticide was introduced in significant part to prevent the criminal law from being brought into disrepute.[12] In the criminal law, the offence/defence is distinctive in that it is restricted by type of defendant and type of victim: only a mother who kills her very young biological child may plead it or be convicted of it.[13] With the passage of the Infanticide Acts 1922 and 1938, all killings of newborn children by mentally incapacitated mothers were taken outside the reach of both the offence of murder and the defence of insanity. In England and Wales, the infanticide provision operates to substitute liability for infanticide in place of murder (or manslaughter) where the 'balance' of the defendant woman's mind was disturbed at the time of the act or omission leading to the death of her child under the age of 12 months.[14]

By contrast with the extensive public and political debates that took place in England and Wales, the introduction of infanticide laws in Australian jurisdictions was less spectacular. In Australia, criminal law is largely reserved to the States and Territories, and thus it was up to individual States to enact infanticide laws.[15] Infanticide laws were introduced in three States – NSW, Victoria and Tasmania – in the mid-twentieth century (and later in Western Australia, as I discuss in section III of this chapter. In the absence of high-profile cases, the introduction of infanticide laws was less an urgent response to a perceived need to deal with such cases differently, and more a matter of keeping the law up to date and in good working order. That is, the introduction of infanticide was a matter of good

[11] See further A Loughnan, *Manifest Madness: Mental incapacity in the criminal law* (Oxford University Press 2012) ch 8; see also D Seaborne Davies 'Child-Killing in English Law' (1937) 1 *MLR* 203.

[12] See Loughnan (n 11) 215.

[13] Infanticide is both a charge and a plea – it is both a stand-alone homicide offence and a partial defence to a charge of murder or manslaughter. I have argued elsewhere that this means that the infanticide doctrine itself is most accurately understood as either/both partially exculpatory and partially inculpatory: see further Loughnan (n 11) ch 8.

[14] Infanticide Act 1938 (England and Wales), as amended by the Coroners and Justice Act 2009 (England and Wales).

[15] Australia has nine criminal jurisdictions, encompassing both codified criminal law and the common law of crime, and including a growing body of Federal criminal law; for discussion in relation to criminal responsibility, see A Loughnan, *Self, Others and the State: Relations of Criminal Responsibility* (Cambridge University Press 2019) ch 5.

legal housekeeping rather than an expression of the inadequacy of the law without infanticide provisions, and it was not clear that parliamentarians had a particular type of infanticide case in mind in the enactment of the laws. The infanticide provisions were enacted in Tasmania in 1934, in Victoria in 1949 and in NSW in 1951.[16] In each jurisdiction, the new provisions were included in larger omnibus Bills enacting a number of reforms to the criminal law that had been recommended by parliamentary law review bodies (this was also the case in Western Australia in the 1980s). Thus, in NSW, the introduction of infanticide was part of a general Bill aimed at keeping 'laws in line with modern conditions'.[17] In addition, given the still emergent nature of a distinctively Australian criminal law, in these jurisdictions, frequent references were made to the need to bring the law into line with that of England and Wales.[18]

Australian parliamentary debates on the infanticide provisions within these large omnibus Bills reveal the largely uncontroversial nature of the laws. In the mid-century, in NSW, Victoria and Tasmania, the punishment for murder was the death penalty, and abortion was a criminal offence. In this context, infanticide was a merciful addition to the criminal law. There is no information about how common the practice of infanticide was at this time, but the tenor of the discussions in parliament suggests that the numbers were not so high as to cause alarm. In speaking about the Bill containing the new offence in Victoria, one minister stated that 'it is felt that, on many occasions, the person so charged is guilty of neither murder nor manslaughter. In any event the Government believes that punishment for murder is much too severe to meet such case'.[19]

In the words of one member of the NSW parliament, 'it is much more humane to charge a woman with the offence of infanticide than to allow her to stand trial on the capital charge of murder'.[20] A Victorian parliamentarian noted that while the seriousness of the crime of a mother killing her child could not be denied, 'in certain circumstances' the charge and punishment of murder is 'too severe'.[21] In NSW, the new offence was regarded as a 'wise' provision that was likely to 'reduce human unhappiness'.[22] As in England and Wales, parliamentarians noted that 'juries have been reluctant to bring in capital verdicts against unfortunate women who have been through a most trying experience, but who nevertheless showed criminal intent'.[23] As these comments indicate, the charge of murder and the death

[16] See Criminal Code Act 1934 (Tas) (inserting s 165A into the Criminal Code (Tas)); Crimes Act 1949 (Vic), s 4(1) (subsequently amended by Crimes (Homicide) Act 2005 (Vic), s 5); Crimes (Amendment) Act 1951 (NSW), s 2(d). The Tasmanian provision was amended in 1973 to remove the reference to 'newly born': see for discussion *R v Taylor* [1969] Tas SR 1.

[17] *Hansard*, NSW Legislative Assembly 27 September 1951, vol 196, col 3272.

[18] See eg *Hansard*, NSW Legislative Assembly 27 September 1951, vol 196, col 3275.

[19] *Hansard*, Victoria Legislative Council 11 May 1949, vol 229, col 902.

[20] *Hansard*, NSW Legislative Assembly 2 October 1951, vol 196, col 3320.

[21] *Hansard*, Victoria Legislative Assembly 30 March 1949, vol 229, col 68.

[22] *Hansard*, NSW Legislative Assembly 27 September 1951, vol 196, cols 3263 and 3272 respectively.

[23] *Hansard*, Victoria Legislative Assembly 28 April 1949, vol 229, col 580.

penalty were seen as inappropriate for these women, who attracted sympathy rather than condemnation.[24]

Against a backdrop of the strong social norms around gender, sex and family that characterised the mid-century period in Australia (and elsewhere), the requirement that is at the heart of the law of infanticide, that women have a 'disturbance of mind' following birth or lactation, was readily accepted. At this time, the risk of 'insanity' before and after birth was regarded as 'well known'.[25] In speaking for the relevant Bill in Victoria, one member of parliament expressed compassion for a mother who is, in his words, 'not in full possession of her mental faculties' after childbirth.[26] In NSW, one parliamentarian offered support for the new provision of infanticide by reference to women's 'natural' pathology:

> The status and dignity of any institution can always be judged by the manner in which it refers to and deals with women. This is a test that should be applied in any matter where women are concerned, and there is a matter in hand which has to be tested. Women are, by ordinance of nature, subject to certain fundamental disabilities. The Attorney-General, in creating this new offence and bringing the Act into line with the law of England, has done something for the status of women in this country.[27]

As this comment indicates, the creation of an infanticide provision was appropriate because it responded to women's natural infirmities – on the basis that they are 'by ordinance of nature, subject to certain fundamental disabilities' – and an enhancement of the criminal law. While this parliamentarian's views about women's pathology were becoming less acceptable at this time, the sympathy for women charged with murder of their babies that these views encoded was more widespread. As scholars have argued, this sympathy was based in compassion for women's familial and social personal circumstances, as well as appreciation of their psychological state.[28]

In introducing infanticide in parliament, there were some concerns expressed that the new offence/defence would prevent women charged with the murder of their children from securing the benefit of an acquittal based on insanity.[29] But there was generalised recognition that 'puerperal insanity' – a discrete disease, characterised by depression, hallucinations and anxiety that had first developed

[24] The death penalty was abolished in Australia progressively during the 20th century, with the last execution taking place in 1967. The Commonwealth abolished the death penalty in 1973: see Death Penalty Abolition Act 1973 (Cth) (Australia).

[25] *Hansard*, NSW Legislative Assembly 3 October 1951, vol 196, col 3347.

[26] *Hansard*, Victoria Legislative Council 19 May 1949, vol 229, col 1250.

[27] *Hansard*, NSW Legislative Assembly 27 September 1951, vol 196, col 3275.

[28] See, eg, R Lansdowne, 'Child killing and the offence of infanticide: the development of the offence and its operation in New South Wales, 1976–1980' (LLM thesis, University of New South Wales 1987); and R Lansdowne, 'Infanticide: Psychiatrists in the Plea Bargaining Process' (1990) 16 *Monash University Law Review* 41.

[29] See, eg, *Hansard*, NSW Legislative Assembly 2 October 1951, vol 196, col 3318; *Hansard*, NSW Legislative Council 10 October 1951, vol 197, cols 3505–06.

in the early modern period – was a specific kind of condition.[30] This condition was thus appropriately addressed via a distinct legal response. In the words of one parliamentarian, it is a condition that 'may border on insanity and can often – though it does not necessarily – amount to insanity'.[31] In another comment, one parliamentarian stated:

> In ninety-nine cases out of 100 these charges are the result of a sickness or mental disturbance, and in most instances the prisoner deserves sympathy rather than condemnation. This attempt to bring the crimes of unfortunate mothers into proper perspective is worthy of commendation.[32]

As this statement suggests, the offence/defence of infanticide licensed 'sympathy rather than condemnation' for women defendants.[33]

As was the case elsewhere, at this time, in its operation in both clinical and legal contexts, 'puerperial insanity' had an open-textured or porous character, and such a psychiatric diagnosis stretched in practice to encompass a woman's circumstances and biology as well as her mental condition.[34] In the legal context, reliance on psychiatric labels was a key way in which women charged with infanticide were constructed as abnormal, and through which aspects of personal circumstances that would not otherwise be relevant were able to be considered in court.[35] As Alan Norrie argues in relation to the creation of infanticide, its separation from murder and its presentation in 'medical terms' enabled the law to 'maintain a general punitive stance to a social problem, laced with an unthreatening show of compassion in the individual(ised) case'.[36] The 'stretchy' or elastic aspect of infanticide is crucial in the operation of the law, as I discuss in section II below.

The last Australian jurisdiction to introduce an infanticide provision was Western Australia. This State introduced an infanticide provision in 1986.[37] At the time the provision was enacted, both murder and wilful murder (separate offences under the State's Criminal Code) were subject to mandatory penalties of life in prison. Again, the introduction of an infanticide provision was unspectacular,

[30] See further JP Eigen, 'Criminal Lunacy in Early Modern England: Did Gender Make a Difference?' (1998) 21(4) *International Journal of Law and Psychiatry* 412; A Loughnan, 'The Strange Case of the Infanticide Doctrine' (2012) 32(4) *OJLS* 685.

[31] *Hansard*, NSW Legislative Council 10 October 1951, vol 197, col 3504.

[32] *Hansard*, NSW Legislative Assembly 27 September 1951, vol 196, col 3278.

[33] See also *Hutty* (n 8) (the first infanticide case in Victoria, in which Justice Barry suggested that, going forward, infanticide rather than murder was the appropriate charge for a woman accused of killing her young child).

[34] See, eg, KJ Kramar, *Unwilling Mothers, Unwanted Babies: Infanticide in Canada* (UBC Press 2005); T Ward, 'The Sad Subject of Infanticide: Law, Medicine and Child Murder 1860–1938' (1999) 8(2) *Social and Legal Studies* 163; and KM Brennan '"Traditions of English Liberal Thought": A History of the Enactment of an Infanticide Law in Ireland' (2013) 50 *Irish Jurist* 100.

[35] See further Loughnan (n 11) 220–21.

[36] See A Norrie, *Crime, Reason and History: A Critical Introduction to Criminal Law* (Butterworths 2001) 191.

[37] See Criminal Law Amendment Act 1986 (WA), creating s 281A of the Western Australian Criminal Code.

although there was some debate about the appropriateness of creating a distinct category of offence/defence for women.[38] The amendment arose as part of the ongoing review of the Western Australian Criminal Code by the then State government, and seems to have been given consideration because the offence/defence was in place in comparable jurisdictions.[39] In expressing support for the Bill containing the new provision, one member stated that '[t]he tremendous strain that women go through in society today should be recognised', and also commented that

> [i]t is a shame that, although this charge has been on the Statute books of the United Kingdom and other European countries since 1938 – certainly since before the Second World War – it was not until a review of the Criminal Code that it was decided to introduce this charge here.[40]

As this indicates, infanticide was introduced in Western Australia in order to bring the State up to date in its approach to women who kill their biological children. As I discuss in section III, the infanticide provision was repealed in Western Australia in 2008.

As enacted, Australian infanticide laws were substantially the same as the English law. In general, to be liable for infanticide, a woman must have caused the death of a 'newly born' child, when her 'balance of mind' was 'disturbed' by the effect of childbirth or lactation. In Victoria, the law (which has now been amended, as I go on to discuss) provided that a mother who, 'notwithstanding' the effects of the infanticide provision, would have been liable for murder of a child aged 12 months or younger, 'but at the time of the act or omission the balance of her mind was disturbed by reason of her not having fully recovered from the effect of giving birth to the child, or by reason of the effect of lactation consequent upon the birth of the child', would be convicted of infanticide instead. A woman found guilty of infanticide was liable to be punished as if she had been convicted of manslaughter (for which the maximum penalty was 15 years' imprisonment at the time of the offence/defence was introduced). In NSW, section 22A of the Crimes Act 1900 (NSW) was expressed in the same terms.[41] The terms of the Western Australian provision were similar to those provisions in place in NSW and Victoria, with any woman convicted of infanticide subject to a maximum prison term of seven years.[42] In Tasmania, the wording of the provision is different in that no reference is made to lactation, but the age limit is the same.[43] Each of these three laws provided that infanticide was both a stand-alone homicide offence and a partial defence to a charge of murder.

[38] See, eg, *Hansard*, Western Australia Legislative Council 16 October 1986, vol 261, col 3155.

[39] *Hansard*, Western Australia Legislative Council 7 October 1986, vol 260, cols 2703–04.

[40] *Hansard*, Western Australia Legislative Council 16 October 1986, vol 261, col 3153.

[41] See Crimes Act 1900 (NSW), s 22A. The reference to lactation was removed in 2020, as I go on to discuss below.

[42] Criminal Law Amendment Act 1986 (WA), creating s 287A of the Western Australian Criminal Code.

[43] See Criminal Code (Tas), s 165A.

Like the infanticide provision in operation in England and Wales, Australian laws have three distinctive legal features. The first is that the mens rea or fault element of the offence/defence is not evident on the face of the infanticide provision. But in recent decades it has become clear that the inclusion of the term 'wilful' in the infanticide provision means that the mens rea is either intent or recklessness.[44] The second distinctive legal feature of infanticide relates to the relationship between the requirement that the defendant woman's mind be 'disturbed' and the actus reus of killing, the external element of the offence. As a number of commentators note, the connection required is merely temporal: the infanticide law does not specify that a defendant woman's mental disturbance must *cause* her to kill her child.[45] This creates what Nigel Walker has referred to as a 'virtual presumption' that the woman actor was not fully responsible by reason of mental illness.[46] The third distinctive legal feature of infanticide relates to the precise significance of its actus reus or external element, the act of killing. The external element of infanticide is more than a mere threshold for liability. As I have suggested elsewhere, the act of killing her child over-determines a defendant woman's criminal responsibility. That is, by eliding a distinction between the descriptive aspects of infanticide (a woman kills her infant at the same time as having a mind disturbed by childbirth or lactation) and its evaluative aspects (this action under these conditions warrants partial liability), the act of killing becomes an instantiation of abnormality and a finding of partial rather than full responsibility follows.[47]

The inclusion of the infanticide offence/defence in Australian law marked a major development in criminal law. As I have argued elsewhere, based on the pathologisation of women's violence, the laws constituted the first recognition, on the face of the criminal law, of partial responsibility for crime.[48] In this context, the creation of specific infanticide provisions in Australian jurisdictions 'authorised' the special and lenient treatment of women convicted of killing their newborn children.[49] These provisions worked to channel a group of women homicide defendants away from the law of murder, which, until the second half of the century, attracted a mandatory death penalty, and into the realm of manslaughter, which attracted sentencing discretion. I labelled the laws 'a cul-de-sac of specialness and leniency in the law of homicide'.[50] This cul-de-sac has proved durable

[44] See *R v Gore (Lisa Therese) (Deceased)* [2007] EWCA Crim 2789.

[45] See, eg, H Allen, *Justice Unbalanced: Gender, psychiatry, and judicial decisions* (Open University Press 1987).

[46] N Walker and S McCabe, *Crime and Insanity in England*, vol 1 (Edinburgh University Press 1967) 135. Based on my analysis of the social type, the infanticidal woman, I suggest that infanticide operates via an implicit assumption that the defendant woman's actus reus of killing is caused or determined behaviour: see Loughnan (n 11) ch 8.

[47] See further Loughnan (n 11) 214–16.

[48] See generally Loughnan (n 15) ch 6. Dimished responsibility – a partial defence to murder only – had yet to be introduced in England and Wales or Australia: see ibid, ch 9.

[49] ibid 168–71.

[50] ibid 170.

and, despite the discrediting of the 'scientific' basis for the law – based around mental disorder following childbirth – infanticide remains on the statute books in three Australian jurisdictions.[51] As I discuss in section II, this retention does not equate to frequent use in legal practice, with infanticide typically raised as a plea in response to a charge of murder, if it is raised at all.

II. The Mixed Picture of Infanticide in Australia

In the Australian jurisdictions in which infanticide provisions are part of the criminal law, their use can be described as limited. As I discuss in this section, based on my assessment of the cases in which infanticide is raised and those cases in which it is not raised but where the external element of the offence/defence is satisfied, it is clear that infanticide is not often charged, with prosecutors tending to rely on charges of murder and manslaughter instead.[52] While infanticide it is more often pleaded by the defence, defendants also raise other defences, such as substantial impairment by reason of abnormality of mind (diminished responsibility), where this is available. While the cases in which infanticide is charged or pleaded seem to attract sympathy rather than condemnation, other cases of child killing have this feature, and it is difficult to be precise about what separates these cases from others in which a woman kills her very young child.

In those Australian jurisdictions in which it is available, infanticide is rarely charged by the prosecution. The charge is reserved for what are perceived to be the most deserving of cases, in which the defendant attracts sympathy rather than condemnation. For example, in *DPP v QPX*, the defendant pleaded guilty to the infanticide of one twin and recklessly causing serious injury to the other twin while suffering from 'significant emotional and psychological compromise'.[53] In sentencing QPX, the judge stated that her moral culpability was 'either non-existent or of such a low degree as to be negligible'.[54] Similarly, in *R v Cooper*, the defendant woman suffocated her 7-month-old daughter.[55] Cooper was a young woman who had been diagnosed with severe depression, was in a violent relationship with the father of her daughter and had been abused as a child. At the time of

[51] See New South Wales Law Reform Commission, *People with Cognitive and Mental Health Impairments in the Criminal Justice System* (Law Com No 135, 2012) (which concluded that the 'statutory offence/defence of infanticide affords an appropriate and compassionate criminal law response to the complex and tragic set of circumstances that may result in a mother killing her infant' [5.49]). For the empirical profile of infanticide in Australia, see L Bartels and P Easteal, 'Mothers Who Kill: The Forensic Use and Judicial Reception of Evidence of Postnatal Depression and Other Psychiatric Disorders in Australian Filicide Cases' (2013) 37 *Melbourne University Law Review* 297.

[52] My empirical study confirms the findings of the NSW Law Reform Commission: see NSWLRC, *Partial Defences to Murder: Provocation and Infanticide* (Report No 83, 1997) [3.13].

[53] *DPP v QPX* [2014] VSC 189 [27].

[54] ibid.

[55] *R v Cooper* [2001] NSWSC 769.

the killing, Cooper had just moved from the women's refuge where she was staying into accommodation where she was the sole carer for her children.[56] In sentencing Cooper to a good behaviour bond of four years, Justice Simpson stated:

> This is a tragic case. The life of a child has been lost almost before it began. That happened in circumstances where little real culpability can be attributed to the perpetrator. It happened because Ms Cooper lacked the resources – mainly emotional, but also intellectual and probably financial – to manage the family for whom she was responsible.[57]

As this suggests, Cooper was a pitiful defendant, showing 'little real culpability'. It is notable that the exculpatory factors in this case include aspects of Cooper's social context (eg economic disadvantage) as well as her mental state (severe depression). This reflects the elastic or stretchy feature of the medical basis of infanticide, 'disturbance of mind', mentioned in section I.

In some of the cases in which infanticide is charged, the defendant is depicted as a victim herself. In *DPP v UA*, the defendant woman, a refugee from Somalia, stabbed her 13-month-old during a psychotic episode related to underlying schizophrenia.[58] She was charged with infanticide and pleaded guilty. Agreeing with the prosecution and defence that a term of imprisonment was not appropriate, the judge stated that 'the question of your safety, the safety of your family and the community would have to be at the forefront of any disposition'.[59] The defendant was sentenced to a community corrections order of 30 months. In *R v Azzopardi*, the defendant woman, Leanne Azzopardi, drowned her baby in the bath.[60] She was subsequently diagnosed with severe postnatal depression.[61] She pleaded guilty to the charge and was sentenced to a community order of 18 months.[62] The sentencing judge, Justice Kellam, referred to the defendant's situation and stated:

> In particular you have suffered considerably. Your marriage has finished. The dreams and aspirations that you had when you fell pregnant are now a memory only, and are likely to remain so for a considerable period of time, if not for the rest of your life.[63]

As this comment suggests, the defendant is herself regarded as a victim. This idea that infanticide defendants are themselves victims is a theme of the operation of the laws in other jurisdictions, with scholars arguing that women are judged for

[56] ibid [23].
[57] ibid [24].
[58] *DPP v UA* [2018] VSV 423. While the defendant's schizophrenia was an underlying condition, rather than a postpartum condition, expert evidence indicated the risk of psychotic episodes was heightened during the postpartum period as a result of UA's refusal of antipsychotic medication, the stress of caring for a young family in circumstances of socioeconomic disadvantage, and four pregnancies in five years (ibid [12]). She was sentenced to a community corrections order of 30 months.
[59] ibid [19].
[60] *R v Azzopardi* [2004] VSC 509.
[61] ibid [22].
[62] ibid [31].
[63] ibid [26].

who they are (including in relation to their status as an otherwise 'good' mother) rather than for what they have done.[64]

With infanticide charged in only a handful of cases, a number of women who have killed a child or children are charged with murder or manslaughter. For example, in *R v NLH*, the 18-year-old defendant, who was a victim of childhood sexual abuse and in an abusive relationship, killed her 7-week-old baby while suffering from postnatal depression.[65] Infanticide was not raised and NLH pleaded guilty to manslaughter, being sentenced to four years and two months' imprisonment. While this defendant seems sympathetic, it is notable that the sentencing judge observed that NLH failed to get help for the child after she became aware that the child was seriously hurt, and commented that, while the depression was significant, 'it was not to the extent that the offender was completely debilitated to a degree sometimes seen in similar cases'.[66] Similarly, in *R v Rowe*, the defendant was charged with murder when her 7-month-old baby died after she gave him methadone to settle him.[67] Infanticide was not raised by the defence, and Rowe, who had a long history of drug use, was convicted of manslaughter by the jury and sentenced to five and a half years in prison.[68] It is difficult to determine precisely what marks these cases out from others in which infanticide is either charged or pleaded, but factors such as consciousness of guilt (evident in lies and failing to seek help for the child in *NLH*) and culpability and lack of contrition (evident in *Rowe*) may play into the strategic decision making of prosecution and defence counsel. I pick up this point again in section IV.

Infanticide is more frequently pleaded by the defence than charged by the prosecution. In cases in which expert medical evidence supports the defence, the prosecution seem likely to accept the plea of guilty.[69] For example, in the NSW case of Tanya Soutter, the defendant was charged with murder after she shook her 8-month-old son and threw him to the floor.[70] Expert medical evidence indicated that Soutter suffered from severe postnatal depression and was in a violent relationship with the baby's father.[71] Soutter's plea of guilty to infanticide

[64] See, for discussion, Milne (n 8); see also KM Brennan, '"A Fine Mixture of Pity and Justice": The Criminal Justice Response to Infanticide in Ireland, 1922–1949' (2013) 31 *Law and History Review* 793.

[65] See *R v NLH* [2010] NSWSC 662.

[66] ibid [99]–[100].

[67] *R v Rowe* [2007] NSWSC 300.

[68] ibid [35].

[69] The preference of the prosecution to accept a plea to infanticide rather than charge it seems to reflect in part the perceived difficulty of discharging the burden of proof in infanticide. As the NSW DPP stated in its submission to the NSW Law Reform Commission review of the law of mental incapacity, 'one reason why infanticide is not used as a substantive offence is because the prosecution would then be required to prove as part of its case that the accused suffered from a disturbance of the mind': see NSWLRC (n 52) [3.13].

[70] Editorial, 'Murder accused granted bail' *Goulburn Post* (Goulburn, 25 January 2007) at www.goulburnpost.com.au/story/961744/murder-accused-granted-bail/.

[71] Editorial, 'Mum gets suspended sentence for infanticide' *Australian Broadcasting Corporation* (Sydney, 27 February 2008) at www.abc.net.au/news/2008-02-27/mum-gets-suspended-sentence-for-infanticide/1056296.

was accepted by the prosecution and she was sentenced to two years' imprisonment, which was suspended.[72] Similarly, in *R v Nikat*, the defendant suffocated her baby daughter aged 14 months.[73] She was diagnosed with depression, which, according to expert witnesses, began after the defendant's arrival in Australia from Fiji and was made worse by the pregnancy, separation from her husband and stress of raising her child.[74] The plea of guilty to infanticide was accepted and Nikat was sentenced to a 12-month community corrections order.[75] Another example is provided by *R v ZZMM*,[76] in which the defendant woman, who was 19 at the time, gave birth alone at home. She was diagnosed with a 'rare but recognised' mental condition, denial of pregnancy, and was held to be in a state of dissociation and acute stress at the time of the birth.[77] Her plea of guilty to infanticide was accepted by the prosecution and she was sentenced to a one-year community corrections order.

In accounting for the limited or non-use of infanticide, it might be assumed that the failure of some women defendants to admit the killing or killings of a child or children is a stumbling block. A notable example of such a case is provided by the high-profile matter of *R v Folbigg* from NSW.[78] In 2003, Kathleen Folbigg was convicted of the homicides of her four children, who died between 1989 and 1999.[79] Although three of the children were aged less than 12 months old at the time they died, and Folbigg had been diagnosed with depression following the first of the children's deaths, she was not charged with infanticide and it was not pleaded by the defence, as Folbigg maintained that each of the children died of natural causes. At trial, the prosecution relied on numerous entries from Folbigg's diary that were alleged to reveal her consciousness of guilt, as well as forensic evidence that demonstrated the low likelihood of deaths absent human intervention. Folbigg's appeals to the Court of Appeal, and the High Court, against her convictions were dismissed.[80] Following a petition initiated by the University of Newcastle Legal Centre, and having marshalled significant support from leading medical experts, Folbigg's convictions were the subject of a special inquiry held in 2019.[81] The inquiry concluded that new expert medical evidence (which related to the children's genetic susceptibility

[72] ibid.

[73] *R v Nikat* [2017] VSC 713. In Victoria, following reform, infanticide extends to cover an infant under the age of 2 years. I discuss this reform in section III of this chapter.

[74] ibid [33].

[75] ibid [44].

[76] *R v ZZMM* [2015] VSC 524.

[77] ibid [7]–[8].

[78] *R v Folbigg* (2005) 152 A Crim R 35.

[79] Folbigg was charged with three counts of murder, one count of manslaughter and an additional charge of maliciously inflicting grievous bodily harm with intent in relation to one of the children who died subsequently.

[80] *Folbigg v The Queen* [2007] NSWCCA 371; *Folbigg v The Queen* [2005] HCATrans 657.

[81] See New South Wales Department of Communities and Justice, *Report of the Inquiry into the convictions of Kathleen Megan Folbigg* (2019); *Folbigg v Attorney General New South Wales* (2021) 391 ALR 294.

to cardiac arrest) did not raise a reasonable doubt about Folbigg's guilt. At the time of writing, and following a call by Folbigg's lawyers for another coronial inquest into the deaths of her four children,[82] another special inquiry into Folbigg's convictions was held in early 2023, with a finding that there was reasonable doubt about her convictions, and, in June 2023, Folbigg was pardoned.[83]

But even in cases in which individual women admit to killing a child, and there is evidence of mental disorder, the defence do not necessarily plead infanticide, relying instead on other defences. For example, in the case of *R v Schoultz*, the defendant, who had been diagnosed with multiple mental-health issues, including depression and cannabis-use disorder, admitted shaking her baby, causing the injuries leading to her death.[84] Schoultz pleaded guilty to manslaughter on the basis of substantial impairment (as diminished responsibility is known in NSW[85]), a partial defence to murder only, and received a prison sentence of seven years.[86] In *R v MD*, the defendant was charged with murder after slashing her 6-week-old baby's throat.[87] At trial, the defence raised evidence that MD suffered from a major depressive episode with psychotic features, and sought to rely on the mental illness defence. The judge found the elements of this defence – at the time, a disease of the mind, leading to a defect of reason, and meaning the defendant could not understand what she was doing or that it was wrong – were made out and held MD not guilty by reason of mental illness.[88] Similarly, in *R v Doolan*, the defendant drowned her 5-week-old son in the bath.[89] The judge found the defendant was suffering from acute psychosis at the time of the killing, and acquitted her on the basis of mental Illness.[90] In some instances, other defences may also be available to a defendant who commits the external element of the offence/defence of infanticide.[91] These cases indicate that other mental incapacity defences are absorbing some of the space otherwise available under infanticide, pointing up

[82] R Brown, 'Kathleen Folbigg's lawyers request inquest into deaths of her four children' *Australian Broadcasting Corporation* (Sydney, 5 March 2022) at www.abc.net.au/news/2022-03-05/kathleen-folbigg-lawyers-want-inquest-into-childrens-deaths/100885100.

[83] See Attorney-General Michael Daley, 'Kathleen Folbigg Pardoned' (Press Release, 8 June 2023) at https://www.dcj.nsw.gov.au/news-and-media/media-releases/2023/kathleen-folbigg-pardoned.html.

[84] See *R v Juanita Leslie Schoultz* [2007] NSWSC 809.

[85] See Crimes Act 1900 (NSW), s 23.

[86] See also *R v RG* [2006] NSWSC 21 (in which the defendant pleaded guilty to the manslaughter of her 7-month-old daughter, despite expert medical evidence that RG had a psychotic disorder that would have lent support to a full defence of mental impairment).

[87] *R v MD* [2016] NSWSC 1286.

[88] ibid [67]–[68].

[89] *R v Doolan* [2010] NSWSC 147.

[90] ibid [139]. Doolan was also under the influence of drugs at the time of the killing, but expert evidence suggested she had an underlying condition independent of the effects of the drugs (ibid [134]).

[91] eg *R v Wiseman* (Supreme Court of Victoria, 27 April 1972), in which the defendant drowned her two children in the bath in a state of dissociation and was acquitted on the basis of automatism; *R v Wiseman* (Supreme Court of Victoria, 27 April 1972), cited in Law Reform Commission of Western Australia, *Project 97 – a review of the law of homicide* (2007) 113.

the importance of examining infanticide in the wider context of homicide laws, as I do in this chapter.

It must be acknowledged that the use and non-use of infanticide provisions in individual cases is a matter of prosecutorial and defence strategic decision making, and this is not able to be detected on the face of reported judgments. For instance, it is possible that changes to internal practices in prosecution services, including preferences for charging the more serious offence open on the facts, have impacted on the operation of infanticide laws.[92] Certainly, as the NSW Law Reform Commission (NSWLRC) observed, prosecutorial discretion not to prosecute may be exercised in relation to the killings of newborns (neonaticide), explaining their almost complete absence from criminal statistics.[93] Beyond prosectutorial policies and discretion, factors such as defence awareness of the laws, the availability of expert evidence and the defendant's mental-health history, as well as the sympathy she attracts, seem likely to help explain the use and non-use of infanticide provisions. The retention of the laws despite their limited and uneven usage is discussed in section IV of this chapter.

On my analysis, I suggest that, taken in the aggregate, the review of cases offered here exposes a deep dynamic – reduced legal and social tolerance for the act of infanticide – which is reflected in increased punitiveness in individual cases. In the current era, against the background of increased access to abortion services and a highly moralised climate around childrearing,[94] infanticide defendants and their acts seem less likely to attract compassion and understanding. In the words of the Law Commission for Western Australia:

> Unlike their pre-20th century counterparts, contemporary women generally have various options – such as legal abortion – to deal with an unwanted pregnancy and many more contraceptive means of preventing pregnancy. The social stigma attached to unmarried mothers is also less evident and governments in Australia recognise that single mothers will often require financial support. Further, new mothers are closely monitored by healthcare professionals who are alert to symptoms of post-natal depression and readily refer at-risk women for psychological counselling.[95]

As this indicates, in the current era, women are regarded as having choice around reproduction, and assistance from the state, meaning that the protection provided by infanticide laws is less necessary and less desirable. The provision of access to abortion and other options changes the social context in which infanticide laws operate, removing one of the features of the legal landscape that was present at the time the laws were enacted in Australia. The Law Commission of Western

[92] Factors such as these, including the significance of individual practitioner attitudes to infanticide, have been canvassed by others: see R Lansdowne, 'Infanticide: Psychiatrists in the Plea Bargaining Process' (1990) 16 *Monash University Law Review* 41.

[93] New South Wales Law Reform Commission, *People with cognitive and mental health impairments in the criminal justice system: Criminal responsibility and consequences* (Law Com No 138, 2013) [5.17].

[94] See for discussion Milne (n 8) ch 3.

[95] Law Reform Commission of Western Australia (n 91) 110.

Australia went on to recommend the removal of the infanticide provision from the State's Criminal Code, as I now turn to discuss.

III. Recent Reforms

In recent years, infanticide provisions have been subject to significant critique,[96] and in some instances to reform of the law. These reforms have both restricted the scope of infanticide (through abolition in one jurisdiction) and expanded it (through reform in other jurisdictions). These apparently contradictory developments in the law testify to the contradictory status of infanticide in the current era, in which the laws encode a veneer of leniency for all mothers who kill their children but, in practice, are reserved for a small set of cases.

Of the jurisdictions that enacted infanticide laws, only one – Western Australia – has abolished the provision. As already discussed, Western Australia was the last of the four Australian jurisdictions to make infanticide a separate offence. The offence/defence was removed from the WA Criminal Code in 2008 after a recommendation by the Law Reform Commission of Western Australia.[97] The Commission noted that infanticide had been pleaded by the defence just once since the provision was introduced in 1986, and never charged by the prosecution.[98] In recommending removal of the offence/defence from the law, the Commission cited the undesirability of laws that apply only to specific groups of people based on their sex, the overlap with the defence of mental impairment, the absence of scientific support for a biological link between childbirth and mental impairment, and the arbitrariness of the 12-month age limit for the child victim.[99] In the Commission's view, although murder retains a manadatory life sentence, other defences and existing sentencing rules were sufficient to accommodate a merciful approach in appropriate cases.[100]

Two other jurisdictions have reviewed the operation of infanticide provisions and opted to retain the offence/defence. In NSW, infanticide has been considered on two occasions 15 years apart. In 1997, as part of a review of partial defences to murder, the NSWLRC recommended the abolition of the infanticide offence.[101] This recommendation was not put into effect, however. The infanticide provision

[96] See, eg, Victorian Law Reform Commission, *Defences to Homicide: Final Report* (Law Com No 94, 2004) 256–58.

[97] See Law Reform Commission of Western Australia (n 91). This was part of a larger reform of homicide law in which murder and wilful murder were combined together, the partial defence of provocation was abolished and a new offence of unlawful assault causing death was introduced.

[98] ibid 112. The case in which an infanticide plea was entered by the defence, and accepted by the prosecution, was the unreported decision of *R v Smith* (INS 148 of 2001).

[99] See Law Reform Commission of Western Australia (n 91) 108–09, 115–17.

[100] ibid 116, 117.

[101] See NSW Law Reform Commission Report, *Partial Defences to Murder: Provocation and Infanticide Contents* (Law Com No 83, 1997).

was reviewed again in 2013 as part of a review of mental incapacity in criminal law. At that point, the Commission stated:

> Although the arguments are finely balanced we conclude in favour of retention. In the very few cases where the defence is used:
>
> - infanticide affords an appropriate and compassionate criminal law response to the complex and tragic circumstances that may result in a mother killing her infant
> - stakeholder opinion was strongly in favour of retention, and
> - infanticide provisions respond appropriately to a particular set of circumstances that may not, in all cases, be adequately dealt with by the partial defence of substantial impairment.[102]

In line with broader changes to update the language of the criminal law relating to mental incapacity, the NSWLRC recommended amending this formulation to require that, at the time of the conduct causing the death of the child, the defendant had a 'mental health impairment consequent on or exacerbated by her having given birth to that child'.[103] The NSWLRC also recommended that the infanticide provision no longer refer to lactation, as 'lactational insanity' is not recognised as a medical condition.[104]

In Victoria, not only has infanticide has been retained, but the scope of the offence/defence has been expanded. Infanticide was first reviewed in the 1990s when the Victorian Law Reform Commission (VLRC) concluded that it should be retained because 'the killing of a young child by its natural mother constitutes a distinctive form of human tragedy which should be reflected in the offence for which the accused is convicted'.[105] In 2004, the VLRC reviewed infanticide again, and again recommended that the offence/defence should be retained but reformulated to indicate tha suffering from a disturbance of mind as the result either of not having recovered from the effect of giving birth or any disorder consequent on childbirth.[106] The VLRC also recommended that the upper age limit of the child should be extended to 2 years, on the basis that 'extending the age might ensure that all the deserving cases are given access to infanticide'.[107] Further, the VLRC recommended that the lenient sentencing regime attached to infanticide be extended to incorporate killings of any other children killed at the same time as the youngest child.[108] This last recommendation met with considerable opposition and it was not incorporated into the amendments passed by parliament. Had this reform been implemented it would have covered the situation of Akon Guode,

[102] New South Wales Law Reform Commission (n 93) [0.19].

[103] ibid [0.20]. This recommendation was enacted in the Mental Health and Cognitive Impairment Forensic Provisions Act 2020 (NSW).

[104] See Crimes Act 1900 (NSW), s 22A. These changes were enacted in the Mental Health and Cognitive Impairment Forensic Provisions Act 2020 (NSW).

[105] Cited in Victorian Law Reform Commission (n 96) xii.

[106] ibid recommendations 47 and 48.

[107] ibid [6.41]. This recommendation was incorporated into the Crimes Act 1949 (Vic) in 2005: see *Crimes (Homicide) Act* 2005 (Vic).

[108] See Victorian Law Reform Commission (n 96) [6.41], recommendation 49.

canvassed at the start of this chapter and to which I return in the Conclusion in section IV.

These different approaches to reform of the law of infanticide indicate the contradictory status of offence/defence in the current era. At present, the laws are retained 'on the books', but infanticide is rarely charged and only slightly more frequently pleaded by the defence. That is, while, with the exception of Western Australia, law reform bodies are unwilling to remove the option to charge infanticide, or to allow the defence to plead infanticide in response to a murder charge, the limited and uneven use or non-use of infanticide persists. This seems to be a case of having one's cake and eating it too – retaining the option to charge infanticide and for the defence to raise it, thus avoiding the appearance of punitiveness that might come with abolition, but without substantive reliance on the laws. To me, this indicates that the laws encode a veneer of leniency for all mothers who kill their children, while in practice they are reserved for only a small set of cases.

IV. Conclusion

This chapter re-examined the introduction of the offence/defence of infanticide into Australian criminal laws and assessed the operation of the laws in the decades since they were first enacted to the present. I examined two sets of cases – those in which infanticide was either charged or pleaded, and those in which the external element of the offence/defence was satisfied despite reliance on other homicide provisions – which together provide a holistic understanding of infanticide in Australia. Based on this examination, I argued that there has been a decline in social and legal tolerance for infanticide up to the current era, and this is reflected in increased punitiveness in individual cases. My analysis revealed that the legal reliance on infanticide provisions is limited and uneven, with prosecutors tending to rely on charges of murder and manslaughter instead, and defence counsel raising other defences.[109] Given the apparent reluctance by prosecution services to charge infanticide and considering law reform recommendations to retain the offence/defence despite limited and uneven usage, this chapter argued that the laws encode a veneer of leniency for all mothers who kill their children but are in practice reserved for only a small set of cases.

To conclude, it is appropriate to return to the two high-profile cases with which this chapter began. The cases of Akon Guode and Kelli Lane demonstrate the dramatic and tragic circumstances that characterise cases in which mothers kill their children. They are also stark instances of the increased punitiveness marking individual cases. As mentioned in section I, while Guode was convicted of infanticide, she was given a custodial sentence in relation to the offence (and the offences

[109] This is similar to the operation of infanticide in England and Wales: see Brennan and Milne, ch 1 of this volume, and Mackay, ch 3 of this volume.

against her older children), the first time such a sentence had been handed down for infanticide in Victoria. Further, although all of the killings with which Guode was charged occurred at the same moment in time (and thus with the same 'disturbed' mental state), the special (that is, lenient) sentencing regime that applies to infanticide was quarantined and not permitted to reduce the prison sentence she received for the murder of two of her other children and the attempted murder of the third child.[110] At the conclusion of her long prison term, Guode faces deportation from Australia.[111] In the case of Lane, the prosecution itself remains controversial, with questions raised about the conduct of the police practice, the rigorous or even zealous nature of the Crown case (which was pursued in the absence of the baby's body) and the adequacy of the defence.[112] While there is some evidence that Lane's case has spurred moves to enact baby safe-haven laws in Australia,[113] the overall picture the cases paint is of reduced social and legal tolerance for infanticide.

References

Books

Allen, H, *Justice Unbalanced: Gender, psychiatry, and judicial decisions* (Open University Press 1987).

Kramar, KJ, *Unwilling Mothers, Unwanted Babies: Infanticide in Canada* (UBC Press 2005).

Loughnan, A, *Manifest Madness: Mental incapacity in the criminal law* (Oxford University Press 2012).

——, *Self, Others and the State: Relations of Criminal Responsibility* (Cambridge University Press 2019).

Milne, E, *Criminal Justice Responses to Maternal Filicide: Judging the Failed Mother* (Emerald Publishing Ltd 2021).

Norrie, A, *Crime, Reason and History: A Critical Introduction to Criminal Law* (Butterworths 2001).

Walker, N and McCabe, S, *Crime and Insanity in England*, vol 1 (Edinburgh University Press 1967).

[110] This was the issue for the High Court on appeal: see *The Queen v Guode* [2020] HCA 8. By majority, the court held that the 'unique sentencing regime' that applied to infanticide should be kept separate from the sentencing that applied to the other homicide offences.

[111] See A Cooper, 'Akon Guode faces deportation after serving jail term, court told' *The Age* (Melbourne, 9 March 2017) at www.theage.com.au/national/victoria/akon-guode-faces-deportation-after-serving-jail-term-court-told-20170309-guuqas.html.

[112] For example, the trial judge, Anthony Whealy QC, who is now retired, is on record calling for an investigation into allegations that police withheld covert recordings from the defence: see C Meldrum-Hanna and J Balendra, 'Keli Lane trial judge calls for investigation into withheld police recordings' *Australian Broadcasting Corporation* (Sydney, 19 March 2019) at www.abc.net.au/news/2019-03-19/keli-lane-trial-judge-calls-for-investigation-police-recordings/10912430.

[113] See for discussion L Bartels, 'Safe Haven Laws, Baby Hatches and Anonymous Hospital Birth: Examining Infant Abandonment, Neonaticide and Infanticide in Australia' (2012) 36 *Criminal Law Journal* 19.

Journal Articles

Antolak-Saper, N, 'The Role of Mercy in Infanticide' (2023) 35 *Current Issues in Criminal Justice* 65.
Bartels, L, 'Safe Haven Laws, Baby Hatches and Anonymous Hospital Birth: Examining Infant Abandonment, Neonaticide and Infanticide in Australia' (2012) 36 *Criminal Law Journal* 19.
Bartels, L and Easteal, P, 'Mothers Who Kill: The Forensic Use and Judicial Reception of Evidence of Postnatal Depression and Other Psychiatric Disorders in Australian Filicide Cases' (2013) 37 *Melbourne University Law Review* 297.
Brennan, K, '"A Fine Mixture of Pity and Justice": The Criminal Justice Response to Infanticide in Ireland, 1922–1949' (2013) 31 *Law and History Review* 793.
——, '"Traditions of English Liberal Thought": A History of the Enactment of an Infanticide Law in Ireland' (2013) 50 *Irish Jurist* 100.
Eigen, JP, (1998) 'Criminal Lunacy in Early Modern England: Did Gender Make a Difference?' 21(4) *International Journal of Law and Psychiatry* 412.
Lansdowne, R, 'Infanticide: Psychiatrists in the Plea Bargaining Process' (1990) 16 *Monash University Law Review* 41/.
Loughnan, A, 'The Strange Case of the Infanticide Doctrine' (2012) 32 *OJLS* 685.
Seaborne Davies, D, 'Child-Killing in English Law' (1937) 1 *MLR* 203.
Ward, T, 'The Sad Subject of Infanticide: Law, Medicine and Child Murder 1860–1938' (1999) 8 *Social and Legal Studies* 163.

Newspaper Articles

Cooper, A, 'Akon Guode faces deportation after serving jail term, court told' *The Age* (Melbourne, 9 March 2017) at www.theage.com.au/national/victoria/akon-guode-faces-deportation-after-serving-jail-term-court-told-20170309-guuqas.html.
Editorial, 'Mother starved her three-month-old baby girl to death – and then wrapped the body up and left it to rot inside a cooler bag in a shed' *Daily Mail* (Australia, 7 December 2016) at www.dailymail.co.uk/news/article-4008680/Mother-starved-three-month-old-baby-girl-death-wrapped-body-left-rot-inside-cooler-bag-shed.html (accessed 20 March 2022).
Editorial, 'Murder accused granted bail' *Goulburn Post* (Goulburn, 25 January 2007) at www.goulburnpost.com.au/story/961744/murder-accused-granted-bail/ (accessed 20 March 2022).
Daley, M, 'Kathleen Folbigg Pardoned' (Press Release 8 June 2023) at https://www.dcj.nsw.gov.au/news-and-media/media-releases/2023/kathleen-folbigg-pardoned.html.

Online Resources

Brown, R, 'Kathleen Folbigg's lawyers request inquest into deaths of her four children' *Australian Broadcasting Corporation* (5 March 2022) at www.abc.net.au/news/2022-03-05/kathleen-folbigg-lawyers-want-inquest-into-childrens-deaths/100885100 (accessed 20 March 2022).

Editorial, 'Mum gets suspended sentence for infanticide' *Australian Broadcasting Corporation* (27 February 2008) at www.abc.net.au/news/2008-02-27/mum-gets-suspended-sentence-for-infanticide/1056296 (accessed 20 March 2022).
Meldrum-Hanna, C, and Balendra, J, 'Keli Lane trial judge calls for investigation into withheld police recordings' *Australian Broadcasting Corporation* (19 March 2019) at www.abc.net.au/news/2019-03-19/keli-lane-trial-judge-calls-for-investigation-police-recordings/10912430 (accessed 20 March 2022).
Menagh, J, 'Mother Cassandra Doohan who murdered her baby Anastasia Hand fails to avoid life jail term' *Australian Broadcasting Corporation* (10 September 2019) at www.abc.net.au/news/2019-09-10/mother-who-shook-baby-to-death-jailed-for-life-for-murder/11495094 (accessed 20 March 2022).

Reports

Law Reform Commission of Western Australia, *Project 97 – A Review of the Law of Homicide* (2007).
New South Wales Department of Communities and Justice, *Report of the Inquiry into the Convictions of Kathleen Megan Folbigg* (2019).
New South Wales Law Reform Commission, *Partial Defences to Murder: Provocation and Infanticide Contents* (Law Com No 83, 1997).
——, *People with Cognitive and Mental Health Impairments in the Criminal Justice System* (Law Com No 135, 2012).
——, *People with Cognitive and Mental Health Impairments in the Criminal Justice System: Criminal Responsibility and Consequences* (Law Com No 138, 2013).
Victorian Law Reform Commission, *Defences to Homicide: Final Report* (Law Com No 94, 2004).

Theses

Lansdowne, R, 'Child killing and the Offence of Infanticide: The Development of the Offence and its Operation in New South Wales, 1976–1980' (LLM thesis, University of New South Wales 1987).

8

Capital Punishment and Infanticide Law in Ireland

LYNSEY BLACK AND DAVID M DOYLE

The example of Ireland offers an illuminating case study on the offence of infanticide. Irish law reform on this offence category occurred through the Infanticide Act 1949. Prior to this legislation, the law made no distinction between the murder of an infant and the murder of an adult or a child. Anyone convicted of the murder of an infant, including mothers convicted for the murder of their own infant, were sentenced to death, the mandatory sentence for murder in Ireland at this time. While Ireland shared a 'common law' with England and Wales, including a reliance on key criminal law statutes that underpinned the relevant offences, it was much slower to reform this particular area of law. This chapter explores the factors underlying this divergence from the English example, suggesting reasons why, although England and Wales introduced infanticide law reforms in 1922 and again in 1938, Ireland took this step only in 1949. This chapter looks at the Irish case, outlining the particularities of infant murder in Ireland, the consequences of this in terms of women convicted of murder, the route to reform and the discourses this move elicited, before closing with a brief overview of the post-reform landscape. The chapter explores some of the key arguments against the introduction of a standalone infanticide offence in Ireland. These include its arbitrariness in applying only to the mother of an infant victim, and the related context of the medical rationale that (ostensibly) underpinned the offence, as well as the need to preserve the sanctity of infant life.

The chapter draws on extensive historical newspaper and archival research from materials held in the National Archives of Ireland in Dublin, with a particular emphasis on records from the Department of Justice, Department of Taoiseach (Irish Prime Minister) and the Office of the Attorney-General. Notably, the chapter examines the prisoner files of women who were either charged with or convicted of infanticide-related offences between 1923 and 1949.[1] Although a substantial

[1] The conditions of access to the archival material that forms the basis of this chapter include a stipulation to refrain from identifying the defendants by name. The full names of individuals quoted in this chapter are available in the original material.

body of historical research has been conducted on women who were convicted of infanticide-related offences in the Central Criminal Court, this chapter is unique in the wide-ranging research access that we obtained to previously restricted files not only on these prisoners, but also on other women (and men) who were charged and convicted of infanticide-related offences in the Circuit Criminal Courts during this period.[2] These unexplored records provide an additional and 'nuanced' understanding of the criminal justice response to what was colloquially referred to as 'infanticide' during a chronological period in which there was 'dramatic' decline in baby killing in Ireland.[3] Furthermore, the files give a 'voice' to these 'women and their stories'[4] and provide us with a rare and partial glimpse into 'an ordinary person's negotiation of what was usually buried within the confines of the private life'.[5] These glimpses reveal details of women's lives that would otherwise have faded into obscurity, and offer an important sense of the lives of poor and marginalised women in Irish twentieth-century society, a group traditionally neglected in the historiography.

The chapter is divided into five sections. Section I outlines the context for infanticide law reform in Ireland, overviewing the criminal justice responses to infant murder before 1949. This section also considers the intermittent discussion, and lack of urgency, about creating a standalone homicide offence for infanticide. Section II focuses on the consequences of this failure to reform, namely, those cases of women who were sentenced to death for the murder of their infants between 1922 and 1949. However, as section III goes on to demonstrate, the state responses to this particular cohort exhibit the fundamental disjointedness between law on the books (a murder conviction and death sentence) and law as it operated in practice in these cases. This section also examines the treatment of women condemned to death for infant murder, such as their swift commutation and their post-commutation disposals, including the lengths of time that they spent in prison and religious institutions. Section IV explores in more detail some of the opposition to infanticide law reform, and focuses on a number of cases that correspond with one of the primary objections registered against introducing legislation in Ireland along similar lines to the English Infanticide Act of 1938, namely, the proposed restriction of the offence to the mother of the infant victim. This section also explores the ostensible medical rationale for the offence, and considers further the need of

[2] If the birth mother and/or others were charged with concealment of birth or child abandonment only, the case was tried in the Circuit Criminal Court rather than the Central Criminal Court.

[3] I O'Donnell, 'Unlawful Killing Past and Present' [2002] *The Irish Jurist* 56, 67. The decline in baby killing was established many years before contraception became widely available and preceded the legalisation of abortion in Britain, which gave Irish women who could afford it the option to travel. For a discussion of abortion in the early decades of the Irish state, see C Rattigan, '"Crimes of Passion of the Worst Character": Abortion Cases and Gender in Ireland, 1925–50' in M Gialanella Valiulis (ed), *Gender and Power in Irish History* (Irish Academic Press 2009) 115.

[4] L Earner-Byrne, 'The Rape of Mary M: A Microhistory of Sexual Violence and Moral Redemption in 1920s Ireland' (2015) 24(1) *Journal of the History of Sexuality* 75, 97; Mother and Baby Homes Commission of Investigation, *Final Report* (Stationery Office 2020) para 9.2.

[5] Earner-Byrne (n 4) 97.

policymakers to foreground concerns over the sanctity of infant life. The chapter concludes in section V with a brief overview of the post-reform criminal justice landscape and the decline in baby killing in the second half of the twentieth century.

I. Infant Murder in Ireland and the Route to Infanticide Law Reform

Although not a recognised offence in Ireland until 1949, the criminal justice response to what was commonly referred to as 'infanticide' had assumed a predictable pattern in the decades before reform. As Farrell has written, looking at the period from 1850 to 1900, despite a considerable number of suspected infant murders, few of these cases resulted in a murder conviction, and for those that did, no executions occurred.[6] In the two decades prior to independence, suspected infant murder was also generally dealt with leniently, with lesser charges preferred in many cases. Rattigan found that of 71 cases of suspected infant murder in the years 1900 to 1921, 38 women were convicted of concealment of birth. The next most common outcome was acquittal, which occurred in 10 cases, while only three women were found guilty of murder and sentenced to death.[7] This approach to infant murder – which saw a preference for lesser charges in many cases and a considerable number of acquittals – was the status quo on independence, resulting in a de facto lenient approach to what could, in many cases, have been processed as murder. Similarly, from independence until reform in 1949, Brennan found that of 160 cases in which women were charged with infant murder, most were ultimately convicted on a lesser charge.[8] Decisions taken by the Attorney-General at the earliest stages of criminal prosecution meant that a charge of murder was pursued only if the evidence was overwhelming. The common usage of the term 'infanticide' in Ireland therefore reflected a discrete criminal justice position. In other words, while there was no distinct homicide offence for baby killing, suspected infanticide offenders received different treatment from other persons appearing before the courts on a murder charge.

Nonetheless, despite Irish inaction on the question of law reform in this area, and even though this cohort of offender received differential treatment in practice, there was occasional debate on the matter and the question of whether the law should be reformed. In the 1920s, following the enactment of the first change to the law in England and Wales, references were made in Irish courtrooms to the situation prevailing across the water. In 1924, a young woman appearing in the Central Criminal Court pleaded guilty to a charge of murdering her baby. One

[6] E Farrell, *'A Most Diabolical Deed': Infanticide and Irish Society, 1850–1900* (Manchester University Press 2013).

[7] C Rattigan, *'What Else Could I Do?': Single Mothers and Infanticide, Ireland 1900–1950* (Irish Academic Press 2012).

[8] K Brennan, 'Punishing Infanticide in the Irish Free State' (2013) 3 *Irish Journal of Legal Studies* 1.

reason cited by counsel as to why her guilty plea should be rejected was the 1922 reform in England and Wales.[9] Some petitioners who wrote on behalf of women also referenced the desirability of legal reform. Following Elizabeth H's conviction for the murder of her infant in 1927, the Religious Society of Friends wrote to the Minister for Justice to ask whether it was proposed to introduce a law to remove the necessity of passing capital sentence in these cases. The Department of Justice replied that 'The advisability of introducing legislation to deal with the crime of infanticide is at present under discussion between the Minister for Justice and the Attorney General.'[10]

Reform was to take a slow path, however. In 1939, the Department brought together a committee of judges (the Sullivan Committee) to devise a programme for restricting the scope of the death penalty.[11] Two years later, the Committee recommended the creation of a specific infanticide offence. The Secretary at the Department of Justice, Stephen Roche, disappointed at the conservative nature of the Committee's proposals, observed that this amounted to little more than 'the reconciliation of the law with common-sense'; this, presumably, referred to the fact that it was already common practice that infanticide offenders were treated differently and that even those women convicted of infant murder did not risk the carrying out of the sentence of death.[12] Although the eventual reform in 1949 followed the 1938 English template, Roche also expressed some reservation about the arbitrary 12-month limit on the applicability of infanticide and of its restriction to the mother of the infant victim. Against Roche's disappointment at the overly restrictive nature of this proposal, though, are comments made by Conn Ward in the Department of Local Government and Public Health, who argued that only women suffering from the medical condition of puerperal insanity should be afforded differential treatment.[13] This requirement would have been a particularly restrictive approach and out of line with the law in England and Wales. These and other objections to the introduction of a standalone infanticide offence are explored more fully later in the chapter.

McAvoy has observed that that it was 'clear that the introduction of infanticide legislation was not perceived as a priority issue',[14] and it was to be another eight years before the Committee's recommendation was enacted. The eventual Infanticide Act 1949 incorporated the same terminology as the English law of 1938.[15] This Act allowed for an offence of infanticide where it could be shown

[9] Anon, 'Virginia Girl's Trial' *Anglo-Celt* (15 November 1924) 1.

[10] National Archives of Ireland (NAI) JUS 234/2016, Letter from Religious Society of Friends, 15 December 1927 and Department of Justice response, 21 December 1927.

[11] G O'Brien, 'Capital Punishment in Ireland, 1922–1964' in NM Dawson (ed), *Reflections on Law and History* (Four Courts Press 2006) 223.

[12] NAI, DT S7788A, 25 August 1941.

[13] NAI, DT S7788A, Department of Local Government and Public Health memorandum relating to Insanity as a Defence in Criminal Cases and Infanticide, 2 February 1944.

[14] Cited in Rattigan (n 7).

[15] K Brennan, '"A Fine Mixture of Pity and Justice": The Criminal Justice Response to Infanticide in Ireland, 1922–1949' (2013) 31 *Law and History Review* 793.

that the mother's 'mind was disturbed by reason of her not having fully recovered from the effect of giving birth to the child or by reason of the effect of lactation consequent upon the birth of the child'.[16] The primary rationale underpinning the reform was identified by Brennan as the need to realign the law with practice, with humanitarian motivations as a lesser consideration.[17] Nevertheless, and as explored in section IV, the stated rationale was clearly medical, relating to mental disturbance and the physical toll of labour and lactation. Crucially, Brennan has also noted the slight difference between the English and Irish infanticide laws, in the Irish statute's requirement that the woman first be charged with murder, and surmises that this particularity may be attributable to the influence of the Archbishop of Dublin, Charles McQuaid, one of Ireland's most powerful religious figures at this juncture.[18] These nuances of the Irish infanticide debate are explored more fully later in the chapter. However, before we deal with the opposition to and particularities of reform, we first turn to look at the consequences of the failure to reform, namely, the cases of those women convicted of the murder of an infant and sentenced to death, from independence in 1922 until 1949. Sections II and III examine these cases, while also demonstrating that the Irish criminal justice system developed discrete responses to these women in the decades prior to 1949.

II. Infant Murder and Capital Convictions

From 1922 until reform in 1949, women who were convicted of the murder of an infant were sentenced to death – as death remained the mandatory sentence for murder until the Criminal Justice Act 1964. The category of infant murder accounted for most of the women sentenced to death in post-independence Ireland, ensuring that the delayed legal reform of the law materially shaped the profile of capital cases and created a gendered profile of condemned persons. While the Irish police (*An Garda Síochána*) pursued suspected cases of infant murder rigorously,[19] as already outlined, women prosecuted for this offence were typically shown leniency by the courts with regard to the ultimate charge.[20] Despite this attrition, 12 women were convicted of the murder of their infant and sentenced to death (these cases are outlined in Table 8.1). Over half of the 22 women sentenced to death in Ireland post-independence had been convicted of infant murder.[21]

[16] Infanticide Act 1949, s 1(3). This has subsequently been amended by s 22 of the Criminal Law (Insanity) Act 2006, to replace the reference to lactation with the wording 'by reason of a mental disorder'.

[17] Brennan (n 8).

[18] K Brennan, 'Traditions of English Liberal Thought: A History of the Enactment of an Infanticide Law in Ireland' (2013) 50 *Irish Jurist* 100.

[19] Rattigan (n 7).

[20] Brennan (n 8).

[21] DM Doyle and I O'Donnell, 'Capital Punishment in Post-Independence Ireland' (2012) 33 *The Journal of Legal History* 65, 74–75.

Table 8.1 Women convicted of infant murder and sentenced to death, 1922–49

Name	Convicted	Age	Location	Victim	Marital Status	Work
Elizabeth D	3 June 1926	40	Co Wicklow	Own infant	Widow	Farm labourer
Mary K	28 Oct 1926	22	Co Westmeath	Own infant	Unmarried	Domestic
Elizabeth H	12 Dec 1927	30	Co Westmeath	Own infant	Unmarried	In home
Mary Anne K	10 June 1929	23	Co Roscommon	Own infant	Married	Former domestic
Deborah S	13 June 1929	21	Co Kerry	Own infant	Unmarried	Domestic
Catherine A	25 June 1929	26	Co Wexford	Own infant	Married	Former domestic
Christina R	27 Nov 1930	28	Co Dublin	Own infant	Unmarried	Domestic
Margaret F	3 March 1931	25	Co Clare	Own infant	Unmarried	Domestic
Elizabeth E	28 March 1935	28	Co Roscommon	Own infant	Unmarried	None
Rose E	28 March 1935	20	Co Roscommon	Infant of sister	Unmarried	None
Mary S	15 Nov 1938	50	Co Monaghan	Grandchild	Widow	Farmer
Kate O	22 Nov 1943	36	Co Westmeath	Own infant	Unmarried	Former domestic

Note: Data based on archival material from the National Archives of Ireland.

Of these 12 women, 10 were capitally convicted for the murder of their own infant and two had killed an infant within the family (Mary S had killed her 18-year-old daughter's newborn infant, and Rose E had killed the infant of her sister Elizabeth). Of the 11 infant victims,[22] most were 'illegitimate', born outside the protections of marriage, or otherwise involved a crisis pregnancy. These included the case of Catherine A, who married the infant's father while she was pregnant, and that of Mary Anne K, whose husband claimed that he was not the father of her infant. Roughly half of the infants were newborns when they died and had been killed almost immediately following birth. The infants of Mary Anne K, Christina R, Elizabeth E, Elizabeth D and Mary K lived for periods of approximately two to three weeks, reflecting the fact that they had been born in institutions and were not killed until their mothers were discharged.[23] The proportion of institutional birth was higher for the cohort of women who were convicted on the murder charge and sentenced to death compared to women prosecuted for infant murder but

[22] Two sisters were capitally convicted for infanticide.

[23] Elizabeth D in Rathdrum County Home, Mary K in Mullingar County Home, Mary Anne K in Roscommon County Home, Christina R in the South Dublin Union and Elizabeth E in Roscommon County Home.

convicted of lesser offences.[24] Cases involving institutional birth presented clearer evidence of deliberation, and afforded prosecution counsel the ability to introduce witnesses to speak to the health of the baby at the point of discharge. Following the conviction of Christina R, the judge noted privately that '[t]his is not an ordinary case of infanticide, inasmuch as the murder did not take place until some 20 days after the birth of the child'.[25] This delay led the Secretary at the Department of Justice to claim that Christina R had acted 'in cold blood'.[26]

III. A Discrete Category: Reprieve from Capital Conviction and Post-Commutation Disposal

While the law made no difference in cases of infant murder, in practice, the criminal justice system in Ireland responded to infant murder offenders in a very different way. Put otherwise, a discrete category of offender was fashioned. Once murder convictions were achieved in the 12 cases outlined in section II, rationales for mercy and commutation were immediately sought. This was evident, for instance, in the case of Mary K, in which it was stated that 'The Department of Justice strongly recommend that the sentence should not be carried out and state that it would be against all our precedents to do so'.[27] The expectation of reprieve had been cemented as standard practice (something that stretched back to the nineteenth century)[28] and there was little concern that women capitally convicted for killing an infant would be executed.[29] Rather, the 12 condemned women had their sentence of death commuted to penal servitude for life. Reprieve thus was the inevitable pathway for women sentenced to death for infant murder.

Many of the cases attracted considerable sympathy, and the women were often viewed with pity.[30] The reasons given for reprieve included the often tender age of the condemned and the difficult circumstances of childbirth, as many women gave birth alone.[31] The women were also frequently represented as mentally 'defective', a label that further justified a speedy reprieve. Their categorisation as mental defectives reflected a commonly assumed link between 'weak-mindedness' and

[24] L Black, *Gender and Punishment in Ireland: Women, Murder and the Death Penalty, 1922–64* (Manchester University Press 2022).

[25] NAI, DT S6096, Letter from Justice O'Byrne, 27 November 1930.

[26] NAI, JUS 234/3332, Letter from Stephen Roche, 17 November 1933.

[27] NAI, DT S5195, Memorandum, 4 November 1926.

[28] Farrell (n 6).

[29] This reflected wider official reluctance to execute women in 20th-century Ireland. L Black, '"On the other hand the accused is a woman …": Women and the Death Penalty in Post-independence Ireland' (2018) 36 *Law and History Review* 139. For the employment of English executioners in Ireland, see I O'Donnell, and DM Doyle, 'A Family Affair? English Hangmen and a Dublin Jail, 1923–54' (2014) 18 *New Hibernia Review* 101.

[30] DM Doyle and L O'Callaghan, *Capital Punishment in Independent Ireland: A Social, Legal and Political History* (Liverpool University Press 2019) 106.

[31] Black (n 24).

illegitimate pregnancy.[32] In some cases, it was argued that the strain of a death sentence would be particularly injurious to women possessed of such weakness. Justice O'Byrne endorsed Mary K's reprieve because he felt it was a case 'in which the strain of a capital sentence, if continued for any length of time, may have serious results on the physical and mental health of the prisoner'.[33] As a result, there was considerable urgency in these cases to formalise reprieve as quickly as possible. In Department of Taoiseach memoranda following the sentencing of Catherine A, it was noted that the Minister for Justice 'would like to get an early decision on the matter'.[34] Catherine A's death sentence was commuted just three days after it had been handed down. The women condemned to death for infant murder during the 1920s and 1930s – a period of 'moral panic' about sexual morality in the independent Irish state – experienced the shortest waiting period between conviction and commutation.[35] While reform of the law was not forthcoming, the Irish criminal justice system developed a discrete response to these cases.

Despite the moral overtones of these crimes, there was an almost instinctive tendency by the Government and the judiciary to look with pity upon these women. This tendency underpinned the practice that had developed in cases of suspected infant murder or infanticide-related offences, extending to women ultimately convicted of this offence as well as to women convicted of alternative offences. The sentences imposed on the women convicted of the lesser infanticide-related offences varied considerably. For instance, Anne O'H, a 30-year-old single domestic servant, was released six months after her conviction for abandoning her 12-day-old child in Longford in April 1941. The baby girl was healthy when leaving the hospital, but was subsequently found alive in a ditch about a mile and a half from Longford. The child was taken to Longford Hospital where she died a month later. Rattigan observes that most single women who were tried for infanticide in the Central Criminal Court between 1922 and 1950 were 'young, unmarried, seduced and abandoned, driven to infanticide by shame and desperation',[36] and this statement is equally applicable to many of the women who pleaded guilty to the lesser charges of manslaughter, concealment of birth or child abandonment. The 'stigma attached to illegitimacy' played a pivotal role in the decision taken by many of these women to 'murder or conceal the births of their offspring',[37] and this too appeared to be the primary motivation to kill in this case.[38] Moreover, Anne O'H had 'fallen more than once'[39] – she had given birth to an illegitimate child about four years previously in England, and that child had been in a home since

[32] M Luddy, 'Moral Rescue and Unmarried Mothers in Ireland in the 1920s' (2001) 30 *Women's Studies* 797.

[33] NAI, DT S5195, Memorandum, 4 November 1926.

[34] NAI, DT S5891, Letter from Department of the President, 28 June 1929.

[35] Black (n 24).

[36] Rattigan (n 7) 19.

[37] Farrell (n 6) 17, 26.

[38] NAI, JUS 18/4816, Connolly to Commissioner, 22 July 1941.

[39] Commission on the Relief of the Sick and Destitute Poor, including the Insane Poor, *Report* (Dublin 1927) 68.

birth.[40] Fortunately for Anne O'H, the Medical Officer certified that the abandonment and exposure had nothing to do with the cause of death, and she was released in October 1941.[41]

At the other end of the spectrum, Margaret D was sentenced to four years' penal servitude for the manslaughter of her 22-day-old female infant in Roscommon in 1940.[42] After being discharged from the Roscommon County Home, she travelled by bus to Castlerea carrying the child in her arms. After disembarking from the bus, Margaret D entered a grove on the Roscommon side of Castlerea. She subsequently returned home that evening without the infant, but the next day the Gardaí traced her movements and discovered the 'dead body of the child … concealed beneath the trunk of an old, decayed tree and completely covered with grass'.[43] A post-mortem examination revealed that strangulation was the cause of death and that a portion of the child's garment was found knotted tightly around the child's neck.[44] Margaret D was released on licence from prison in July 1943,[45] but she 'decided' to reside in Our Lady's Home, Henrietta Street, Dublin.[46] Somewhat peculiarly, a 'military escort' was considered for transporting Margaret D from prison to Dublin.[47]

The recourse to the detention of women and girls in religiously run institutions was one feature of the criminal justice response to infanticide-related offences in independent Ireland that marked it out from Northern Ireland and England and Wales. This peculiarity was another of the features of the punishment landscape that saw infanticide fashioned as a discrete offence prior to its formal legal creation in 1949. As Rattigan observed, from independence in 1922, the sentencing patterns for such offences in Northern Ireland and the Irish Free State diverged markedly.[48] From a common origin point, at which religious institutions were little used as a site of punishment, these soon became an integral part of Ireland's penal landscape, in contrast to Northern Ireland. Although it was suggested by the Department of Local Government and Public Health's Inspector of Boarded Out Children, Miss Fitzgerald-Kenney, that the existence of 'these homes have done much to prevent infanticide',[49] many women 'agreed' to enter religious institutions – such as the Magdalen Laundries and mother and baby homes or other religious homes – at the direction of the criminal justice agencies and actors following the commission of infanticide-related offences. In recent years, various

[40] NAI, JUS 18/4816, Connolly to Commissioner, 22 July 1941.
[41] ibid.
[42] NAI, JUS 18/4361, Prisoner's Record, 25 October 1940.
[43] NAI, JUS 18/4361, Letter from J Lyons, 11 December 1940.
[44] ibid.
[45] NAI, JUS 18/4361, Governor of Mountjoy to Secretary of Department of Justice, 21 July 1943.
[46] NAI, JUS 18/4361, Governor of Mountjoy to Secretary of Department of Justice, 5 July 1943.
[47] NAI, JUS 18/4361, Governor of Mountjoy to Secretary of Department of Justice, 25 October 1940.
[48] Rattigan (n 7); Following the Government of Ireland Act 1920, six counties in the northeast of the island became Northern Ireland and remained within the United Kingdom; the remaining 26 counties became the Irish Free State, later to become the Republic of Ireland.
[49] Mother and Baby Homes Commission of Investigation, *Final Report* (October 2020) 19.

government-commissioned inquiries have probed the extent of state complicity in this network of religious sites in which thousands of women and girls spent time.[50] The McAleese Report, for instance, explored state involvement in the Magdalen Laundries, and found that the criminal justice system accounted for at least 8.1 per cent of entries to these institutions following 1922.[51]

Of the 12 women convicted of infant murder and reprieved, the surviving evidence reveals that six were subsequently transferred from prison to a religious institution.[52] A Department of Justice 'working rule', which had developed from the late-1920s, provided official guidance on procedures for such women:

> As a working rule in infanticide cases I think that the mother convicted should be kept in prison for a period of two years and then placed in a home … Each case therefore must be examined on the merits, in some cases the above mentioned period may have to be abridged in others extended. It applies only to average cases.[53]

Other women convicted of infanticide-related offences also served their punishment in religious sites. Disposal to some form of religious detention became more popular for this cohort in the years post-independence, as the prison decreased in importance as a place of punishment for women in Ireland.[54] For example, Margaret D, who pleaded guilty to concealment of birth before the Central Criminal Court in 1936, was sentenced to either six months' imprisonment with hard labour or two years in Our Lady's Home Henrietta Street, while Kate R, who was convicted of manslaughter for poisoning her baby daughter with strychnine in 1938, was sentenced to 12 months' confinement in Mary Magdalen's Convent in Donnybrook.[55] Similarly, in the case of Kathleen M, the judge asked the Minister for full remission of sentence owing to the 'extenuating circumstances' and the fact that Kathleen M, was 'agreeable [to] enter Good Shepard's Convent'.[56] Although difficult to quantify precisely 'the actual period of detention for most inmates',[57] it certainly appears that many of these girls and women spent longer in confinement than the preponderance of prisoners in the formal criminal justice system.[58]

[50] McAleese Report, *Inter-Departmental Committee to Establish the Facts of State Involvement with the Magdalen Laundries* (Department of Justice and Equality 2013); Mother and Baby Homes Commission of Investigation (n 49).

[51] McAleese Report (n 49). This Report noted (ibid 204) that most women who entered the laundries from the criminal justice system had not committed serious crimes, 'The majority of placements of women in the Magdalen Laundries by the criminal justice system followed convictions for more minor or petty crimes, particularly those dealt with in the District Court.'

[52] Black (n 24).

[53] This 'working rule' was found on various files within the archives, see NAI Department of Justice 234/2016 (Elizabeth H); Department of Justice 234/2603 (Catherine A); Department of Justice 234/3332 (Christina R).

[54] C Quinlan, *Inside: Ireland's Women's Prisons Past and Present* (Irish Academic Press 2011); M Rogan, *Prison Policy in Ireland: Politics, Penal Welfarism and Political Imprisonment* (Routledge 2011).

[55] NAI, JUS 18/2426, Boyle Fawsitt to Secretary of the Department of Justice, 28 November 1938.

[56] Telegram, O'Brien Moran, 23 July 1927.

[57] L Earner-Byrne, *Mother and Child: Maternity and Child Welfare in Dublin, 1922–60* (Manchester University Press 2017), 187.

[58] E O'Sullivan and I O'Donnell, *Coercive Confinement in Post-Independence Ireland: Patients, Prisoners and Penitents* (Manchester University Press 2012) 41; Rattigan (n 7) 210.

That said, there is evidence that some women were permitted to leave these convents before serving their full sentences.[59] Máire Ní C, for instance, was released almost two years prematurely on foot of a petition that revealed that her father was terminally ill and anxious to see her. Máire Ní C had pleaded guilty to the manslaughter of her unnamed infant in 1941, and Black J suspended her sentence of three years' penal servitude subject to her entering into a recognisance to keep the peace for three years and, as part of this recognisance, entering the convent at Henrietta Street Dublin with the 'usual conditions'.[60] McAvoy has noted that Probation Officer Elizabeth Carroll is explicitly referred to in many of the extant infanticide records,[61] and in this case Miss Carroll expressed her opinion that as the girl had been in the convent for over a year, she had benefited by her experience there and might be permitted to go home.[62] The President of the High Court sympathised with the situation, and on foot of the approval of the trial judge,[63] Black J, the Minister for Justice wrote to the Sisters of Charity of St Vincent de Paul Convent on Henrietta Street, requesting that the 'inmate be released to return to her home forthwith'.[64]

Following the reform of 1949, Brennan has documented what appears to be a decreasing reliance on religiously run institutions as places of punishment in infanticide cases. Of those cases in which a sentence could be ascertained, just 10 per cent of women were sentenced to a period of time in a religious institution; Brennan writes that, if accurate, 'this would be a striking change in practice' from the post-1922 decades.[65] The reliance on religious institutionalisation for these women suggests some of the ideological underpinning of the law on infanticide in Ireland. This moral and religious dimension is explored further in section IV, in discussion of the objections raised to the proposed reform of the law on infant murder. Despite law reform in Britain in 1922 and 1938, these sections have demonstrated how the Irish route towards special accommodation for these cases was marked by a degree of leniency in terms of the charge preferred, with the swift reprieve of those small numbers of women who were convicted of infant murder, and with a highly gendered penal arrangement, in which women's custody was often delegated to congregations of religious sisters rather than prison. Alongside occasional discussion of a change in the law, Ireland developed what was perceived by many as an appropriately 'lenient' criminal justice response, one that left the law untouched but diverted many women away from the prison towards religious detention.

[59] Rattigan (n 7) 210.

[60] NAI, JUS 18/5617, Clárathóir Chónde to Roche, 22 June 1941. For an overview of the procedure see Brennan (n 8) 11–12.

[61] Cited in Rattigan (n 7) 215.

[62] NAI, JUS 18/5617, Clárathóir Chónde to Roche, 22 June 1941.

[63] NAI, JUS 18/5617, Clárathóir Chónde to Roche, 22 June 1941.

[64] NAI, JUS 18/5617, O'Connor to The Reverend Mother, Sisters of Charity, 22 June 1942.

[65] K Brennan, 'Murderous Mothers and Gentle Judges: Paternalism, Patriarchy, and Infanticide' (2018) 30 *Yale Journal of Law and Feminism* 139, 161.

IV. Reservations about the 1938 English Act and Belated Irish Reform

Ireland enacted infanticide law reform in 1949 – 27 years after the first English reform, 11 years after the further reform of the law in England and Wales, and eight years after the Sullivan Committee had recommended reform. Since at least the 1920s, commentators in Ireland had been calling for some amelioration in the continued capital status of infant murder. Why did law reform take such a long time? This chapter now turns to explore some of the key objections to infanticide law reform, reflecting on the discussions that took place particularly following the enactment of the English Act of 1938. Further, and in light of the discrete and lenient treatment such women received, why was there a need for the law to be reformed at all? The development of an informal and ad hoc response to infanticide offenders caused as many problems as it solved. It ameliorated the immediate harshness of the law – most women were charged with lesser offences, and for women prosecuted for infant murder, most were ultimately convicted of lesser offences if they were not acquitted. For the few women convicted of murder and sentenced to death, commutation was speedily arranged. Yet the increasing gap between the law and how it operated in practice in this regard must have worked on the minds of policymakers. Brennan has argued that 'the Irish approach to infanticide from the time of independence and up to the present day has been based on implicit shared social norms about the "appropriate" outcome in cases where women killed their newborn infants'.[66] She concludes that the law 'had little impact on the outcome'.[67] The amelioration measures put in place prior to reform reflected contemporary social norms, and allowed the legal status quo to be retained until 1949.

Perhaps underpinning the delayed infanticide reform was the need for Irish lawmakers to reinforce the sanctity of infant life. As previously discussed, when the 1949 law was enacted, it differed from the English example in one respect – the need to first charge a woman with murder. Brennan suggests that this Irish distinction was shaped by the sway of the Catholic Church.[68] This influence was felt despite the fact that, as Maguire writes, the Catholic Church remained largely silent on the question of infanticide.[69] Nevertheless, Maguire demonstrates the extent to which the views of the Catholic Church were heard, put forward by the imposing political figure of Éamon de Valera during discussions on the infanticide bill.[70] In the immediate post-1922 years, there was greater emphasis on the need for

[66] K Brennan, 'Social Norms and the Law in responding to Infanticide' (2018) 38 *Legal Studies* 480, 481.

[67] ibid.

[68] ibid 480–99.

[69] MJ Maguire, *Precarious Childhood in Post-Independence Ireland* (Manchester University Press 2010) 181–83.

[70] Éamon de Valera was the most prominent Irish politician of the post-independence decades, serving as a member of the Irish parliament, as Irish prime minister, and finally as President of Ireland.

the law to symbolically reinforce the sanctity of infant life.[71] This move occurred within a newly independent society that sought to differentiate itself from Britain by, among other things, its adherence to the Catholic Church's values and morality. The maintenance of the legal status quo therefore appeared to serve a need to symbolically reassert the sanctity of infant life in a period of Church-inspired moral panic surrounding illegitimacy.[72] Although the capital sentence would not be carried out in these cases, it could be argued that the passing of a death sentence and the preservation of this punishment in law satisfied the calls for some that reform would cheapen infant life.

At the time that the Sullivan Committee was convened in 1939, however – following further English reform of infanticide – the Department of Justice appeared ready to accept that something must be done on the matter of the law on infant murder. On foot of the Committee's subsequent and by then relatively uncontroversial recommendation that an offence of infanticide should be introduced in Ireland, one of the key issues raised by Secretary Roche at the Department of Justice was that it was entirely arbitrary to restrict such an offence to the mother of an infant victim who kills her child before the age of 12 months. This was one of the few documented objections during this period of policy discussion. Indeed, it was not really an objection to infanticide law reform and Roche did not view it as a reason to retain the status quo. Rather, it was a pragmatic point to consider in terms of the reality of cases appearing before the courts. We investigate it here because it not only sheds light on the complexity of legislating for infanticide, but it also elucidates the medical rationale that underpins the offence and the extent to which this, perhaps, was a 'cover' for social norms, pragmatic considerations and/or humanitarian concerns. The hesitance to adopt the English approach, which restricted the offence in this manner, appeared to be influenced by the cases that Roche invoked in which family members and relatives had assisted the mothers in killing their infants.[73] One of the striking features of infant killing in the early decades of Irish independence was the 'degree to which the relatives of single women were involved in the death of an illegitimate infant and the disposal of its body'.[74] Although most of the women charged with infanticide-related offences acted alone,[75] a number of women were charged or convicted jointly with relatives.

The most high-profile case, and the one that Secretary Roche appeared to reference in his objection, was that of sisters Elizabeth and Rose E, who were found guilty in the Central Criminal Court of the murder of an infant female, Mary Theresa E, the daughter of Elizabeth, and sentenced to death. Elizabeth had given birth to her daughter in Roscommon County Home on 2 October 1934. These 'catch-all institutions'[76] had persisted as the 'chief refuge for many women who found

[71] Luddy (n 32).
[72] D Ferriter, *The Transformation of Ireland, 1900–2000* (Profile 2004) 322–23.
[73] Brennan (n 18) 106.
[74] Rattigan (n 7) 232.
[75] Brennan (n 8) 7.
[76] O'Sullivan and O'Donnell (n 58) 15–18.

themselves pregnant outside marriage' post-independence.[77] It appears, however, that the behaviour of unmarried mothers towards their neonates was monitored more carefully within these institutions than that of their married counterparts,[78] and medical staff at the Roscommon Home expressed concern about Elizabeth's apparent negligence in the care and feeding of the infant. Throughout her confinement in the Home, the only person to visit her was her 18-year-old sister Rose. Elizabeth, like many other Irish women who found themselves in a similar predicament, had concealed her pregnancy from her parents and neighbours.[79] That Elizabeth 'would strive to conceal a pregnancy is hardly surprising, given the level of hostility towards unmarried mothers in Ireland during this period'.[80] The sisters were convicted of murder and sentenced to death on 28 March 1935, and an extant Department of Justice Memorandum reveals that the Minister for Justice recommended that, as with other women so condemned, the death sentences imposed on Elizabeth and Rose E should be commuted to penal servitude for life.[81] The jury also added a strong recommendation to mercy to their verdict, and the private observations of the trial judge, O'Byrne J, were in accordance with the jury's rider:

> In all the circumstances of the case and having regard to the sex and age of the convicts, I consider it is a case in which the recommendation of the Jury might receive favourable consideration.[82]

The sisters were subsequently reprieved,[83] but the case was not soon forgotten. Almost six years later, Roche noted that if the Sullivan Committee's recommendation was adopted and 'another similar case then occurred the position would arise that the elder sister – the mother of the child – would not be tried for murder – though she might be more culpable' but the 'younger sister, a girl of 18, would be so tried, and, inevitably, convicted, and equally inevitably, reprieved'.[84] Roche also observed that the commuted sentence of penal servitude for life was a fiction.[85] In the case of sisters Elizabeth and Rose E, Rose was released in December 1936, less than two years after the killing of her niece.[86] Elizabeth was released in December 1938 after serving the last 15 months of her sentence in Our Lady's

[77] Luddy (n 32) 800.

[78] C Rattigan, '"Done to death by fathers or relatives": Irish Families and Infanticide Cases, 1922–1950' (2008) 13 *The History of the Family* 370.

[79] ibid.

[80] C Rattigan, '"I thought from her appearance that she was in the Family Way": Detecting Infanticide Cases In Ireland, 1900–1921' (2011) 11 *Family and Community History* 134, 143–44.

[81] NAI DJUS/18/885A & B, Memorandum from The Department of Justice as to the Case of Elizabeth and Rose E – Under Sentence of Death, 15 May 1935.

[82] ibid.

[83] NAI DJUS/18/885A & B, the sentences were commuted on 18 May 1935, see Letter from Secretary, Office of the President, 18 May 1935.

[84] NAI DT S7788A, Roche to O'Donoghue, 25 August 1941 (underlining in original).

[85] ibid.

[86] Rose was released on 1 December 1936. See NAI DJUS/18/885A & B, Letter from Ard Cheannphort to Runaidhe, Roinn Dli agus Cirt. Rose E: Convicted of Murder on 28 March 1935, Released on Licence on 1 December 1936, 1 June 1937.

Home, Henrietta Street, Dublin.[87] The case, beyond its notoriety, was important as it revealed the complexity of attempting to legislate for infanticide where the crime might stray beyond the mother and include third parties. Roche's hesitation, therefore, was grounded in the fact that the adoption of English law, with its focus on the mother, may have created anomalies.

Rattigan has highlighted that in most infanticide cases, if the unmarried mother sought help from a family member or confided in a relative it was generally a female.[88] However, in 1936, 23-year-old Mary Anne D and her brother, Martin D, were jointly convicted after pleading guilty to placing Mary Anne D's female infant in 'a suitcase while it was alive and throwing it into the river'.[89] Based on the evidence furnished in the Garda report,[90] it was believed that Mary Anne D's motive for harming her illegitimate infant was due to the fact that it was proving difficult for her to abscond from larceny charges with a new baby. Mary Anne D opted to spend two years in Henrietta Street Convent rather than face six months' imprisonment with hard labour, while Martin D was sentenced to six months with hard labour if he entered recognisance to keep the peace and be of good behaviour for two years. Mary Anne D subsequently petitioned for mitigation with the assistance of her mother, but the request was denied, with the extant correspondence stating that 'the petitioner is a dangerous type of criminal we do not recommend her release from the convent'.[91] This case further outlines the complexity of legislating for infanticide, demonstrating the difficulties a more expansive offence construction would present if widened beyond the scope of the mother.

Despite Secretary Roche's concerns about the arbitrariness of restricting the offence to the mother who kills her infant aged less than 12 months, the very construction of the English, and later the Irish, statute was premised in such a way as to render this objection moot. The crime of infanticide was underpinned by an explicitly medical rationale that related to mental disturbance on the birth of a child. The relationship between insanity and the female reproductive system had been the subject of extensive discourse in the nineteenth century,[92] but very few Irish women who killed their infants in the post-independence period were deemed unfit to plead or found guilty but insane at trial.[93] In 1930, Annie C was charged with murder and concealment of birth, but was subsequently found insane and incapable of pleading before Meredith J in the Central Criminal Court. She was ordered to be detained at the Central Criminal Lunatic Hospital,[94] and despite

[87] NAI DJUS/18/885A & B, J Raftery to Secretary, Department of Justice, 13 December 1938; Governor, Mountjoy Prison, to the Secretary, Department of Justice, 1 September 1937.

[88] Rattigan (n 78) 376–77.

[89] NAI, JUS 18/2507, Somers to Ard Ceannphort, 25 August 1937.

[90] ibid.

[91] ibid.

[92] P Prior, 'Murder and Madness: Gender and the Insanity Defense in Nineteenth-century Ireland' (2005) 9 *New Hibernia Review* 19, 24.

[93] Rattigan (n 7) 205.

[94] NAI, JUS 18/2700, Laurence B to Minister for Justice, 5 July 1938.

numerous petitions by family members seeking her discharge, she would spend almost 27 years in custody. However, this outcome was anomalous, and despite discourses of mental abnormality pervading infanticide cases, very few resulted in insanity verdicts.

Findings of insanity were also infrequent in cases of baby killing in other jurisdictions,[95] but it was not unusual for those detained in the non-criminal justice system institutions in Ireland – especially unmarried mothers and the mentally ill – to spend longer in institutions than those detained in the formal criminal justice system.[96] Infanticide law was therefore founded on a presumption of mental abnormality following childbirth, but this medical rationale was rarely accepted in cases before the courts prior to reform. Furthermore, although the medical rationale appeared to be a somewhat disingenuous basis for the law, extending the parameters of infanticide beyond the scope of the infant's mother would have seriously undermined the medical justification upon which the law was based. As Brennan writes, infanticide offenders post-reform were 'not considered to suffer from a mental illness that required medical intervention'[97] and there was a 'veiled recognition' of the socio-political context in which the offence was committed.[98] The law thus served a dual purpose. It satisfied social norms (that such women should not be convicted of murder) and legal norms (by offering a concession to the need for individualised notions of responsibility).[99]

To explore the question of the medical rationale further, the law as formulated was restricted to the mother of the infant victim because of its grounding in a medical justification. Essentially, the partial defence of infanticide relied on the acceptance that the woman was suffering from mental unbalance at the time of the killing for reasons related to the birth of the child and associated physiological factors such as lactation. For instance, the Infanticide Act of 1922 in England and Wales based its differential treatment of such an offender on the understanding that 'the balance of her mind was then disturbed' as a result of 'the effect of giving birth'. In 1938, while expanding the parameters of the offence to infants aged up to 1 year, the medical rationale remained 'where the mother had not recovered from the effect either of giving birth or of lactation'.

Ward has considered how an offence often understood in lay terms as occurring due to the socio-economic hardships faced by unmarried women, became formalised in law only because of this medical justification.[100] He overviews the legal responses to infanticide in the nineteenth century, arguing that in this period the term meant the killing of a newly born infant by its unmarried mother, for reasons

[95] Rattigan (n 7) 204; K Johnson Kramar, *Unwilling Mothers, Unwanted Babies: Infanticide in Canada* (University of British Columbia Press 2005).

[96] O'Sullivan and O'Donnell (n 58).

[97] Brennan (n 65) 163.

[98] ibid 179.

[99] Brennan (n 66).

[100] T Ward, 'The Sad Subject of Infanticide: Law, Medicine and Child Murder, 1860–1938' (1999) 8 *Social and Legal Studies* 163.

relating to the difficulties of 'illegitimate' motherhood. In essence, then, whatever criminal justice 'leniency' existed (in convictions for manslaughter rather than murder, or the swift reprieve of death sentences when murder convictions were achieved) was premised on a certain pragmatic sympathy for women who found themselves in this position. It was external, not internal, factors that motivated leniency. Ironically, why, then, did the reform of the law on infant killings adopt a medical rationale, when factors external to the woman were generally considered to have been predominant? Ward writes that the attempts through the late nineteenth century to ameliorate the law for infanticidal women always floundered due to reluctance to dilute the law on murder. The developing legal construction of infanticide, first in 1922 and then in 1938, therefore reflected 'a reconstruction of medical concepts to fit the needs of the law'.[101] Medical understandings were twisted, yet the veneer of medical justification was retained to provide an acceptable legal response to women who killed their infants. This was necessary because of the need to preserve the criminal law's commitment to individualised responsibility. Broader societal or structural causes were not acknowledged in the statutory construction of infanticide, although they motivated its creation. The appearance that women were 'getting away with murder'[102] was countered by pointing to the ostensible 'scientific' rationale that dictated the terms and limits of the offence. This was despite the common acknowledgement among contemporary observers and subsequent analysis that in reality the reform was motivated by different concerns. A medical basis, albeit a lay construction of a medical basis, was an acceptable means by which the overwhelming difficulties faced by such women could be catered for in law, while preserving a commitment to individual responsibility. Osborne, viewing the operation of Canada's infanticide law in 1987, acknowledged that there was little evidence to support the medical rationale that underpinned its justification at the time of enactment or since.[103] Yet she disputes the argument that the law should therefore be abolished, by arguing:

> Removing infanticide from the law on the basis of outmoded medical knowledge ignores the fact that the medical rationale was never in vogue or scientifically established. It was simply more conventional, conservative and less contentious than the reasons for the courts' lenient treatment of murdering mothers.[104]

In light of the 'the medicalisation of infanticide',[105] albeit for the purposes of expediency, the extension of infanticide to persons beyond the immediate biological

[101] ibid 174.

[102] R Heberle, 'Disciplining Gender; Or, Are Women Getting Away with Murder?' (1999) 24 *Signs* 1103.

[103] JA Osborne, 'The Crime of Infanticide: Throwing Out the Baby with the Bathwater' (1987) 6 *Canadian Journal of Family Law* 47.

[104] ibid 58.

[105] K Donovan, 'The Medicalisation of Infanticide' [1984] *Crim LR* 259. For further discussion of the history of the medical rationale, see Brennan and Milne, ch 1 of this volume. For further discussion of the medicalisation issue, see Milne and Brennan, ch 6 of this volume.

mother of the infant victim would pose significant problems, inevitably signalling a broader acceptance of societal and structural factors. While such persons appearing before the courts may have been dealt with leniently so far as the law allowed, to extend the infanticide offence to such offenders would have undermined the medical basis that made the law palatable.

The exact justifications and appropriate parameters of infanticide as an offence that troubled some Irish policymakers in the 1940s have remained perennial issues of debate. As Friedman et al noted, despite their proliferation worldwide (largely based on the English law), infanticide laws have been criticised as being simultaneously too expansive, automatically excusing mothers who kill in cases where they should be held culpable, and too restrictive, in their exclusion of the killings of infants aged over 12 months and applicability to biological mothers only.[106] Notwithstanding the arguments made that the causal link between the medical rationale and the killing is spurious at best, over two dozen nations retain infanticide as a partial defence to murder. The offence has appeared to offer a pragmatic solution to the problems of subjecting often vulnerable women to the full rigour of the law. In the Irish context, murder remained a capital offence until the Criminal Justice Act 1964, which saw it restricted to certain political murders and the killing of a police officer or prison officer in the course of their duty.[107] The exemption for infanticide occurred 15 years before any wider amelioration of capital sentencing in Ireland and over 50 years before a diminished responsibility partial defence was introduced in 2006. To broaden this exception to offenders who were not the infant's mother, a reform that came with the imprimatur of the medical profession, may have seemed like a reform too far. While Roche wondered about the case of Rose E, this was something of an anomaly across the cases. In most cases, it was mothers alone who were prosecuted and mothers alone who acted. Other family members, if suspected of being complicit or of turning a very blind eye to domestic matters, could be dealt with by way of lesser charges such as concealment of birth. It would have been disproportionate to legislate for such 'edge cases'.

V. Conclusion

Writing in the American periodical *Holiday* in December 1949, the writer Frank O'Connor noted that infanticide in Ireland is 'appallingly common',[108] but this statement ignored the reality of a declining rate of baby killing that endured until

[106] S Hatters Friedman, J Cavney and PJ Resnick, 'Mothers Who Kill: Evolutionary Underpinnings and Infanticide Law' (2012) 30 *Behavioral Sciences and the Law* 585.

[107] Doyle and O'Callaghan (n 30) 201–44. See also DM Doyle, 'Republicans, Martyrology, and the Death Penalty in Britain and Ireland, 1939–1990' (2015) 54 *Journal of British Studies* 703.

[108] F O'Connor, 'Ireland' in *Holiday* (December 1949) 40, cited in D Ferriter, *Occasions of Sin: Sex and Society in Modern Ireland* (Profile 2009) 249.

the middle of the twentieth century, after which point recorded infanticide virtually disappeared from the criminal statistics.[109] Although in specific years the majority of homicides still involved babies (eg 54 per cent in 1952), the decline in this category of violent death in the second half of the twentieth century – after the enactment of the Act of 1949 – is particularly noteworthy.[110] In the 1950s, for instance, one in six homicides involved the killing of an infant. This fell to one in eight in the 1960s, before plummeting to one in 50 in the 1970s.[111] Similarly, in the UK there was a notable decline. As Elizabeth Parker and Frances Good point out, 'in six years 1973–1978 there were on average 8.7 women convicted of infanticide each year compared with 16.8 per annum for the 1967–1972 period'.[112] Thus, the disappearance of baby killing must be viewed as one of the most striking shifts in lethal violence in twentieth-century Ireland.[113]

The partial defence of infanticide in the Act of 1949 – which allowed a woman who killed her newly born infant due to disturbance of the mind caused by giving birth to be tried and punished as for manslaughter rather than murder – has been described as 'a gender-based concession'.[114] In practice, though, it appears to have simply put the status quo ante on a statutory footing, as juries in the post-independence period generally sympathised with the plight of unmarried women in infanticide cases,[115] and invariably alleviated the excesses of the law not necessarily by a 'high acquittal rate but in a high rate of convictions on lesser charges'.[116] As Ferriter put it, 'there was a recognition of the human dilemma and stark loneliness of the single mother, and a frequent refusal by juries to convict women of infanticide or impose the death penalty or unduly harsh sentences'.[117] The enactment of the 1949 law placed Ireland among a number of jurisdictions who adopted such legislation. A similar offence, for instance, was enacted into New Zealand law in 1961, with the 'passing of the *Crimes Act* of that year',[118] while the United States and Scotland, by contrast, have the 'contemporary distinction of not having such laws'.[119]

[109] Incidence of baby killing had fallen rapidly from the 1850s. See I O'Donnell, 'Lethal Violence in Ireland, 1841 to 2003: Famine, Celibacy and Parental Pacification' (2005) 45 *British Journal of Criminology* 671, 678; Farrell (n 6) 13–23.

[110] O'Donnell (n 109) 678.

[111] ibid 678.

[112] E Parker and F Good, 'Infanticide' (1981) 5 *Law and Human Behaviour* 237.

[113] O'Donnell (n 109) 678. The trend in Ireland and the UK diverges from that in the United States, where 'between 1970 and 1991, the infant homicide rate more than doubled from 4.3 to 9.5 infant deaths per 100,000 children under age one'. See Child Trends Databank, *Infant Homicide: Indicators of Child and Youth Well Being* (February 2008) 3.

[114] T O'Malley, *Sexual Offences: Law, Policy, Punishment* (Round Hall Sweet & Maxwell 1996) 98.

[115] Rattigan (n 7) 198; Ferriter (n 72) 323.

[116] Rattigan (n 7) 201. For Central Criminal Court Cases, see JM Smith, *Ireland's Magdalene Laundries and the Nation's Architecture of Confinement* (University of Notre Dame Press 2007) 194–200.

[117] Ferriter (n 72) 323.

[118] I Lambie, 'Mothers Who Kill: The Crime of Infanticide' (2001) 24 *International Journal of Law and Psychiatry* 71, 75.

[119] Hatters Friedman, Cavney and Resnick (n 106) 587.

What happened to women suspected of killing their infants following the Infanticide Act 1949? Brennan found 31 infanticide convictions from 1950 to 1975, with no convictions since 1973 and no prosecutions since 1984. Sentencing information was available for 29 of the cases, and Brennan concludes that women were treated exceptionally leniently under the reformed law. Although custodial sentences were passed in 62.1 per cent of cases, 88.9 per cent of these were suspended and only two women spent any time in prison following conviction.[120] The 1949 Act was followed by a period of slow, but sustained, decline in baby killing, and remarkably this category of homicide, which had constituted 20 per cent of the total homicides in the 1950s, accounted for 0 per cent by the 1990s.[121] Moreover, there was a corresponding decline in the 'half-way verdict of concealment of birth'[122] and in child abandonment.[123] It is thus clear that newly born infants were much less at risk from their mothers, not to mention other relatives, by the end of the century.[124] The 'Kerry Babies Case'[125] – involving Joanne Hayes and her family – brought the issue of infanticide to the fore again temporarily in the 1980s. In common with the immediate post-independence years, the 1980s in Ireland was also a period of moral panic, but this time about changing gender roles and the sanctity of infant life. The Hayes case coincided with a particularly bitter public debate and referendum on the question of abortion. Nevertheless, despite the fleeting resurgence of infanticide as a topic of public concern, the downward decline in baby killing was inexorable. The most recently recorded infanticide was in 2007.[126]

The law on infanticide remains on the statute books in Ireland. The 1949 Act was amended by the Criminal Law (Insanity) Act 2006. This change saw the medical underpinning for infanticide modified. The amendment saw reference to 'lactation' removed from the 1949 Act and reference inserted instead to 'mental disorder',[127] with an associated definition of the term 'mental disorder' also provided by the 2006 Act as mental illness, mental disability, dementia or any disease of the mind.[128] The medical justification underpinning infanticide was therefore retained, but couched instead in the contemporary language of psychiatry.

[120] Brennan (n 65) 161.

[121] I O'Donnell, 'Violence and Social Change in the Republic of Ireland' (2005) 33 *International Journal of the Sociology of Law* 101, 103.

[122] Cited in Rattigan (n 7) 200.

[123] O'Donnell (n109) 679.

[124] ibid 678.

[125] In 1984, Joanne Hayes concealed the death of her baby on a farm near Tralee, County Kerry. She also confessed to the stabbing of a second child whose body washed up on a beach in Caherciveen around the same time. Scientific evidence showed that she was not the mother of the Caherciveen baby. Joanna was charged with murder, but the Office of DPP subsequently directed that all charges be dropped, and a Tribunal of Inquiry was established to investigate the behaviour of the Gardaí and their handling of the case. See V Conway, *Policing Twentieth Century Ireland: A History of An Garda Síochána* (Routledge 2013) 172–74.

[126] Central Statistics Office, Recorded Crime Offences (Under Reservation), Table CJA01 at www.cso.ie.

[127] Criminal Law (Insanity) Act 2006, s 22.

[128] ibid s 1.

References

Archival Sources

National Archives of Ireland, Department of Justice.
National Archives of Ireland, Department of Taoiseach.

Books

Black, L, *Gender and Punishment in Ireland: Women, Murder and the Death Penalty, 1922–64* (Manchester University Press 2022).
Conway, V, *Policing Twentieth Century Ireland: A History of An Garda Síochána* (Routledge 2013).
Doyle, DM and O'Callaghan, L, *Capital Punishment in Independent Ireland: A Social, Legal and Political History* (Liverpool University Press 2019).
Earner-Byrne, L, *Mother and Child: Maternity and Child Welfare in Dublin, 1922–60* (Manchester University Press 2017).
Farrell, E, *'A Most Diabolical Deed': Infanticide and Irish Society, 1850–1900* (Manchester University Press 2013).
Ferriter, D, *The Transformation of Ireland, 1900–2000* (Profile 2004).
Johnson Kramar, K, *Unwilling Mothers, Unwanted Babies: Infanticide in Canada* (University of British Columbia Press 2005).
Maguire, MJ, *Precarious Childhood in Post-Independence Ireland* (Manchester University Press 2010).
O'Malley, T, *Sexual Offences: Law, Policy, Punishment* (Round Hall Sweet & Maxwell 1996).
O'Sullivan, E and O'Donnell, I, *Coercive Confinement in Post-Independence Ireland: Patients, Prisoners and Penitents* (Manchester University Press 2012).
Quinlan, C, *Inside: Ireland's Women's Prisons Past and Present* (Irish Academic Press 2011).
Rattigan, C, *'What Else Could I Do?': Single Mothers and Infanticide, Ireland 1900–1950* (Irish Academic Press 2012).
Rogan, M, *Prison Policy in Ireland: Politics, Penal Welfarism and Political Imprisonment* (Routledge 2011).
Smith, JM, *Ireland's Magdalene Laundries and the Nation's Architecture of Confinement* (University of Notre Dame Press 2007).

Chapters in Edited Volumes

O'Brien, G, 'Capital Punishment in Ireland, 1922–1964' in Dawson, NM (ed), *Reflections on Law and History* (Four Courts Press 2006) 223.
Rattigan, C, '"Crimes of Passion of the Worst Character": Abortion Cases and Gender in Ireland, 1925–50' in Gialanella Valiulis, M (ed), *Gender and Power in Irish History* (Irish Academic Press 2009) 115.

Journal Articles

Black, L, '"On the Other Hand the Accused is a Woman …": Women and the Death Penalty in Post-independence Ireland' (2018) 36 *Law and History Review* 139.
Brennan, K, '"A Fine Mixture of Pity and Justice": The Criminal Justice Response to Infanticide in Ireland, 1922–1949' (2013) 31 *Law and History Review* 793.
—— 'Punishing Infanticide in the Irish Free State' (2013) 3 *Irish Journal of Legal Studies* 1.
——, 'Traditions of English Liberal Thought: A History of the Enactment of an Infanticide Law in Ireland' (2013) 50 *Irish Jurist* 100.
——, 'Murderous Mothers and Gentle Judges: Paternalism, Patriarchy, and Infanticide' (2018) 30 *Yale Journal of Law and Feminism* 139.
——, 'Social Norms and the Law in responding to Infanticide' (2018) 38 *Legal Studies* 480.
Donovan, K, 'The Medicalisation of Infanticide' [1984] *Crim LR* 259.
Doyle, DM, 'Republicans, Martyrology, and the Death Penalty in Britain and Ireland, 1939–1990' (2015) 54 *Journal of British Studies* 703.
Doyle, DM and O'Donnell, I, 'Capital Punishment in Post-Independence Ireland' (2012) 33 *The Journal of Legal History* 65.
Earner-Byrne, L, 'The Rape of Mary M: A Microhistory of Sexual Violence and Moral Redemption in 1920s Ireland' (2015) 24 *Journal of the History of Sexuality* 75.
Hatters Friedman, S, Cavney, J and Resnick, PJ, 'Mothers Who Kill: Evolutionary Underpinnings and Infanticide Law' (2012) 30 *Behavioral Sciences and the Law* 585.
Heberle, R, 'Disciplining Gender; Or, Are Women Getting Away with Murder?' (1999) 24 *Signs* 1103.
Lambie, I, 'Mothers Who Kill: The Crime of Infanticide' (2001) 24 *International Journal of Law and Psychiatry* 71.
Luddy, M, 'Moral Rescue and Unmarried Mothers in Ireland in the 1920s' (2001) 30 *Women's Studies* 797.
O'Donnell, I, 'Unlawful killing past and present' (2002) 37 *Irish Jurist* 56.
——, 'Lethal Violence in Ireland, 1841 to 2003: Famine, Celibacy and Parental Pacification' (2005) 45 *British Journal of Criminology* 671.
——, 'Violence and Social Change in the Republic of Ireland' (2005) 33 *International Journal of the Sociology of Law* 101.
O'Donnell, I and Doyle, DM, 'A Family Affair? English Hangmen and a Dublin Jail, 1923–54' (2014) 18 *New Hibernia Review* 101.
Osborne, JA, 'The Crime of Infanticide: Throwing Out the Baby with the Bathwater' (1987) 6 *Canadian Journal of Family Law* 47.
Parker, E and Good, F, 'Infanticide' (1981) 5 *Law and Human Behaviour* 237.
Prior, P, 'Murder and Madness: Gender and the Insanity Defense in Nineteenth-century Ireland' (2005) 9 *New Hibernia Review* 19.
Rattigan, C, '"Done to Death by Fathers or Relatives": Irish Families and Infanticide Cases, 1922–1950' (2008) 13 *The History of the Family* 370.
——, '"I thought from her appearance that she was in the family way": Detecting Infanticide Cases in Ireland, 1900–1921' (2011) 11 *Family and Community History* 134.
Ward, T, 'The Sad Subject of Infanticide: Law, Medicine and Child Murder, 1860–1938' (1999) 8 *Social and Legal Studies* 163.

Newspaper Articles

Anon, 'Virginia Girl's Trial' *Anglo-Celt* (Cavan, 15 November 1924) 1.

Reports

Central Statistics Office, *Recorded Crime Offences (Under Reservation)*, Table CJA01 at www.cso.ie.

Child Trends Databank, *Infant Homicide: Indicators of Child and Youth Well Being* (February 2008).

Commission on the Relief of the Sick and Destitute Poor, including the Insane Poor, *Report* (Dublin 1927).

McAleese Report, *Inter-Departmental Committee to Establish the Facts of State Involvement with the Magdalen Laundries* (Department of Justice and Equality 2013).

Mother and Baby Homes Commission of Investigation, *Final Report* (Stationery Office 2020).

9

Infanticide in Sweden – From Condemnation to (Too Much?) Consideration

MARIA KASPERSSON

In Swedish, the term that means the killing of a child under the age of 1 year is 'child manslaughter' or the earlier term 'child murder', and it reflects what is called 'infanticide' in the literature and the law in other jurisdictions. It has been a specific crime since the first 'child murder proclamation' in 1655,[1] with attributes presuming guilt consisting of unmarried mothers who concealed the pregnancy, gave birth in deliberate solitude and hid the dead child. There has been a shift over time in how child murder/manslaughter is viewed and treated, as it has gone from being considered more heinous than murder – and called 'child murder' – to being considered less serious than manslaughter – called 'child manslaughter'.[2] At the same time, there has been a considerable decrease in its prevalence, from an estimated rate of 1–2 per 100,000 inhabitants in the eighteenth century to 0.1 per 100,000 inhabitants between 1920–39[3] and 0.003 per 100,000 inhabitants today.[4] This can be compared with an annual filicide[5] rate of 0.04 per 100,000.[6] A number of reasons have been brought forward to explain this decrease in filicide, including

[1] M Kaspersson, 'Dödligt våld i Stockholm på 1500-, 1700- och 1900-talen' ['Homicide in Stockholm in the sixteenth, eighteenth and twentieth centuries'] (DPhil thesis, Stockholm University 2000) 133f. The proclamation was followed by others until child murder was included in the 1734 Code of Punishments and Misdeeds.

[2] M Kaspersson, 'Homicide and Infanticide in Stockholm 1920–1939' (2003) 3 *Journal of Scandinavian Studies in Criminology and Crime Prevention* 135, 143f.

[3] Kaspersson (n 1) 139f.

[4] Brottsförebyggande Rådet, Table 421, 'Women found guilty of criminal offences, by principal offence and principal sanction, whole country' for the years 1995–2021 (National Council for Crime Prevention, 2022) at www.bra.se/statistik/kriminalstatistik. Population figures from Worldometer, 'The population of Sweden' at worldometers.info/world-population/Sweden-population.

[5] The killing of a child under 15 years of age.

[6] The number of filicides minus infanticide: J Hedlund, T Masterman and J Sturup, 'Intra- and Extrafamilial Child Homicide in Sweden 1992–2012: A Population-based Study' (2016) 39 *Journal of Forensic and Legal Medicine* 91, 93.

infanticide.[7] One important reason is improved birth control.[8] Legal abortion has been available under certain conditions since 1938[9] and has been free since 1974,[10] as is family planning advice and contraceptives in connection with it.[11] There has been an increased acceptance and less shaming of single mothers,[12] and greater tolerance of divorce in society.[13] Welfare support is available for those on a low income, a monthly child allowance is paid to all parents (currently £115 per child) and 480 days of paid parental leave is a legal entitlement.[14] Another factor that might explain the decrease in filicide is improved treatment for mentally ill parents and the expanded prescription of anti-depressant medication.[15]

In Sweden, as elsewhere, research has mainly been carried out on filicide, often without specific attention being paid to infanticide.[16] Given its low prevalence, it is perhaps not surprising. For example, Sturup and Granath have studied child homicide in Sweden, and Somander and Rammer and Hedlund et al have studied intra- and extrafamilial child homicide in Sweden during different time periods.[17] Rying looked at the decline in child homicide since the 1960s, and Trägårdh et al compared male and female homicide, with particular focus on female filicide.[18]

There is not much debate regarding the infanticide law and its application within the legal profession or elsewhere in Sweden. What debate there is concerns whether infanticide is a killing committed in mitigating circumstances and whether the specific crime of infanticide is needed. The aim of this chapter is to provide an insight into a different legal tradition and discuss the Swedish approach

[7] The rate for all filicide decreased from 0.7 per 100,000 in the 1990s to 0.29 in the 2000s: ibid 97.

[8] L Somander and L Rammer, 'Intra- and extrafamilial child homicide in Sweden 1971–1980' (1991) 15 *Child Abuse and Neglect* 45.

[9] The Swedish Code of Statutes (hereinafter 'SFS') 1938:318 *Lag om avbrytande av havandeskap* [Law on termination of pregnancy] (The Swedish Government 1938) allowed abortion on medical grounds (the pregnant woman was ill, or the pregnancy posed a risk to the woman's and/or child's life) and humanitarian grounds (such as the pregnancy's being the result of rape or incest).

[10] The SFS (1974:595) *Abortlag* [Abortion law] (The Swedish Government 1974) allows for abortion until the end of gestational week 18 at the woman's own request.

[11] ibid.

[12] This may vary among the population, with more traditional values held in some segments. A study of migrant values found that issues regarding honour, gender equality, divorce, contraceptives and abortion are the slowest to change among migrants and are held most strongly among those who most recently arrived in Sweden. B Puranen, *Med migranternas röst* [*In the Voice of the Migrants*] Research report 2019/2 (Institutet för framtidsstudier Stockholm 2019).

[13] See Hedlund, Masterman and Sturup (n 6); and M Lehti, J Kääriäinen and J Kivivuori, 'The Declining Number of Child Homicides in Finland, 1960–2009' (2012) 16 *Homicide Studies* 3, 15f for Finland, which is a country very similar to Sweden.

[14] www.sweden.se/life/society/work-lifebalance, www.forsakringskassan.se.

[15] J Sturup and S Granath, 'Child Homicide in Sweden: A Descriptive Study Comparing the 1990s and 2000s' (2015) 19 *Homicide Studies* 175, 183.

[16] See M Kaspersson, '"You Always Hurt the One You Love": Homicide in A Domestic Context' in N Loucks, S Smith-Holt and JR Adler (eds), *Why We Kill. Understanding Violence Across Cultures and Disciplines*, 2nd edn (Routledge 2020) 38 for an overview on filicide research.

[17] Sturup and Granath (n 15); Somander and Rammer (n 8); Hedlund, Masterman and Sturup (n 6).

[18] M Rying, 'Dödligt våld mot barn – mindre nu än förr' ['Lethal violence against children – Less now than before'] (2004) 4 *Välfärd* 18; K Trägårdh et al, 'A Time Trend Study of Swedish Male and Female Homicide Offenders from 1990 to 2010' (2016) 15 *International Journal of Forensic Mental Health* 125.

to infanticide as regards the legal definition, the use of imprisonment and dealing with mentally ill offenders. The Swedish infanticide legislation and the legal process are outlined first, before discussion of issues identified in law enforcement and infanticide research, putting them all into an international context to finish.

For this study, all verdicts of infanticide and attempted infanticide in Sweden in 2000–21, seven in total, were analysed. The principle of public access entitles all Swedish citizens to view official documents.[19] As the verdicts contain personal and sensitive information, cases have been anonymised to protect the women and their families, and to comply with legal requirements.[20]

I. The Development of Swedish Infanticide Legislation over the Past 100 Years

Two different codes have been in effect during the past 100 years. The 1864 Penal Code was in effect until 1965, when it was replaced by the Criminal Code.[21] Both Codes contained sections covering child murder or child manslaughter and are outlined below.

A. The 1864 Penal Code

In the 1864 Penal Code, child murder is covered in Chapter 14: On Murder, Manslaughter and Other Violence, sections 22–25.[22] Child murder was an umbrella term covering different offences where the child was illegitimate and the woman killed it after giving birth in solitude, either with intent or through neglect or failure to provide care. Classified as child murder, but sentenced less harshly, were also cases where the mother gave birth in solitude and then hid the dead child, even if she had not killed it (eg where the child was stillborn). A mitigating factor in the case was if she had not sought solitude, whereas an aggravating factor was if she had. There was also a presumption of guilt if it could not be proved that the child was stillborn or died from reasons other than the woman's actions

[19] P Asp, 'The Prosecutor in Swedish Law' (2012) 41 *Crime and Justice: A Review of Research* 141, 143.

[20] To comply with SFS (2003:460) *Lag om etikprövning av forskning som avser människor* [Law on ethical approval of research concerning humans] (The Swedish Government 2003), limited case information is provided and pseudonyms are used: see Table 9.1 in section II of this chapter. Quotations without source references are from the verdicts.

[21] M Brush, 'The Swedish Penal Code of 1965' (1968) 1 *Duke Law Journal* 67, 67. Confusingly, Brush translates the Swedish name *Brottsbalken* as Penal Code, when the literal translation is Criminal Code, which is also the generally accepted translation and avoids confusion with the 1864 Penal Code. N Jareborg, 'The Swedish Sentencing Law' (1994) 2 *European Journal on Criminal Policy and Research* 67, 67.

[22] R Bergendahl, 'Straffrätt' ['Criminal law'] in R Malmgren (ed), *Rättskunskap för blivande lands-fiskaler* [*Introduction to Criminal Justice for Police Superintendents*] (CW Lindströms Bokhandel 1925) 3, 153ff.

or inactions.[23] Depending on the presence of mitigating or aggravating circumstances, the sentence for child murder or attempted child murder was hard labour (imprisonment) for between six months and up to six years. The shorter penalties were for cases where there were mitigating circumstances at hand – such as where the child was stillborn or killed accidentally – and the maximum penalty of six years' imprisonment was for intentional killings. This maximum penalty of six years was the minimum for killings classified as manslaughter.[24] Previous regulations had treated child murder as a crime that was more heinous than the murder of people older than infants, and it was punished more harshly with the death penalty.[25] The 1864 Penal Code now treated it more leniently.[26] In the commentaries to the Penal Code, it is stated that the purpose of the child murder offence was 'to produce, to a certain extent, a milder punishment of murder, attempted murder, manslaughter … that is by such a woman committed against the child'.[27] The legal view was that it was unnatural to kill your child, but it was due to extreme situations and circumstances, and the courts showed sympathy to these women.[28] Many of the social circumstances that led to infanticide were therefore considered as mitigation by the courts, as society was responsible for provoking infanticide by shaming and stigmatising unmarried mothers.[29] For example, courts referred to issues regarding need, shame, and the financial and social difficulties related to having an illegitimate child.[30] The mental state of the woman at the time of birth was also taken into account, and during the meetings of the 1810 Law Committee it was pointed out that the 'woman's physical and mental state at the time of the act' should be taken into account.[31] Women who were considered insane were not subject to punishment and were acquitted.[32] This means that an early connection

[23] Kaspersson (n 2) 135. Kaspersson (n 1) 188. In two cases in the 1920s, the accused women were acquitted by the district court as the autopsy concluded the failure of care was not intentional – one had not sought solitude at birth, in the other case the baby was suffocated by the bed sheets.

[24] Bergendahl (n 22) 153.

[25] Kaspersson (n 1) 135f. The death penalty for child murder was harsher than for murder – as well as being beheaded, the woman's right hand was also severed.

[26] The death penalty for child murder was abolished in 1864, the last execution taking place in 1830: H Hagelin, 'Kvinnovärldar och barnamord' ['Women's Worlds and Child Murder'] (DPhil thesis, University of Gothenburg 2010) fn 11. The death penalty had been regularly commuted to hard labour (imprisonment) since the end of the 18th century, Kaspersson (n 1) 135.

[27] Bergendahl (n 22) 153.

[28] Kaspersson (n 1) 195. See K Brennan '"A Fine Mixture of Pity and Justice": The Criminal Justice Response to Infanticide in Ireland, 1922–1949' (2013) 31 *Law and History Review* 793 for similar views in Ireland.

[29] See T Ward, 'The Sad Subject of Infanticide: Law, Medicine and Child Murder, 1860–1938' (1999) 8 *Social & Legal Studies* 163, 173 on how this differs from the English Infanticide Act 1922, where the socio-economic circumstances were generally taken into account but could not be explicitly stated in the Act itself; and K Brennan, '"Traditions of English Liberal Thought": A History of the Enactment of an Infanticide Law in Ireland' (2013) 50 *Irish Jurist* 100 for a similar situation in Ireland.

[30] Kaspersson (n 2) 144.

[31] The 1810 Law Committee was appointed to 'discern, simplify and improve the laws' due to the increased need to modernise the 1734 Code of Punishments and Misdeeds. Kaspersson (n 1) 135.

[32] The 1864 Penal Code, ch 5, s 5 states that acts committed by someone who is 'senseless' or has lost their mental capacity due to illness or old age shall be 'free from punishment'. Bergendahl (n 22) 65.

was made in practice between childbirth and mental illness, as the courts took the woman's mental state into consideration when sentencing, even if it was not yet explicitly stated in law.[33] The growing belief in psychiatric treatment, reformation and the improvement of offenders in Sweden resulted in the 1931 Mental Illness Act.[34] Indicted offenders were now commonly seen as not responsible for their actions and unfit for imprisonment, and were subject to 'care in a mental hospital not to endanger public security' instead.[35] Of the eight women convicted of child murder in Stockholm in 1920–40, three were subject to psychiatric treatment instead of imprisonment because they had been in a 'state of depression', 'lacked in psychiatric development' or had been 'bereft of [their] senses' due to illness.[36] The connection between childbirth and mental illness was eventually made explicit in the 1965 Criminal Code.

B. The 1965 Criminal Code

Work to modernise the criminal law and replace the 1864 Penal Code began in the 1930s, with the new Criminal Code taking effect in 1965.[37] A major change in the Criminal Code was that the concept of responsibility as formulated in the 1864 Penal Code was removed.[38] Unlike most countries that require a person to be culpable in order to be considered legally responsible for a criminal act (as in the *M'Naghten* rules[39]), the Swedish system does not acquit offenders of legal responsibility. The court must prove the criminal intent of offenders even if they are suffering from mental disorder. There is therefore a difference in how child manslaughter (and other homicides) is processed. There are two stages, one establishing guilt and one deciding on the sentence. Any mental disturbance resulting from the birth is considered at the sentencing stage – if an offender is suffering from severe mental disorder, the sanction of forensic psychiatric care replaces imprisonment[40] – rather than being used as a defence in the establishment of guilt. This will be discussed in more detail in section II.C.ii.

The Committee preparing the new Criminal Code[41] discussed whether infanticide needed a separate section. It was suggested that it did not, as the general

[33] Kaspersson (n 1) 189.

[34] Kaspersson (n 2) 145.

[35] Bergendahl (n 22) 65.

[36] Kaspersson (n 1) 189.

[37] Brush (n 21) 72; Jareborg (n 21) 67.

[38] Brush (n 21) 86.

[39] C Elliot and F Quinn, *Criminal Law*, 12th edn (Pearson Education 2018) 356.

[40] P Höglund et al, 'Accountability and Psychiatric Disorders: How do Forensic Psychiatric Professionals Think?' (2009) 32 *International Journal of Law and Psychology* 355, 355f; M Kindström Dahlin et al, 'Mentally Disordered Offenders: Legal and Criminological Perspectives' (2009) 32 *International Journal of Law and Psychology* 377, 377f.

[41] Swedish Government Official Reports (hereinafter 'SOU') 1953:14, *Förslag till brottsbalk* [*Proposed Criminal Code*] (Norstedts 1953). The Committee was appointed in 1938 and presented its report in 1953: Brush (n 21) 72.

provisions in the Criminal Code, Chapter 29: On Determination of Penalties and Remission of Sanctions, allow for mitigating circumstances to be considered in terms of sentencing, which could be applied instead of including the mitigation in a separate child manslaughter section.[42] However, the Committee argued that due to 'the few cases where infanticide was committed because of a severe mental disturbance connected to the birth', it was considered justified 'with regard to tradition'[43] to 'retain a particular type of crime as an expression of the more lenient judgement that seems natural when a new mother abuses her child'.[44] This illustrates the general assumption from the start of the twentieth century, made by psychiatrists, that pregnancy and childbirth could cause mental disturbance.[45] It also shows how the view of infanticide changed and became more associated with mental illness.[46] It did not become wholly medicalised within the Code, which will be discussed in section II.B, as social circumstances were also explicitly stated in the child manslaughter section, continuing the tradition from the 1864 Penal Code to take these into consideration.

The 1965 Criminal Code, Chapter 3: On Offences Against Life and Health, section 1, defines 'murder'[47] as the normal case of intentional killing, and the sentence is at least 10 and at most 18 years' imprisonment, or life imprisonment in the most serious cases.[48] Section 2 defines 'manslaughter'[49] as a murder that is considered less serious – for example, it was not planned or it was due to provocation – and the sentence is at least six and at most 10 years' imprisonment.[50] Elsewhere in the Criminal Code,[51] aggravating and mitigating circumstances are outlined, and these are applied to determine the seriousness of the crime and the length of the prison sentence.

[42] Swedish Government Bill no 10 1962 *Förslag till Brottsbalk* [*Proposed Criminal Code*] (His Majesty 1962) pt B 70.

[43] ibid pt B 12.

[44] ibid pt B 77.

[45] M Oberman, 'Mothers Who Kill: Coming to Terms with Modern American Infanticide' (2004) 8 *DePaul Journal of Health Care Law* 3, 15f.

[46] HL Stangle, 'Murderous Madonna: Femininity, Violence, and the Myth of Postpartum Mental Disorder in Cases of Maternal Infanticide and Filicide' (2008) 50 *William & Mary Law Review* 699, 717.

[47] The Criminal Code, ch 3, s 1 states (original emphasis): 'A person who takes the life of another person is guilty of *murder* and is sentenced to imprisonment for a fixed term of at least ten and at most eighteen years, or for life. As grounds for life imprisonment, particular consideration is given to whether the act was preceded by careful planning, was characterised by particular cunning, aimed to promote or conceal other offences, involved severe suffering for the victim or was otherwise particularly ruthless.'

[48] The sentence was 10 years or life until 2009 when it was changed to 10 to 18 years or life. National Council for Crime Prevention, *Dödligt våld i Sverige 1990–2017* [*Homicide in Sweden 1990–2017*], BRÅ Report 2019:6, Stockholm, Fritzes, 2019) 5.

[49] The Criminal Code, ch 3, s 2 states (original emphasis): 'If, in view of the circumstances that occasioned the act or for some other reason, an offence referred to in Section 1 is considered less serious, the person is guilty of *manslaughter* and is sentenced to imprisonment for at least six and at most ten years.'

[50] L Waltersson, 'Förmildrande omständigheter vid straffvärdesbedömningen – en studie av 29 kap. 3 § BrB' ['Mitigating circumstances when deciding the penalty value – a study of The Criminal Code, Chapter 29, Section 3'] (LLB Dissertation, Gothenburg University/Handelshögskolan 2011) 21.

[51] Chapter 29: On Determination of Penalties and Remission of Sanctions, s 2 covers aggravating circumstances, s 3 covers mitigating circumstances.

Section 3 covers 'child manslaughter', which is a so-called 'privileged'[52] form of manslaughter:

> A woman who kills her child at birth or at some other time when she is in a disturbed state of mind or severe distress on account of giving birth to the child is guilty of child manslaughter and is sentenced to imprisonment for at most six years.

The crime is now called 'child manslaughter' instead of 'child murder', justified by the fact that it is treated more leniently than manslaughter and that should be reflected in the wording.[53] As in the 1864 Penal Code, the maximum penalty for child manslaughter – six years – is the minimum for manslaughter.

A new element in the child manslaughter section is that it covers the killing of a child by any mother, married or not.[54] It therefore includes a larger population than before. Of the seven cases that were tried between 2000 and 2021, three women were married, one was cohabiting, two were in relationships and in one case the relation with the father was not stated. It means that most modern cases would not have been considered child manslaughter before 1965.

The section covers two situations: when a child is killed 'at birth' (referred to as neonaticide in the literature[55]), the timing of the killing automatically makes it a child manslaughter crime;[56] and when a child is killed 'at some other time', when the mother is disturbed by the birth (known as infanticide in the literature[57]). How long after birth is covered by 'at some other time' is not clearly specified, but it is claimed that the mind can be disturbed throughout the whole time a mother is

[52] A privileged crime is a form of a particular crime that is punished less harshly than other forms of the crime, eg child manslaughter is punished less harshly than manslaughter and murder. C Elwing, P-E Wallén and E Aspelin, *Brott och brottmål* [*Crimes and Criminal Cases*], 7th edn (Norstedts 1993) 36. This privilege was first granted for child murder by the 1864 Penal Code due to the social condemnation of illegitimate children. SOU 2014:18, *Straffskalorna för allvarliga våldsbrott* [*Sanctions for Serious Violent Crimes*] (Fritzes, 2014) 195.

[53] SOU 1953:14, *Proposed Criminal Code* 125.

[54] Some objected to the inclusion of married women in the child manslaughter section because 'the reasons for retaining child murder as a privileged crime, foremost the woman's feelings of shame in combination with abandonment, cannot be pleaded by married women'. Swedish Government Bill no 10 1962, *Proposed Criminal Code*, pt B 77.

[55] Neonaticide is the killing of a child by its mother within 24 hours after birth. For research on neonaticide, see S Amon et al, 'Potential Predictors in Neonaticide: the Impact of the Circumstances of Pregnancy' (2012) 15 *Archives of Women's Mental Health* 167, 170; C Klier et al, 'Repeated Neonaticide: Differences and Similarities to Single Neonaticide Events' (2019) 22 *Archives of Women's Mental Health* 159; PT d'Orbán, 'Women who Kill their Children' (1979) 134 *British Journal of Psychiatry*, 560, 561ff; T Porter and H Gavin, 'Infanticide and Neonaticide: A Review of 40 Years of Research Literature on Incidence and Causes' (2010) 11 *Trauma, Violence & Abuse* 99; H Putkonen et al, 'Classifying Filicide' (2016) 15 *International Journal of Forensic Mental Health* 198.

[56] C Sitte-Durling, 'Barnadråp – voffor gör di på detta viset?' ['Child manslaughter – why are they doing like this?'] in L Heuman, M Leijonhufvud and A Norée (eds), *Festskrift till Suzanne Wennberg* (Nordstedst Juridik 2009) 337, 340, 342 criticises this unconditional right to more lenient punishment.

[57] Infanticide is the killing of a child under the age of 1 year by its mother. For research on infanticide, see GB Palermo, 'Murderous Parents' (2002) 46 *International Journal of Offender Therapy and Comparative Criminology* 123; d'Orbán (n 55) 565; Porter and Gavin (n 55) 100f; Putkonen et al (n 55) 205.

breastfeeding.[58] The section also explicitly states that child manslaughter is not due only to 'a disturbed state of mind' due to childbirth, but that it could also be due to 'severe distress'. This distress (actual or perceived) can be of an economic or other kind and is caused by the birth, such as the mother's facing financial difficulties after the child is born because she is not able to work.[59] This continues and confirms the practice of the 1864 Penal Code to see social circumstances as mitigating, and it also makes it explicit that it is not only the woman's mental state that can be seen as mitigation in child manslaughter, but also her social situation, which will be discussed in section II.B.

II. The Criminal Justice Process

In this section, the Swedish criminal justice process is outlined to identify similarities and differences in dealing with child manslaughter.

The prosecutor, aided by the police, leads the criminal investigation once there is a suspect. The prosecutor has a duty to prosecute if it is believed it will lead to a conviction – there is no public interest test whether to prosecute.[60] Waiver of prosecution can be granted only in specific situations,[61] and in the period 2000–21, of seven child manslaughter prosecutions, none was waived.[62] Decisions in the Swedish district court system are decided by a professional judge and three politically elected lay judges.[63] At the trial, the court has to establish the defendant's guilt and the crime label (see section II.B) and then decide on the sanction.[64]

A. Establishing Guilt

As already mentioned, the first stage of a criminal trial is to decide whether the defendant is guilty and, if so, of what crime they are to be convicted.[65] No matter

[58] SOU 1953:14, *Proposed Criminal Code* 125.
[59] ibid.
[60] Asp (n 19) 147–48.
[61] These are that the offender is young (the age of criminal responsibility in Sweden is 15; N Jareborg, 'Sweden. Criminal Responsibility of Minors' (2004) 75 *Revue Internationale de Droit Pénal* 511), the offence would not result in imprisonment, other crimes have been committed, or due to mental disturbance *and* if the waiver would not disregard any 'compelling public or private interest': Asp (n 19) 156.
[62] Brottsförebyggande Rådet, Table 501B, 'Waiver of Prosecution, women, by principal offence and section of the legislation under which the decision was taken' for the years 2000–2021 (National Council for Crime Prevention 2022) at www.bra.se/statistik/kriminalstatistik. During the period, of the female perpetrators, only one case of manslaughter (due to mental disturbance) and one of murder (due to the youth of the offender) were waived.
[63] P Carlsson and M Persson, *Processrättens grunder* [*The Foundations of Procedural Law*], 7th edn (Iustus Förlag 2004).
[64] Brush (n 21) 85.
[65] ibid.

whether the defendant might have acted due to mental illness, it needs to be established whether the defendant intended to commit the crime charged, or whether it was due to criminal negligence.[66] In all seven child manslaughter cases, the court established that the woman had intended to kill the child. For example, in one case, where the newborn child of university student Ulrika had been found wrapped in plastic bags, the court found that she had acted intentionally, as it 'is obvious that [Ulrika] realised that the child would suffocate when she put it in a plastic bag and thereafter tied it'.

B. Deciding the Crime Label

In tandem with establishing the defendant's guilt, the court also decides the crime label. The prosecutor decides what crime to charge the defendant with, but it is the court that decides what crime the defendant will be convicted of, and it does not have to accept the prosecutor's label. A murder charge, for example, might be commuted to manslaughter due to circumstances uncovered during the trial.[67] A case can also be prosecuted under alternative headings put forward by the prosecutor, the court deciding the final label.[68] It has not been within the scope of this research to trace murder and manslaughter cases to see if these were initially prosecuted with child manslaughter as an initial or alternative charge, but it is possible that some were, and then the women were convicted of murder or manslaughter, especially in cases where other people were involved as suspects.[69]

As can be seen in Table 9.1, in four of the seven cases, the prosecutor's labelling of the crime was agreed by the court. In the three cases where alternative charges were put forward by the prosecutor, it is interesting to see how the court reasoned, as it decided on the more leniently sanctioned child manslaughter crime rather than murder or manslaughter in all of them. In Valentina's case, the alternative charge was manslaughter, but because her mental state was affected by childbirth, the court concluded 'she should consequently not be convicted of manslaughter, but of child manslaughter'. In the case of Olivia, it is possible the prosecutor proposed the alternative charge of murder as Olivia suffered from postpartum psychosis at her previous birth and had tried to stab her husband. There is a high risk of reoccurrence of postpartum psychosis,[70] and Olivia, her husband and her

[66] Intent specifies an act committed 'with sense and will', where the perpetrator wanted to commit the crime and knew that the act was criminal or could lead to criminalised consequences, such as death. Negligence makes someone criminally responsible if the perpetrator realised there was a risk of death, had neglected to clarify the risks of the act for themselves and they had the ability to realise the consequences of a certain act. Elwing, Wallén and Aspelin (n 52) 26–29.

[67] Asp (n 19) 153f.

[68] ibid.

[69] SOU 1953:14 *Proposed Criminal Code* 125 states that the more leniently sanctioned crime of child manslaughter 'is not applicable to anyone but the mother'. Other killings of infants are either murder or manslaughter.

[70] Oberman (n 45) 40–41; and Stangle (n 46) 699.

medical team were all aware of it. As Stangle argues, a woman who is aware of this risk would be 'more culpable than another mother who has never experienced postpartum symptoms'.[71] However, the court decided against the murder charge as the killing of the child was connected to Olivia's mental state, which, in turn, had been triggered by the birth; therefore the conviction was for child manslaughter.

Table 9.1 Child manslaughter verdicts in Sweden 2000–21

Name of defendant (Pseudonym)	*Age of victim*	*Charged with*	*Convicted of*	*Sentence*
Valentina	6 hours	Manslaughter or Child manslaughter	Child manslaughter	Forensic psychiatric care
Gunilla 1	At birth	Two counts of Child manslaughter	Two counts of Child manslaughter	Prison 3 years
Gunilla 2	At birth			
Klara	At birth	Child manslaughter	Child manslaughter	Forensic psychiatric care
Ulrika	At birth	Murder or Child manslaughter	Child manslaughter	Prison 3 years
Laura	11 weeks	Attempted Child Manslaughter	Attempted Child manslaughter	Forensic psychiatric care
Natalie	10 weeks	Child manslaughter	Child manslaughter	Forensic psychiatric care with special discharge review
Olivia	5.5 weeks	Murder or Child manslaughter	Child manslaughter	Forensic psychiatric care with special discharge review

Note: Data based on analysis of the verdicts.

Ulrika was tried for 'murder, or alternatively child manslaughter'. The district court eventually deemed it to be child manslaughter, as it was 'established that [Ulrika] killed her child in connection to the birth'. The court further argued that it could not be ascertained that Ulrika had planned to kill the child and therefore had concealed her pregnancy; instead, the court argued that her 'action seems rather to have been provoked by the stress the pregnancy presented' – all pointing to the connection to the birth, making the killing a child manslaughter.

The verdict of child manslaughter in Ulrika's case was appealed by the prosecutor, who was of the opinion that she should be convicted of murder and

[71] Stangle (n 46) 721.

sentenced to life imprisonment or 10 years. She found the aggravating aspects of the killing – that Ulrika had concealed the pregnancy, had put the baby alive in three plastic bags, each individually tied, and that she did not call for help until she feared for her own life – were such as to outweigh the mitigating factor that the killing had been in connection with the birth.[72] The Appeal Court did confirm the child manslaughter verdict, however, and concluded:

> [Ulrika] killed her child very close to the birth and before the placenta had been expelled. [She further] had not called for help until she understood she might die herself from bleeding etc. With regard to this and taking into account that no one had known about her pregnancy and that she therefore felt herself unable to call for assistance [Ulrika] must also be considered to have been in such severe distress as is mentioned in the [child manslaughter] section after she had given birth to the child alone in her home.

In the four cases where the killing took place in connection with the birth (see Table 9.1), the courts paid attention to whether mental disturbance or severe distress was present and had caused the killing. Despite the criticism put forward in other countries that 'the legislative connection between childbirth and mental disorder may now be so firmly fixed in the public consciousness that reduced liability for women who kill their children is virtually automatic',[73] it is clear that this connection – for which there is little medical evidence[74] – is not questioned by the courts. To illustrate, in the case of Valentina, who had suffocated her 6-hour-old son in the maternity ward, the court states there is 'almost a presumption that a woman who kills her newborn child was in a disturbed state or in severe distress', and it concludes that 'such a tragic event must be given an explanation that in the main can be traced to the woman's psychological state at the time of birth'.

At the same time, even if all the prosecuted cases were considered to be child manslaughter in the end, including when alternative charges were brought, there was sometimes a reluctance to label a killing at birth as child manslaughter rather than murder or manslaughter. This was seen especially when premeditation (see Gunilla below) or negligence were present. The child manslaughter crime does not preclude premeditation – it is considered an aggravating circumstance when it comes to sentencing and would result in a longer sentence – but the connection to the birth is the deciding factor. The court therefore decides whether the timing of the killing has greater weight than the premeditation, the neglect or any other factors (see Ulrika above).

For example, in the case of Klara, the court deliberated around the intentionality of her act versus the timing of it. The court pointed out that Klara had given birth before and therefore understood what was happening when she went into

[72] Radio P4 Uppland, 'Domen om barnadråp överklagas' ['The child manslaughter verdict is appealed'] *Sveriges Radio* (19 August 2004).

[73] J Osborne, 'The Crime of Infanticide: Throwing Out the Baby with the Bathwater' (1987) 6 *Canadian Journal of Family Law*, 47, 58.

[74] V Dobson and B Sales, 'The Science of Infanticide and Mental Illness' (2000) 6 *Psychology, Public Policy, and Law* 1098, 1100; Stangle (n 46) 722.

labour. She claimed that she had not known she was pregnant and therefore was shocked when she gave birth, but it did not remove her responsibility, the court argued, and it ruled that while she perhaps did not directly intend to kill the child, she was still completely indifferent to the fact that the child would die when it was dropped on the ground face down and covered in snow in freezing temperatures. The district court said she therefore could not be absolved of having committed an intentional crime, but as 'the act was carried out in immediate connection to the birth of the child' it should be deemed child manslaughter.

The practice of considering the killing to be child manslaughter because it is committed in connection with the birth – which is what the child manslaughter section sets out – has been highlighted in the legal debate.[75] Sitte-Durling finds it problematic that the timing of the act automatically qualifies it as child manslaughter rather than murder or manslaughter,[76] since this means that women who had planned to kill their children and did so at birth would be sentenced more leniently, with at most six years' imprisonment, which is the minimum for manslaughter.[77] For example, Gunilla, who had killed two newborn babies six years apart, had 'decided to kill the child immediately after birth' in both instances, strangling them with the belt from her dressing-gown. The court concluded that both killings took place in connection with the birth, and therefore that 'the circumstances are such that [she] is guilty of child manslaughter'.

When Sitte-Durling is critiquing the connection between killing at birth with the less serious crime of child manslaughter, she is arguing in a similar vein to much international debate. Stangle points to how the English Infanticide Acts and other laws based on them disregard 'the possibility that a mother could premeditate and deliberately choose to kill her infant', rather than kill the child because of mental disturbance, and that her actions should therefore not automatically be treated as infanticide.[78] Mason, when discussing the English Infanticide Act, points out that there might be reasons other than mental disturbance for a woman to kill that are not considered, such as unwillingness to become a mother or a desire to pursue a career.[79] However, Sitte-Durling's argument that the courts are uncritically labelling these killings as child manslaughter is weakened when looking at the Swedish cases. First, because the courts are following the law to the letter and,

[75] N Jareborg et al, *Brotten mot person och förmögenhetsbrotten* [*Crimes against the Person and Property Crimes*], 2nd edn (Iustus Förlag AB 2015) 24–25, commenting on the child manslaughter section.

[76] The prison sentence for manslaughter is at least six years and at most 10, depending on mitigating or aggravating factors, the average prison sentence being seven years. Involuntary manslaughter – called 'causing the death of another' (ch 3, s 7) – is sanctioned with fines or up to six years' imprisonment. Involuntary manslaughter rarely results in prison sentences (for 16% of the women found guilty of it) unless considered more serious, and the average prison sentence is then four years. See Table 9.2 and National Council for Crime Prevention (n 47) 62f.

[77] Sitte-Durling (n 56) 337, 341.

[78] Stangle (n 46) 719.

[79] J Mason, 'The Myth of Madness: Murderous Mothers and Maternal Infanticide' (2021) 85 *The Journal of Criminal Law* 441, 450.

second, because even when the killing was planned – as in Gunilla's case – it does not appear to be committed in a cold-hearted and calculated manner but have more to do with fear and social isolation.[80] Gunilla mentioned that she 'had had troubles with her economy' when she was expecting the first victim. She wanted to tell her social worker she was pregnant with the second victim but did not want her mother to know she had given birth to so many children.[81] She tried contraceptive pills 'but they didn't work so well', and it was too late for abortion. Similarly, university student Ulrika deliberately concealed her pregnancy. She did not want to admit to being pregnant again because she did not want to give another child up for adoption, worrying what future children might think of her, and it was too late for an abortion. She also feared she would be persuaded to keep the child, which social services had tried last time. Oberman talks about the road to neonaticide in terms of missed opportunities to discover the women were pregnant, that options such as abortion and adoption were not options – as in the cases of Gunilla and Ulrika – and finds that these cases are distinctly different from more premeditated homicides.[82] What is happening, then, is that the Swedish courts utilise the option they have available to take into account the social factors that can cause 'severe distress' when they label a killing that took place in connection with the birth as child manslaughter; and when they do, it does not seem to be a case of letting women 'get away with murder' as Pearson, for example, argues.[83]

C. Deciding the Sanction

If it is established the woman killed the child intentionally, recklessly or by neglect, the court proceeds to decide the sanction. Unlike many other countries, such as England and Wales, the presence of a mental disturbance is not a prerequisite for child manslaughter, and the sanction for child manslaughter is either imprisonment or forensic psychiatric care.[84] Any severe mental disturbance resulting from the birth generally precludes imprisonment,[85] and the court therefore must establish whether the woman suffered from severe mental disturbance at the time of the killing. Initially, the court can order a so called 'section 7 assessment'[86] – a medical

[80] R Farooque and FA Ernst, 'Filicide: A Review of Eight Years of Clinical Experience' (2003) 95 *Journal of the National Medical Association* 90, 91; S Amon et al, 'Neonaticide in the Courtroom – Room for Improvement? Conclusions Drawn from Austria and Finland's Register Review' (2020) 29 *Child Abuse Review* 61, 62.

[81] She had a son when she was 17 who was still living with her. Two children were given up for adoption, two were killed at birth and a further pregnancy was terminated.

[82] Oberman (n 45) 68–76. See also Amon et al (n 55); and Klier et al (n 55).

[83] P Pearson, *When She Was Bad. How Women Get Away With Murder* (Virago, 1997) 88–91.

[84] Jareborg (n 21) 67f.

[85] The 1965 Criminal Code, ch 30, s 6, stipulates that a 'person who commits an offence under the influence of a serious mental disturbance is preferably sentenced to a sanction other than imprisonment'.

[86] Referring to s 7 in SFS (1991:2041) *Lag om särskild personutredning i brottmål m. m.* [*Law on special personal assessments in criminal cases, etc*] (The Swedish Government 1991).

examination of the accused by a psychiatrist to establish whether further assessment is required. If further assessment is necessary, the court orders a forensic psychiatric assessment, given that the crime warrants a prison sentence and there is either an admission of guilt or convincing evidence of the defendant's guilt.[87] The National Board of Forensic Medicine authorises forensic psychiatric assessment teams[88] to provide the courts with 'expert opinions'[89] on whether defendants committed the crime under the influence of a severe mental disorder and whether they still suffer from it;[90] if not, the length of the prison sentence is determined.

i. Deciding the Sanction – Prison

In Sweden, the sanction for each crime in the Criminal Code is stated as a range, with a specific maximum and minimum sentence. These so-called penalty scales reflect the relative seriousness of the specific offences.[91] For child manslaughter, the maximum is six years' imprisonment. When a minimum is not stated it is six months.[92] Depending on the presence of aggravating or mitigating circumstances, the court decides the length of the prison sentence within this range.[93]

As a comparison for the discussion below, Table 9.2 shows the outcome for all women found guilty of homicide in Sweden in 2000–21. Regarding the child manslaughter verdicts, Table 9.1 shows that Gunilla and Ulrika, who had committed neonaticide, were sentenced to three years' imprisonment. Based on the forensic psychiatric assessments, the courts found that the women were suffering from a mental disturbance at the time of the act, but not severe enough to warrant psychiatric care. In the case of Gunilla, the court concluded, after much deliberation,[94] that 'the disturbance [she] is seen to suffer from … cannot be considered a severe mental disturbance in the meaning of the law'; and in the case of Ulrika, the court stated that she 'committed the act due to a mental disturbance but which is not severe'. In both cases it was therefore concluded that there was no medical reason to commit them to psychiatric care and hence the sanction should be imprisonment.

When deciding the appropriate length of the prison sentence, the court needs to consider the penalty value of the crime.[95] This is done by assessing 'the damage,

[87] SOU 2002:3, *Psykisk störning, brott och ansvar* [*Mental disturbance, crime and responsibility*] (Fritzes 2002) 149f.

[88] Teams consist of forensic psychiatrists, psychologists, social workers and healthcare staff. A Andersson, 'Rättspsykiatrisk vård som påföljd' ['Forensic Psychiatric Care as Sanction' (LLM Dissertation, Gothenburg University/Handelshögskolan 2011) 22.

[89] Brush (n 21) 87f finds it an advantage that experts can 'testify within the language of their profession' without having to get involved in legal matters.

[90] Höglund et al (n 40) 356.

[91] Jareborg (n 21) 70f.

[92] The so-called 'general prison minimum', SOU 2014:18, *Sanctions* 37.

[93] ibid 45.

[94] Two different assessments agreed that Gunilla suffered from a mental disturbance but disagreed whether this was severe or not.

[95] Asp (n 19) 155 and Jareborg (n 21) 75.

Table 9.2 Women found guilty of homicide in Sweden 2000–21, distributed according to crime label

	Crime label				
	Murder	**Manslaughter**	**Child Manslaughter**	**Causing the Death of Another (Involuntary manslaughter)**	**Total**
No/% of total	190/43%	96/22%	6/1%	145/33%	437
Of which prison, No/%	122/64%	67/70%	2/33%	24/16%	215
Average prison sentence in years	10*	7	3	4	
	15**				

* Until 2008, the sentence for murder was imprisonment for 10 years or life; 14% of prison sentences for murder were life sentences.

** In 2009 a change in the law made the sentence for murder imprisonment for 10 to 18 years or life; since 2009, 5% of prison sentences for murder have been life sentences.

Sources: BRÅ, Table 421, 'Women found guilty of criminal offences, by principal offence and principal sanction, whole country' for the years 2000–21 (National Council for Crime Prevention 2022) at www.bra.se/statistik/kriminalstatistik; National Council for Crime Prevention, *Dödligt våld i Sverige 1990–2017* [*Homicide in Sweden 1990–2017*] (BRÅ Report 2019:6, Fritzes 2019).

violation or danger involved in the act, what the accused realised or ought to have realised in this respect, and their intentions and motives'.[96] To illustrate, Gunilla was found guilty of two counts of child manslaughter. and the court concluded that the crime 'is of such a kind and has such a high penalty value that no other sanction than prison can be considered'. The court noted that even 'if one of the cases was committed a long time ago (9 years) there are predominant reasons for a longer imprisonment'. Gunilla received a three-year sentence, half of the maximum sentence of six years for child manslaughter. One would have thought the fact she had killed two children should merit a sanction at the top of the available penalty scale, but instead the court refers to the forensic psychiatric assessments that stated she had suffered from a mental disturbance at the time of the killings and therefore 'had a greatly reduced ability to control her actions'. The court assumed that she would get psychological care in prison.

[96] The 1965 Criminal Code, ch 29, s 1. The whole chapter is devoted to defining the 'penalty value' – s 2 covers aggravating circumstances, s 3 mitigating circumstances and s 4 previous offences.

Two years later, Ulrika was also sentenced to three years' imprisonment for killing one child. The court reasoned that she killed her child due to the stress factor of the pregnancy, but the act 'has despite this such a high penalty value that no other sanction than prison can be chosen'. Child manslaughter is so rare it is likely the court would have looked to previous cases for guidance, and Gunilla's case was the only previous one with a prison sentence.[97] It is therefore not strange that both women were sentenced to imprisonment, but perhaps the fact that the length of the prison sentence was the same, despite different number of victims, is odd. One would have thought the penalty value in Gunilla's case would have been considered higher, as she had killed two children.[98] It is also interesting to note that in these two cases with prison sentences (see Table 9.1), there is still a psychological element involved. Both women were seen to suffer from a mental disturbance, only it was not severe enough to warrant forensic psychiatric care.

ii. Deciding the Sanction – Forensic Psychiatric Care

If a psychiatric assessment concludes that the suspected offender was suffering from a severe mental disturbance both at the time of committing the act and at the time of assessment, the sentence is forensic psychiatric care to accommodate the offender's need for care.[99] Up until a legal change in 2008, courts were not allowed to sentence a mentally disturbed offender to prison, but now a prison sanction is allowed if there are 'exceptional grounds'[100] to impose one.[101] It was not argued for in any of the child manslaughter cases.

If there is a risk that the offender will relapse into serious crime because of the mental disturbance, forensic psychiatric care with special discharge review can be imposed.[102] When assessing the need for a special discharge review, the risk of danger to someone else's life, health or security should be considered, as well as the need to protect society.[103] Decisions regarding discharge and temporary leave[104]

[97] S Wilderoth, 'Det straffar sig – fast mindre on mamma dödar dig. En kritisk analys av barnadråpsbrottet' ['Crime will be punished – but less if mummy kills you. A critical analysis of the crime of child manslaughter'] (LLB Dissertation, Lund University 2017) 24 points out that with no precedential Supreme Court cases, it is likely that the court in Ulrika's case looked at how the court in Gunilla's case judged the penalty value.

[98] See ibid 23f.

[99] D Morad, 'Rättspsykiatrisk vård med särskilt utskrivningsprövning' ['Forensic Psychiatric Care with Special Discharge Review'] (LLM Dissertation, Örebro University 2022) 19. If the offender has recovered by the time of sentencing, the sanction may be imprisonment (ibid 16).

[100] The 1965 Criminal Code, ch 30, s 6, outlines these exceptional grounds as: the high penalty value of the crime; no or limited need for psychiatric care; self-inflicted mental disturbance (alcohol or drugs); and other circumstances.

[101] SOU 2002:3, *Mental disturbance* 144.

[102] The 1965 Criminal Code, ch 31, s 3.

[103] Morad (n 99) 19.

[104] In Sweden, forensic psychiatric care patients (and prisoners) can be granted temporary leave to go home and visit family, etc to help with rehabilitation and to maintain social relationships. S Johansson, 'Vägen ut – en studie av permission och utskrivning vid LRV-vård' ['The way out – a study

for forensic psychiatric care are made by a psychiatrist and, in cases with special discharge review, by a county administrative court.[105]

Five women (see Table 9.1) were found to suffer from a severe mental disturbance caused by the birth of their children both at the time of the killing and at the time of assessment; they were sentenced to forensic psychiatric care. Two of these cases involved neonaticides and the diagnosis was vague in these instances – unspecified severe mental disturbance in the case of Klara and 'due to her mental state and personal circumstances in general' in the case of Valentina. The vagueness of the psychiatric diagnoses in these two cases can support the claim made in research that neonaticide is not connected to mental illness, as postpartum psychosis and depression take a while to develop and the hormones involved in childbirth do not cause mental illness.[106] It has also been pointed out in Sweden that there is a difficulty in aligning the legal concept of 'mental disturbance' with psychiatric diagnoses, which gives the courts scope to use more vague labels.[107]

The remaining three women who were sentenced to forensic psychiatric care had committed infanticide. Laura was already in psychiatric care due to postnatal depressive psychosis when she attempted to drown her 10-week-old baby on a home visit. Two women, both diagnosed with postpartum psychosis, one with an added diagnosis of PTSD, were sentenced to forensic psychiatric care with special discharge review. Olivia had previously suffered postpartum psychosis after the birth of her third child and attempted to stab her husband, and had now suffered it again after the birth of her fourth child, which she had drowned. The court therefore concluded 'there is a risk that [Olivia] will relapse into crime of a serious nature'. Natalie had killed her son and attempted to kill herself, and was given special discharge review because of the suicide risk.

To conclude, five out of seven women were seen to suffer from a severe mental disturbance, such as postnatal psychosis, and were sentenced to forensic psychiatric care (see Table 9.1). Mental disturbance was also found in the remaining two cases, but not considered severe enough to prevent a prison sentence. This seems to go against discussions in much international debate questioning whether mental disturbance is present in killings at birth, as it generally takes longer to develop.[108] It can be due to a lack of alignment between psychiatric and legal definitions, but also, when there is a choice between prison or care, even diagnoses not considered severe can be referred to when deciding the sentence, as they can still be considered mitigating.

of temporary leave and discharge from forensic psychiatric care'] (LLB Dissertation, Lund University 2001); K Livstedt, 'Förutsättningar för permission från kriminalvårdsanstalt' ['Conditions for temporary leave from prison'] (LLB Dissertation, Lund University 2001).

[105] Kindström Dahlin et al (n 40) 378.

[106] Dobson and Sales (n 74) 1105f; SH Friedman, J Cavney and PJ Resnick, 'Mothers Who Kill: Evolutionary Underpinnings and Infanticide Law' (2012) 30 *Behavioral Sciences and the Law* 585; Porter and Gavin (n 55) 107.

[107] See Andersson (n 88); and Morad (n 99) 20f for problems around differences in legal and psychiatric definitions.

[108] Dobson and Sales (n 74) 1104f.

III. Infanticide Debate

Apart from issues relating to the criminal justice process discussed in section II, there are two more general issues in the legal debate regarding infanticide: whether infanticide is mitigated manslaughter; and whether it requires a specific section. These issues are found in the international debate as well, but Swedish scholars rarely make references to countries outside Scandinavia.[109]

A. Is Infanticide a Less Serious Homicide?

This is the classic sticking point – should a mother's killing of her newborn, or very young, child be treated more leniently than other forms of homicide? There is generally an agreement on the more lenient treatment of mothers suffering from postpartum psychosis.[110] When it comes to neonaticide, some commentators view it as murder (when there is intent) that should not be covered by infanticide laws,[111] while others consider it a mitigated form of killing that needs to be recognised as such.[112] The reason for these diverging opinions, Oberman argues, is because there is a 'profound sense of confusion, ambivalence and general unwillingness to equate these homicides with murder', at the same time as there is no proper justification for the mitigation of infanticide mothers.[113] In similar vein, Stangle points to 'a dangerous societal ambivalence toward mothers who kill' that is promoting empathy towards these women without considering that their acts can be a conscious choice.[114]

In Sweden, it is neonaticide without severe mental disturbance for which imprisonment is the sanction (see Table 9.1) that has been focus of discussion, and it is argued that this offence is no less serious than murder or manslaughter.[115] Wilderoth refers to regulations regarding aggravating circumstances in the 1965 Criminal Code,[116] and specifically highlights two points in the list of aggravating circumstances: (i) the accused exploited another person's defenceless position or difficulty defending themselves (point 3); and (ii) the offence was liable to damage the security and trust of a child in their relationship with a family member (point 8). She applies these points to the cases of Gunilla and Ulrika and concludes

[109] SOU 2014:18, *Sanctions* 201–03 includes a 'Nordic outlook'.

[110] Wilderoth (n 97) 22. See also KE Nelson, 'Postpartum Psychosis and Women Who Kill Their Children: Making the Punishment Fit the Crime' (2004) 23 *Developments in Mental Health Law* 23, 32f; M Spinelli, 'Infanticide and American Criminal Justice (1980–2018)' (2019) 22 *Archives of Women's Mental Health* 173, 176; Mason (n 79) 454.

[111] See Pearson (n 83) 90f; Stangle (n 46); Osborne (n 73).

[112] Amon et al (n 80) 69f. For the USA, see Spinelli (n 109) 173.

[113] Oberman (n 45) 27, 58. See also Mason (n 79) 454.

[114] Stangle (n 46) 704.

[115] Sitte-Durling (n 56) 341f; Wilderoth (n 97) 22ff, 32.

[116] The 1965 Criminal Code, ch 29, s 2.

they should not have been considered instances of child manslaughter as it is more serious when a parent kills their child. However, neither district court brought in these arguments. Wilderoth finds this particularly remarkable in the case of Ulrika, as point 8 – regarding child abuse in close relationships – had taken effect the year before her trial.[117] The court deliberated whether Ulrika's case involved child manslaughter or murder, but did not bring these aggravating circumstances into the discussion. Nielsen, when discussing aggravating factors in murder, points out that these circumstances mainly refer to instances of ongoing domestic abuse,[118] which means they do not apply to these killings at birth.

Views put forward in the international debate regarding mitigation of infanticide, namely, that women get more lenient sentences – or no sentence at all – because of the assumed connection between childbirth and mental disturbance,[119] are found in Sweden as well. Both Sitte-Durling and Wilderoth find that Swedish offenders 'get away with it' when they are sentenced for child manslaughter.[120] When one looks at these cases – as has been done in this chapter – and taking into account that not all the women were sentenced to forensic psychiatric care, the main impression is either one of women who are suffering from postpartum mental disturbances, justifying psychiatric care, or where the social circumstances – the severe distress – were such that sentencing these women to prison, albeit for a shorter term, hardly seems like they are 'getting away with it'.

B. Does Infanticide Require a Specific Section?

The second part of the debate regards whether a specific infanticide section is needed, and again, references are mainly made to other Nordic countries. The debate is mostly in terms of the low prevalence of infanticide, the infanticide section's being outdated and that the general rules regarding mitigation elsewhere in the 1965 Criminal Code suffice. There has also been a suggestion that a section on mitigated homicide should be introduced, which would include child manslaughter.

Apart from a few legal scholars, the main debate on infanticide took place in the 2014 Swedish Government Official Report reviewing the sanctions for certain serious violent crimes.[121] It discussed infanticide and described it as having a

[117] The changes proposed in the Swedish Government Bill 2002/3:53, *Stärkt skydd för barn i utsatta situationer m.m.* [*Increased Protection for Children in Vulnerable Situations, etc*] (The Swedish Government 2003) took effect in 2003 and Ulrika was tried in 2004.

[118] V Nielsen, 'En tanke om vad som är försvårande vid mord – straffmätning med fokus på försvårande omständigheter relaterat till normalstraffet' ['A thought of what is aggravating in murder – the meting out of punishment with focus on aggravating circumstances related to the standard sentence'] (LLB Dissertation, Stockholm University 2016) 40f.

[119] Mason (n 79) 451.

[120] Sitte-Durling (n 56) 340f; and Wilderoth (n 97) 27f.

[121] SOU 2014:18, *Sanctions*. The remit was whether the sentences for murder and manslaughter and some other violent crimes needed to be made harsher.

strong connection to historic circumstances. In the 1864 Penal Code, infanticide was considered as mitigating due to the discrimination against and stigmatisation of unmarried mothers. In the 1965 Criminal Code, infanticide was seen as the result of 'biologically normal physical and psychological causes', but it also included considerations of 'severe distress' that referred to social and economic issues.[122] The Report concludes that infanticide as a phenomenon has largely lost its relevancy today, and the rarity of the crime and the possibility of mitigation therefore makes the infanticide section superfluous.[123] The Report refers to Norway, where the specific child manslaughter section, covering neonaticide only, was removed from the new Penal Code that took effect in 2015.[124] The justification followed the same lines as the Swedish and international debate: these offences are rare today, social factors are much less important and the general rules regarding mitigation can be applied in such cases.[125]

Regarding the concept of 'severe distress', legal commentators find it outdated and cannot see what circumstances apply now that contraception, abortion, adoption and welfare support are widely available and the stigma of being an unmarried mother is much weaker. Also, it is argued, 'severe distress' should not have greater weight when killing your newborn baby than in any other type of killing.[126] The previous concerns regarding shame and abandonment no longer apply. Mason also finds that the social difficulties that were considered when the laws were made are largely irrelevant today as new mothers find themselves in very different circumstances.[127] Legal practice speaks against the claim that the concept of 'severe distress' is outdated, however. As has been demonstrated, the Swedish courts still take such issues into consideration and accept these as mitigating, even if the legal debate does not. It demonstrates the point made by Friedman et al that there is still a 'desire to spare women with difficult social circumstances'.[128] The social conditions are different today, but it is possible that courts just have adapted 'severe distress' to encompass modern-day stressors – such as inability to take action or seek help and lack of social support.[129]

In other countries, claims have been made that the existing rules on mitigation and diminished responsibility would suffice instead of retaining a specific infanticide section.[130] In Sweden, Wilderoth asks why infanticide is singled out as needing a specific section when all other types of intentional homicide are

[122] SOU 1953: 14, *Proposed Criminal Code* 103.

[123] SOU 2014:18, *Sanctions* 204.

[124] SOU 2014:18, *Sanctions* 202 at www.lovdata.no.

[125] The Norwegian Government Bill, *Om lov om endringer i straffeloven 20. Mai 2005 nr. 28* [*On the Law on Changes in the Penal Code 20 May 2005 no 28*] (The Norwegian Government, Bill Ot.prp. no 22, 2008–2009) 204.

[126] Jareborg et al (n 75) 25; Sitte-Durling (n 56) 341; Wilderoth (n 97) 26.

[127] Mason (n 79) 448.

[128] Friedman, Cavney andResnick (n 106) 593.

[129] See Klier et al (n 55).

[130] See Dobson and Sales (n 74) 1108f; Porter and Gavin (n 55) 107 and Friedman, Cavney and Resnick (n 106) 594f.

covered by the provisions on murder and manslaughter and the rules on mitigating circumstances.[131] These rules, however, do not allow treatment as lenient as under the child manslaughter section, since issues in connection with childbirth are not included, and that is therefore an argument to retain the separate section.

Instead of a child manslaughter section, the same Report[132] also suggested the introduction of a crime called 'manslaughter under mitigating circumstances', inspired by such a provision in the Finnish Penal Code,[133] even though Finland also has the crime of child manslaughter.[134] Apart from infanticide, the crime of 'manslaughter under mitigating circumstances' would include killing in self-defence, euthanasia, assisted suicide and killing of abusive partners or family members. However, the recommendation was rejected by the Government.[135] Wilderoth adds that there is a fundamental difference between infanticide and the other suggested mitigated manslaughters, as the child victim had not asked to be killed, nor provoked the killing by their actions apart from being born.[136] This qualitative difference, therefore, contrary to what Wilderoth argues, supports the retaining of the specific crime of child manslaughter in order not to conflate the offences, as is the case in Finland. None of these suggestions to repeal the child manslaughter section in Sweden has resulted in any changes as it seems practice is prevailing over the legal critics. The courts may not question the section on the rare occasions when it is applied, but as they found that the women committing child manslaughter were either suffering from severe mental disturbance or affected by severe distress of different kinds, it seems the section is fit for purpose.

IV. Conclusions

Infanticide is a rare crime in Sweden. Between 2000–21 there were seven convictions – six for completed and one for attempted child manslaughter – but it is possible that there were more cases where the sentence was for manslaughter or murder. The child manslaughter section in the 1965 Criminal Code covers killing both in connection with the birth and at a time after the birth when the mother's mind was still affected by the birth. The woman can be affected by mental disturbance and also by other forms of severe distress.

[131] Wilderoth (n 98) 32. Rules on mitigation are set out in the 1965 Criminal Code, ch 29, s 3.

[132] SOU 2014:18, *Sanctions* 204f.

[133] The Finnish Penal Code, ch 21, s 3 outlines the crime of 'manslaughter under mitigating circumstances': SOU 2014:18, *Sanctions* 203. There are special sections on 'mercy killings' in Denmark, Iceland and Norway as well, but they are less inclusive: ibid.

[134] The Finnish Penal Code, ch 21, s 4. See Lehti, Kääriäinen and Kivivuori (n 13) 6.

[135] The Swedish Government Bill 2016/17:108, *Straffskalorna för vissa allvarliga våldsbrott* [*Sanctions for Certain Serious Violent Crimes*] (The Swedish Government 2017) 17.

[136] Wilderoth (n 97) 30.

The Swedish legal process differs from that in most other countries with regard to mental illness. Rather than affecting the criminal responsibility for the act committed, any mental disturbance affects the sentencing decision instead. If there is severe mental disturbance, psychiatric care will almost always be ordered instead of imprisonment.[137] Five out of the seven women convicted in Sweden were sentenced to forensic psychiatric care. the two women who were sentenced to prison had committed neonaticide and were seen to suffer from mental disturbance, but not severely enough to warrant psychiatric care.

The limited legal debate has focused on two main issues: whether infanticide is a less serious homicide; and whether a specific infanticide section is required. It has been argued that the child manslaughter section is superfluous and outdated, because of the low number of cases and because changes in society have reduced the circumstances that tended to lead to infanticide. Suggestions to repeal the law or to create a new category of 'mitigated manslaughter' have been rejected. It has also been argued that the general rules on mitigation in the 1965 Criminal Code can be utilised – an argument put forward in other jurisdictions as well.[138] The general view is that infanticide warrants more lenient treatment than allowed for by the rules of mitigation, which is why the section is retained, but legal commentators express harsher views than the district courts and the Court of Appeal.[139]

In an international comparison, the Swedish model allows both for differentiation between child manslaughter cases where mental disturbance is present or not, and for differentiation between the severity of the mental disturbance in different cases, leading to a prison sentence when the disturbance is not severe. Stangle highlights how existing infanticide laws based on the English and Welsh Infanticide Act 1938 do not distinguish between women who suffer from severe forms of postpartum psychosis and those who have 'baby blues' or depression with postpartum onset.[140] Sweden avoids the situation where women are labelled 'mad' and treated more leniently in court even when they are not mentally ill, as it recognises that the crime can be committed due to severe distress as well.[141] It also means that in Sweden, child manslaughter does not automatically equal mental illness – a crucial aspect of much criticism of infanticide laws.

Apart from all these points that have some connection with the debate in other countries, it is worth highlighting what is *not* debated in Sweden. First, there is a lack of debate on the fact that the child manslaughter section separates the crime out for special treatment (that it is a 'privileged' crime, treated less harshly than

[137] Interestingly, this is what Nelson (n 110) suggests for the US, but for infanticide only, not neonaticide (ibid 35): 'Only after a woman has been found guilty of the murder of her children should attention turn to whether the presence of a postpartum psychosis should result in reduced sentencing.'

[138] Stangle (n 46) 726ff; Dobson and Sales (n 74) 1108; Mason (n 79).

[139] This harsher view among legal commentators than in the courts and public, is found in the English-speaking debate as well. See Dobson and Sales (n 74) 1100ff; Friedman, Cavney and Resnick (n 106) 594; Stangle (n 46) 724ff; Porter and Gavin (n 55) 107f; Mason (n 79) 453f.

[140] Stangle (n 46) 721.

[141] Friedman, Cavney and Resnick (n 106) 593; Mason (n 79) 447.

other homicides) and singles out women (specifically mothers) from men.[142] Second, there is no specific discussion of whether there is a medicalisation of infanticide that removes women's agency, perpetuating myths around motherhood and leading to the sentencing of women more leniently as they are seen as controlled by their biology and incapable of murdering their children;[143] there are, however, related discussions regarding female violent criminals in general, and how they are more likely than men to be sentenced to forensic psychiatric care.[144]

Infanticide has rarely been studied on its own in Sweden, unless from a historical perspective,[145] but issues such as those discussed here, regarding the justification for a separate infanticide ruling, the view of mental disturbance and the difference between legal practice and legal theory, point to scope for further, more critical assessment of the infanticide cases. From a feminist point of view, too, further study is called for to identify how law might contribute to female subordination and to a modification of legal approaches to gender issues.[146]

To conclude, in Swedish legal practice, infanticide, including neonaticide, is seen as a lesser form of homicide. Some issues are resolved in the Swedish model – such as the differentiation between cases with or without mental disturbance, as well as levels of mental disturbance and the possibility to take social circumstances into account – but the fundamental question is the same: should a mother's killing of a newborn or very young child constitute a lesser form of homicide? Do we need an infanticide section? In defence of retaining it, Oberman comments that having an infanticide section would incorporate the dominant lenient response to neonaticide without simultaneously treating women, by virtue of their biology, as less than full citizens.[147] It may be argued that the Swedish model achieves this.

References

Books

Carlsson, P and Persson, M, *Processrättens grunder* [*The Foundations of Procedural Law*], 7th edn (Iustus Förlag 2004).

Elliot, C and Quinn, F, *Criminal Law*, 12th edn (Pearson Education 2018).

Elwing, C, Wallén, P-E and Aspelin, E, *Brott och brottmål* [*Crimes and Criminal Cases*], 7th edn (Norstedts 1993).

[142] Oberman (n 49) 60ff; Stangle (n 46) 717ff.

[143] Pearson, *When She Was Bad* 79ff; Stangle (n 46) 705ff; Mason (n 79) 445ff.

[144] For an overview see M Sjöö and M Varmin, 'Rättsväsendets resonemang gällande kvinnor och rättspsykiatrisk vård som påföljd' (The arguments of the criminal justice system regarding women and forensic psychiatric care as a sanction) (BSc Dissertation, Stockholm University, 2018).

[145] See Kaspersson (n 1); Kaspersson (n 2); and Hagelin, 'Women's Worlds'.

[146] Stangle (n 46) 706.

[147] Oberman (n 45) 98.

Jareborg, N et al, *Brotten mot person och förmögenhetsbrotten* [*Crimes against the Person and Property Crimes*], 2nd edn (Iustus Förlag 2015).
Pearson, P, *When She Was Bad. How Women Get Away With Murder* (Virago 1999).

Chapters in Edited Volumes

Bergendahl, R, 'Straffrätt' ['Criminal law'] in Malmgren, R (ed), *Rättskunskap för blivande landsfiskaler* [*Introduction to Criminal Justice for Police Superintendents*] (CW Lindströms Bokhandel 1925) 3.
Kaspersson, M, '"You always hurt the one you love": Homicide in a Domestic Context' in Loucks, N, Smith Holt, S and Adler, J (eds), *Why We Kill. Understanding Violence Across Cultures and Disciplines*, 2nd edn (Routledge 2020) 34.
Sitte-Durling, C, 'Barnadråp – voffor gör di på detta viset?' ['Child manslaughter – why are they doing like this?'] in Heuman, L, Leijonhufvud, M and Norée, A (eds), *Festskrift till Suzanne Wennberg* (Nordstedst Juridik, 2009) 337.

Journal Articles

Amon, S et al, 'Potential Predictors in Neonaticide: the Impact of the Circumstances of Pregnancy' (2012) 15 *Archives of Women's Mental Health* 167.
——, 'Neonaticide in the Courtroom – Room for Improvement? Conclusions Drawn from Austria and Finland's Register Review' (2020) 29 *Child Abuse Review* 61.
Brennan, K, '"A Fine Mixture of Pity and Justice:" The Criminal Justice Response to Infanticide in Ireland, 1922–1949' (2013) 31 *Law and History Review* 793.
——, '"Traditions of English Liberal Thought": A History of the Enactment of an Infanticide Law in Ireland' (2013) 50 *Irish Jurist* 100.
Brush, M, 'The Swedish Penal Code of 1965' (1968) 1 *Duke Law Journal* 67.
d'Orbán, PT, 'Women who Kill their Children' (1979) 134 *British Journal of Psychiatry* 560.
Dobson, V and Sales, B, 'The Science of Infanticide and Mental Illness' (2000) 6 *Psychology, Public Policy, and Law* 1098.
Farooque, R and Ernst, FA, 'Filicide: A Review of Eight Years of Clinical Experience' (2003) 95 *Journal of the National Medical Association* 90.
Friedman, SH, Cavney, J and Resnick PJ, 'Mothers Who Kill: Evolutionary Underpinnings and Infanticide Law' (2012) 30 *Behavioral Sciences and the Law* 585.
Hedlund, J, Masterman, T and Sturup, J, 'Intra- and Extrafamilial Child Homicide in Sweden 1992–2012: A Population-based Study' (2016) 39 *Journal of Forensic and Legal Medicine* 91.
Höglund, P et al, 'Accountability and Psychiatric Disorders: How do Forensic Psychiatric Professionals Think?' (2009) 32 *International Journal of Law and Psychology* 355.
Jareborg, N, 'The Swedish Sentencing Law' (1994) 2 *European Journal on Criminal Policy and Research* 67.
——, 'Sweden. Criminal Responsibility of Minors' (2004) 75 *Revue Internationale de Droit Pénal* 511.
Kaspersson, M, 'Homicide and Infanticide in Stockholm 1920–1939' (2003) 3 *Journal of Scandinavian Studies in Criminology and Crime Prevention* 135.

Kindström Dahlin, M et al, 'Mentally disordered offenders: Legal and criminological perspectives' (2009) 32 *International Journal of Law and Psychology* 377.
Klier, C et al, 'Repeated Neonaticide: differences and similarities to single neonaticide events' (2019) 22 *Archives of Women's Mental Health* 159.
Lehti, M, Kääriäinen, J and Kivivuori, J, 'The Declining Number of Child Homicides in Finland, 1960–2009' (2012) 16 *Homicide Studies* 3.
Mason, J, 'The Myth of Madness: Murderous Mothers and Maternal Infanticide' (2021) 85 *The Journal of Criminal Law* 441.
Nelson, K, 'Postpartum Psychosis and Women Who Kill Their Children: Making the Punishment Fit the Crime' (2004) 23 *Developments in Mental Health Law* 23.
Oberman, M, 'Mothers Who Kill: Coming to Terms with Modern American Infanticide' (2004) 8 *DePaul Journal of Health Care Law* 3.
Osborne, J, 'The Crime of Infanticide: Throwing Out the Baby with the Bathwater' (1987) 6 *Canadian Journal of Family Law* 47.
Palermo, GB, 'Murderous Parents' (2002) 46 *International Journal of Offender Therapy and Comparative Criminology* 123.
Porter, T and Gavin, H, 'Infanticide and Neonaticide: A Review of 40 Years of Research Literature on Incidence and Causes' (2010) 11 *Trauma, Violence & Abuse* 99.
Putkonen, H et al, 'Classifying Filicide' (2016) 15 *International Journal of Forensic Mental Health* 198.
Rying, M, 'Dödligt våld mot barn – mindre nu än förr' ['Lethal violence against children – Less now than before'] (2004) 4 *Välfärd* 18.
Somander, L and Rammer, L, 'Intra- and extrafamilial child homicide in Sweden 1971–1980' (1991) 15 *Child Abuse and Neglect* 45.
Spinelli, M, 'Infanticide and American Criminal Justice (1980–2018)' (2019) 22 *Archives of Women's Mental Health* 173.
Stangle, HL, 'Murderous Madonna: Femininity, Violence, and the Myth of Postpartum Mental Disorder in Cases of Maternal Infanticide and Filicide' (2008) 50 *William & Mary Law Review* 699.
Sturup, J and Granath, S, 'Child Homicide in Sweden: A Descriptive Study Comparing the 1990s and 2000s' (2015) 19 *Homicide Studies* 175.
Trägårdh, K et al, 'A Time Trend Study of Swedish Male and Female Homicide Offenders from 1990 to 2010' (2016) 15 *International Journal of Forensic Mental Health* 135.
Ward, T, 'The Sad Subject of Infanticide: Law, Medicine and Child Murder, 1860–1938' (1999) 8 *Social & Legal Studies* 163.

Parliamentary Papers

The Norwegian Government Bill, *Om lov om endringer i straffeloven 20. Mai 2005 nr 28* [*On the Law on Changes in the Penal Code 20 May 2005 no 28*] (The Norwegian Government, Bill Ot.prp. nr 22, 2008–2009).
The Swedish Government Bill nr 10, 1962, *Förslag till Brottsbalk* [*Proposed Criminal Code*] (His Majesty 1962).
The Swedish Government Bill 2002/3:53, *Stärkt skydd för barn i utsatta situationer m.m.* [*Increased Protection for Children in Vulnerable Situations, etc*] (The Swedish Government 2003).

The Swedish Government Bill 2016/17:108, *Straffskalorna för vissa allvarliga våldsbrott* [*Sanctions for Certain Serious Violent Crimes*] (The Swedish Government 2017).

Reports

National Council for Crime Prevention, *Dödligt våld i Sverige 1990–2017* [*Homicide in Sweden 1990–2017*] (BRÅ Report 2019:6, Fritzes 2019).
Puranen, B, *Med migranternas röst* [*In the Voice of the Migrants*], Research Report 2019/2 (Institutet för framtidsstudier 2019).
Swedish Government Official Reports SOU 1953:14, *Förslag till brottsbalk* [*Proposed Criminal Code*] (Norstedts 1953).
Swedish Government Official Reports SOU 2002:3, *Psykisk störning, brott och ansvar* [*Mental Disturbance, Crime and Responsibility*] (Fritzes 2002).
Swedish Government Official Reports SOU 2014:18, *Straffskalorna för allvarliga våldsbrott* [*Sanctions for Serious Violent Crimes*] (Fritzes 2014).

Theses

Andersson, A, 'Rättspsykiatrisk vård som påföljd' ['Forensic Psychiatric Care as Sanction'] (LLM Dissertation, Gothenburg University/Handelshögskolan 2011).
Hagelin, H, 'Kvinnovärldar och barnamord' ['Women's Worlds and Infanticide'] (DPhil thesis, University of Gothenburg 2010).
Johansson, S, 'Vägen ut – en studie av permission och utskrivning vid LRV-vård' ['The way out – a study of temporary leave and discharge from forensic psychiatric care'] (LLB Dissertation, Lund University 2001).
Kaspersson, M, 'Dödligt våld i Stockholm på 1500-, 1700- och 1900-talen' ['Homicide in Stockholm in the Sixteenth, Eighteenth and Twentieth Centuries'] (DPhil thesis, Stockholm University 2000).
Livstedt, K, 'Förutsättningar för permission från kriminalvårdsanstalt' ['Conditions for temporary leave from prison'] (LLB Dissertation, Lund University 2001).
Morad, D, 'Rättspsykiatrisk vård med särskilt utskrivningsprövning' ['Forensic Psychiatric Care with Special Discharge Review'] (LLM Dissertation, Örebro University 2022).
Nielsen, V, 'En tanke om vad som är försvårande vid mord – straffmätning med fokus på försvårande omständigheter relaterat till normalstraffet' ['A thought on what is aggravating in murder – the meting out of punishment with focus on aggravating circumstances related to the standard sentence'] (LLB Dissertation, Stockholm University 2016).
Sjöö, M and Varmin, M, 'Rättsväsendets resonemang gällande kvinnor och rättspsykiatrisk vård som påföljd' ['The arguments of the criminal justice system regarding women and forensic psychiatric care as a sanction'] (BSc Dissertation, Stockholm University 2018).
Waltersson, L, 'Förmildrande omständigheter vid straffvärdesbedömningen – en studie av 29 kap. 3 § BrB' ['Mitigating circumstances when deciding the penalty value – a study of The Criminal Code, Chapter 29, Section 3'] (LLB Dissertation, Gothenburg University/Handelshögskolan 2011).
Wilderoth, S, 'Det straffar sig – fast mindre on mamma dödar dig. En kritisk analys av barnadråpsbrottet' ['Crime will be punished – but less if mummy kills you. A critical analysis of the crime of infanticide'] (LLB Dissertation, Lund University 2017).

10

A Crazy Quilt: Infanticide in the United States

SUSAN AYRES

Society is horrified when a mother kills her child because 'early dependence on mother figures makes us especially vulnerable to the fear that an evil mother in human form can elicit'.[1] We expect that women will nurture their children and experience positive pregnancies; however, for many women, pregnancy is a time of ambivalence. And for women with an unwanted pregnancy, it may be a negative experience.[2] Yet society silences ambivalent or negative pregnancies just as it silences the vulnerabilities many women face in childrearing.

Unlike many other countries, neither the federal criminal code nor any State criminal code in the United States (US) includes an infanticide law.[3] Instead, mothers who kill their children are usually charged with murder or manslaughter,[4] and sentences range from about six months to life in prison.[5] While some mothers receive probation or a suspended sentence, in rare cases they may receive the death penalty.[6] Many legal scholars believe the US should take a different approach than harsh punishment in these cases. As Michelle Oberman observes,

> each case generates the same tired dialogue regarding the defendant's culpability and the merit and utility of punishment. Society becomes trapped in this ongoing dialogue and therefore never comes to grips with the role played by families and communities in contributing to these infants' deaths.[7]

[1] B Morrissey, *When Women Kill: Questions of Agency and Subjectivity* (Routledge 2003) 1. This chapter examines cases involving mothers, not fathers or other family members.

[2] C Lundquist, 'Being Torn: Toward a Phenomenology of Unwanted Pregnancy' (2008) 23 *Hypatia* 136, 152.

[3] CL Meyer and M Oberman, *Mothers Who Kill Their Children: Understanding the Acts of Moms from Susan Smith to the 'Prom Mom'* (NYU Press 2001) 172.

[4] Other charges include child endangerment/abuse resulting in death, aggravated assault, concealment of a corpse, child neglect, child abuse, illegal disposal of a body, and child abandonment.

[5] See Meyer and Oberman (n 3) 60, 172–73.

[6] See S Ayres, '"[N]ot a story to pass on": Constructing Mothers Who Kill' (2004) 15 *Hastings Women's Law Journal* 39, 94–95.

[7] M Oberman, 'Mothers Who Kill: Coming to Terms with Modern American Infanticide' (1996) 34 *American Criminal Law Review* 1, 52.

Yet, as many recognise, various social factors, such as 'education, employment, housing, and health care', as well as '[p]overty, inequity, isolation, and shame', increase the risk of an individual's involvement in the criminal justice system.[8] Nonetheless, society continues to be outraged by neonaticide and infanticide, and continues to ignore defendants' vulnerabilities, including unwanted pregnancy, mental illness and substance abuse, domestic violence, trauma, disability and poverty, among others.[9]

The argument for creating social safety-nets for individuals facing desperate situations is one made by vulnerability theorists, such as Martha Fineman, who rejects the concept that individuals should be viewed as autonomous and self-sufficient subjects. Rather, Fineman asserts that the universal human condition is one of interdependence and vulnerability; in other words, everyone is vulnerable to change, to 'harm, injury, and misfortune from internal and external forces'.[10] Therefore, it is the state's responsibility to remedy vulnerability and provide individuals with assets for resilience.[11] In terms of an individual's involvement in the criminal justice system, the risk of involvement grows when the individual is faced with vulnerability in 'the web of social institutions in which we are all embedded', as mentioned above.[12] Regarding infanticide and neonaticide, Meyer and Oberman argue that 'a civilised and compassionate society' should take patterns and vulnerabilities into account in responding to and preventing these cases, and should 'creat[e] safety nets to catch mothers who are driven to the edge of despair'.[13] Similarly, in combining vulnerability theory with universal design theory, Jennifer Sarrett argues that society should '[work] towards a *justice* system rather than a criminal justice system' by reforming the web of social institutions that 'increase the risk of justice involvement'.[14] Sarrett's focus on criminal justice reform includes increasing diversionary programmes and reducing incarceration, as well as '[c]reating a culture of compassion and forgiveness between criminal justice professionals and the accused'.[15] Criminal justice professionals should be trained to recognise 'our shared humanity, vulnerability, and capacity to make mistakes and poor choices'.[16]

[8] JC Sarrett, 'A Vulnerability Inspired Universal Design of Justice' (2021) 24 *Punishment & Society* 1, 7.

[9] Meyer and Oberman (n 3) 14, 17.

[10] M Fineman, 'The Vulnerable Subject: Anchoring Equality in the Human Condition' (2008) 20 *Yale Journal of Law & Feminism* 1, 9.

[11] ibid 14–15.

[12] Sarrett (n 8) 7. Sarrett's project focuses on individuals with intellectual, psychiatric and developmental disabilities. The vulnerabilities in this community are similar to the vulnerabilities of an unwanted pregnancy or panic birth, as Emma Milne discusses. See E Milne, *Criminal Justice Responses to Maternal Filicide: Judging the Failed Mother* (Emerald Publishing Ltd 2021) 5, 36–37.

[13] Meyer and Oberman (n 3) 171, 177.

[14] Sarrett (n 8) 9 (emphasis added).

[15] ibid 11, 14.

[16] ibid 14. While I agree with Sarrett's ideas about criminal justice reform, this chapter focuses more narrowly on infanticide and neonaticide.

However, when it comes to neonaticide and infanticide, US society rejects a vulnerability approach. Instead, many prosecutors pride themselves on being tough on crime.[17] As one of the prosecutors in *State v Weaver* claimed when the neonaticide case was reversed and remanded:

> The State is extremely disappointed … however, we are confident the next court to sentence this remorseless murderer will reach the same conclusion as the first sentencing court, and that is that Emile Weaver's crimes were the result of selfish and calculated acts not the result of something beyond her control.[18]

Moreover, like the patchwork 'crazy quilts' American women created in the late 1800s, which contained miscellaneous materials and irregular patches, US laws today present a crazy quilt of offences, defences and sentences – both over time and among similar cases. To complicate matters, State laws differ in terms of mens rea requirements for the different categories of homicide. In some States, for example, premeditation can occur in an instant, and can be inferred based on circumstantial evidence.[19] State laws also differ in terms of sentencing, resulting in 'a patchwork of approaches'.[20] Some States provide mandatory maximum and minimum sentences, while other States provide sentencing guidelines that may be either advisory or binding.[21] In some States, the jury decide the sentence, whereas in others, the judge decides the sentence.[22] The disparity in punishment has been compared to a roller coaster, 'moving from a lenient-to-moderate period to a severe period, then changing to a very lenient period'.[23] Nonetheless, the US is seen as 'the world's most punitive country'.[24]

This chapter builds on previous research to present a sampling of cases in the US, primarily in the twenty-first century, in order to show the harshness and disparity in criminal charges, defences and sentences.[25] The broad term

[17] See A Gruber, *The Feminist War on Crime: The Unexpected Role of Women's Liberation in Mass Incarceration* (University of California Press 2020) 191–92.

[18] 'College Student Who Killed Newborn Infant May Get Parole, Avoid Life Sentence' *Y-City News* (21 December 2022) at https://ycitynews.com/25237/news/college-student-who-killed-newborn-infant-may-get-parole-avoid-life-sentence/ (accessed 10 January 2023); *State v Weaver* 2022 WL 17490776 (Oh 2022).

[19] WR LaFave et al, *Criminal Law*, 6th edn (West Publishing Co 2017) 1014, 1017–18.

[20] ibid 1483.

[21] ibid 1486–87, 1497–1500.

[22] ibid 1490–91. Additionally, it should be noted that in some States, judges are appointed; in other States, judges are elected and may run on 'tough-on-crime' platforms. For instance, the Ohio judge who presided in the Emile Weaver case ran on a 'tough-on-crime' platform. He was quoted in the media as saying, 'I'm a conservative, no-nonsense, tough-on-crime judge. My opponent is not.' See 'College Student Who Killed Infant May Get Parole, Avoid Life Sentence' (n 18).

[23] NJ Finkel et al 'Commonsense Judgments of Infanticide, Murder, Manslaughter, Madness, or Miscellaneous' (2000) 6 *Psychology Public Policy & Law* 1113, 1133 (cited in Ayres (n 6) 72, fn 258).

[24] MJ Walker Wilson, 'Retribution as Ancient Artifact and Modern Malady' (2020) 24 *Lewis & Clark Law Review* 1339, 1346.

[25] The names of adult defendants are not anonymised in this chapter since US trial court records for adult defendants are styled by defendants' names and are publicly available. Due to space limitations, this chapter describes overall trends but provides only a sample of cases in each section. Prior and more thorough surveys may be found in various sources cited in this chapter.

'infanticide' is used for child-murder cases, and the more specific term 'neonaticide' is used for the killing of a child in the first 24 hours after birth.[26] This chapter also describes the more recent use of genetic genealogy to solve cold cases of neonaticide. It concludes by considering how the absence of an infanticide offence and expanded defences results in an incoherent, unjust and irrational approach that ignores women's vulnerabilities and fails to acknowledge the patterned nature of these cases.

I. A Sampling of Neonaticide Cases

In the US, an estimated 150 to 300 neonaticides occur annually, and over 100 infants are abandoned.[27] Researchers have surveyed the demographics of neonaticide cases as well as the sentences for these cases. For instance, a study of 55 cases of neonaticide from 1992 to 2009 found that the average age of the woman was 21.7, the median age was 18, 33 per cent of the women had other living children, 43 per cent had been pregnant previously, and 96 per cent concealed the pregnancy from their families or denied it, although 44 per cent had told someone else about their pregnancy.[28] Surveys of US neonaticides also show a broad sentencing range and a wide array of charged offences. For example, Meyer and Oberman's survey of 37 neonaticide cases from 1990–99 found that some of the women were not charged, while others were charged with first-degree murder, second-degree murder, involuntary manslaughter, negligent manslaughter, negligent homicide, child abuse and felony child endangerment.[29] Meyer and Oberman's survey found that neonaticide sentences 'varied between outright acquittal to life imprisonment. Some were required to participate in psychotherapy while others were asked to perform community service.'[30]

Studies have also found that many neonaticide cases display common patterns and vulnerabilities. For instance, many women concealed or psychologically denied an unwanted pregnancy, gave birth alone and panicked during the

[26] See Oberman (n 7) 19, 31. This chapter discusses these broad categories so the reader may draw comparisons between the US and countries that have infanticide Acts; however, the US criminal system does not distinguish between infanticide and neonaticide. Rather, cases are generally considered homicides.

[27] See PJ Resnik, 'Murder of the Newborn: A Psychiatric Review of Neonaticide' (1970) 126 *American Journal of Psychiatry* 1414; Meyer and Oberman (n 3) 46; Child Welfare League of America, 'Baby Abandonment: The Role of Child Welfare Systems' (2003) 2, 12. Both estimates are thought to be low, because many cases are never discovered.

[28] JL Shelton et al, 'Neonaticide: A Comprehensive Review of Investigative and Pathologic Aspects of 55 Cases' (2011) 26 *Journal of Family Violence* 263, 266–27.

[29] Meyer and Oberman (n 3) 58.

[30] ibid 58–59.

ordeal; some experienced dissociation during labour.[31] As one decision states regarding 'the circumstances that lead to this tragic crime':

> Such a mother is often in an overwhelming state of desperation at the time of her infant's birth and lacks adequate resources to mentally handle the situation of delivering a child. She often conceals and denies her pregnancy, lacks insight into the situation, shows poor judgment, is cognitively immature with limited intelligence, and lacks sufficient coping skills.[32]

In addition, other vulnerabilities described in prior surveys include shame, pregnancy resulting from rape or incest, domestic violence, addiction, mental illness, low IQ and undocumented status.[33]

A brief look at several cases show the common patterns and vulnerabilities in neonaticide.[34] For instance, Dana Deegan, a young Native American woman, was sentenced to 121 months' imprisonment for second-degree murder for the death of her newborn, abandoned after birth.[35] Dana was struggling to care for other children, and her own childhood had been filled with physical and sexual abuse. As a child, she was removed from her family and placed in abusive foster homes, where she began a relationship with her foster mother's son, who had raped and beaten her. She had no money; she was severely depressed, suffered PTSD and psychologically denied her pregnancy. When Dana had 'sought help from individuals and institutions, they failed to assist or protect her'.[36] Similar vulnerabilities can be seen in Racquel Phifer, who gave birth when she went into labour at the end of an unwanted pregnancy in a state of desperation when she was 19 years old. Racquel abandoned the baby in a dumpster and was sentenced to 10 years in prison for second-degree murder.[37] Racquel had been raped when she was 11, and had been suicidal and depressed since she was 16. She had dropped out of high school and found it hard to keep jobs.[38] Likewise, CMG was a 15-year-old mother sentenced to 12 years imprisonment after she went into labour and put the baby in a gym bag.[39] The pregnancy was the result of incest, and CMG suffered depression

[31] S Ayres, 'Who Is to Shame? Narratives of Neonaticide' (2007) 14 *William & Mary Journal of Women & the Law* 55, 58; S Ayres and P Manjunath, 'Pregnancy Denied, Pregnancy Rejected in *Stephanie Daley*' (2016) 12 *Law, Culture and the Humanities* 132, 134.

[32] *US v Deegan* 605 F3d 625, 643 (2010) (dissent).

[33] Meyer and Oberman (n 3) 43–44, 49–50, 57–60; Ayres, 'Who Is to Shame' (n 31) 69, 97, 103. Milne describes similar vulnerabilities, and refers to these concealed and denied pregnancies as 'crisis pregnancies': Milne (n 12) 36–37.

[34] These patterns and profiles are discussed more fully below in the case of Emile Weaver.

[35] *US v Deegan* (n 32) 627.

[36] ibid 639–42.

[37] Ayres, 'Narratives of Neonaticide' (n 31) 102–03. Both Dana and Racquel pled guilty to second-degree murder after being charged with first-degree murder.

[38] ibid.

[39] *CMG* 180 SW3d 836 (2005). She was sentenced for delinquent conduct for the offence of capital murder.

and PTSD, and was on the border of mental retardation, with a mental/emotional age of an 8- to 11-year-old.[40]

Evidence of these vulnerabilities is not typically presented in these criminal trials; rather, the primary defences involve challenges to causation and mens rea.[41] Examples of challenges to causation include the case of Katie McCoy, a 19-year-old college student, who gave birth in her dormitory bathroom and was found not guilty of murder based on expert testimony that the baby asphyxiated because of problems during labour.[42] Similarly, Maria Gabriel (aged 33) was found not guilty of first-degree murder based on expert testimony that the baby died not from asphyxiation due to smothering, but from aspiration of meconium.[43] And Karla Emaus (aged 35) was found not guilty because the evidence did not show beyond a reasonable doubt that the baby was born alive.[44]

In addition to causation, defendants may present defences based on their mental state during pregnancy and childbirth. For instance, Dana Deegan presented evidence of both denial and dissociation.[45] Evidence of dissociation during childbirth may disprove culpability or mitigate the sentence.[46] When a woman dissociates, it is similar to 'a trance state, a hypnotic state, a fugue state in which a person can perform fairly complex acts … without quite knowing what … she is doing'.[47] She may also go into a state of panic and terror, which may also negate mens rea.[48] Likewise, evidence of psychological denial or concealment of pregnancy may also be presented to negate mens rea (for example, of premeditation) or to mitigate punishment.[49] However, case law suggests that these mental-state defences rarely succeed, and that defences based on neonaticide syndrome have generally not been admissible because courts hold that the syndrome lacks

[40] ibid 839.

[41] See *People v Ehlert* 811 NE2d 620 (2004) (Supreme Court of Illinois held evidence insufficient to show that newborn was born alive; conviction for first-degree murder reversed); *State v Usnick* 585 SW3d 298 (2019) (Missouri Court of Appeals reversed conviction for involuntary manslaughter based on state's failure to prove cause of death).

[42] B Barrouquere, 'Mother Charged in Baby's Death' *The Kentucky Post* (Covington, KT, 26 October 2007). She was found guilty of tampering with physical evidence; J MacDonald, 'Jury finds woman not guilty in death of newborn' *Wave* (23 March 2009, updated 22 April 2009) at www.wave3.com/story/10055909/jury-finds-woman-not-guilty-in-death-of-newborn/ (accessed 10 April 2023).

[43] J Coen, 'Verdict near in baby-slaying case' *Chicago Tribune* (Chicago, IL, 16 June 2003); Anon, 'Woman cleared in baby's death' *Chicago Tribune* (Chicago, IL, 19 June 2003).

[44] M Higgins, 'Newborn slayings difficult to prove' *Chicago Tribune* (Chicago, IL, 6 August 2003).

[45] *US v Deegan* (n 32) 629, 644.

[46] See eg, *Fields v Kentucky* 44 SW3d 355 (2001) (defendant was tried for killing her newborn while she was in a dissociative state during labour; in a bizarre twist, this evidence was used to mitigate the charge of intentional murder and to convict her of first-degree manslaughter under a theory that she was acting under extreme mental or emotional distress, the Model Penal Code's version of a heat-of-passion killing; her sentence for 20 years was affirmed).

[47] E Dulit, 'Girls Who Deny Pregnancy: Girls Who Kill the Neonate' [2000] *Adolescent Psychiatry* 219, 223.

[48] Meyer and Oberman (n 3) 66.

[49] S Hatters Friedman, A Heneghan and M Rosenthal, 'Characteristics of Women Who Deny or Conceal Pregnancy' (2007) 48 *Psychosomatics* 11.

scientific validity.[50] Nonetheless, an Ohio court recently considered evidence of 'pregnancy-negation syndrome', as discussed below in the Emile Weaver case.[51] Finally, defences based on insanity are unusual in neonaticide cases, unless the mother had a pre-existing history of severe mental illness.[52]

A comparison of two Ohio cases sets in stark contrast the 'crazy quilt' of outcomes for neonaticide. Both cases involved young women attending Muskingum University but occurred more than 10 years apart – Emile Weaver's case in 2015 and Jennifer Bryant's in 2002.

Jennifer, who was 21 years old at the time, claimed she did not know she was pregnant and delivered the baby alone. She believed the baby was stillborn and put the body in the trash.[53] She was indicted and pleaded guilty to involuntary manslaughter, endangering a child and abuse of a corpse.[54] We know less about the facts surrounding her case than Emile's because Jennifer entered a guilty plea. During the court hearing for sentencing, Jennifer gave a statement that the baby was stillborn; her mother testified that she was 'a good girl'; and a psychologist testified that in neonaticides, women do not bond with the baby and thus it was normal that they did not show 'a great deal of remorse'.[55] Although the maximum sentence was 10 years, and although 'autopsy results showed the baby was born alive and died of suffocation', Jennifer was sentenced to three years in prison and was granted early release after seven months, with an agreement to perform three years of community service by creating a website and giving talks about her experience.[56]

In contrast to Jennifer's sentence of three years, Emile Weaver was sentenced to life imprisonment, although in 2022 the Ohio Supreme Court reversed and remanded the case for sentencing based on ineffective assistance of counsel.[57] Emile, who was 20 years old at the time, delivered a baby in the toilet at her college sorority house in 2015.[58] Emile turned down a plea bargain,[59] and at

[50] *State v McMillen* 197 Wash App 1039 (2017) [8]; *People v Wernick* 215 AD2d 50 (1995), *aff'd* 674 NE2d 322 (1996) (rejecting evidence of a neonaticide syndrome); ML Perlin, '"She Breaks Just Like a Little Girl": Neonaticide, the Insanity Defense, and the Irrelevance of "Ordinary Common Sense"' (2003) 10 *William & Mary Journal of Women & the Law* 1, 23–24.

[51] *State v Weaver* (2022) (n 18) [39] (as discussed below, it is unclear whether courts will permit syndrome evidence since the state did not object to the testimony during the post-conviction hearing).

[52] Meyer and Oberman (n 3) 43.

[53] J Smola, 'Young women in Muskingum County who killed newborns got very different sentences' *The Columbus Dispatch* (Columbus, OH, 10 July 2016) at www.dispatch.com/story/news/crime/2016/07/09/young-women-in-muskingum-county/23587584007/ (accessed 14 May 2022).

[54] ibid.

[55] D Wilson, 'Mom says she thought baby dead already' *The Columbus Dispatch* (Columbus, OH, 23 May 2003).

[56] ibid; D Wilson, 'Woman Who Killed Infant Wins Freedom' *The Columbus Dispatch* (Columbus, OH, 28 January 2004).

[57] *State v Weaver* (2022) (n 18).

[58] Smola (n 53); *State v Weaver* 93 NE3d 178 (2017) [3].

[59] Apparently, her first attorney counselled her to accept a plea bargain, and withdrew as counsel when Emile refused to do so. *State v Weaver* 2021 WL 1177317 (2021) (slip op [35]). Presumably, she refused to enter a plea bargain because she hoped for an acquittal or lesser sentence than she ultimately received.

trial, a jury found her guilty of aggravated murder, gross abuse of a corpse and tampering with evidence.[60] In Ohio, the definition of aggravated murder states that '[n]o person shall purposely, and with prior calculation and design, cause the death of another'[61] and '[n]o person shall purposely cause the death of another who is under thirteen years of age at the time of the commission of the offense'.[62] It is unclear from the various court decisions and documents if Emile was found guilty of the more general aggravated murder offence (purposely and with prior calculation and design) or the more specific aggravated murder of a child (purposely). The trial court sentenced Emile to life without parole for the aggravated murder charge, to three years for gross abuse of a corpse and to one year for tampering with evidence; in support of the sentence 'the trial court concluded that appellant was not remorseful, that she had committed "the worst form of the offense," and that she had caused emotional hardship to her sorority sisters'.[63]

Emile did not challenge the sufficiency of the evidence for the aggravated murder verdict. This evidence included that Emile knew about her pregnancy, and concealed it from her roommate, sorority sisters and family.[64] After giving birth alone and putting the baby first in a pail then in a trash bag next to the sorority's dumpster, Emile texted her ex-boyfriend (the purported father), 'no more baby'; 'taken care of'.[65] Later, when the sorority house manager saw the bathroom, she sent a group text: 'Attention: Housemates, whoever made the mess in the study bathroom needs to clean it up ASAP … It looks like a murder scene.'[66]

In addition to this, the jury heard other evidence from which they could have inferred culpability for a purposeful murder, such as testimony from sorority sisters (who had confronted Emile about being pregnant) that in the past months Emile had been drinking alcohol and falling down the stairs without catching herself, and that a week before the birth she played in the annual dodgeball tournament, 'fell hard' and 'caught the hurtling ball right in her stomach'.[67] The jury also heard that in the weeks before she gave birth, Emile was taking a herbal supplement, black cohosh, which is thought to induce labour.[68]

Other evidence showed that early in the semester, Emile took a pregnancy test at the university clinic in order to obtain birth-control pills. Her pregnancy test turned out to be positive; however, she 'didn't respond to the clinic's calls,

[60] *State v Weaver* (2017) (n 58) [8]–[10].
[61] Ohio Rev Code Ann §2903.01 (West 2019).
[62] ibid.
[63] *State v Weaver* (2017) (n 58) [10]. Emile's aggravated murder conviction required a mandatory life sentence, but carried the option of parole in 20 years (which she did not receive): Smola (n 53).
[64] Some of her sorority sisters testified they thought she was pregnant, but when they had asked her, she denied it. A Ronan, 'What did Emile Weaver know?' *Elle* (16 January 2020) at elle.com/life-love/a29998766/neonaticide-emile-weaver-sorority/ (accessed 14 May 2022).
[65] *State v Weaver* (2021) (n 59) (slip copy [36]).
[66] Ronan (n 64).
[67] ibid.
[68] ibid (there were 20 pills left in the 100-pill bottle).

voice mails or text messages'.[69] The clinic sent her a certified letter, which she never opened.[70] Moreover, Emile had told her ex-boyfriend that she 'might be pregnant', but he asked her to keep it secret.[71] When he agreed to drive her to an abortion clinic, they had to turn back because of an ice storm, and she did not subsequently seek an abortion.[72] Emile testified at trial that 'she had lied about her pregnancy because she was scared, "felt like [she] had no one," and was "worried about … getting in trouble"'.[73] She also 'did not "completely" believe she was pregnant because she did not show the normal signs of pregnancy', that is, weight gain, morning sickness and lack of menstruation.[74]

After sorority sisters discovered the dead newborn in a trash bag, Emile denied to first responders that she had given birth.[75] However, when a detective later interviewed her (from 10:26pm to 3:45am), she described her labour and gave 'different versions as to whether [the baby] was born alive and the type of movements or noises she made'.[76] It wasn't until after this intensive questioning that Emile received any medical treatment or counselling – three days after giving birth, her mother found her weak and bleeding, and took her to a hospital to be treated for infection.[77]

At trial, the defence's theory, which the jury rejected, was that Emile did not know she was pregnant and that the baby had died of natural causes.[78] After unsuccessful direct appeals of the judgment, Emile appealed to the Ohio Supreme Court for review of post-conviction relief based on ineffective assistance of counsel.[79] One argument she made for ineffective assistance was that during sentencing, her lawyer failed to present evidence about neonaticide, especially its 'social and cultural causes', which would have contextualised the crime and would have provided 'grounds to mitigate her individual culpability'.[80] The Ohio Supreme

[69] ME Miller, '"No more baby": Sorority sister gets life term for tossing newborn into trash to die' *The Washington Post* (Washington, DC, 28 June 2016) at www.washingtonpost.com/news/morning-mix/wp/2016/06/28/no-more-baby-sorority-sister-gets-life-term-for-tossing-newborn-into-trash-to-die/ (accessed 15 May 2022).

[70] Ronan (n 64).

[71] ibid.

[72] ibid. In other cases of neonaticide, young women were turned away or somehow thwarted when they sought an abortion. See S Ayres, 'When Women Kill Newborns: The Rhetoric of Vulnerability' in K Cole (ed), *Feminist Challenges or Feminist Rhetoric? Locations, Scholarship, Discourse* (CSP 2014) 83, 84–85 (discussing the case of Nicole Beecroft).

[73] *State v Weaver* (2022) (n 18) (slip copy [4]).

[74] ibid.

[75] *State v Weaver* (2017) (n 58) [6].

[76] ibid.

[77] Ronan (n 64).

[78] Miller (n 69) (a pathologist testified the baby was born alive).

[79] *State v Weaver* (2022) (n 18).

[80] *State v Weaver* (2021) (n 59) [7]–[9]. During the post-conviction hearing, the trial court rejected the testimony of Dr Diana Lynn Barnes regarding 'negated pregnancy' ('a term which encompasses both pregnancy denial and pregnancy concealment') and the likelihood that Emile was dissociating when she gave birth (ibid [13]–[15]). The trial court found that Dr Barnes 'was not credible' and that Emile's attorney had 'brought the issue of neonaticide to the court's attention' during the sentencing hearing (ibid [18]).

Court agreed that the trial court arbitrarily dismissed expert testimony about neonaticide as a mitigating factor, and that Emile's trial counsel was ineffective for failing to present this evidence during sentencing.[81] Although her counsel had mentioned 'neonaticide', the Ohio Supreme Court found that he failed to define the term, to 'explain the social and cultural causes of neonaticide and provide a personality and demographic profile of women … and the pattern of behaviors that are typical', and to 'describe how Weaver and her actions fit into this profile and pattern, thereby contextualizing her actions as those of extreme panic rather than premeditation'.[82]

Emile's original sentence of life without parole differed wildly from Jennifer's sentence of three years. Even if Emile were re-sentenced to life with the possibility of parole, what accounts for these greatly different sentences? The cases were not heard by the same judge, and news accounts suggest that the judge who sentenced Jennifer was not re-elected, in part because the community viewed Jennifer's sentence as too lenient.[83] Additionally, the two cases were separated by the passage of over 10 years, reflecting the roller-coaster analogy of lenient-to-harsh sentences mentioned above. Moreover, Jennifer's possibly culpable statements to investigators were suppressed, whereas Emile's were not; Jennifer entered a guilty plea to a lesser homicide, whereas Emile's guilt was decided by a jury. Finally, and most importantly, Emile's life sentence for aggravated murder was mandatory under Ohio law (although the judge could have entered the option of parole).

Now that Emile's sentence has been reversed and remanded, upon Emile's retrial for sentencing, evidence of pregnancy-negation syndrome,[84] or simply evidence of the social context and causes of neonaticide, may result in a reduction of her sentence to allow for the possibility of parole. It is hard to predict whether the trial court will allow expert testimony about syndrome evidence if the state challenges it as not being generally accepted as 'a legitimate syndrome with clinical dimensions' in the field of psychiatry or medicine.[85] However, even if the trial court were to exclude expert testimony of syndrome evidence on remand, expert testimony that Emile fit the typical pattern and profile of neonaticide might mitigate

[81] *State v Weaver* (2022) (n 18) [39]–[42], [48]–[58].

[82] ibid [50].

[83] 'College Student Who Killed Newborn Infant May Get Parole, Avoid Life Sentence' (n 18).

[84] During Emile's post-conviction hearing, Dr Diana Barnes explained that 'pregnancy negation' included both denied and concealed pregnancies, and that women with this syndrome would negate and detach from their bodies, experiencing fewer signs of pregnancy, and would be surprised when labour began. Dr Barnes testified that the typical profile was 'young, immature women who have suffered traumatic childhood events and who are experiencing social isolation and fear the reaction of others.' *State v Weaver* (2022) (n 18) [13].

[85] J Macfarlane, 'Criminal Defense in Cases of Infanticide and Neonaticide' in M Spinelli (ed), *Infanticide: Psychosocial and Legal Perspectives on Mothers Who Kill* (APA 2002) 133, 161, 147, 157. As noted above, the state did not challenge Dr Barnes' testimony in the post-conviction hearing before the trial court (see n 84): *State v Weaver* (2022) (n 51) [12]. In another case claiming ineffective assistance of counsel for failure to present evidence of a neonaticide syndrome, the Court of Appeals in Washington State rejected the claim because it held that such evidence was inadmissible: *State v McMillen* (n 50) 8.

her sentence because, as already noted, according to the Ohio Supreme Court, it 'could have framed [her] actions not as premeditated, but those of desperation and panic from an immature and isolated young woman'.[86] For example, as Dr Clara Lewis stated in the affidavit Emile attached to her post-conviction petition:

> [Emile] fit the typical personality and demographic profile [in that] women who commit neonaticide 'tend to be immature, isolated, worried about the judgment of others on issues ranging from sex to abortion to unwed motherhood' and they generally 'receive no prenatal care, suffer from pregnancy denial, make no plans for their labor or deliver, and labor alone on toilets without medical care.' And when the baby arrives, 'their denial shatters and panic ensues,' leading these women to respond with 'poorly concealed acts of desperation.'[87]

As this overview of US neonaticide cases indicates, the criminal justice system generally disregards the vulnerabilities and patterned response in women's unplanned and concealed or denied pregnancies. These cases also show how society fails to provide individuals with assets for resilience, and rather than responding to the vulnerability of neonaticide compassionately, by allowing greater use of defences for denial and dissociation, continues to punish these women and girls harshly. As one dissenting judge wrote, concerning Dana Deegan's prison sentence of over 10 years, 'And what about the failures of society to assist Ms Deegan in her travail? … [W]here were the government and social agencies during the many instances of physical, verbal, and sexual abuse suffered by Ms Deegan as a child and young adult?'[88] Similar questions have been asked about the failure of schools and universities, as well as of families, to assist students suspected of concealing or denying a pregnancy.[89]

II. A Sampling of Infanticide Cases

Prior surveys have categorised cases of infanticide based on motivations for the act.[90] For instance, Meyer and Oberman developed the following four categories: abuse-related (children killed during an assault, but not purposeful); due

[86] *State v Weaver* (2022) (n 18) (para 5-8).

[87] ibid [8]–[10].

[88] *US v Deegan* (n 32) 652 (dissent). Some legal theorists argue that 'the state bears some responsibility' for crimes of neonaticide when it holds women solely responsible without contextualising the circumstances: Milne (n 12) 97 (summarising argument of Karen Brennan).

[89] Meyer and Oberman (n 3) 45, 56–57, 64.

[90] See ibid 20–31 (discussing classification schemes by prior researchers in the US and Europe); eg, Philip Resnick found five categories of acutely psychotic, altruistic, unwanted child, accidental, and spouse revenge – PJ Resnick, 'Child Murder by Parents: A Psychiatric Review of Filicide' (1969) 126 *American Journal of Psychiatry* 325, 329; Geoffrey McKee found five different categories, ie 'detached mothers, abusive/neglectful mothers, psychotic/depressed mothers, retaliatory mothers, and psychopathic mothers' – GR McKee, *Why Mothers Kill: A Forensic Psychologist's Casebook* (Oxford University Press 2006) 31).

to neglect; assisted/coerced (children killed by mother and/or her partner); and purposeful.[91] While these categories are conceptually useful to help predict or prevent infanticide, in practice they are not so distinct. What appears to be death based on neglect, for example, may be tried and sentenced as purposeful murder, as shown by the Melissa Lucio case discussed below.

Just as for neonaticides, offences and sentences for infanticides in the US also make up an unpredictable 'crazy quilt'. As Margaret Ryznar observes, 'these cases produce significant sentencing inconsistencies, ranging from two years imprisonment to the death penalty. Furthermore, these crimes are frequently overcharged and under-convicted.'[92] For instance, Patricia Michaelis was sentenced to 10 to 15 years for involuntary manslaughter of her 10-week-old daughter, who died of hyperthermia when Patricia covered her with an electric blanket she knew was malfunctioning. Her infant died during the night, and the next morning at the hospital, Patricia's blood sample tested positive for marijuana and methamphetamine.[93] The judge stated 'With this sentence, this court intends to provide a deterrent to others who would use drugs while ignoring the needs of others.'[94] Another mother, Stevie Buckley, was convicted of manslaughter for the death of her 6-month-old infant, who died of starvation and dehydration. Stevie received a 10-year sentence with five years suspended.[95] Like Patricia, Stevie suffered from substance abuse and alcohol addiction; she was 18 at the time she was arrested.[96] Another 18-year-old mother, Elizabeth Potts, was convicted of involuntary manslaughter and sentenced to three years' imprisonment when she and her husband allowed their 2-month-old to sleep in a car seat wearing a snowsuit and covered with a plush blanket.[97] The next morning, when the infant was blue and having trouble breathing, they took her to the hospital; she later died from 'hypoxic injuries to the brain' due to suffocation.[98] Both Elizabeth and her husband were charged with involuntary manslaughter; her husband accepted a guilty plea to child endangerment and received a two-year sentence. As part of the plea, he agreed to testify as a witness in Elizabeth's trial, although by then they had

[91] Meyer and Oberman (n 3) 36–38 (the survey included cases from 1990–99 and uses the term 'filicide' to mean the killing of one's child); see also Ayres (n 6) 70–109 (surveying Texas cases of neonaticide and infanticide from 1899 to 2001 using the categories developed by Meyer and Oberman).

[92] M Ryznar, 'A Crime of Its Own? A Proposal for Achieving Greater Sentencing Consistency in Neonaticide and Infanticide Cases' (2013) 47 *University of San Francisco Law Review* 459, 461–62.

[93] *Michaelis v State* 115 P3d 1098 (2005) [4], [8]; Anon, 'Rawlins mother gets prison time in baby death' *AP Alert-Wisconsin* (Madison, WI, 23 January 2004).

[94] 'Rawlins mother gets prison time in baby death' (n 93).

[95] *State v Buckley* 792 NW2d 518 (2010) [1], [2]; J Michael, 'Supreme Court upholds Buckley's manslaughter conviction' *Bismarck Tribune* (Bismarck, ND, 22 December 2010) at https://bismarcktribune.com/news/local/crime-and-courts/north-dakota-supreme-court-upholds-stevie-buckley-s-manslaughter-conviction/article_16d66b70-0d52-11e0-ac99-001cc4c03286.html (accessed 12 April 2023).

[96] *State v Buckley* (n 95) [2].

[97] *People v Potts* 2020 IL App (4th) 170256-U (2020) [1], [5], [7]–[9]; E Brady-Lunny, 'Mother receives 3 years in baby's death' *The Pantagraph* (Bloomington, IL, 22 February 2017).

[98] *People v Potts* (n 97) [5], [10], [23].

divorced.[99] Another mother, Renee Mitchell, who physically abused her 3-month-old and told officers that she acted out of frustration, was sentenced to 25 years to life for second-degree murder.[100]

These cases demonstrate not just the disparities in sentences, but also how society ignores the vulnerabilities of women accused of infanticide. As Milne observes, society views 'these cases as an individual "problem"', but this ignores how 'wider social circumstances' and vulnerabilities 'contribut[e] to circumstances that lead to the "crimes"'.[101] These vulnerabilities include the mother's 'childhood exposure to aggression and adult domestic violence', poverty, addiction, lack of support, depression or other psychological problems.[102] Additionally, immigrant mothers who commit infanticide face unique vulnerabilities due to their status, including isolation, assimilation, financial difficulties and, in some cases, a negative stigma about mental illness.[103]

Many of these vulnerabilities constellated in the case of Melissa Lucio, which seized national and international attention. Melissa, a mother in south Texas, received the death penalty for killing her 2-year-old daughter, Mariah, and was sentenced to be executed.[104] She would be the first Latina executed in Texas. The child's death occurred in 2007, and Melissa was sentenced in 2008. The case was reviewed by State and federal courts over the next 14 years. The Innocence Project became involved in Lucio's post-conviction defence,[105] and Sabrina van Tassel produced a documentary, *The State of Texas v Melissa*.[106] Many are convinced that Lucio was wrongfully convicted based on a false confession, and the trial was tainted as a political ploy by a district attorney who was running for re-election.[107]

Melissa's death sentence represents the far end of the spectrum in terms of society's harsh response to mothers accused of killing their children. Melissa experienced multiple vulnerabilities stemming from childhood. For instance, from the ages of 6 to 8 years, she was sexually abused by her mother's lover; she married when she was 16 and had five children with 'a physically and emotionally abusive

[99] E Brady-Lunny, 'B-N father sentenced in infant's death' *The Pantagraph* (Bloomington, IL, 21 May 2016).

[100] *People v Mitchell* 289 AD2d 776, 777 (2001).

[101] Milne (n 12) 145–46.

[102] Meyer and Oberman (n 3) 93, 103, 112, 114, 126–28.

[103] ibid 90. See *Modarresi v State* 488 SW3d 455 (2016) (immigrant mother in arranged marriage who had suffered bipolar disease since she was a teenager convicted of killing her infant).

[104] *Lucio v State* 351 SW3d 878, 881 (2011); cert denied, *Lucio v Texas* 556 US 1036 (2012).

[105] The Innocence Project is a non-profit organisation that 'works to restore freedom for the innocent, transform systems responsible for unjust incarceration, and advance the innocence movement'; see at https://innocenceproject.org/.

[106] S van Tassel, *The State of Texas v Melissa* (Vito Films, Tahli Films, Andaman Films, 2020).

[107] 'New Filing: Melissa Lucio, Who Suffered a Lifetime of Abuse, is Innocent and Her Execution Date Should be Withdrawn' *Innocence Project* (8 February 2022) at https://innocenceproject.org/new-filing-melissa-lucio-suffered-lifetime-abuse-innocent-execution-date-withdrawn/ (accessed 13 April 2022) (article points out that the district attorney was subsequently found guilty of bribery and extortion, and is serving a federal prison sentence).

alcoholic'; when her first husband left her, she moved in with Robert Alvarez, another abusive man whom she called her husband.[108] Together, they had seven children.[109] Melissa had addiction problems, and, as in most abuse-related killings surveyed by Meyer and Oberman,[110] at the time of Mariah's death, Child Protective Services (CPS) had been involved with the family for almost 10 years. As one dissenting justice wrote, 'the tragedy of Mariah's death unfolded against the depressingly familiar background of the State's struggle with CPS's systemic failures'.[111] The children were removed by CPS in 2004, when Mariah tested positive for cocaine not long after her birth.[112] In early 2007, several months after the children had been returned, paramedics were called to the home.[113] Melissa told them Mariah had fallen down the stairs.[114] Upon arrival at the hospital, Mariah was pronounced dead.[115]

Later, Melissa was taken in for questioning that lasted from about 10:00pm until after 3:00am. After three hours of police questioning, a Texas Ranger (Escalon) took over.[116] By the time Escalon questioned Melissa, she had been shown 'dozens of photographs of the child'[117] and she had maintained that while she sometimes spanked her daughters, she did not know who caused Mariah's injuries.[118] Escalon testified that he believed that based on her demeanour, she was 'hiding the truth'.[119] He pressed Melissa to tell him 'everything', and after more questions she said, 'I just did it'.[120] The state seized on this ambiguous statement as a confession to the child's death.

[108] *Lucio v Lumpkin* 987 F3d 451, 490–91 (2021) (Higginbotham CJ, dissenting). Alvarez may not have been her legal husband but Texas legalises informal or common law marriage; he was the father of seven of Melissa's children: *Lucio v State* (2011) (n 104) 880.

[109] *Lucio v State* (2011) (n 104) 878 n1.

[110] Meyer and Oberman (n 3) 129–30.

[111] *Lucio v Lumpkin* (2021) (n 108) 492 (Higginbotham CJ, dissenting).

[112] ibid. CPS records indicate that although Melissa was ordered to attend substance abuse counselling and parenting courses, she seldom complied. She also had issues with income and housing – and 'the family was homeless at least once.' CPS were also aware of behavioural problems with her children, 'including physical aggression to the point of violence and sexual misbehavior' and incidents in which the older children had beaten the younger ones.

[113] *Lucio v State* (2011) (n 104) 880.

[114] ibid 880–81. The child had bruises all over her body, bite marks on her back, an arm that had been broken two to seven weeks earlier, and patches of scalp where her hair had been pulled out.

[115] ibid 880.

[116] ibid. The Texas Ranger Division, the 'Texas Rangers', are 'the primary criminal investigative branch of' the State of Texas's Department of Public Safety. The organisation, among other things, investigates major felonies alone or in concert with local and federal law-enforcement authorities. 'Texas Rangers' *Texas Department of Public Safety* at www.dps.texas.gov/section/texas-rangers/texas-rangers (accessed 13 April 2022).

[117] *Lucio v Lumpkin* (2021) (n 108) 517, fn 4 (Higginson CJ, dissenting).

[118] *Lucio v Davis* 783 Fed Appx 313 (2019) (unpub slip 3).

[119] *Lucio v State* (2011) (n 104) 881.

[120] *Lucio v Davis* (2019) (n 118) 3–4; *Lucio v State* (2011) (n 104) 882. After Melissa admitted she would spank the child, Escalon said 'Melissa. I'm being straight with you. And I need you to be completely honest with me. OK? It's just you and I. OK? I'm meeting you halfway. OK? … OK? … it's OK … You did it? Who did it?' *Lucio v Lumpkin* (2021) (n 108) 518, fn 4 (Higginson CJ, dissenting).

In the US, police interrogation techniques are more confrontational than in England.[121] The problem of false confessions in the US has been highlighted by DNA exonerations, which have shown a 15 to 25 per cent rate of false confessions.[122] Police are known to use various techniques to elicit a confession and, as Richard Leo observes, there is a 'rush to judgment [of guilt] when there are ambiguous injuries or death to a child'.[123] Interrogators 'seek to influence, persuade, manipulate, and deceive suspects into believing that their situation is hopeful and that their best interest lies in confessing'.[124] The US Supreme Court has not held that interrogation trickery and deception automatically invalidate a confession.[125] Other psychological techniques also cause false confessions, including implicit or explicit promises of a lower sentence if the suspect confesses, or wearing down the suspect to the point at which 'the suspect subjectively feels that he has no choice but to comply … to put an end to the intolerable stress of continued interrogation'.[126] A suspect may be more easily worn down because of sleep deprivation, or because he or she has cognitive disabilities or psychopathology or personality disorders.[127]

During Melissa's trial, the court excluded expert testimony that because she had been abused both as a child and as an adult, her confession was not voluntary.[128] Specifically, a social worker would have testified regarding Melissa's 'body language' during the interrogation, and would have explained why Melissa 'would have given police … information in that statement that was not correct'.[129] A psychologist would also have testified regarding the circumstances surrounding her confession. However, on direct appeal, the court held that the defence had failed to preserve error because the testimony proffered at trial did not comport with the claim raised on appeal that 'since she was an abused woman, she would agree with anything a policeman would say'.[130]

Melissa's defence also challenged the cause of death; however, the jury rejected their theories and found her guilty of intentionally causing Mariah's death. During the sentencing portion of trial, the jury found that Melissa would commit future

[121] SM Kassin et al, 'Police-Induced Confessions: Risk Factors and Recommendations' (2010) 34 *Law & Human Behavior* 3, 13.

[122] RA Leo, 'Police Interrogation, False Confessions, and Alleged Child Abuse Cases' (2017) 50 *University of Michigan Journal of Law Reform* 693, 699.

[123] ibid 697.

[124] ibid 703.

[125] Kassin (n 121) 13–14. As Richard Leo points out, '[m]any people do not know that police detectives can legally lie by pretending to have incriminating evidence that does not exist, is fabricated, or is exaggerated': Leo (n 122) 712.

[126] Leo (n 122) 709.

[127] Kassin (n 121) 21.

[128] *Lucio v State* (2011) (n 104) 897. This testimony was raised by the defence after the innocence/guilt stage of trial.

[129] ibid 897–99.

[130] ibid 900–03. Although defence counsel told the trial court that the psychologist would testify that, as a battered woman, Melissa 'takes blame for everything that goes on in the family', the psychologist's proffer of testimony was very vague and did not mention abuse or battering.

criminal acts of violence that would be a continuing threat to society, and on direct appeal the court affirmed her conviction for the death penalty.[131]

Melissa subsequently lost a writ of habeas corpus in State court[132] and in federal district court.[133] Her writ of certiorari to the US Supreme Court was denied.[134] As her execution date came near, Texas legislators urged the governor to grant clemency, jurors in her case publicly favoured clemency and, in the days before, as the Texas Board of Pardons and Paroles considered her request in order to make a recommendation to the governor, the highest appellate State court halted the execution and sent the case back to the trial court to consider various claims, including the reliability of her confession.[135]

Thus, whereas the last execution of an English mother who killed her children was in 1849 for infanticide and 1832 for neonaticide,[136] a US mother found guilty of killing her children may still be charged with capital murder and sentenced to death in 28 US jurisdictions.[137] Some would say this reflects the community's moral condemnation. Certainly, Melissa was portrayed as an evil mother who deserved the death penalty. However, her trial could also be viewed as an example of race and class discrimination.[138] Was Melissa seen as a poor Latina with a drug-abuse problem who was not the right kind of mother?[139] As a dissenting judge wrote, 'we execute few with means'.[140] Melissa's sentence, like those of Dana Deegan and Racquel Phifer, shows how the US criminal law system and society focus more on pinpointing an individual's responsibility and punishment than on considering vulnerabilities – such as addiction, domestic violence, childhood trauma, poverty, psychological problems and others – that could mitigate a defendant's acts or invalidate a confession.

One of the major vulnerabilities raised as a defence in US infanticide cases is mental illness. A defendant may use evidence of postpartum psychosis to show that the death was accidental, as in Heidi Anfinson's trial for the drowning

[131] ibid 903–04.

[132] *Lucio v Lumpkin* (2021) (n 108) 461. The Texas Court of Criminal Appeals subsequently denied habeas relief when Lucio filed objections to the lower court's findings: ibid 462.

[133] ibid 456, 463.

[134] *Lucio v Lumpkin* 142 S Ct 404 (2021) (Mem).

[135] *Ex parte Lucio* 2022 WL 1211313 (2022).

[136] Milne (n 12) 111.

[137] See at www.ncsl.org/research/civil-and-criminal-justice/death-penalty.aspx#:~:text=Capital%20punishment%20is%20currently%20authorized,government%20and%20the%20U.S.%20military (accessed 17 May 2022).

[138] See JB Gonzales Rose, 'Toward a Critical Race Theory of Evidence' (2017) 101 *Minnesota Law Review* 2243.

[139] See J Huckerby, 'Women Who Kill Their Children: Case Study and Conclusions Concerning the Differences in the Fall from Maternal Grace by Khoua Her and Andrea Yates' (2003) 10 *Duke Journal of Gender & Policy* 149; DE Roberts, 'Crime, Race, and Reproduction' (1993) 67 *Tulane Law Review* 1945; DE Roberts, 'Prison, Foster Care, and the Systemic Punishment of Black Mothers' (2012) 59 *UCLA Law Review* 1474; Milne (n 12) 146.

[140] *Lucio v Lumpkin* (2021) (n 108) 491 (CJ Higginbotham, dissenting).

of her 15-day-old son.[141] A defendant may also introduce evidence of postpartum psychosis to argue that she lacked the mens rea for the offence, as in Narjes Modarresi's trial for drowning her 2-month-old son.[142] In some jurisdictions, the defendant may raise the defence of diminished capacity.[143]

Although the insanity defence succeeds very rarely, in only a fraction of 1 per cent of all criminal cases, it succeeds in one-half to one-third of infanticide cases.[144] Most cases raising an insanity defence are resolved by plea agreements.[145] For example, Sabrina Maiden's plea of not guilty by reason of insanity was accepted by the trial court in Louisiana, when all three experts found that she was legally insane at the time of her 2-month-old's death.[146] Likewise, a Texas trial court accepted a plea of not guilty by reason of insanity in the killing of a 3-week-old based on reports by all three experts that Otty Sanchez was legally insane.[147]

However, just as there is not one crime for acts of infanticide, there is not one national test for legal insanity. Most States and the federal system use a form of the antiquated *M'Naghten* test,[148] and 14 States use the modernised Model Penal Code or ALI test.[149] Juries continue to find psychotic and delusional mothers guilty of murder, especially under the *M'Naghten* test, based on evidence such as 'disposing of the body, calling 911, or confessing in a cold and calm manner'.[150] Thus, a mother such as Andrea Yates, who drowned her children while suffering from

[141] *Anfinson v State* 758 NW2d 496 (2008) (conviction reversed and remanded because it was ineffective assistance of counsel not to investigate postpartum depression to show the death was an accident).

[142] *Modarresi v State* 488 SW3d 455 (2016) (the jury rejected her claim that her psychotic episode negated an intent to kill).

[143] See *Anfinson* (n 141). It should be pointed out that diminished capacity or diminished responsibility varies greatly in the jurisdictions that allow the defence.

[144] S Hatters Friedman and R Sorrentino, 'Commentary: Postpartum Psychosis, Infanticide, and Insanity – Implications for Forensic Psychiatry' (2012) 40 *Journal of the American Academy of Psychiatry and the Law* 326; S Ayres, 'Newfound Religion: Mothers, God, and Infanticide' (2005) 33 *Fordham Urban Law Journal* 335, 350, fn 130 (citing Perlin (n 50) 13–15). For example, Cheyenne Greer was found not guilty by reason of insanity for smothering her 3-month-old daughter with a pillow: *People v Greer* 2014 WL 4260795 (2014).

[145] EL Johnston, 'Delusions, Moral Incapacity, and the Case for Moral Wrongfulness' (2022) 97 *Indiana Law Journal* 297, 300.

[146] 'Judge accepts insanity plea from mother charged in baby's death *WAFB9* (23 January 2014) at www.wafb.com/story/24530862/judge-accepts-insanity-plea-from-mother-charged-in-babys-death/ (accessed 21 May 2022).

[147] C Kapitan, 'Mom who mutilated newborn enters plea' *MySA* (1 July 2010) at www.mysanantonio.com/news/local_news/article/Mom-who-mutilated-newborn-enters-plea-845553.php#:~:text=A%20San%20Antonio%20mother%20who,a%20maximum%2Dsecurity%20mental%20facility (accessed 21 May 2022).

[148] The *M'Naghten* test requires proof that at the time of the offence, as a result of mental disease or defect, the defendant was unable to understand the nature and quality of his act or was unable to distinguish right from wrong. Jurisdictions have slight variations from the traditional test, eg, instead of the word 'understand', a jurisdiction may use the word 'appreciate'. See *Kahler v Kansas* 140 SCt 1021, 1025 (citing *R v M'Naghten* (1843) 8 ER 718, 10 Cl & F 200), 1051 (Appendix) (2020).

[149] *Kahler* (n 148) 1046, 1057 (Appendix). The Model Penal Code or ALI test requires proof that due to mental disease or defect, a defendant lacked the capacity either to appreciate the wrongfulness/criminality of his conduct or to conform his conduct to the requirements of the law.

[150] Ayres (n 144) 351.

postpartum psychosis and delusions that she was being ordered to kill her child, may nonetheless be convicted if the trier of fact finds that she knew her actions were wrong.[151]

A more recent example is the jury's rejection of Dung Ngoc Thi-Zeluff's insanity defence for the capital murder of her 5-month-old daughter.[152] Dung was mandatorily sentenced to life without parole upon a guilty verdict (because the state had not sought the death penalty).[153] Dung had a history of mental illness. Six years before her pregnancy, she had been hospitalised for a suicide attempt.[154] She was hospitalised again when she was eight months pregnant, when she had threatened her husband with a knife and had threatened to kill herself and the foetus.[155] When the baby was several months old, Dung was again hospitalised for threatening to kill herself and the baby, and just prior to the baby's death, Dung had a car collision that may have been another suicide attempt.[156] Due to her threats, CPS investigated, and accepted a family safety plan that Dung could not be 'alone or unsupervised' with the baby.[157]

Yet two months after Dung's last hospitalisation, Dung and her mother were spending the evening together when Dung took the baby into a bedroom for a diaper change, locked the door and strangled the baby to death.[158] The psychiatrist who evaluated her and testified in her defence opined that Dung had a severe depressive disorder for which she was on medication,[159] and that at the time of the baby's death she 'was suffering from postpartum depression and psychosis' and had acted under the delusion that 'she couldn't care for the baby, [so] the best option for the baby was to be dead'.[160] The jury nonetheless found her guilty of murder.[161]

In affirming the verdict, the appellate court considered testimony and circumstantial evidence showing that under the *M'Naghten* test, Dung knew what she was doing was wrong. This included the state expert's opinion that she was not legally insane but had borderline personality disorder, that she was 'stone-faced' when

[151] *Yates v State* 171 SW3d 215 (2005). Yates' conviction was reversed, and on retrial she was found not guilty by reason of insanity: Anon, 'Jury Finds Yates Insane, Not Guilty' *Houston Chronicle* (Houston, TX, 26 July 2006).

[152] *Dung Ngoc Thi-Zeluff v State* 2019 WL 3047283 (2019).

[153] ibid.

[154] ibid 3.

[155] ibid 4.

[156] ibid. Dung told the psychiatrist who evaluated her that 'she intentionally drove her car off the road to kill herself, though she denied this to other professionals'. Additionally, the CPS caseworker testified that Dung 'had made multiple threats to harm her child throughout the course of her pregnancy and since the child was born in May': ibid.

[157] ibid.

[158] ibid 2. Her husband was not at home when the death occurred.

[159] There was also testimony from Dung's siblings that she had quit taking medicine for depression because she was nursing the baby, and testimony from the psychiatrist that after the car collision, Dung was prescribed Tylenol 3 with codeine, which can exacerbate depression: ibid 4.

[160] ibid 5.

[161] ibid 1, 5–6.

police arrived, had removed two wedding rings and placed them on the end table because 'she no longer felt like a good wife or mother', had told an officer the act was 'evil' and had apologised to the baby for her actions.[162]

As these examples show, proving legal insanity is notoriously difficult. The outcome of Dung's case explains why another accused mother, such as Sarah Henderson, might accept a plea offer reducing a capital murder charge to intentional murder, even when two out of three experts concluded she was legally insane at the time of death of her two daughters, aged 5 and 7.[163] Rather than risk a death sentence if a jury failed to find she was legally insane, Sarah accepted a plea agreement for murder with a sentence of life without parole.[164] Her case illustrates the disconnect between the treatment of severe mental illness in the medical and legal fields. In cases in which a severely mentally ill mother is harshly punished for the death of her child, how does this serve justice?

As these infanticide cases demonstrate, the US criminal justice system does not give weight to the vulnerabilities of women who kill their children, nor does society create social safety nets to decrease risks of involvement in the criminal justice system. Before turning to possible reforms, the next section of this chapter discusses the recent trend of prosecuting cold cases.

III. The Quest to Solve Baby Doe Cases

In addition to prosecuting current cases of neonaticide, many States are now prosecuting Baby Doe cold cases using new investigative techniques involving forensic or genetic genealogy. This includes women who are being prosecuted for neonaticides that occurred decades ago. First developed in the early-2000s in the UK and various US States,[165] genetic genealogy uses familial DNA from databases such as Ancestry, 23andMe, or the public domain website GEDmatch, to build a genealogy tree based on partial matches to the DNA of the victim in the cold case.[166] The genealogy tree often points to suspects whose DNA is not on any criminal database. Investigators then obtain the suspect's DNA (sometimes surreptitiously) in order to make an arrest. For example, a 1987 Washington State cold case of the

[162] ibid 2–3, 6.

[163] LA Campbell, 'Henderson County woman pleads guilty to murder of her 2 children, sentenced to life in prison' *tylerpaper.com* (Tyler, TX, 17 July 2019).

[164] ibid. The district attorney commented that it was risky for her to go to trial because 'sanity is a determination made by the jury' and she was facing the death penalty. Moreover, the district attorney said that the offer of life without parole was based on her husband's wish that she 'spend the rest of her life in prison instead of receiving the death penalty'.

[165] JL Entrikin, 'Family Secrets and Relational Privacy: Protecting No-So-Personal, Sensitive Information from Public Disclosure' (2020) 74 *University of Miami Law Review* 781, 869, 871 (describing the discovery of the Golden State Killer in the US and the 'Dearne Valley Shoe Rapist' in the UK). 'Genetic genealogy' is also referred to as 'forensic genealogy'.

[166] ibid 869–70. See also R Khatchadourian, 'Family Secrets' *The New Yorker* (22 November 2021) 36, 42 (describing the technique called 'the Methodology').

murder-rape of a young woman and murder of her boyfriend was not solved until 2018, when a suspect was identified through genetic genealogy.[167] Officers then tailed the man identified as a probable suspect and picked up a coffee cup he had dropped out of his truck. The DNA on the cup matched that of the murder and murder-rape that had occurred 30 years earlier.[168]

Despite celebrated successes, the use of genetic genealogy is rife with ethical and privacy issues, including a lack of legislative oversight. There are concerns that it should be restricted to heinous crimes,[169] a fear that it 'disproportionately targets minorities' (who 'have a two-times higher chance of being incorrectly targeted')[170] and a claim that law enforcement violates the Fourth Amendment in surreptitiously collecting an individual's DNA from a discarded item.[171] While a handful of States have enacted legislation to control access to familial DNA, most have not.[172] Despite these concerns, States continue using genetic genealogy to solve cold crimes, and many families and communities feel relieved when a long unsolved violent murder case is finally closed.

As mentioned above, genetic genealogy is increasingly being used to investigate cold cases of infant abandonment or neonaticide. South Dakota was one of the first States to solve a cold case that had occurred almost 40 years earlier, when a baby had been abandoned in 1981 near a cornfield.[173] When there was no evidence leading authorities to a suspect, it was filed as a cold case. In 2009, with advances in DNA, detectives exhumed the body and sent it to a forensics lab to obtain a DNA profile.[174] In 2019, a genetic genealogy search narrowed in on Theresa Bentaas, a 57-year-old grandmother and paralegal in Sioux Falls.[175] After

[167] Khatchadourian (n 166) 36–38.

[168] ibid.

[169] SH Katsanis, 'Pedigrees and Perpetrators' (2020) 21 *Annual Review of Genomics and Human Genetics* 535, 550.

[170] See SD Hodge, Jr, 'Familial DNA Is One of the Newest Forensic Techniques – But It Raises Thorny Ethical and Legal Issues' (2020) 66 *The Practical Lawyer* 23.

[171] JW Hazel and C Slobogin, 'A World of Difference? Law Enforcement, Genetic Data, and the Fourth Amendment' (2021) 70 *Duke Law Journal* 705, 736. As discussed below, this practice has occurred in the Baby Doe cases.

[172] As at the time of writing, California, Maryland, Montana and Utah have enacted limits on investigative use. JK Kadish and H Schafer, 'California Enacts New Privacy Law for Genetic Data' (30 September 2022) XI no 285 *National Law Review* at www.natlawreview.com/article/california-enacts-new-privacy-law-genetic-data (accessed 2 Mar 2022). All of the new laws require that customers of genetic databases consent to disclosing genetic data to law enforcement. V Hughes, 'Two New Laws Restrict Police Use of DNA Search Method' *New York Times* (New York, 31 May 2021) at www.nytimes.com/2021/05/31/science/dna-police-laws.html (accessed 12 April 2023).

[173] J Diaz, '40-Year-Old Cold Case of South Dakota Baby Ends with Conviction' *New York Times* (New York, 11 October 2021) at nytimes.com/2021/10/11/us/theresa-bentaas-conviction-manslaughter.html (accessed 23 May 2022).

[174] ibid; C Hauser, 'A Dead Baby Was Found in a Ditch in 1981. DNA Helped Charge the Mother With Murder' *New York Times* (New York, 12 March 2019) at www.nytimes.com/2019/03/12/us/sioux-falls-baby-theresa-bentaas.html (accessed 24 May 2022).

[175] J Schuppe, 'Police lifted DNA from her trash and charged her with a baby's 1981 killing. She says that was illegal' *NBC News* (14 March 2020) at www.nbcnews.com/news/us-news/police-lifted-dna-her-trash-charged-her-baby-s-1981-n1158416 (accessed 17 April 2022).

police obtained a warrant to collect a DNA sample from Theresa, she confessed that she had concealed her pregnancy, delivered alone in her apartment when she was 19 and abandoned the baby.[176]

Theresa was arrested and charged with first- and second-degree murder and first- and second-degree manslaughter.[177] She entered an Alford Plea to first-degree manslaughter.[178] At sentencing, the state requested a 40-year sentence, with the possibility of parole in 10 years.[179] In mitigation, a psychiatrist testified that Theresa had 'complete pregnancy denial' and was unaware of her pregnancy until she was in labour.[180] Additionally, the psychiatrist testified that Theresa described the newborn as 'pale, grey and lifeless' and did not think the child was alive because there was no crying or breathing.[181] The judge sentenced Theresa to 10 years in prison, with nine years suspended.[182]

Theresa is not the only mother who has been charged in a cold case of neonaticide based on genetic DNA. Christine Marie Warren was arrested in 2021 in Washington State and charged with second-degree murder for the death of a newborn found in the trash of a gas station convenience store in 1997.[183] She was 27 at the time, and in denial about her unplanned pregnancy; when she went into labour, she panicked.[184] Christine pleaded guilty to first-degree manslaughter and was sentenced to five years of community custody.[185] Another woman, Angela Renee Siebke, was charged with first-degree murder for the death of a baby discovered in 1992 in the Mississippi River.[186] At the time, she was 17.[187] By the time of

[176] ibid.

[177] S Zhang, 'An Abandoned Baby's DNA Condemns His Mother' *The Atlantic* (13 March 2019) at www.theatlantic.com/science/archive/2019/03/38-years-later-dna-leads-to-teenager-who-abandoned-her-baby-in-a-ditch/584683/ (accessed 17 April 2022).

[178] Diaz (n 173). In an Alford Plea the defendant enters a guilty plea without admitting to the commission of the crime.

[179] A Galvan and A Todd, 'Theresa Bentaas Sentenced to 10 Years in Prison with 9 Years Suspended in Relation to the Baby Andrew Case' *Argus Leader* (Sioux Falls, SD, 3 December 2021) at www.argusleader.com/story/news/crime/2021/12/02/baby-andrew-theresa-bentaas-sentencing-hearing-sioux-falls-1981-cold-case/8826498002/ (accessed 19 January 2023).

[180] ibid.

[181] ibid.

[182] ibid. The judge 'said he struggled for weeks to determine the sentence'. A McDade, 'Judge Torn Over Woman's Sentence, Says It Isn't Clear Whether She Tried to Kill Her Newborn' *Newsweek* (2 December 2021) at www.newsweek.com/judge-tornover-womans-sentence-says-it-isnt-clear-whether-she-tried-kill-her-newborn-1655649 (accessed 12 April 2023).

[183] G Horcher, 'Mystery solved: DNA leads to the mother of a baby found dead in trash can in 1997' *KIRO 7 News* (15 March 2021) at www.kiro7.com/news/local/seattle-police-use-genealogy-website-make-arrest-23-year-old-cold-case/NQYMS7AGTNAV5ED5JCNNKGGNNY/ (accessed 17 April 2022).

[184] ibid.

[185] Staff, 'Seattle woman receives 60 months of community custody for 1997 killing of newborn son' *KING 5* (6 January 2023) at www.king5.com/article/news/crime/seattle-woman-sentenced-1997-murder-newborn/281-952705b5-7abe-4a40-a480-e58484115995 (accessed 7 January 2023).

[186] T Loewy, 'Mother of "Baby April" sentenced to two years, credited with time served' *Quad City Times* (Davenport, IA, 15 February 2022) at https://qctimes.com/news/local/crime-and-courts/mother-of-baby-april-sentenced-to-two-years-credited-with-time-served/article_419dbf5e-0d7d-52be-b0a3-b8f3a1e383de.html (accessed 21 September 2022).

[187] ibid.

her arrest 18 years later, she had six children.[188] She claimed the baby was stillborn, and pleaded guilty to endangering the life of a child. Angela was sentenced to two years' imprisonment.[189]

The investigation and prosecution of these Baby Doe cold cases demonstrates the entrenched position in the US of viewing neonaticide like any other case of murder. Yet, as argued above, this is an unjust approach that fails to consider vulnerabilities and the patterned nature of these cases. Perhaps the judge in Theresa Bentaas's case took her pregnancy denial into account, but did not seem to take into account that both the baby and Theresa '[were] victims of their situation, victims of the culture and the stigma of a young, unwed pregnant girl in 1981', as Theresa's daughter stated to the judge when pleading for a lenient sentence.[190] Similarly, Christine Marie Warren, who also pleaded guilty to first-degree manslaughter, denied her unwanted pregnancy and panicked during childbirth. Although she did not receive a prison sentence, she did receive five years of community custody (ie probation), while Angela Siebke received a prison sentence of two years. Angela was 17 and was living alone, having been abandoned by her family because the unborn child was interracial.[191]

To investigate and harshly charge these cold cases 30 to 40 years later seems arguably inconsistent with the goal of using genetic genealogy to solve heinous murders.[192] In contrast to typical cold cases, in which a family will feel relief to learn the identity of a killer, in Baby Doe cases the family *is* the killer.[193] These investigations result in 'families shattered by these discoveries'.[194] As forensic genealogist Margaret Press asserted, 'Ultimately it's about punishment, not about closure for a family.'[195] Although the state has an interest in vindicating the death of a newborn, the vulnerabilities of the mother should be taken into account when prosecutors exercise discretion in charging and recommending sentences. Given these vulnerabilities of youth, an unwanted pregnancy, denial or concealment, isolation and giving birth alone in a situation of panic, would these women and society be better served by a more compassionate approach, such as non-prosecution or mental-health treatment? Some might argue that society's interest in human life requires that these women be punished; however, as argued above, a more compassionate response would take these vulnerabilities into account as mitigation.

[188] ibid.

[189] ibid.

[190] McDade (n 182).

[191] Loewy (n 186).

[192] Katsanis (n 169) 550; J Ford-Monroe, 'Why Familial Searches of Civilian DNA Databases Can and Should Survive *Carpenter*' (2021) 72 *Hastings Law Journal* 1717, 1738. However, public surveys have supported using the techniques to investigate violent crimes, crimes against children and missing persons: Katanis (n 169) 555.

[193] E Mullin, 'DNA Is Now Solving Decades-Old Newborn Killings' *Future Human* (16 December 2020) at https://futurehuman.medium.com/dna-is-now-solving-decades-old-newborn-killings-67dd0f9ccf82 (accessed 17 April 2022). As investigators said of Theresa's case when it was finally solved, 'it's not share the joy [with the family], because there's nothing to be joyous about': Zhang (n 177).

[194] Mullin (n 193).

[195] Zhang (n 177).

IV. Conclusion

Up until now, only one State (Texas) has ever introduced legislation for an infanticide offence, which proposed making infanticide a category of homicide punished as a State jail felony (up to two years' jail time). The 2009 bill defined 'infanticide' like the English Act:

> A person commits an offense if the person willfully by an act or omission causes the death of a child to whom the person gave birth within the 12-month period preceding the child's death and if, at the time of the act or omission, the person's judgment was impaired as a result of the effects of giving birth or the effects of lactation following the birth.[196]

The proposed bill was subsequently amended to allow defendants to raise infanticide as a mitigating defence for a murder conviction.[197] The legislation was motivated by Texas trials, including that of Andrea Yates, in which mothers killed their children when in a psychotic, delusional state.[198] The proposed infanticide legislation was unsuccessful, and has not been re-introduced.[199] Although some legal scholars have criticised infanticide statutes as being based on outdated medical views that medicalise childbearing and deprive women of agency,[200] other legal scholars justify the need for them on a practical basis.[201]

In 2018, another State took steps to recognise postpartum psychosis as a defence. Illinois amended its Post-Conviction Act to allow for a sentence reduction for an imprisoned woman who 'was suffering from post-partum depression or post-partum psychosis which was either undiagnosed or untreated … and [where] this temporary mental illness tended to excuse or justify the defendant's criminal

[196] HB 3318, 81st Reg Sess (Tex 2009). See W Hundley, 'Proposed bill would recognise postpartum psychosis as a defense for moms who kill infants' *The Dallas Morning News* (Dallas, TX, 23 March 2009) (quoting an expert on postpartum disorders who stated that 'women who suffer from postpartum disorder need treatment, not imprisonment' but 'infanticide with no jail time would not fly. Our country is not ready for that').

[197] HB 3318 (n 196).

[198] Hatters Friedman and Sorrentino (n 144) 327. Under the proposed Infanticide Act, a mother such as Andrea Yates might be convicted of this lesser offence rather than capital murder for the death of a child under the age of 1 year, but not for older children killed at the same time. Although Andrea Yates was initially convicted of capital murder, on retrial she was found not guilty by reason of insanity.

[199] See B Lewis, 'A New Model Law Offers Hope: Postpartum Disorders and the Law' (March 2018) *The Champion* 20, 24 at www.nacdl.org/Article/March2018-ANewModelLawOffersHopePostpart (accessed 22 May 2022).

[200] Ayres (n 72) 83, 86; Milne (n 12) 71–72.

[201] Meyer and Oberman (n 3) 58, 172, noting that 'Although the quasi-scientific basis of this [British Infanticide Act] has been widely criticized, few have questioned the wisdom of its lenience.' See Milne (n 12) 150–51 (Milne makes the important point that the debate between women's agency and social contexts for offending is a false dichotomy because patriarchal foundations of law deprive women of the ability to 'choose': 'When a woman's back is against the wall and she can see only bad options (including deciding to negate/ignore/deny the pregnancy in the hope that it goes away), we cannot think of this as her having "choices"': ibid 150).

conduct'.[202] In order to apply for this post-conviction relief, the evidence must not have been presented at trial.[203] Although the Post-Conviction Act was subsequently amended to delete this provision, Illinois had also amended its sentencing guidelines in 2018 to take into account postpartum depression or psychosis as a factor in mitigation for sentencing.[204] A supporter of the post-conviction statute hoped that it would serve as 'a developmental model for legislatures throughout the United States', because while it was not a 'panacea' in cases of infanticide, 'Its limited application may make it more palatable to other legislatures.'[205]

So far, the majority of States have shown more interest in prosecuting decades-old cold cases than in passing legislation that would mitigate culpability or sentences based on women's vulnerabilities. As mentioned, the US continues to be tough on crime. Infanticide and neonaticide continue to be treated like other murder cases in the US and most jurisdictions continue to use the antiquated *M'Naghten* test for insanity. This chapter proposes that criminal justice reforms are needed. States should reform laws for insanity, enact infanticide laws, permit evidence of factors that would mitigate a charge of murder, such as expanded defences including the social and cultural causes of neonaticide, and incorporate more diversionary programmes into sentencing.[206] Meanwhile, because the US Supreme Court has held that the Constitution does not confer a right to abortion,[207] some worry that 'young women across much of the country will have fewer options for dealing with an unplanned pregnancy'.[208] At such a time, when half the States are restricting or banning abortion,[209] they are unlikely to consider an infanticide offence. Rather, some argue that US society has regressed to what Caren Morrison describes as a culture of 'fetal coverture' over women, that is, 'the abandonment of the woman's legal existence in favor of that of the unborn'.[210] In the US, mothers who kill their children may remain at the mercy of a tough-on-crime mentality and the 'crazy quilt' of offences and sentences for their acts.

[202] C Perez-Tineo, 'Criminal Prosecution and the Postpartum Period: A Call for More Effective Application of the Insanity Defense' (2019) 28 *Annals of Health Law Advance Directive* 203, 217.

[203] ibid.

[204] *People v Weiss* 2022 Il App 210557-U (2022).

[205] Lewis (n 198) 22, 24.

[206] As mentioned above, while this chapter focuses on infanticide and neonaticide, I agree with the proposals made overall by Sarrett in her call for a more just system, and for the application of a 'cultural humility approach' of compassion and forgiveness in the criminal justice system. Sarrett (n 8) 14.

[207] *Dobbs v Jackson Women's Health Org* 142 S Ct 2228 (2022).

[208] A Rubin, 'Woman is Charged in Death of Newborn Abandoned in 1985' *New York Times* (New York, 26 June 2022) at www.nytimes.com/2022/06/26/us/mother-arrested-cold-case-baby.html (accessed 12 April 2023); Ronan (n 64) (Dr Resnick, an expert on neonaticide, 'said that if abortion becomes unavailable or more difficult to access, he'd foresee an increase in neonaticides'); Milne (n 12) 96 (citing Karen Brennan's work on gendered harm and the contributing causes of Irish neonaticides, such as a 'lack of reproductive autonomy, including access to contraception and abortion' and other social factors).

[209] 'Tracking the States Where Abortion is Now Banned' *New York Times* (New York, 23 September 2022) at www.nytimes.com/interactive/2022/us/abortion-laws-roe-v-wade.html.

[210] C Myers Morrison, 'State Abortion Bans: Pregnancy as a New Form of Coverture' (2022) 108 *Virginal Law Review Online* 381, 395 at https://virginialawreview.org/articles/state-abortion-bans-pregnancy-as-a-new-form-of-coverture/ (accessed 12 April 2023). Milne also discusses society's 'foetus first' perspective and questions whether this response 'is about protecting "children," or … about controlling women?': Milne (n 12) 153–56, 158.

References

Books

Gruber, A, *The Feminist War on Crime: The Unexpected Role of Women's Liberation in Mass Incarceration* (University of California Press 2020).
LaFave, WR et al, *Criminal Procedure*, 6th edn (West Publishing 2017).
McKee, G, *Why Mothers Kill: A Forensic Psychologist's Casebook* (Oxford University Press 2006).
Meyer, CL and Oberman, M, *Mothers Who Kill Their Children: Understanding the Acts of Moms from Susan Smith to the 'Prom Mom'* (NYU Press 2001).
Milne, E, *Criminal Justice Responses to Maternal Filicide: Judging the Failed Mother* (Emerald Publishing Ltd 2021).
Morrissey, B, *When Women Kill: Questions of Agency and Subjectivity* (Routledge 2003).

Chapters in Edited Volumes

Ayres, S, 'When Women Kill Newborns: The Rhetoric of Vulnerability' in Cole, K (ed), *Feminist Challenges or Feminist Rhetoric? Locations, Scholarship, Discourse* (CSP 2014) 83.
Macfarlane, J, 'Criminal Defense in Cases of Infanticide and Neonaticide' in Spinelli, M (ed), *Infanticide: Psychosocial and Legal Perspectives on Mothers Who Kill* (APA 2002) 133.

Journal Articles

Ayres, S, '"[N]ot a story to pass on": Constructing Mothers Who Kill' (2004) 15 *Hastings Women's Law Journal* 39.
——, 'Newfound Religion: Mothers, God, and Infanticide' (2005) 33 *Fordham Urban Law Journal* 335.
——, 'Who Is to Shame? Narratives of Neonaticide' (2007) 14 *William & Mary Journal Women & the Law* 55.
Ayres, S and Manjunath, P, 'Denial and Concealment of Unwanted Pregnancy' (2012) 26 *Journal of Civil Rights & Economic Development* 197.
—— and ——, 'Pregnancy Denied, Pregnancy Rejected in Stephanie Daley' (2016) 12 *Law, Culture and Humanities* 132.
Dulit, E, 'Girls Who Deny Pregnancy: Girls Who Kill the Neonate' [2000] *Adolescent Psychiatry* 219.
Entrikin, JL, 'Family Secrets and Relational Privacy: Protecting No-So-Personal, Sensitive Information from Public Disclosure' (2020) 74 *University of Miami Law Review* 781.
Fineman, M, 'The Vulnerable Subject: Anchoring Equality in the Human Condition' (2008) 20 *Yale Journal of Law & Feminism* 1.
Finkel, NJ et al, 'Commonsense Judgments of Infanticide, Murder, Manslaughter, Madness, or Miscellaneous' (2000) 6 *Psychology, Public Policy, & Law* 1113.
Ford-Monroe, J, 'Why Familial Searches of Civilian DNA Databases Can and Should Survive Carpenter' (2021) 72 *Hastings Law Journal* 1717.

Friedman, SH, Heneghan, A and Rosenthal, M, 'Characteristics of Women Who Deny or Conceal Pregnancy' (2007) 48 *Psychosomatics* 11.

Hatters Friedman, S and Sorrentino, R, 'Commentary: Postpartum Psychosis, Infanticide, and Insanity – Implications for Forensic Psychiatry' (2012) 40 *Journal of the American Academy of Psychiatry and the Law* 326.

Hazel, JW and Slobogin, C, 'A World of Difference? Law Enforcement, Genetic Data, and the Fourth Amendment' (2021) 70 *Duke Law Journal* 705.

Hodge, SD, 'Familial DNA Is One of the Newest Forensic Techniques – But It Raises Thorny Ethical and Legal Issues' (2020) 66 *The Practical Lawyer* 23.

Huckerby, J, 'Women Who Kill Their Children: Case Study and Conclusions Concerning the Differences in the Fall from Maternal Grace by Khoua Her and Andrea Yates' (2003) 10 *Duke Journal of Gender Law & Policy* 149.

Johnston, EL, 'Delusions, Moral Incapacity, and the Case for Moral Wrongfulness' (2022) 97 *Indiana Law Journal* 297.

Kassin, SM, et al, 'Police-Induced Confessions: Risk Factors and Recommendations' (2010) 34 *Law & Human Behavior* 3.

Katsanis, SH, 'Pedigrees and Perpetrators' (2020) 21 *Annual Review of Genomics and Human Genetics* 535.

Khatchadourian, R, 'Family Secrets' *The New Yorker* (22 November 2021) 36.

Leo, RA 'Police Interrogation, False Confessions, and Alleged Child Abuse Cases' (2017) 50 *University of Michigan Journal of Law Reform* 693.

Lundquist, C, 'Being Torn: Toward a Phenomenology of Unwanted Pregnancy' (2008) 23 *Hypatia* 136.

Oberman, M, 'Mothers Who Kill: Coming to Terms with Modern American Infanticide' (1996) 34 *American Criminal Law Review* 1.

Perez-Tineo, C, 'Criminal Prosecution and the Postpartum Period: A Call for More Effective Application of the Insanity Defense' (2019) 28 *Annals of Health Law Advance Directive* 203.

Perlin M '"She Breaks Just Like a Little Girl": Neonaticide, the Insanity Defense, and the Irrelevance of "Ordinary Common Sense"' (2003) 10 *William & Mary Journal of Women and the Law* 1.

Resnik, PJ, 'Child Murder by Parents: A Psychiatric Review of Filicide' (1969) 126 *American Journal of Psychiatry* 325.

——, 'Murder of the Newborn: A Psychiatric Review of Neonaticide' (1970) 126 *American Journal of Psychiatry* 1414.

Roberts, DE, 'Crime, Race, and Reproduction' (1993) 67 *Tulane Law Review* 1945.

——, (2012) 'Prison, Foster Care, and the Systemic Punishment of Black Mothers' 59 *University of California at Los Angeles Law Review* 1474.

Rose, JBG, 'Toward a Critical Race Theory of Evidence' (2017) 101 *Minnesota Law Review* 2243.

Ryznar, M, 'A Crime of Its Own? A Proposal for Achieving Greater Sentencing Consistency in Neonaticide and Infanticide Cases' (2013) 47 *University of San Francisco Law Review* 459.

Sarrett, Jennifer C, 'A Vulnerability Inspired Universal Design of Justice' (2021) 24 *Punishment & Society* 1.

Shelton, JL et al, 'Neonaticide: A Comprehensive Review of Investigative and Pathologic Aspects of 55 Cases' (2011) 26 *Journal of Family Violence* 263.

Wilson, MJW, 'Retribution as Ancient Artifact and Modern Malady' (2020) 24 *Lewis & Clark Law Review* 1339.

Zabel, J, 'The Killer Inside Us: Law, Ethics, and the Forensic Use of Family Genetics' (2019) 24 *Berkeley Journal of Criminal Law* 47.

Newspaper Articles

Anon, 'Woman cleared in baby's death' *Chicago Tribune* (Chicago, IL, 19 June 2003).

——, 'Rawlins mother gets prison time in baby death' *AP Alert-Wisconsin* (Madison, WI, 23 January 2004).

——, 'Jury Finds Yates Insane, Not Guilty' *Houston Chronicle* (Houston, TX, 26 July 2006).

Barrouquere, B, 'Mother Charged in Baby's Death' *The Kentucky Post* (Covington, KT, 26 October 2007).

Brady-Lunny, E, 'B-N father sentenced in infant's death' *The Pantagraph* (Bloomington, IL, 21 May 2016).

——, 'Mother receives 3 years in baby's death' *The Pantagraph* (Bloomington, IL, 22 February 2017).

Campbell, L, 'Henderson County woman pleads guilty to murder of her 2 children, sentenced to life in prison' *Tyler Morning Telegraph* (Tyler, TX, 17 July 2019) at https://tylerpaper.com/news/local/henderson-county-woman-pleads-guilty-to-murder-of-her-2-children-sentenced-to-life-in/article_85c0bf12-a8d1-11e9-b26a-e3f1794c5802.html (accessed 19 May 2022).

Coen J, 'Verdict near in baby-slaying case' *Chicago Tribune* (Chicago, IL, 16 June 2003).

Diaz, J, '40-Year-Old Cold Case of South Dakota Baby Ends with Conviction' *New York Times* (New York, 11 October 2021) at nytimes.com/2021/10/11/us/theresa-bentaas-conviction-manslaughter.html (accessed 23 May 2022).

Galvan, A and A Todd, 'Theresa Bentaas Sentenced to 10 Years in Prison with 9 Years Suspended in Relation to the Baby Andrew Case' *Argus Leader* (Sioux Falls, SD, 3 December 2021) at www.argusleader.com/story/news/crime/2021/12/02/baby-andrew-theresa-bentaas-sentencing-hearing-sioux-falls-1981-cold-case/8826498002/ (accessed 19 January 2023).

Hauser, C, 'A Dead Baby Was Found in a Ditch in 1981. DNA Helped Charge the Mother with Murder' *New York Times* (New York, 12 March 2019) at www.nytimes.com/2019/03/12/us/sioux-falls-baby-theresa-bentaas.html (accessed 24 May 2022).

Higgins, M, 'Newborn slayings difficult to prove' *Chicago Tribune* (Chicago, IL, 6 August 2003).

Hughes, V, 'Two New Laws Restrict Police Use of DNA Search Method' *New York Times* (New York, 31 May 2021) at www.nytimes.com/2021/05/31/science/dna-police-laws.html (accessed 12 April 2023).

Hundley, W, 'Proposed bill would recognise postpartum psychosis as a defence for moms who kill infants' *The Dallas Morning News* (Dallas, TX, 23 March 2009).

Loewy, T, 'Mother of "Baby April" sentenced to two years, credited with time served' *Quad City Times* (Davenport, IA, 15 February 2022) at https://qctimes.com/news/local/crime-and-courts/mother-of-baby-april-sentenced-to-two-years-credited-with-time-served/article_419dbf5e-0d7d-52be-b0a3-b8f3a1e383de.html (accessed 21 September 2022).

Michael, J, 'Supreme Court upholds Buckley's manslaughter conviction' *Bismarck Tribune* (Bismarck, ND, 22 December 2010) at https://bismarcktribune.com/news/local/crime-and-courts/north-dakota-supreme-court-upholds-stevie-buckley-s-manslaughter-conviction/article_16d66b70-0d52-11e0-ac99-001cc4c03286.html (accessed 12 April 2023).

Miller, ME, '"No more baby": Sorority sister gets life term for tossing newborn into trash to die' *The Washington Post* (Washington, DC, 28 June 2016) at www.washingtonpost.com/news/morning-mix/wp/2016/06/28/no-more-baby-sorority-sister-gets-life-term-for-tossing-newborn-into-trash-to-die/ (accessed 15 May 2022).

Rubin, A, 'Woman Is Charged in Death of Newborn Abandoned in 1985' *New York Times* (New York, 26 June 2022) at www.nytimes.com/2022/06/26/us/mother-arrested-cold-case-baby.html (accessed 12 April 2023).

Smola, J, 'Young women in Muskingum County who killed newborns got very different sentences' *The Columbus Dispatch* (Columbus, OH, 10 July 2016) at www.dispatch.com/story/news/crime/2016/07/09/young-women-in-muskingum-county/23587584007/ (accessed 14 May 2022).

'Tracking the States Where Abortion is Now Banned' *New York Times* (New York, 23 September 2022) at www.nytimes.com/interactive/2022/us/abortion-laws-roe-v-wade.html.

Wilson, D, 'Mom says she thought baby dead already' *The Columbus Dispatch* (Columbus, OH, 23 May 2003).

——, 'Woman who killed infant wins freedom' *The Columbus Dispatch* (Columbus, OH, 28 January 2004).

Online Resources

Child Welfare League of America, *Baby Abandonment: the Role of Child Welfare Systems* (2003), http://www.cwla.org/programs/baby/babymongraph.pdf [https://web.archive.org/web/20131017144313/http://www.cwla.org/programs/baby/babymonograph.pdf].

'College Student Who Killed Newborn Infant May Get Parole, Avoid Life Sentence' *Y-City News* (21 December 2022) at https://ycitynews.com/25237/news/college-student-who-killed-newborn-infant-may-get-parole-avoid-life-sentence/ (accessed 10 January 2023).

'Judge accepts insanity plea from mother charged in baby's death' *WAFB9* (23 January 2014) at www.wafb.com/story/24530862/judge-accepts-insanity-plea-from-mother-charged-in-babys-death/ (accessed 21 May 2022).

Horcher, G, 'Mystery solved: DNA leads to the mother of a baby found dead in trash can in 1997' *KIRO 7 News* (15 March 2021) at www.kiro7.com/news/local/seattle-police-use-genealogy-website-make-arrest-23-year-old-cold-case/NQYMS7AGTNAV5ED5JCNNKGGNNY/ (accessed 17 April 2022).

Kadish, JK and Schafer, H, 'California Enacts New Privacy Law for Genetic Data' (2022) XI no 285 *National Law Review* at www.natlawreview.com/article/california-enacts-new-privacy-law-genetic-data (accessed 2 March 2022).

Kapitan, C, 'Mom who mutilated newborn enters plea' *MySA* (1 July 2010) at www.mysanantonio.com/news/local_news/article/Mom-who-mutilated-newborn-enters-plea-845553.php#:~:text=A%20San%20Antonio%20mother%20who,a%20maximum%2Dsecurity%20mental%20facility (accessed 21 May 2022).

Lewis, B, 'A New Model Law Offers Hope: Postpartum Disorders and the Law' (March 2018) *The Champion* 20 at www.nacdl.org/Article/March2018-ANewModelLawOffersHopePostpart (accessed 22 May 2022).

McDade, A, 'Judge Torn Over Woman's Sentence, Says It Isn't Clear Whether She Tried to Kill Her Newborn' *Newsweek* (2 December 2021) at www.newsweek.com/judge-torn-over-womans-sentence-says-it-isnt-clear-whether-she-tried-kill-her-newborn-1655649 (accessed 12 April 2023).

MacDonald, J, 'Jury finds woman not guilty in death of newborn' *Wave* (23 March 2009, updated 22 April 2009) at www.wave3.com/story/10055909/jury-finds-woman-not-guilty-in-death-of-newborn/ (accessed 10 April 2023).

Morrison, CM, 'State Abortion Bans: Pregnancy as a New Form of Coverture' (2022) 108 *Virginia Law Review Online* 381 https://virginialawreview.org/articles/state-abortion-bans-pregnancy-as-a-new-form-of-coverture/ (accessed 12 April 2023).

Mullin, E, 'DNA Is Now Solving Decades-Old Newborn Killings' *Future Human* (16 December 2020) at https://futurehuman.medium.com/dna-is-now-solving-decades-old-newborn-killings-67dd0f9ccf82 (accessed 17 April 2022).

'New Filing: Melissa Lucio, Who Suffered a Lifetime of Abuse, is Innocent and Her Execution Date Should be Withdrawn' *Innocence Project* (8 February 2022) at https://innocenceproject.org/new-filing-melissa-lucio-suffered-lifetime-abuse-innocent-execution-date-withdrawn/ (accessed 13 April 2022).

'Our Work' *Innocence Project* at https://innocenceproject.org/about/ (accessed 15 May 2022).

Ronan, A, 'What did Emile Weaver know?' *Elle* (16 January 2020) at elle.com/life-love/a29998766/neonaticide-emile-weaver-sorority/ (accessed 14 May 2022).

Schuppe, J, 'Police lifted DNA from her trash and charged her with a baby's 1981 killing. She says that was illegal' *NBC News* (14 March 2020) at www.nbcnews.com/news/us-news/police-lifted-dna-her-trash-charged-her-baby-s-1981-n1158416 (accessed 17 April 2022).

'Seattle woman receives 60 months of community custody for 1997 killing of newborn son' *KING 5* (6 January 2023) at www.king5.com/article/news/crime/seattle-woman-sentenced-1997-murder-newborn/281-952705b5-7abe-4a40-a480-e58484115995 (accessed 7 January 2023).

'States and Capital Punishment' (National Conference of State Legislatures) at www.ncsl.org/research/civil-and-criminal-justice/death-penalty.aspx#:~:text=Capital%20punishment%20is%20currently%20authorized,government%20and%20the%20U.S.%20military (accessed 17 May 2022).

'Texas Rangers' *Texas Department of Public Safety* at www.dps.texas.gov/section/texas-rangers/texas-rangers (accessed 13 April 2022).

Zhang, S, 'An Abandoned Baby's DNA Condemns His Mother' *The Atlantic* (13 March 2019) at www.theatlantic.com/science/archive/2019/03/38-years-later-dna-leads-to-teenager-who-abandoned-her-baby-in-a-ditch/584683/ (accessed 17 April 2022).

INDEX

www.ingramcontent.com/pod-product-compliance
Ingram Content Group UK Ltd.
Pitfield, Milton Keynes, MK11 3LW, UK
UKHW020244290926
15470UKWH00002B/736

9 781509 961641